Building a neighborly c

Manchester University Press

To our children,
Tatsuji (Dazhi), Yo, Dawen, Edward, and Sandra,
with love.

Building a neighborly community

Post-Cold War China, Japan, and Southeast Asia

Daojiong Zha and Weixing Hu

Manchester University Press
Manchester and New York
distributed exclusively in the USA by Palgrave

Published by Manchester University Press
Oxford Road, Manchester M13 9NR, UK
and Room 400, 175 Fifth Avenue, New York, NY 10010, USA
www.manchesteruniversitypress.co.uk

Distributed in the United States exclusively by
Palgrave Macmillan, 175 Fifth Avenue,
New York, NY 10010, USA

Distributed in Canada exclusively by
UBC Press, University of British Columbia, 2029 West Mall,
Vancouver, BC, Canada V6T 1Z2

British Library Cataloguing-in-Publication Data is available

Library of Congress Cataloging-in-Publication Data is available

ISBN 978 0 7190 7065 5 paperback

First published by Manchester University Press in hardback 2006

This paperback edition first published 2013

The publisher has no responsibility for the persistence or accuracy of URLs for any external or third-party internet websites referred to in this book, and does not guarantee that any content on such websites is, or will remain, accurate or appropriate.

Printed by Lightning Source

Contents

Preface

From the establishment of the Asia–Pacific Economic Cooperation (APEC) forum in 1989 to the first East Asia Summit in December 2005, there has been a flurry of diplomatic projects aimed at creating an 'East Asian Community'. These have included the Association of Southeast Asian Nations (ASEAN) + 1 dialogue mechanisms (with Japan, South Korea, and China), the ASEAN Regional Forum (ARF, since 1994), the ASEAN + China, South Korea, and Japan leaders' meeting (ASEAN + 3, since 1997), the three-way leaders' meeting among China, Japan, and South Korea (1999–2004, at the sidelines of ASEAN annual meetings, with a possibility of resumption in the future), and Asia Cooperation Dialogue (since 2001). This list does not include the numerous 'track two' and 'track three' activities across the region on a daily basis. Community building in East Asia is certainly full of dynamism.

In dealing with the aftermath of the Asian financial crisis in 1997, East Asian states have demonstrated that they are capable of pooling their resources for the common good of the entire region. Moving from issue-based cooperation to a rule-based region-wide architecture of cooperation, however, has proven elusive. Practitioners of the East Asian style of community building take pride in relying on coordination and consensus in pursuing cooperation, which in turn is based on the level of comfort with each other, fostering the level of closeness with each other, while sticking to openness in agenda setting and membership. There can be little disguising the fact that East Asian nations are still far from their shared vision of acting in unison. As the one-day East Asia Summit in Kuala Lumpur in December 2005 demonstrated, the half-empty portion of the glass in regional cooperation continues to be disagreement over state membership of a regional institution that was initially conceived to move in the direction of formal regionalism, in the style of the European

Union. It is plain to see that the various formal and informal mechanisms East Asian states have created have not had a tangible impact on reducing long-standing inter-state tensions.

This book presents our observations of the post-Cold War community-building exercises in East Asia; the focus is on what has made up the half-full portion of the glass in regional cooperation. We believe China, South Korea, Japan, and ASEAN states have sought to construct a neighborly community. The fundamental differences between a neighborly community and the kind of community that has emerged in Europe and North America are:

1 qualification for membership is not conditional
2 the process of routine interactions is itself one of reassurance
3 the aim of inter-state interactions is to foster acceptance of each other
4 change in a member's foreign policy behavior is something to cope with.

In a nutshell, member states are just the same as neighbors within a village. Nobody, however undesirable his or her behavior, can be wished away. Through interactions, a state practices conflict avoidance. Despite the fact that, at the time of writing (January 2006), Sino-Japanese diplomatic tensions were on the rise, thus casting doubt on the future of community building in East Asia, we maintain that the basic pattern of conflict avoidance will prevail.

Both of us have benefited from observing East Asian intra-regional diplomacy from being at the center of activities. In 1997, Weixing came to teach in Hong Kong, where he was in a prime location to study how Southeast Asian states interact with their Northeast Asian neighbors, China and Japan in particular. His research trips to Southeast Asia, China, and Japan, in addition to hosting visitors from these countries in Hong Kong, have kept him up to date on all the events in the region. Also in 1997, Daojiong moved to teach in Japan and stayed until early 2003. In particular, the International University of Japan, where Daojiong served for four years, had a large number of students who were government officials from Southeast Asian countries. Teaching and supervising those students' theses was in and of itself a process of learning. The years Daojiong spent in Japan saw a non-stop unfolding of diplomatic dramas between Tokyo and Beijing, particularly in the wake of the first Chinese head of state's visit to Japan, in 1998. Since taking his present position in Beijing in 2003, Daojiong has been actively involved in China's regional policy discussions with domestic and international academics, government officials, and foreign diplomats.

A word about our focus of inquiry in terms of state actors is in order. We decided not to have a chapter on South Korea's role in the regional community-building process, mainly because neither of us is familiar with the Korean language, which severely limits our capacity to gain a sense of Korean perspectives. In factual terms, South Korea and Australia, as middle powers, have played significant roles in shaping the evolution of regional diplomacy. But in our book we do make reference to South Korea's role where appropriate.

Throughout the text in this book, we present both Chinese and Japanese persons' names with the family name first, as is the customary practice in their home countries.

We are grateful to Professor Emil Kirchner, of the Department of Government, University of Essex, for encouraging us to proceed when we started to conceive of writing the present book in the summer of 2002, when we met at a conference in Beijing. The anonymous reviewers for Manchester University Press deserve our deep gratitude for helping us sharpen our focus and, in the case of the reviewer of the entire manuscript, for pointing out some factual errors therein.

In the course of writing this book, we have benefited from the advice and support of many individuals whom we consulted about parts and the entirety of the book. It is impossible to name them all. We would like especially to thank, Kent Calder, William Callahan, James Cotton, Kenten Clymer, Paul M. Evans, Harry Harding, Higashi Nobuyuki, Jia Qingguo, Jin Canrong, Jin Xide, Ryosei Kokubun, James K. Chin, Chung-in Moon, Qin Yaqing, Song Xining, Takagi Seiichiro, Takahara Akio, Tang Shiping, James T. H. Tang, Nick Thomas, Wang Jisi, Yuan Ming, Zhang Xiaojin, Zhang Yunling, and Zhu Liqun for their intellectual and personal support. In the last three years Weixing has also benefited a great deal from the China–ASEAN project at the Center of Asian Studies at the University of Hong Kong, and he would like to express his gratitude to its Director, Professor Siu-lung Wang, for his precious support. Similarly, he would also like to acknowledge research grants (CRCG) from the University of Hong Kong which made his research trips possible. Daojiong thanks the Renmin University of China for administrative and research support, including grants provided by the University's Asian Research Center and the University's support in acquiring research grants from China's National Social Science Research Fund.

Our students deserve our appreciation for supporting our journey in writing this book, including sharing with us their opinions and perspectives on issues discussed herein. Some of our ideas were tested in the classroom and we valued our students' ideas and feedback, especially from our postgraduate seminars on East Asian international relations and political economy. A few people deserve our special thanks for providing research assistance. Kim Beng Phar, Victor Chan, and Jacqueline Mui provided valuable research assistance at various stages of producing this book. Our colleagues in the School of International Relations, Renmin University, and the Department of Politics and Public Administration, University of Hong Kong, supported us both intellectually and by sharing many of the administrative tasks we otherwise would have to perform.

Last but not least, Tony Mason, Editor at Manchester University Press, his assistant, Lucy Nicholson, and the Press's freelance copy-editor, Ralph Footring, deserve our most profound gratitude for being so patient with us in the process of producing the complete manuscript. Their inspiration and devotion to detail is truly exemplary in the world of academic publishing.

We also want to thank our families for their encouragement and unconditional support as we juggled teaching, administration, and writing over the last two years. Our children deserve special appreciation for frequently putting up with having absent fathers, and it is to them that we dedicate this book.

Abbreviations

ACFTA	ASEAN–China Free Trade Area
ADB	Asian Development Bank
AFTA	ASEAN Free Trade Area
AMF	Asian Monetary Fund
APEC	Asia–Pacific Economic Cooperation
ARF	ASEAN Regional Forum
ASEAN	Association of Southeast Asian Nations
ASEAN-5	Indonesia, Malaysia, the Philippines, Singapore, Thailand
ASEAN-6	Brunei Darussalam, Indonesia, Malaysia, the Philippines, Singapore, Thailand
ASEAN-10	Brunei Darussalam, Cambodia, Indonesia, Laos, Malaysia, Myanmar/Burma, the Philippines, Singapore, Thailand, Vietnam
ASEM	Asia Europe Meeting
EAEC	East Asian Economic Caucus
EAEG	East Asian Economic Group
EAS	East Asia Summit
EASG	East Asia Study Group
EAVG	East Asia Vision Group
EEZ	exclusive economic zone
EPA	Economic Partnership Agreement
EU	European Union
GATT	General Agreement on Tariffs and Trade
IAI	Initiative for ASEAN Integration
IMB	International Maritime Bureau
IMF	International Monetary Fund
IMO	International Maritime Organization
IR	international relations

MCEDSEA	Ministerial Conference on Economic Development in South-east Asia
NAFTA	North American Free Trade Agreement
NATO	North Atlantic Treaty Organization
NIE	newly industrialized economy
ODA	Overseas Development Assistance
OECD	Organization for Economic Cooperation and Development
PAFTA	Pacific Free Trade Area
PMC	Post-Ministerial Conference
PRC	People's Republic of China
SARS	severe acute respiratory syndrome
SEANWFZ	Southeast Asia Nuclear Weapons-Free Zone (treaty)
SEATO	Southeast Asia Treaty Organization
TAC	Treaty of Amity and Cooperation
UN	United Nations
UNCLOS	United Nations Convention on the Law of the Sea
WTO	World Trade Organization
ZOPFAN	Zone of Peace, Freedom and Neutrality

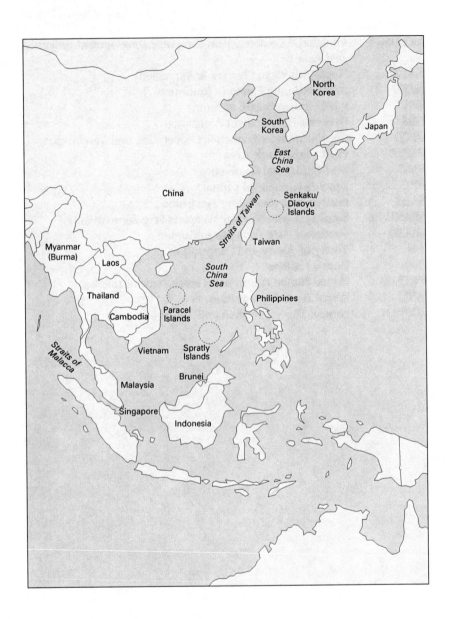

Regions of East Asia discussed in the text.

Chapter 1

Introduction

This book looks at how China, Japan, and Southeast Asian states have pursued a regional community in the post-Cold War era, comprising an intra-regional political interface combined with economic diplomacy. The end of the Cold War created new strategic opportunities for East Asian countries to cultivate a regional environment conducive to their development and security. The United States remains committed to and continues to be vital for the region's security and stability. At the same time, its post-Cold War East Asian policy orientation leaves space wide open for East Asian states to learn how to associate with each other, short of upsetting US dominance in the security field. The most significant post-Cold War change in the East Asian geostrategic landscape is the rise of China, perceived and real, and a corresponding relative decline of Japan. Against this background, both China and Japan reached out to the Southeast Asian states, trying to shape the course of change in the region according to their own designs. The member states of the Association of Southeast Asian Nations (ASEAN), in order to avoid becoming a victim of Sino-Japanese rivalry in East Asia, took the initiative to socialize China and Japan through the 'ASEAN way' of diplomacy, and they have indeed made ASEAN the hub of the East Asian community-building process.

This book provides a historically informed analysis of East Asian regionalism at the turn of the century. We hope to help readers to appreciate the historical and ideational linkages behind research generalizations about East Asian regionalism and behind the more eye-catching newspaper headlines. The thrust of our argument is as follows. East Asia's path toward structured regionalism can best be described as one of building a neighborly community. The neighborly community in East Asia is quite different from those seen in Europe and North America. Although there have been various programs and activities in regional community building,

East Asian states are still far from having a shared vision of acting in unison. Although the process does rely, as elsewhere, on consultation and consensus building in pursuit of cooperation, closeness, and openness with each other to whatever degree is comfortable, the East Asian neighborly community in the making is characterized by the following features.

First, the community's membership and responsibilities derive from geography, not conformity in political systems, levels of economic development, or societal/cultural mainstreams, and certainly not in ideological orientation in foreign policy. A common-sense analogy is of households within a village. Whatever misgivings one household may hold about another, none can be evicted. The kind of neighborhood the village is to be has to be nurtured, not imposed or escaped from.

Second, the community is not a highly institutionalized structure. Nor is it a supranational entity, in either form or substance. It is, rather, just a mechanism to coordinate how the members interact with each other. In other words, a European Union (EU) approach to managing inter-state relationships is not what China, Japan, and Southeast Asian countries have aimed for. Whether or not they should be going in that direction is another matter.

Third, built on the principles and rules of the 'ASEAN way' of diplomacy, state interactions within the community-building process indicate a willingness to cultivate acceptance of each other as being more reliable actors than those outside the region. Such reliability rests on repeated assurance of benign intent, rather than on treaty-binding demands on state behavior.

Fourth, change of foreign policy behavior on the part of fellow members in such a community is something that must be coped with. By way of everyday interactions, one member reminds the others of the value of being taken seriously and thus proceeds in the hope that conflict will not be necessary.

In this introductory chapter we review key developments in East Asian regional diplomacy in the post-Cold War era. We then lay out the conceptual framework for our study of post-Cold War community building in East Asia. Preliminary to this, Table 1.1 provides a quick reference to the states that are the focus of this book.

The end of the Cold War in East Asia

Viewed in the wider Asia–Pacific context, arguably 'the Cold War [in the East Asian region] ended in the mid-1970s with the [United States] opening to China and the end of the Vietnam War'.[1] Normalization of Sino-Soviet relations after Mikhail Gorbachev and Deng Xiaoping met in Beijing in May 1989 signified that the end of the Cold War in East Asia was moving on a path of no return. In September 1989, Vietnam began

Table 1.1 ASEAN, China, and Japan: basic data

	Total area (km²)	Population (1,000s)	GDP (2004, US$ millions)	Trade (2004, US$ millions)
China	9,598,000	1,288,000	1,400,000	841,400
Japan	378,000	127,600	4,300,000	855,700
ASEAN				
Brunei	5,765	373	5,181	6,585
Cambodia	181,035	13,589	4,517	5,414
Indonesia	1,890,754	216,410	258,266	122,339
Laos	236,800	5,760	2,439	1,004
Malaysia	330,257	25,580	117,776	221,471
Myanmar	676,577	54,745	10,463	5,034
Philippines	300,000	82,664	86,407	76,940
Singapore	697	4,240	106,884	363,431
Thailand	513,254	64,469	163,525	190,446
Vietnam	330,363	82,022	45,277	55,261

GDP, gross domestic product.

The GDP figures for Cambodia, Laos, and Myanmar are rough estimates using GDP real growth and inflation.

The trade figures for Laos, Malaysia, Myanmar, and the Philippines are estimates based on the available data until the third quarter of 2003, using simple extrapolation.

The GDP and trade figures for China and Japan are 2003 data, from *World Bank Development Indicators Database 2005*.

Sources: *ASEAN Statistical Pocketbook 2005*; *World Bank Development Indicators Database 2005*.

to withdraw from its Soviet-backed invasion of Cambodia. By the end of 1991, East Asia, like the rest of the world, no longer had to live under the shadow of the Soviet Union.

The Cold War in East Asia did not end in as clear-cut a fashion as it did in Europe, however. The most obvious difference is that division lines on the Korean peninsula and across the Taiwan Straits persist. Struggles over the future of the divided Chinese and Korean nations continue to involve actors outside the region and serve as constant reminders of the volatile nature of peace and stability throughout the whole of Northeast and Southeast Asia.[2] The United States was the prime actor in setting up the Cold War security structure for the East Asian region and the end of the Cold War has not altered US dominance in regional security. As Ikenberry has observed, 'for half a century East Asian regional order has been built around the mutual strategic embrace of America and its Asian partners'.[3] In short, in East Asia the end of the Cold War did not usher in a completely new era.

Nonetheless, there have been at least two major changes in the political economy of the East Asian region. First, there has been a reconfiguration of big power relationships. The key actors in the region are China, Japan, and the United States. But the nature of the triangular relationship profoundly changed in 1989, when China's place in the liberal international and regional order began to be seriously questioned. Gone is the geostrategic imperative for China, Japan, and the United States to coordinate in deterring the Soviet Union[4] and the three governments have since failed to locate a commonly subscribed strategic basis for collective action. Instead, among the three powers, the pursuit of one set of bilateral ties often becomes a source of contention between the other two.[5] Both China and Japan found themselves having to be more creative in managing their strategic relations with the smaller powers in East Asia in order to make up for the loss in geostrategic certainty that was characteristic of the Cold War era. Uncertainty in big power strategic relations in the region is a major source of concern for Southeast Asian nations and informs ASEAN's initiative to establish the ASEAN Regional Forum (ARF) and to expand its own member-ship. The ARF serves the purposes of socializing the big powers into annual dialogue and providing assurance for each of its participants. Expansion of ASEAN membership implies a growth in group power in negotiating with powers outside the Southeast Asian region.

Second, immediately after the end of the Cold War in East Asia, economic power became the main basis for interactions among the key actors in the region. Japan faced the task of regaining growth following the burst of its economic bubble in 1989. More than a decade later, Japan is still strug-gling to revive its domestic economy, to make the country once again the driving force of regional economic growth. Although by the end of 2005 the Japanese economy had started to move on a more stable path of sustained growth, its continuance was by no means assured. China makes maintenance of high growth the basis for strengthening its domestic gover-nance capacity as well as for promoting its 'comprehensive national power' in international competition. A key component of the Chinese strategy for economic growth has been to attract a continuous inflow of international investment capital. In trade with the rest of the region, China's strategy is to tolerate deficits with its Northeast and Southeast Asian trading partners, which in turn allows it to claim leadership in making region-wide growth possible. Southeast Asian states have had to compete with China and other markets that were off limits to international investment capital during the Cold War era. Southeast Asian complaints about international (mainly Western) insensitivities to their needs notwithstanding, ASEAN economies remain linked with the international economic system, even in the wake of the financial crisis of 1997. In addition, ASEAN states agreed to quicken the pace of intra-regional economic integration by activating the ASEAN Free Trade Area (AFTA) ahead of the original schedule.

Northeast Asian and Southeast Asian economies are all heavily depen-dent on the US import and financial markets for their individual growth.

The Clinton administration made promoting US economic interests overseas a key strategy for eliminating the trade and fiscal deficits that had troubled the US economy for decades. It managed to achieve fiscal balance while in part tolerating the widening imbalance in US trade with East Asia. Were it not for the terrorist attacks on 11 September 2001, the Bush administration might equally have made trade with and investment in East Asia a key part of its diplomacy toward the region. Arguably, indeed, the Bush administration has not lessened US interests in strengthening economic ties with East Asia, in spite of observations from both sides of the Pacific about a single issue (i.e., anti-terrorism) dominating the US policy orientation toward the region.

There is, meanwhile, an important area of continuity in the East Asian region. Out of all the strategic plans and reviews by the United States of its post-Cold War policy for East Asia, the one option that has been missing is any attempt to construct a truly region-wide security regime, as it did for Europe by way of enlarging the North Atlantic Treaty Organization (NATO). As a matter of fact, the United States chose to shun a comprehensive role as a provider of the region's security *and* economic welfare. Instead, it has by and large restricted its role to maintaining the same security order it had established before the Cold War's end. This ensures that China, Japan, and Southeast Asian states face the challenge of learning to associate with each other based on the assumption that the United States will not act as the final arbiter when an intra-regional dispute arises.

A lot more can be said about the end of the Cold War in East Asia. In line with the focus of the book, we now turn to a closer examination of the impact of the Cold War's end on countries within the region.

For Japan, the security and political structures elaborated in the wake of the Second World War still serve as the basis for its foreign policy, including its East Asian policy.[6] Japan continues to make its bilateral alliance with the United States the foundation of its foreign policy behavior. Japan's success in the capitalist world economy has not translated into encouragement within the region for Japan to manage regional political and security affairs in a fashion commensurate with its economic power. In the Cold War era, Japan managed to claim representation of Southeast Asian interests in major international organizations and institutions. Immediately after the end of the Cold War, Japan gave priority to its campaign to be accepted as a 'normal state', including making itself the second largest contributor to the United Nations (UN) and the largest aid donor among the industrialized states. In 1994, Japan failed to win support from the region for its bid for a permanent seat on the UN Security Council.[7] In 2005, on the occasion of the sixtieth anniversary of the UN, Japan teamed up with Germany, India, and Brazil to jointly campaign for permanent membership of the Security Council. By the summer, however, it became clear Japan's bid was running into fierce resistance from China and South Korea. Southeast

Asian countries chose to stay out of an obvious political rivalry among Northeast Asian states. The resultant choice for Japan seems limited: it has to continue to rely on its alliance with the United States as the key vehicle for its foreign policy alongside a continuation of its drive to win a permanent seat on the UN Security Council.

For China, the geostrategic 'Great Triangle' games Washington and Beijing played *vis-à-vis* Moscow did not contribute to Beijing's wish to enlist Washington's support in its national unification drive. Instead, the Taiwan Relations Act passed by the US Congress in 1979 binds successive US administrations to permanently intervene in interactions between Beijing and Taipei. The Taiwan Straits crisis of 1995–96, related to China's military exercises in response to a warming of ties between Taipei and Washington, proved that it is the United States, not China, which dictates the definition of the status quo across the Straits. Furthermore, China's actions here had the unintended consequences of making the United States and Japan enlarge the geographical scope of their bilateral alliance activities to include the Taiwan Straits. The crisis also provided Japan with a much needed external cause for changing its domestic laws to give it greater freedom to dispatch its armed forces beyond its borders. Strategic rivalry between China and Japan has intensified. In early 2005, Japan publicly declared Taiwan as a 'common strategic objective' in its relations with the United States and thus gave its rivalry with China a more structural nature. Southeast Asian countries chose to stay out of this Sino-Japanese rivalry over Taiwan. From the mid-1990s, China made Southeast Asia the center of its foreign policy campaign of building a neighborly community, but Southeast Asian countries continue to have reservations about a comprehensive role for China in the sub-region. In the regional economic scene, on the one hand, the Chinese market has served as the locomotive of growth in intra-regional trade, but, on the other hand, China's move away from an autarkic, command economy and its adoption of an export-driven growth strategy, a hallmark of the East Asian model of growth, have had mixed receptions in East Asia. As a matter of fact, as later parts of this chapter elaborate, China, the impressive gains it has achieved in its Southeast Asian diplomacy notwithstanding, still has to wrestle with the challenge of whether its rise has been accepted as a positive contribution to regional order.

For Southeast Asia, the time for ASEAN countries to demonstrate their resilience individually and collectively did not end with the end of the Cold War. In regional diplomacy ASEAN managed to realize its dream of incorporating all ten continental and maritime Southeast Asian states into its membership by 1999. ASEAN had begun to protect itself by signing up external powers as its dialogue partners during the Cold War era. The fact that ASEAN has kept enlarging the number of dialogue partners after the Cold War's end actually serves as a good indicator of the persistence of its sense of insecurity. ASEAN continues to be wary of either China or Japan attempting to replace the United States' role in the provision of regional security. For much of its history, ASEAN managed to maintain intra-member cohesion in presenting a unified front. But that cohesion was insufficient to deter China from occupying the Mischief Reef in the Spratly Archipelago in the South China Sea. It took ASEAN an entire decade to have China agree to sign a code of conduct over the South China Sea. In regional economic integration, ASEAN moved way ahead of both China and Japan by launching AFTA in 1992. However, facilitation of trade among AFTA members continues to rely on aid from the outside world, particularly Japan and the Japan-led Asian Development Bank (ADB) for infrastructure development, a basic requirement for increasing the flow of goods across the borders of AFTA member economies. ASEAN as a group was helpless when the Asian financial crisis broke out in 1997. In a similar vein, ASEAN has proved to be ineffective in dealing with the region's non-traditional security challenges, such as the environment, drug, health, and maritime piracy. Indeed, there is no shortage of evidence pointing to the contrast between ASEAN's activism in intra-regional diplomacy and its continuing lack of capacity in moving beyond its Cold War agenda of preserving resilience.

Pessimism is a key theme in the predictions generated by realist inter-national relations research about the evolution of East Asian intra-regional political–economic relations after the Cold War's end. In the early 1990s, East Asia was seen to be heading for inter-state conflicts similar to those in nineteenth-century Europe. Evidence pointing to this pessimistic scenario can be easily amassed. The sovereignty dispute between China and Japan over the Senkaku/Diaoyu Islands, political and military confrontation across the Taiwan Straits, continuation of the complex South China Sea territorial disputes, among other potential points of dispute kept calm under the Cold War structure of superpower rivalry, come readily to mind as evidence of volatility. Within East Asia, nation-states differ greatly in their domestic political–economic structures, history, culture, and demo-graphics. In terms of intra-regional history, imperial Japan tried to create a 'Great East Asian Co-prosperity Sphere'. China in the 1950s and 1960s supported communist insurgent movements in Southeast Asia, in addition to involving itself in the handling of ethnic Chinese strife in a number of Southeast Asian countries. Both Japan and Southeast Asian countries remain wary of any prospect of a return to the regional tributary system centered upon imperial China. Nation building remains a real challenge for many of the states in East Asia, which have a short history of conducting inter-state relations following principles that evolved out of European and North American practices in the international system.[8]

Contrary to the pessimistic predictions of anarchy emerging in East Asia, however, since the end of the Cold War the region has not seen the outbreak of inter-state war. Both China and Japan participated in post-Cold War conflict resolution projects in Cambodia and Indonesia (which resulted in the independence of East Timor). The two East Asian big powers also supported ASEAN's designs for regionalism. A stable regional security environment has contributed to the steady increase in intra-regional trade and investment. According to a World Bank study:

> from 1975 to 2001, East Asia's share of global exports expanded more than three-fold (to just under 19 percent), and doubled from 1985 to 2001. Intra-regional exports, expressed as a share of world trade, experienced an even sharper expansion rising more than six-fold during 1975–2001.[9]

In the process, the percentage of Southeast Asian exports that went to China steadily grew, while there was a corresponding decline in the proportion of exports going to Japan. However, as trade between China and Japan steadily grew in the same period, on top of the role the Japanese market plays in technology and capital transfers, the trend in market-based regional economic integration has continued and deepened. The phenomenon does not put an end to the intellectual debate about economic interdependence and international conflict.[10] However, more than a decade of no-war peace in East Asia does call for a pause in insisting on the theoretical conviction that war is due to break out sooner or later.

Optimistic predictions about post-Cold War East Asia have also proven to be premature.[11] In the region's political scene, none of the Cold War geostrategic and political tensions between the countries in East Asia has dissipated. Ideally, China and Japan would reach a reconciliation with each other, in the same fashion as Germany and France after the end of the Second World War, to provide joint leadership for integration. But the reverse has been true. Diplomatic and political difficulties between the two countries have intensified since 1995. Beyond expressing a wish for political tensions between China and Japan to be reduced, the smaller countries in the region are by and large helpless. Across the region, reference to a shared East Asian identity based on purportedly 'Asian values' remains largely a rhetorical exercise.

In the region's economic scene, a supposedly uniquely East Asian model of development failed the test presented by the Asian financial crisis of 1997. The crisis cast serious doubt on the 'flying geese' pattern of regional growth, with Japan leading the flock, Korea, Taiwan, and Singapore in the middle, and 'tiger economies' in Southeast Asia joining the newly industrialized nations. Moreover, the outburst of dynamism in market interactions between China, Hong Kong, and Taiwan had not led to the emergence of a uniquely Chinese economic area.[12] Among these three economic entities, the market terms set by the World Trade Organization (WTO) matter but cannot override the preferential (in the case of the Chinese mainland toward Taiwan, Hong Kong, and Macau) and discriminatory (in the case of Taiwan toward the Chinese mainland) trade policies put in place for competing political agendas. East Asia also lags behind North America and Europe in the formation of a regional trade bloc. AFTA exists and is actively engaging economies outside the region to form webs of free trade arrangements. But AFTA is very weak in fostering intra-regional integration. Both Japan and China find it more acceptable to launch bilateral free trade schemes with their smaller Southeast Asian trading partners than with each other. Projects for a three-way free trade area among China, Korea, and Japan, and eventually linking that with AFTA, remain a distant dream. More to the point is the fact that, the race to free trade arrangements notwithstanding, virtually all East Asian economies are choosing to go down the path of 'liberalization without political pain'.[13] More serious reform on the domestic front would have meant growth in importing capacity, lessening the competitive ('crowding out') effect in the region-wide markets and beyond.

In short, strategic, political, and economic interactions among China, Japan, and Southeast Asia in the post-Cold War era defy simple description. Clear-cut explanations of the recent past and predictions of the future represent even more of a challenge. What is clear is that the United States will continue to preserve the security order in the region and that states will have to continue to live with the Cold War regional security structure. What is also clear is that East Asian markets are becoming increasingly integrated. What remains uncertain in the political economy of community building in East Asia is how these nation-states can move beyond coping with each other, to cultivate a region that is more predictable and manageable for their collective welfare.

China on the rise, Japan in decline?

With the United States choosing not to reshape the post-Cold War East Asian regional geopolitical and economic scene, attention naturally turns to China and Japan, the two actors with the potential to shape change – again, short of upsetting the military dominance of the United States – in the entire region. But the end of the Cold War in many ways threw China and Japan back into the complexities of the regional political and economic ties that existed before the end of the Second World War.

China's rise

The 'rise of China' is a reference often used to describe major change in China's relative position in the international political–economic system at different points of history. In the post-Cold War era, the phrase becomes relevant in part as a result of an academic inability to predict change inside China and by extension its influence outside.[14] In the immediate wake of the events of the summer of 1989, global and regional concern about a possible collapse of China resulted from the outburst of internal strife symbolized by the month-long political uprising in Tiananmen Square. China's domestic governance also showed signs of retrenching to the kind of autarkic socialism the Chinese government had worked to get out of. China's principal architect of the reform project, Deng Xiaoping, was ailing and an entire generation of revolution-era officials had to leave the task of managing daily governance to a new generation of politicians and bureaucrats. Yet China did not have an institutionalized mechanism for leadership transition.[15] In other words, China changed from being a possible example for getting out of communism/socialism to being a concern to its neighbors due to its internal weaknesses, real and perceived.

The image of China on the verge of collapse was soon overtaken by the image of a China that was rapidly ascending in the international system. The contrast between fast economic growth in China and continuing decay in the Russian and Eastern European economies was only too obvious. The World Bank's 1993 recalculation of the size of the Chinese economy and its prediction that it might overtake that of the United States by 2010 provided an important trigger for contemplating the future of China. The ethnic Chinese business networks that link China and Southeast Asia with Hong Kong and Taiwan provide yet another important source of continued economic growth in China. In other words, China's pursuit of wealth and power did not necessarily have to rely on smooth political ties with the West.[16]

The perception of China's rise, put in the context of the entire Asia–Pacific region and that of the international system more generally, leads to considerations of implications in the areas of security and political ideologies. For the United States, debates throughout the 1990s about an appropriate strategy toward China centered upon containment or engagement.[17] For Japan, perceptions of China on the rise provided a strong rationale to modify its bilateral alliance with the United States to include regional and global issues.[18] For Southeast Asia, however, the rise of China invoked the image of dominance that is rooted in imperial Chinese history. As a Singaporean scholar observed:

> In fact, China could remind its Asian neighbors of the once powerful tributary system of the Ming and Qing Dynasties, when the 'Middle Kingdom' was in fact at the center of an Asian system of trade, cultural eminence and respect. Though Beijing may have no aspirations of re-creating such a system, just as Japan had failed to create its Asian Sphere of Co-Prosperity during World War II, this 'Middle Kingdom' mentality cannot be totally neglected today.[19]

This line of argument maintains that China represents a more serious threat to security in the region than Japan. Among the reasons given are that China is more likely to use force and is less vulnerable to economic coercion. In addition, the government is authoritarian, unstable, and anxious to redress the status quo, and is capable of mobilizing military forces with comparative ease. Southeast Asian nations are then recommended to consider three possible strategies to prepare for the Chinese challenge. One strategy is to suppress China's economic growth. Another is to foster regionalism with China through strategic economic engagement. Still another strategy is to cooperate in China's growth with the hope that a balancing of military forces with China does not prove necessary.[20]

For a good part of the 1990s, China chose to respond to the rhetoric of the 'China threat' in the region by launching two projects. First, it launched a relentless rhetorical offensive by denouncing suggestions that China was either intending to be a threat or materially posing a threat to its Asian neighbors as 'Cold War mentality', a purposeful distortion of history, and quite possibly a Western scheme to derail the improvement in China's ties with Southeast Asian nations, which was made possible by the end of the Cold War.[21] The rhetorical exercise made reference to Chinese restraint from conquering China's Southeast Asian neighbors back in the fifteenth century, when Ming Dynasty official Zheng He traveled throughout the region and beyond, taking with him a powerful force that could have easily subjugated the lands and peoples his entourage came in contact with. But instead, since then, China has made the sharing of Chinese wealth, through trade and commerce, with its neighbors the centerpiece of building up its neighborhood. The end of the Cold War, then, only opens space for China to continue with its long-held tradition of restraint from warfare with its neighbors.[22]

Second, China made clear to Southeast Asian countries, beginning with its negotiations with Indonesia toward normalization of diplomatic ties in 1989, that it had changed its domestic laws to put an end to granting dual nationality status to overseas Chinese.[23] China intervened in Southeast Asian politics by siding with the ethnic Chinese in the 1950s and 1960s. Concerns about China using the ethnic Chinese as Trojan horses remained throughout the Cold War era. With the end of the Cold War, Southeast Asia's ethnic Chinese entered the 'China threat' debate because of perceptions about the wealth they hold, as well as distrust of their political loyalty when China re-entered the regional economy.[24]

In the mid-1990s China began to engage ASEAN diplomatically as a group. But that process moved tentatively and slowly. ASEAN began to feel the true impact of China's rise in 1997. In the wake of the regional financial crisis, China offered Thailand and Indonesia loans of US$1 billion each. It also encouraged the Hong Kong government, newly returned to Chinese sovereignty, to do likewise. Indeed, from the late 1980s relations among all the ASEAN states and China improved markedly. China has used the economic crisis to forge closer relations with states that have historically been suspicious of it. China and ASEAN share a desire to achieve economic growth through expanded trade and investment. Engagement with China fits well into ASEAN's strategic framework. Still, although there is no monolithic ASEAN perception of China's rise, in general terms, a rising China's overtures are met with ambivalence.[25]

Its impressive records of economic growth notwithstanding, China has a short history of practicing multilateral diplomacy over regional security issues. The first time Chinese delegates took part in region-wide security dialogue was only in 1993.[26] Since the ASEAN + China formula of dialogue was established in 1996, China has continually encouraged ASEAN to play a leading role in the various schemes to institutionalize dialogue among nation-states in the region.

As part of its strategy for reassuring Southeast Asia of its benign intentions, in 2001 China launched the Bo'ao Forum for Asia. The Forum, modeled on the World Economic Forum in Davos, Switzerland, is meant to socialize China's Asian neighbors into a better understanding of China. The Forum features former Australian prime minister Robert Hawk – an architect of Asia–Pacific Economic Cooperation (APEC) – former Japanese prime minister Morihiro Hosokawa, and former Philippine president Fidel Ramos as co-founders. The inclusion of Ramos is particularly noteworthy because he had been a staunch champion of the 'China threat' thesis, in part because China clashed with the Philippines over sovereignty of the Spratly region in 1995, while Ramos was in office. It then came as little surprise when, in 2003, China used the Forum to present its vision of China's rise bringing peace and prosperity to the rest of the region.

Zheng Bijian, the key advocate of China's 'peaceful rise' strategy, presents a China that is still far away from achieving the great power status to which it aspires. Zheng argues that, 'according to China's strategic plans, it will take another 45 years – until 2050 – before it can be called a modernized, medium-level developed country'. Pointing to the rapid rise in Chinese imports from Southeast Asia, India, and other economies in recent years, Zheng argues that 'China's peaceful rise will further open its economy so that its population can serve as a growing market for the rest of the world, thus providing increased opportunities for – rather than posing a threat to – the international community'. Finally, 'China's development depends on world peace – a peace that its development will in turn reinforce'.[27] Indeed, the Chinese themselves recognize the numerous domestic economic and social changes China is facing today and some even invoke 'Latin Americanization' of China as one prospect for the country.[28] There is room for cautioning against rushing to the conclusion that the continuing rise of China in material terms is inevitable.

In short, measured in material terms, the end of the Cold War has seen China getting stronger. But the very fact that China decided it was necessary to emphasize its peaceful intent indicates that it has yet to win regional acceptance as a responsible and welcomed neighbor.

Japan's decline

The image of Japan on the decline since the end of the Cold War is both factual and perceived. The factual dimension stems from the loss in momentum of economic growth when 'bubble economy' collapsed in 1989. Japan entered the 1990s seeing a mounting list of challenges in the evolving international environment. Ever since the 1960s, Japan had prospered by taking advantage of the international economic system based on free and open markets. It actively worked to support that system. The end of the Cold War saw European unification gaining momentum, bringing with it a possible rise in trade protectionism. The North American free trade arrangement was expanding to include Mexico, thereby creating yet another trade bloc. Yet, in Japan's own neighborhood, China, South Korea, and some countries in Southeast Asia would not welcome an assertive Japanese role in shaping the region into a similar bloc. The United States was pressuring Japan to shoulder a greater share of global defense burdens, yet the rest of East Asia feared any military expansion by Japan. In short, Japan faced a problem not only of rejuvenating domestic economic growth but also of finding acceptance in its own neighborhood.[29]

By 1998, as Japanese macroeconomic statistics showed the country was entering its first recession for almost twenty-five years, the new catch phrase for describing its decline was Japan's 'lost decade'.[30] Failure to revise its economic and financial systems exacerbated Japanese insecurity for much of the 1990s. Among other major developments, Japan saw uncertainties in its alliance with the United States, partly because US president Clinton and Chinese president Jiang Zemin declared a 'constructive strategic partnership' between the United States and China in 1998. This happened in the wake of serious US opposition to Chinese military behavior in the Taiwan Straits from 1995 to 1996. A 'Japan passing' phenomenon seemed to be at work. It would have made sense for the United States, if it was going to prioritize Japanese interests, to continue giving the Taiwan issue a high priority and simply to tolerate strains in relationships with China. But this it did not do, preferring instead its constructive strategic partnership. Moreover, in spite of the economic woes Japan was going through, 'Japan bashing' by the West extended from the Japanese handling of its domestic economic and political sphere to how Japan responded to the Asian financial crisis of 1997.[31] As Yoichi Funabashi observes:

> Historically, Japan has played a unique role as the most socioeconomically advanced country in Asia, competing with the West on [a] relatively equal footing. This status as a 'member of the club' of modernized nations inspired belief in Japan's role 'bridging' the gap between the West and Asia. But now Japan finds disturbing similarities between its own problems and the rest of Asia's. Throughout the region, the lack of transparency and accountability in both financial markets and politics has been cited as a factor in the economic

crisis. The acute awareness that these are shared problems has exploded the myth of Japanese uniqueness. At the same time, the concept of 'bridging' has proved unnecessary. Western businesses deal with all Asia directly, without needing Japanese intermediaries. Although it thinks of itself as exceptional, Japan has found itself subject to the rules that govern the rest of Asia.[32]

However, the image of Japan's decline is only partially true, in the sense that Japan, as one of the very few 'like-minded' Asian countries in the international political–economic system, has been instrumental in reshaping Asia in the Western image after the collapse of the Soviet Union. As a matter of fact, in spite of its difficulties in regaining momentum in economic growth, Japan has maintained its status as the second largest economy in the world. Its economic aid to Southeast Asia, the main destination of its Overseas Development Assistance (ODA) program, far surpasses Chinese economic aid. In 2004, the total volume of Japanese trade with ASEAN ($136 billion) still surpassed the total value of China–ASEAN trade (US$105.9 billion). Both the Chinese and the ASEAN economies continue to rely heavily on machinery, technology, and managerial input from Japan.[33] Above all, without Japanese initiatives and commitment, East Asia could not have achieved its success in creating regional financial mechanisms for dealing with financial crisis – should another financial crisis arise.

Since the end of the Cold War, Japan has actively sought regional acceptance as a 'normal state'. Indicators of that normalcy include a country whose foreign policy would no longer have to be prefaced with apologies to its East Asian neighbors over imperial Japan's wars. Partly because of ASEAN countries' worries about a rising China and preference for Japan not only as a source of growth but also as a model of development, Japan's East Asian policies made important political inroads in its neighborhood. After the 1995 'no war' resolution by the Japanese legislature, Southeast Asian countries increasingly down-played the need for Japan to continue to apologize for its actions in the Second World War. China routinely protests against Japanese politicians paying homage at the controversial Yasukuni Shrine in Tokyo and claims to be speaking for the peoples of Asia. But Southeast Asian government leaders have chosen not to echo these Chinese sentiments. A case in point is that in 2001, when the Japanese prime minister again aroused sharp criticism from China by visiting the Shrine, in Southeast Asia only Singapore's deputy prime minister, Lee Hsien Loong, commented, by reminding Japan that it should have learnt from how Germany has interacted with the rest of Europe over its Nazi history.[34] Although there was no outright criticism from Southeast Asia of China for taking issue with Japan in this way, Japan can take comfort in seeing no chorus involving China and Southeast Asian countries.

Post-Cold War Japan did try to upgrade its leadership role in the East Asian economy from being primarily a supplier of capital and technology, and a major importer, to one in the realm of development ideology. Japan's sponsorship of the World Bank's 1993 *East Asian Miracle: economic growth and public policy* study was indicative of its resolve to forge a common East Asian 'voice' in debating with other key powers about economic development paradigms on a global scale. In other words, the challenge put to America and Europe was that their insistence on liberal political ideologies for growth and the 'Washington consensus' for narrowing the north–south gap might not be the best and only option for world development.[35] The outbreak of the Asian financial crisis, however, put a halt to the attraction of an East Asian model of growth. On the other hand, it is still too early to conclude that the debate over development ideologies, which has significant implications in international economic policy making, is permanently over.

Amid pervasive perceptions in Japan about China's rise and Sino-American relations resulting in 'Japan passing', Japan acted assertively to deal with its China problem. Immediately after the end of the Cold War, China found itself engulfed in differences with Western countries over its human rights record. Japan took the lead among G7 nations to ease economic sanctions on China in the wake of the Tiananmen Square incident of 1989. A reform-oriented China serves Japan's economic and security interests more directly than it does other G7 members. Nonetheless, there can be no mistake that Japan began to side with the West in upholding human rights as a principle in its foreign policy.[36] Then, in 1995, Japan applied its own economic sanctions to China in protest against the latter's nuclear testing activities. This changed the nature of Japan's China policy from one guided by commercial interests only to include an active agenda of preventing China becoming a superpower.[37] China defined its military exercises in the Taiwan Straits in 1995 and 1996 as acts of self-defense against permanent separation of the Chinese nation. Japan has since made defense of Taiwan a key issue in its security policy making.[38] Indeed, entering the new century, bilateral relations between China and Japan have developed into a geostrategic rivalry.

In short, the perception of the decline post-Cold War Japan has to be seriously questioned. That description is in fact restricted to Japan's economic performance since the bubble burst. Also, it arguably results more from Western, particularly American, reappraisal of Japanese domestic governance and frustration over unmet expectations of Japan playing a larger role in shaping the regional security environment. As J. Arthur Stockwin argues, 'Japan still matters'.[39]

Growing regional institutions for cooperation

The above discussion on a parallel post-Cold War development within the East Asian region, that is, the rise of China and Japan in decline, leads us to a third noticeable trend in the region: the growth in regional institutions for cooperation. This trend began in the economic sphere, and growing economic integration has gradually shored up regional institution building and increased acceptance of the concept of 'East Asia' as a region.

Since the beginning of the 1980s, East Asia has been on par with Europe and North America, the three making up the tripolar world of trade, with over 85 percent of total world trade moving between them. In Europe, member states agreed on the Maastricht Treaty in 1992, making the EU the first to reach the highest level of regional integration worldwide. In North America, the North American Free Trade Agreement (NAFTA), also signed in 1992, began to serve as a powerful instrument for integrating the Canadian, US, and Mexican economies into one. In contrast, in East Asia the launching of the AFTA began in 1993 but its provisions were far less rigorous in effecting change in the marketplace than what the EU or NAFTA was able to accomplish.[40] Still, AFTA includes member states of Southeast Asia only; the more dynamic and competitive worldwide economies of China, Japan, and South Korea were left out of the arrangement. In fact, the idea had been to establish an institutional arrangement that would include member economies of both Southeast and Northeast Asia, but politics had prevented them from forming an East Asian regional economic institution.

In December 1990, Malaysian prime minister Mahathir bin Mohamad put forward precisely an 'Asians only' economic grouping of sorts, known as the East Asian Economic Caucus (EAEC), a modified version of his earlier proposition for an East Asian Economic Group. Mahathir's original vision was to build an exclusive East Asian grouping under the Japanese economic umbrella. In so doing, Kuala Lumpur was counting on Japanese endorsement, without which the new grouping would lose its reason for existence. But Japanese support was slow in coming, in part for fear of upsetting US sensitivities over being left outside an institution linking Southeast and Northeast Asia. By the time Japanese prime minister Kiichi Miyazawa visited Malaysia in 1993, it had become clear that Japan had chosen to side with the United States over the EAEC controversy.[41]

In place of an EAEC, the Clinton administration endorsed the idea of an APEC forum, and this officially started in 1989. The founding members of APEC included the more dynamic nation-states of Southeast Asia.[42] With China, Taiwan, and Hong Kong joining APEC in 1991 and the decision by the Clinton administration in 1993 to elevate the annual APEC meeting exercise to include an informal head-of-state summit, APEC effectively took off as the grouping with the widest geographical coverage for East Asia. APEC survived and grew in membership and agenda, in part thanks to the first Clinton administration's investment in the grouping as a vehicle for pursuing economic security for America. The most significant progress APEC has achieved under the notion of 'open regionalism' is perhaps the 1995 Bogor declaration, which specifies a deadline of 2010 for developed member economies and 2020 for the developing members to implement their pledges for synergistic trade liberalization. However, the Asian financial crisis of 1997 brought an end to Southeast Asia's rapid economic growth, and had devastating effects on the regional economy. During the crisis, Washington turned its back on Southeast Asia's request for financial assistance, and helped Mexico instead. This seriously undermined ASEAN states' confidence in Washington's economic leadership in East Asia. APEC, as the only region-wide economic organization, also proved to be irrelevant, and failed to produce an institutional response to the financial crisis.[43]

The Asian financial crisis was a major turning point for East Asian states, both Southeast and Northeast, when they saw the desirability of an East Asian regional approach to regional financial and economic problems. During the crisis, Beijing's pledge not to devalue the renminbi was widely hailed by regional countries. Tokyo's financial rescue package under the Miyazawa initiative to Southeast Asian countries was welcomed by the region. The financial crisis not only proved that ASEAN and Northeast Asia were deeply interconnected, but also served as a 'centripetal force' in the development of regional institutions.[44] As a result, this revived momentum for regional cooperation led to the beginning of the ASEAN + 3 (ASEAN states plus China, Japan, and South Korea) dialogue process in 1998, and, under the ASEAN + 3 framework, the Chiang Mai initiative in 2000 (see below).

East Asian regionalism is principally driven by economic forces, and regional institution building is largely promoted by ASEAN. Since the failure of the pioneering EAEC, however, ASEAN never really gave up on its attempt to engineer a regional institution that is more 'East Asian' in membership and in agenda setting. ASEAN started its official bilateral dialogue with Japan in 1977, and it made South Korea a dialogue partner in 1991. To expand its scope of consultation with Northeast Asia, ASEAN had China as a dialogue partner. These additions to the 'ASEAN + 1' formula completed ASEAN's drive to institutionally socialize the three Northeast Asian countries around the ASEAN orbit of diplomacy. In the immediate wake of the Asian financial crisis of 1997, the 'ASEAN + 3' formula of intra-regional dialogue came into being and has since held annual meetings unabated. In this connection, given the icy diplomatic rows between China and Japan over Japanese governmental attitudes towards commemoration of the Second World War, the 'ASEAN + 3' formula has been invaluable for China and Japan to maintain the minimum amount of direct communication at the highest level of their respective leaderships.

ASEAN did provide the much-needed institutional venue for China and Japan to demonstrate they can work with Southeast Asian nations on an equal footing. Although an Asian Monetary Fund (AMF), a Japanese initiative in the immediate wake of the Asian financial crisis of 1997, failed to take off, consultations under the ASEAN + 3 aegis have led to materialization of the Chiang Mai initiative in 2000 (see more about the initiative in Chapter 4). The Chiang Mai initiative, designed to function as a regional financial safety net, consists of bilateral currency swap arrangements between the central banks of China, Japan, and South Korea and those of the stronger economies of Southeast Asia. The initiative was a determined East Asian attempt to respond jointly to the slow and rigid response by the International Monetary Fund (IMF) to the Asian financial crisis, which cast serious doubt in East Asia over its reliability as a responsive lender of last resort. The currency swap scheme materialized as planned and has since expanded in membership as well as amounts of capital committed.

Another key development since the Asian financial crisis has been the growth of free trade agreements within the region. One of the most active countries in this regard is Singapore, which has entered five bilateral free trade agreements (with Japan, the US, New Zealand, Australia, and the European Free Trade Association[45]) since 2001.[46] Japan, South Korea, China, and Thailand are also active in proposing and negotiating with countries in the region over bilateral free trade agreements. The rising trend of bilateral arrangements is attributed to the institutional failures of APEC, AFTA, and the WTO in pushing ahead their respective trade liberalization agendas. Some scholars believe the growing bilateral free trade agreements are forging micro- and macro-networking linkages that could lead to a new lattice form of economic cooperation in the region.[47] As the bilateral agreements became a major vehicle for regional trade liberalization and networking, both Japan and China did not want to miss out. In January 2001, Japan and Singapore signed the first free trade agreement linking Northeast and Southeast Asian economies. In 2002, China and ASEAN signed a framework agreement for economic cooperation, aimed at the creation of a free trade area by 2010. As a matter of fact, China and Japan have since been in a race of sorts in reaching out to Southeast Asian economies by using free trade agreements as an instrument.[48]

East Asian regionalism – that is, the move toward regional integration and institution building – is still in a nascent stage by European and North American standards. In an institutional sense, the East Asian focus on a phased-in approach to trade and financial integration implies a reluctance to accept the kind of transfer of sovereignty that is characteristic of the European process. In a similar vein, the legal nature of NAFTA is also absent in the various schemes created in East Asia to promote trade liberalization. When there are indeed elements indicating a willingness to get into the legal realm, East Asian countries are more willing to deal with the use of law as a matter of tactics rather than principle.[49] The intricate nature of intra-regional politics in East Asia is such that Asian regionalism could not possibly have moved along the paths taken in either Europe or

North America. Nonetheless, the steps East Asian countries have taken on the path toward regional integration have been remarkable. This is particularly true given the shifts in US policy toward the region since the end of the Cold War.

The role of the United States in perspective

The conventional and in many ways still predominant interpretation of postwar political–economic development in East Asia is that the United States holds primacy in the evolution of the regional political economy. This approach points to the postwar bipolar competition between the United States and the Soviet Union in the East Asian region. The eight years of US occupation of Japan (1945–52) were instrumental in trans-forming the Japanese political and social structure from one of militarism to one of democracy and pursuit of growth through peaceful means. The US commitment to rolling back the spread of communism and its military presence, through fighting the two land wars in Asia (Korea, 1950–53 and Vietnam 1965–73), provided an important impetus for the takeoff of the Japanese economy, which in turn filled the role of providing leadership in the economic development of the entire region. For the entire Cold War era, there was no wavering in the US commitment to security and economic development in maritime East Asia.[50]

Indeed, the United States' pursuit of strategic influence in the western Pacific during the Cold War era was a key exogenous factor in the growth of the regional economy. The US-led security order in maritime East Asia, despite the brief Soviet presence in Vietnam, also provided the necessary region-wide stability for Japan to pursue a 'flying geese' pattern of growth linking the Japanese and Southeast Asian economies. Economic dynamism in maritime East Asia in the late 1970s also worked as a major exogenous factor contributing to China's re-entry into the regional and global economy. China's emulation of other East Asian countries' strategy of export-led growth could not have been successful without the regional security and economic order established by the United States.

On the other hand, the end of the Cold War has seen the United States having continuous difficulty in forming a consistent East Asian strategy. About the only consistent dimension in post-Cold War US policy toward East Asia is its maintenance of the 'hub and spokes' security arrangement, with the United States as the 'hub' linking to the 'spokes' – the military bases in Japan and South Korea, treaty alliances with the Philippines and Australia, and bilateral agreements allowing the presence of US military installations in Southeast Asian countries. The United States' handling of its bilateral relationships with its allies frequently leaves its East Asian partners searching for confirmation of US commitment. As a matter of fact, it has become customary for US observers to remind their government of the need to better recognize the changing realities in East Asia and develop policies that are more fitting.[51]

In the mid-1990s, the United States failed the test of meeting East Asian expectations for delivering leadership when it was most needed. Its handling of the Asian financial crisis of 1997 indicated that the United States had a single focus in its overall East Asian policy: preserving its design for a unipolar region in the security sphere. That strategy includes stemming the rise of China, ensuring peaceful relations across the Taiwan Straits, and enhancing ties with its traditional allies. Southeast Asia ranked rather low on its list of regional priorities. For example, the United States was swift in organizing international resources to rescue Latin American economies caught in financial crises, but it was slow in encouraging the IMF and World Bank, in which it has the largest weight in decision making, to carry out the duties they were designed to fulfill in relation to Southeast Asia. Worse still, IMF and World Bank policy measures for addressing Southeast Asian financial woes were not only inadequate but also failed to take account of local realities.[52] With hindsight, one can argue that there could not have been a proper response that would have been satisfactory to all the affected parties, as both endogenous and exogenous factors were at work in the crisis. One can even argue that geostrategic proximity made it natural for China and Japan to act more quickly than did the United States, for a continuation of societal instability was bound to have been more directly felt in China and Japan than in the US. Nonetheless, the fact that EU countries together contributed more to the rescue package the IMF organized speaks volumes about the United States' lack of interest in being the leader in non-military affairs in the East Asian region.[53]

In the wake of the crisis, the United States blocked the formation of Japan's proposal for an AMF, for fear of losing its control over the process, on top of serious ideological differences in dealing with the development challenge in East Asia.[54] But since then Japan has been able to gather support from its Asian neighbors and to socialize the United States into allowing the establishment of institutional mechanisms short of an outright rejection of the original AMF notion, at least not in name. Consequently, there is a point in arguing that Japan has demonstrated that it can provide the kind of regional leadership where the United States has failed.[55]

In a similar vein, China took advantage of the Asian financial crisis to increase its influence in the political–economic sphere in Southeast Asia as well. China's commitment not to enter into a round of currency devaluation won it praise from all circles in Southeast Asia. In addition, to Southeast Asia the contrasting images of a weaker yet caring China and a stronger yet ambivalent or outright negligent United States in the immediate wake of the financial crisis cannot be sharper. Banking on the new momentum from this demonstration to Southeast Asia that its rise does not pose a threat to its smaller neighbors, China quickly moved to negotiate a free trade agreement with the enlarged ten-member ASEAN. The process began in 2001 and was completed in only two years. China's free trade project with ASEAN, particularly its decision to include opening itself to ASEAN exports of agricultural products in an 'early harvest' package, was also a challenge to Japan for influence in Southeast Asia.

The United States further contributed to the momentum of intra-regional political–economic interactions in East Asia, but by default. After the 11 September 2001 attacks on New York and Washington, DC, the Bush administration made anti-terrorism the overriding issue in its East Asian diplomacy. A case in point is how the administration approached APEC, the institution that is the most inclusive in membership. In 2001, Bush reoriented the agenda of the APEC leaders' summit in Shanghai away from trade and investment and toward terrorism. It is a focus that has remained in each APEC summit since, while many members, including those in Southeast Asia, would prefer not to be so overwhelmed by the US agenda. At the 2003 summit, the United States managed to have the 'war on terror' in APEC's final declaration. It stated that transnational terrorism and the proliferation of weapons of mass destruction pose 'direct and profound challenges to APEC's vision of free, open and prosperous economies'. It further stated that anti-terrorism initiatives by APEC members were not only 'advancing the prosperity of our economies but also the complementary mission of ensuring the security of our people'.[56] At the 2004 APEC meeting in Santiago, combating terrorism once again featured in the post-meeting declaration.[57]

In short, a decade and a half after the end of the Cold War, the United States continues to be instrumental in preserving peace and stability in East Asia. However, it is no longer setting the pace of change within the region. Worse still, by refusing to sign ASEAN's Treaty of Amity and Cooperation, a key ASEAN condition for membership in the East Asia Summit (EAS) of 2005, the United States has indicated a continuation of its preference for relying on bilateral diplomacy in dealing with East Asian countries. Thereby, the United States has prompted East Asian states to seek frameworks for intra-regional cooperation.

East Asia moving toward a neighborly community

This brings us to our overall argument in this book. The end of the Cold War created new strategic opportunities for countries in East Asia to cultivate a regional environment conducive to enhancing their respective development and security prospects. The United States has remained committed to region-wide strategic security and its hub-and-spoke security architecture is still vital for regional order. But the United States has not been as comprehensively committed to managing the course of change in intra-regional political and economic dynamics in East Asia. On the contrary, since the end of the Cold War the United States has often served as the trigger for East Asian nations seeking a means to ameliorate differences among themselves and to enhance regional welfare. East Asian countries do not seek to challenge, collectively or otherwise, US predominance in the military sphere. What they do want is to enlarge the space for intra-regional cooperation on diplomatic, economic, and social issues in building an East Asian neighborly community.

The East Asian neighborly community building is a multi-level and multi-layered construction process with the aim of developing a framework within which to manage the growing regionalism in East Asia. In this process there is norm building as well as functional cooperation. By using the concept of 'building a neighborly community', we intend to depict four unique features of East Asian regionalism. First, the movement toward a neighborly community describes the dynamism and trajectory of intra-regional diplomacy. In so doing we advocate research attention to how East Asian countries have pursued political–economic interactions with each other. Over the past decade and a half, a pattern of intra-regional diplomacy has emerged. Eligibility for participation in intra-regional discussions is based on geographical proximity and political/diplomatic necessity, rather than similar political systems and/or shared ideological beliefs. Regional organizations, loose by European and North American standards, use consensus building as the operational modality. Participating member states can agree to disagree and escape sanction at the same time. Short of consensus, member states pursue the lowest common denominator. There is little room for creation of the type of supranational constitution seen in Europe. As part of consensus building, no nation-state can expect to have the kind of hegemonic role the United States plays in North and South America for regional cooperation. The result, then, is that a sense of regionalism comes from appreciating each other's positions and policies. That appreciation, in turn, prevents retaliatory measures when one nation-state's behavior is not in tune with other nation-states' expectations. Simply put, a nation-state functions just as a neighbor in a village; the neighbors may not like it but they have to live with it. Through interactions based on respect and care for each other's interests, the community becomes stable.

Second, the process of moving toward an East Asian neighborly community has been peaceful because it allows room for small states, South Korea in Northeast Asia and ASEAN states in Southeast Asia, to initiate ideas and projects to prompt the big powers (China and Japan) to act in the interest of the region. Indeed, East Asia has thrived on the group diplomacy ASEAN has pursued since the 1970s. ASEAN's dialogue partnership arrangements with China and Japan function to keep the two big powers informed about the small nation-states' wish for stability. Since an initiative for region-wide cooperation originates in ASEAN, it becomes easier for China and Japan to respond in kind because the two big powers have less of a reason to see such an initiative in terms of bilateral competition. In a similar vein, South Korea played a role much larger than might have been expected (from its size) in getting APEC to include China, Taiwan, and Hong Kong (which has its own representation, separate from China, in that body) as equal members. It was South Korea that initiated the 'ASEAN + 3' (also called '10 + 3') platform when ASEAN was holding separate 'ASEAN + 1' (also called '10 + 1') meetings in Manila in 1999. In short, in the East Asian neighborly community, it is the small powers that push big powers to move toward regional integration. The ASEAN-centered '10 + 1' and '10 + 3' platforms have become the framework for regional reconciliation and cooperation.

Third, the post-Cold War community-building exercises, though slow and often ineffective by American and European standards, have had the effect of keeping big power rivalry between China and Japan in check. After the Cold War's end, diplomatic difficulties between China and Japan became structural by nature. The persistence of the problem of history is just the most obvious dimension. What is truly at stake is how to respond to each other's changing status in the region. In an ironic way, precisely because Sino-Japanese rivalry keeps resurfacing, both China and Japan find it necessary to respond favorably to ASEAN's initiatives for cooperation in the region. China and Japan may tie their respective acts in regional cooperation to a mode of competition, but the totality is that neither can afford to upset regional stability, for fear of losing ASEAN's support.

Finally, we believe the pattern of regional interactions leading to a neighborly community is going to have a life of its own in the foreseeable future. Although East Asian states have begun to have more and more common interest in regional institution building, there remain areas of contention within the grouping. Structural difficulties between China and Japan do not show signs of early resolution. The United States' reliance on the 'hub and spoke' security order it established in East Asia is likely to continue as well. The role of the United States in many ways helps to prolong the Sino-Japanese rivalry, as it makes it almost impossible for either China or Japan to seek to become the regional hegemon in East Asia. It also leads to difficulty for China and Japan to exercise joint leadership in the region. The most likely engine of regional diplomacy continues to be ASEAN. Against this backdrop, Sino-Japanese rivalry is more about a subtle balance of influence in the region, rather than a traditional struggle for regional hegemonic dominance. Such rivalry, instead of disrupting regional cooperation, will likely allow East Asian states to continue building a neighborly community. Nonetheless, the prospect of East Asia reaching the level of regional integration of the EU will be a very long one.

Organization of the book

This book is not a theory-proposing or theory-testing exercise. What we do offer to do is to contribute to the search for a better understanding of political–economic dynamics in postwar East Asia by making the case that what post-Cold War China, Japan, and Southeast Asian countries have managed to achieve in the region is the fostering of a neighborly community. Such a community is based on a continuing search for a friendlier environment by using regional cooperative institutions as a means to promote trust in each other, rather than as a road to the kind of regional structural integration seen in Europe or North America.

Each chapter is written in a manner that helps the reader to minimize the trouble of making cross-references to other parts of the book. Hence, readers will find some repetition in the description of events.

Following this introduction, Chapter 2 provides a review and critique of regional community building from different theoretical perspectives on the postwar international relations of East Asia, with a focus on predictions offered about post-Cold War Japan, China, and Southeast Asia.[58] As earlier parts of this chapter have touched upon, realism falls short, in that it predicts that post-Cold War East Asian will be embroiled in perpetual conflict. The plea from adherents to the realist school that we need to 'just wait' for them to be proved correct deserves serious questioning now that over a decade of intra-regional developments have pointed to a different, if not opposite, result.[59] The liberal institutional theories either celebrate the prowess of the various institutional arrangements in East Asia to a level they do not deserve, or are too dismissive of their value, simply because there is such a large gap between the East Asia approach to institution building and that of Europe and North America. Constructivists fail the test because their claim for a common Asian identity as a source of power cannot be substantiated when we look at the not-so-subtle reservations China, Japan, and Southeast Asia continue to harbor about each other's intentions. As a matter of fact, political, economic, and cultural diversity within Southeast Asia alone casts serious doubt on the explanatory power of how nation-states in East Asia have responded to events in their own neighborhood. What we do see value in is the kind of 'analytic eclecticism' that is emerging in research on East Asia.[60] As such, we choose to focus on sorting out the key actors, their interests, and their behaviors with regard to some select issues that mainstream international relations theories have tried to account for, although we do not profess to be able to predict the future.

Chapter 3 gives a historical treatment of the evolution of security and political–economic relations between China and Southeast Asia in the postwar period. Developments in the post-Cold War era will be highlighted. The role of the United States as an intervening factor is taken into consideration as well. The chapter discusses China's motivation and objectives in its 'good neighbor' policy toward Southeast Asia after the Cold War, and how China has achieved its goals, bilaterally and multilaterally, in the region. The chapter also assesses how the ASEAN states have responded to the 'rise of China'.

Chapter 4 reviews Japan's pursuit of postwar security and political–economic ties with Southeast Asia, while paying due attention to the changing dynamics of the Japanese–US security alliance and its impact on Japanese foreign policy in general. Without losing our focus on Japan, we also illustrate how China has featured as a factor, and thereby establish a link with Chapter 3.

Chapter 5 continues with our historical treatment by presenting how Southeast Asia has dealt with its two big power neighbors in the postwar era, in light of the changing role of the United States in the entire region. We pay particular attention to the contrasts between how individual ASEAN member states (during the various stages of the grouping's evolution) have pursued their bilateral ties with China and Japan, while making an effort to project a group identity by way of conducting the 'ASEAN way' of diplomacy.

Chapter 6 puts the dispute over territorial waters in the South China Sea into the context of conflict resolution between China and Southeast Asian claimants; it looks at contending definitions of interests and associated conflicts, as well preferences for particular means of conflict resolution. It explores the Japan factor in the South China Sea problem by examining maritime piracy as a major issue of concern for China, Japan, and selected Southeast Asian states. We attempt to shed light on how China, Japan, and ASEAN have turned the Southeast China Sea from a source of conflict to one of community building and why the three have thus far failed to be more effective in dealing with the common security challenges the South China Sea presents.

Chapter 7 examines the trajectory of China, Japan, and Southeast Asia in their attempt to form a regional mechanism for dealing with the economic challenges facing the entire region in the wake of the financial crisis of 1997. It does so by considering the larger background of the rise of China since the 1990s and the associated 'China threat' to Japan (which for most of the period was mired in its 'lost decade') and to Southeast Asia (which had been wounded by a crisis of governance as well by the financial crisis). It considers how the trio (and South Korea) interacted with a heavily US-influenced IMF and World Bank. The chapter also examines the political and security factors behind competing Chinese and Japanese approaches to liberalizing trade with Southeast Asia on the one hand, and Southeast Asian countries' programs in establishing trade liberalization schemes with the other regions of the world on the other.

Chapter 8 discusses the developments in Sino-Japanese relations after the Cold War and how ASEAN has reacted to the deterioration of this relationship. As the driving force of regional community building, ASEAN does not want to see the deteriorating Sino-Japanese relationship affect the intra-regional dynamics toward a neighborly community. Southeast Asian countries do not want to become the victim of Sino-Japanese rivalry in East Asia, either. For nearly a decade, the ASEAN-centered intra-regional process has served as a useful platform on which Beijing and Tokyo can engage with one another.

In the concluding chapter we provide a summary of the findings from the previous chapters, offer our assessment of scenarios for the future, and lay out areas for further study in coming to grips with the post-Cold War dynamics of security and political–economic relations among China, Japan, and Southeast Asia in the new century.

Notes

1 Bruce Cumings, 'The Wicked Witch of the West is Dead. Long live the Wicked Witch of the East', in Michael J. Hogan (ed.), *The End of the Cold War: its meaning and implications*, New York: Cambridge University Press, 1992, p. 94.
2 For an early assessment of the Cold War's end in East Asia, see Stuart Harris and James Cotton (eds), *The End of the Cold War in Northeast Asia*, Melbourne: Longman Cheshire, 1991.
3 G. John Ikenberry, 'American Hegemony and East Asian Order', *Australian Journal of International Affairs*, 58:3 (2004), p. 353.
4 Ezra F. Vogel, Yuan Ming and Tanaka Akihiko (eds), *The Golden Age of the U.S.–China–Japan Triangle, 1972–1989*, Cambridge, MA: Harvard University Press, 2002.
5 Thomas J. Christensen, 'China, the U.S.–Japan Alliance, and the Security Dilemma in East Asia', in G. John Ikenberry and Michael Mastanduno (eds), *International Relations Theory and the Asia–Pacific*, New York: Columbia University Press, 2003, pp. 25–56.
6 Takashi Inoguchi and Purnendra Jain, *Japanese Foreign Policy Today*, New York: Palgrave, 2000.
7 Reinhard Drifte, *Japan's Quest for a Permanent Security Council Seat: a matter of pride or justice?*, New York: Palgrave, 1999.
8 By far the best-known argument along these lines is Aaron L. Friedberg, 'Ripe for Rivalry: prospects for peace in a multipolar Asia,' *International Security*, 18:3 (1993), pp. 5–33. For a summary and theoretical critique of such dire predictions, see David C. Kang, 'Getting Asia Wrong: the need for new analytical frameworks,' *International Security*, 27:4 (2003), pp. 57–85.
9 Francis Ng and Alexander Yeats, *Major Trade Trends in East Asia: what are their implications for regional cooperation and growth?*, World Bank Policy Research Working Paper No. 3084, Washington, DC: World Bank, 2003, p. 2.
10 G. John Ikenberry and Michael Mastanduno (eds), *International Relations Theory and the Asia–Pacific*, New York: Columbia University Press, 2003, particularly chapters 8, 9, and 10.

11 A classic optimistic assessment of East Asian development is World Bank, *The East Asian Miracle: economic growth and public policy*, New York: Oxford University Press, 1993.

12 Randall Jones, Robert King and Michael Klein, *The Chinese Economic Area: economic integration without a free trade agreement*, Paris: OECD, 1992.

13 John Ravenhill, 'The New Bilateralism in the Asia Pacific', *Third World Quarterly*, 24:2 (2003), pp. 299–317.

14 Avery Goldstein, 'The Domain of Inquiry in Political Science: general lessons from the study of China', *Polity*, 21:3 (1989), pp. 517–37.

15 A good example of such concerns is David Shambaugh, 'China in 1990: the year of damage control', *Asian Survey*, 31:1 (1991), pp. 36–49.

16 William H. Overholt, *The Rise of China: how economic reform is creating a new superpower*, New York: W. W. Norton, 1994; and Denny Roy, 'The China Threat Issue Major Arguments', *Asia Survey*, 36:8 (1996), pp. 758–71. See also Herbert Yee and Ian Storey (eds), *The China Threat: perceptions, myths and reality*, London: Routledge Curzon, 2002.

17 A good example of arguments for engagement is Barber B. Conable, Jr. and David M. Lampton, 'China: the coming power', *Foreign Affairs*, 71:5 (1992), pp. 133–49. A particularly unambiguous advocacy for containing China can be found in Gerald Segal, 'Opening and Dividing China', *World Today*, 48:5 (1992), pp. 77–80.

18 Yoichi Funabashi, 'Japan and America: global partners', *Foreign Policy*, 86 (spring 1992), pp. 24–39.

19 Eric Teo Chu Cheow, 'Asian Security and the Reemergence of China's Tributary System', *China Brief*, 4:18 (16 September 2004), p. 7. Available online at www.jamestown.org/images/pdf/cb_004_018.pdf (last accessed April 2006).

20 Thomas Friedman, 'Dust off the SEATO Charter', *New York Times*, 28 June 1995, p. A.19.

21 For one of the earliest Chinese counterarguments against the 'China threat' thesis, see Huai Chengbo, 'Behind the Fear of a "China threat"', *Beijing Review*, 36:9 (1 March 1993), p. 10.

22 Yan Xuetong, 'China's Post-Cold War Security Strategy', *Contemporary International Relations*, 5:5 (1995), pp. 6–7.

23 Rizal Sukma, *Indonesia and China: the politics of a troubled relationship*, London: Routledge, 1999.

24 Wang Gungwu deconstructs these and other myths in *China and Southeast Asia: myths, threats and culture*, East Asian Institute Occasional Paper No. 13, Singapore: Singapore National University Press, 1999.

25 Richard Sokolsky, Angel Rabasa and C. Richard Neu, *The Role of Southeast Asia in U.S. Strategy toward China*, Santa Monica, CA: RAND, 2001, chapter 4.

26 Yan Xuetong, 'Zhongguo de Xinanquan Yu Anquan Hezuo Gouxiang' [China's New Concept on Security and Security Cooperation], *Xiandai Guoji Guanxi* [Contemporary International Relations], November 1997, p. 28.

27 Zheng Bijian, 'China's "Peaceful Rise" to Great-Power Status', *Foreign Affairs*, 84:5 (2005), pp. 18–24.

28 For an English-language summary of Chinese literature on the 'Latin Americanization' of China, see Daojiong Zha, 'Can China Rise?', *Review of International Studies*, 31 (2005), pp. 780–4.

29 A succinct representation of the mood in Japan can be found in Karen Elliot House, 'Japan's Decline, America's Rise', *Wall Street Journal*, 21 April 1992, p. A.16.

30 'The Japan Puzzle', *Economist*, 21 March 1988, p. 15. See also Hiroshi Yoshikawa (translated by Charles H. Stewart), *Japan's Lost Decade*, Tokyo: International House of Japan, 2002; and Gary R. Saxonhouse and Robert M. Stern (eds), *Japan's Lost Decade: origins, consequences and prospects for recovery*, Malden: Blackwell, 2004.

31 Christopher B. Johnstone, 'Strained Alliance: US–Japan diplomacy in the Asian financial crisis', *Survival*, 41:2 (1999), pp. 121–34.

32 Yoichi Funabashi, 'Tokyo's Depression Diplomacy', *Foreign Affairs*, 77:6 (1998), p. 30.

33 For one of the recent studies on Sino-Japanese economic interactions, see Hanns Günther Hilpert and René Haak (eds), *Japan and China: cooperation, competition and conflict*, New York: Palgrave, 2002.

34 Bhubhindar Singh, 'ASEAN's Perceptions of Japan: change and continuity', *Asian Survey*, 42:2 (2002), p. 294.

35 Christopher B. Jonstone, 'Paradigms Lost: Japan's Asia policy in a time of growing Chinese power', *Contemporary Southeast Asia*, 21:3 (1999), pp. 369–70.

36 Seiichiro Takagi, 'Human Rights in Japanese Foreign Policy: Japan's policy toward China after Tiananmen', in James T. H. Tang (ed.), *Human Rights and International Relations in the Asia Pacific Region*, London: Pinter, 1995, pp. 97–111.

37 Michael J. Green and Benjamin L. Self, 'Japan's Changing China Policy: from commercial liberalism to reluctant realism', *Survival*, 38:2 (1996), pp. 35–58.

38 Yoshihide Soeya, 'Taiwan in Japan's Security Considerations', *China Quarterly*, 165 (March 2001), pp. 130–46.

39 J. Arthur Stockwin, 'Why Japan Still Matters', *Japan Forum*, 15:3 (2003), pp. 345–60.

40 For a comparative study, see William D. Coleman and Geoffrey R. D. Underhill (eds), *Regionalism and Global Economic Integration: Europe, Asia and the Americas*, London: Routledge, 1998.

41 For a detailed description of how Japan succumbed to US preferences over the EAEC, see Joseph M. Grieco, 'Realism and Regionalism: American power and German and Japanese institutional strategies during and after the Cold War', in Ethan B. Kapstein and Michael Mastanduno (eds), *Unipolar Politics*, New York: Columbia University Press, 1999, pp. 324–6.

42 The founding member states of APEC were: Australia, Brunei, Canada, Indonesia, Japan, South Korea, Malaysia, New Zealand, the Philippines, Singapore, Thailand, and the United States.

43 Vinod K. Aggarwal and Charles E. Morrison (eds), *Asia–Pacific Crossroads: regime creation and the future of APEC*, New York: St Martin's, 1998.

44 Takashi Terada, 'Constructing an "East Asian" Concept and Growing Regional Identity: from EAEC to ASEAN + 3', *Pacific Review*, 16:2, p. 264.

45 The European Free Trade Association now comprises only Iceland, Liechtenstein, Norway, and Switzerland.

46 Ramkishen S. Rajan, 'Trade Liberalization and the New Regionalism in the

Asia–Pacific: taking stock of recent events', *International Relations of the Asia Pacific*, 10:2 (2005), pp. 217–33.

47 Christopher M. Dent, 'Networking the Region? The emergence and impact of Asia–Pacific bilateral free trade agreement projects', *Pacific Review*, 16:1 (2003), p. 1.

48 Zha Daojiong, 'The Politics of China–ASEAN Economic Relations: assessing the move towards a free trade area', *Asian Perspective*, 26:4 (2002), pp. 53–82.

49 Miles Kahler, 'Legalization as Strategy: the Asia–Pacific case', *International Organization*, 54:3 (2000), pp. 549–71.

50 Yuen Foon Khong, 'The United States and East Asia: challenge to the balance of power,' in Ngaire Woods (ed.), *Explaining International Relations Since 1945*, Oxford: Oxford University Press, 1996, pp. 179–96.

51 One of the more recent examples is James F. Hoge, 'A Global Power Shift in the Making: is the United States ready?', *Foreign Affairs*, 83:4 (2004), pp. 2–7.

52 Joseph E. Stiglitz, 'Failure of the Fund: rethinking the IMF response', *Harvard International Review*, 23:2 (2001), pp. 14–18.

53 Gustav Schmidt, 'Asia, Europe, North America, and the "Asian Capitalist Miracle": changing "power cycles" and evolving roles in regional and international structures', *International Political Science Review*, 24:1 (2003), pp. 67–81.

54 David P. Rapkin, 'The United States, Japan, and the Power to Block: the APEC and AMF cases', *Pacific Review*, 14:3 (2001), pp. 373–410.

55 Saori N. Katada, 'Japan and Asian Monetary Regionalisation: cultivating a new regional leadership after the Asian financial crisis', *Geopolitics*, 7:1 (2002), pp. 85–112.

56 Geoffrey Barker, 'APEC Heads Unite in War on Terror', *Australian Financial Review*, 22 October 2003, p. 1.

57 APEC Economic Leaders' Meeting, Santiago Declaration: 'One Community, Our Future', Santiago, Chile, 20–21 November 2004.

58 Post-Cold War South Korea has played an important role in regional institution building as well. However, compared with China and Japan, the South Korean role is far less in the long term. But we include references to its role when appropriate in the book.

59 David C. Kang, 'Getting Asia Wrong'; and Sorpong Peou, 'Withering Realism? A review of recent security studies on the Asia–Pacific Region', *Pacific Affairs*, 75:4 (2002), pp. 575–84.

60 Peter J. Katzenstein and Nobuo Okawara, 'Japan, Asia–Pacific Security, and the Case for Analytic Eclecticism', *International Security*, 26:3 (2001), pp. 153–85.

Chapter 2

East Asian community building in theoretical perspective

In the introductory chapter, we outlined how China, Japan, and Southeast Asian countries have adopted a pragmatic approach to handling intra-regional political, security, and economic affairs. The end result is what we call neighborly community building. Since the early 1990s we have seen a rising tide of regional organizations and mechanisms for consultation. The East Asian community-building process is a complex one, full of inter-play between politics and economics, and between these and security. As we outlined in the introductory chapter, for the East Asian region the Cold War did not end in a clear-cut fashion. From shortly after the collapse of the Soviet Union, a host of security problems in the region, ranging from the North Korean nuclear stalemate, the tension across the Taiwan Straits, and Sino-Japanese rivalry, to territorial disputes, continued to serve as vivid reminders of deficits in regional security.

The changing balance of power in East Asia has prompted many heated discussions about the possibility of multilateral cooperation in East Asian economic and security affairs. On the economic front, much has been made of the growing international interdependence and deepening market integration in East Asia. East Asian countries are in search of more insti-tutionalized ways of organizing regional economic cooperation. The Asian financial crisis of 1997 prompted some more 'Asianist' views of regional cooperation, which are based on the market-driven integration of national economies and the need for intra-regional policy coordination to manage regional financial welfare. On the security front, East Asian nations have expanded the scope of their discussions to include some non-traditional security issues that are emerging, such as environmental security, energy security, ethnic tension, developmental gaps, demographic pressures on resources and the environment, and political and social instabilities in transition economies. The net result, however, is that East Asian countries have yet to find ways to build a European type of security structure to address their common political and security concerns. Nor is it possible to have a North American type of community, one that is centered upon a single hegemon, in East Asia.

In this chapter we review how mainstream international relations (IR) theories have dealt with the same phenomena and make a case for our preference for a problem-driven approach to studying interactions between China, Japan, and Southeast Asia since the end of the Cold War.

Realists: great power rivalry and inevitable conflict?

The realist approach to international relations is based on analyses of the history of inter-state relations in Europe. As Kenneth Waltz states, 'a general theory of international politics is *necessarily* based on the great powers' (emphasis added).[1] Most realists suggest a rather pessimistic outlook for post-Cold War East Asia. For example, in 1993 Aaron Friedberg wrote in the journal *International Security* that East Asia was 'ripe for rivalry'.[2] Richard Betts saw post-Cold War East Asia 'becoming less stable as an arena of great power interaction.... Superficially, the region appears fairly peaceful at present, but the security order that will replace the Cold War framework is not yet clear.'[3] Indeed, since the early 1990s, security studies on East Asia in the larger Asia–Pacific region have become a growth industry. Many of these studies recognize that a large number of the new developments in East Asia do not fit neatly into conventional IR paradigms, but the dominant research paradigm is realism.[4] After all, as Kenneth Waltz writes about the relevance of realism in describing and analyzing the world after bipolarity, 'theory enables one to say that a new balance of power will form but not to say how long it will take. National and international conditions determine that.'[5]

It is sufficient here to use Friedberg's reasoning as an example of realist predictions about post-Cold War East Asia. According to Friedberg, with the end of superpower rivalry, East Asia, like Europe, is returning to a subsystem 'in which clusters of contiguous states interact mainly with one another'. Unlike Europe, democratic political systems or moves toward them are not the norm in East Asia; in fact, there is a contrasting move toward national chauvinism. Intra-regional economic linkages through trade are growing but are not as strong as those between European economies. Consequently, 'it is simply too early to conclude that war has lost all its appeal, especially in a region as diverse, fast changing, and full of antagonisms and suspicions as Asia will be in the [twenty-first] century'.[6]

Some fifteen years have passed since the collapse of the Soviet Union, and East Asia has not seen the outbreak of a major inter-state war. Tensions do continue, but there is a concurrent movement toward the use of the various formal and informal region-wide mechanisms for addressing divisive issues, or at least for keeping them from escalating into an inter-state military conflict. Of course, fifteen years is short in historical terms, which makes it difficult to refute the explanatory power realists claim for their analysis. Nonetheless, when for over fifteen years the nation-states under study have demonstrated a tendency that challenges realist assumptions, we have good reason to caution against following a straightjacket realist paradigm for studying East Asia.[7]

The rise of great powers is a very popular topic in the realist discussion of East Asian politics. To realist scholars, the history of world politics is commonly told as a story of the rise and decline of great powers, and the rise of China is a structural event that is bound to have fundamental impacts on East Asian politics. This is because danger arises when a rising power, particularly a risk-accepting one, is misidentified and accommodated, as happened with Japan's quest for East Asian hegemony in the 1930s.[8] Nevertheless, some realist theorists do not readily treat China, Japan, or Southeast Asian countries as great powers, at least not in the conventional sense of the term. Therefore, the norm in IR research is to discuss East Asia in contrast to Europe. As a matter of fact, characterization of contemporary Japan and China as great powers – in the context of international or global politics – is more often done within the context of advocating changes to US and European policies over particular issues.

With regard to Japan, by the late 1980s it was generally recognized that it was an economic power, but there was much disagreement about where to place Japan conceptually in the international system, including that of finance.[9] More than a decade after the end of the Cold War, debates are still going on among mainstream IR theorists over whether or not Japan is a great power or should be encouraged to function as a great power in global politics and the management of regional dynamics. Some realists believe that 'Japan will become a great power rival in the short term'. The liberalist internationalists argue that the United States 'remains largely oblivious to the emergence of Japan as a great power rival'.[10] Area studies specialists of Japanese foreign policy agree that, by the beginning of the twentieth century, Japan was still striving to be recognized as a great power in the world.[11]

In mainstream IR research, the question of whether or not China can be viewed as a great power is equally problematic, in spite of the growing amount of literature devoted to discussing the 'rise of China'.[12] Realists see China as an emerging threat, not a great power, particularly not when responsibility is an issue.[13] Liberalist internationalists advocate socializing China into international clubs of great powers so as to encourage acceptable and responsible behavior on the part of China. Area studies specialists of Chinese foreign policy tend to conclude that post-Cold War China seems to behave as if it were a great power already and therefore becomes a source of friction.[14] Even Friedberg has come to be more nuanced, by modifying his predictions made over a decade ago. Now he sees conflict between the rising power (China) and the dominant power (the United States) as one outcome (but not the only one) in the future.[15] In other words, there is no agreement yet over whether or not China can be conceptually characterized as a 'great power' in standard IR research.

Southeast Asian countries, individually or taken as a collective body, come nowhere near the general IR theoretical categorization as great powers at all. In fact, according to Kenneth Waltz, 'it would be ... ridiculous to construct a theory of international politics based on Malaysia and Costa Rica'.[16] Flowing from this logic, the way to watch changes in the East Asian regional security and political scene is to analyze how the small Southeast Asian powers live under the sway of the region's big powers (i.e., China and Japan).

Power analysis provides a good stock of explanations for the state of affairs in regional security. Before and during the Cold War, deep-rooted security problems originating in the long and complex histories of state formation and state interaction among the Northeast Asian countries blocked initiatives for meaningful security cooperation in the region. In Southeast Asia, the establishment of ASEAN in 1967 was in fact a response to the expanding communist influence from the north. ASEAN's founding members, all strong authoritarian regimes, did not have faith in major powers and, rather, took control of their fate by establishing their own organization.[17] It proved impossible to have initiatives coming out of the region itself for the establishment of a region-wide security mechanism.

Moreover, within a realist framework, East Asian states would be expected rarely to adopt multilateral approaches in regional security because the realists tend to view regional cooperation more as a zero-sum game. States would be suspicious of becoming increasingly dependent on others for security. There would be no compromise when national sovereignty collides with international cooperation. States would often gauge cooperation via a relative-gain calculation and would likely choose not to participate in regional cooperative initiatives. Therefore, the only natural outcome was the hegemonic role played by Washington in forcing some security structures on the region after the Second World War.[18] Against the background of a rapid spread of communism in East Asia, which represented a challenge for both Washington and Southeast Asian capitals, the United States initiated the Southeast Asia Treaty Organization (SEATO) to ensure the security and stability of an 'anti-communist bloc'. Apart from limited multilateral security cooperation such as SEATO, the United States always preferred bilateral to multilateral cooperation, to prolong its hegemonic role in the region. Bilateral security cooperation with Japan, South Korea, the Philippines, and Singapore guaranteed the military presence of the United State in East Asia.

While the above is all plausible, realist IR theorization still cannot provide a satisfactory explanation for the lack of war between East Asian states since the end of the Cold War, particularly given the continuation of the deeply rooted problems they have with each other. Part of the explanation lies in the fact that standard IR theories heavily rely on analysis of European experiences and values, and their extensions, historical and contemporary. David Kang sees the Eurocentric nature of IR theories as one of the key causes of the misfit between theoretical insights and the actual evolution of events.[19] Yet, if one chooses to follow the standard realist logic, then one can still certainly find evidence pointing to a security environment of anarchy, and that states seek self-help and engage in balancing behavior as a means of protecting their self-interest. The first and foremost interest for a state is to protect its sovereignty. Indeed, the evolution of history in Asia from ancient times is such that post-Cold War East Asian countries continue to enshrine sovereignty as a top policy agenda.[20]

Territorial sovereignty and conflict avoidance

Sovereignty is a large concept and has both external and internal dimensions. Here we limit our discussion to sovereignty claims over disputed territories in the maritime regions of East Asia, since how a state uses sovereignty to justify its behavior toward another state that claims the same land or offshore areas can be the trigger for war (whether limited or on a larger scale). In East Asia, the government of China stands out as the actor that has been most insistent on the non-violability of its claims to sovereignty. Sovereignty forms a core in China's self-identity, even when the Chinese economy and society have benefited immensely from being part of the forces of globalization.[21] Nevertheless, over the past fifteen years, China demonstrated a discernible shift in terms of whether or not it takes actions that may be viewed as interventions in other states' sovereignty. The strongest evidence comes from increasing Chinese participation in multilateral peace-keeping and peace-making projects. More to the point is that China did not shy away from partaking in such missions in its own neighborhood (Cambodia and East Timor), a fact that seemingly contradicts Chinese insistence on the very high standard of national sovereignty.[22]

What then of China's own territorial sovereignty? Between China and Japan, the postwar history of sovereignty-related territorial disputes begins with fishing rights in the East China and Yellow Seas to the north and the Senkaku/Diaoyu Islands to the south. It is easy for a student of international politics to see the geostrategic significance of the disputed waters for each country. For thousands of years, the maritime boundaries between Japan and China were never clearly marked. The end of the Second World War ushered in a new era for China, Japan, and South Korea to practice the kind of inter-state relations that evolved in modern Europe. But war on the Korean peninsula and intra-Chinese wars from 1945 to 1949 made it impossible for the three countries to start negotiating over demarcation of their maritime boundaries. China in the 1950s began to enforce its claims to the maritime boundaries against Japanese fishing vessels, whose technologies were more advanced than the Chinese. In the absence of formal diplomatic relations, China and Japan worked out a formula whereby they each established an officially non-governmental fisheries council to begin direct negotiations toward a fisheries agreement. The first such agreement was reached in 1955. Although the agreement lapsed between 1958 and 1962, the 'provisional fisheries regime' lasted for twenty years, until a formal governmental-level fisheries agreement was signed in 1975. But the two countries managed to live in peace in the same waters. More to the point is the fact that there was no substantive difference between the 1975 version and its 'non-governmental' predecessor of 1955.

In 1996, both China and Japan ratified the UN Convention on the Law of the Sea (UNCLOS). In the same year, Japan initiated and China agreed to enter into a new fisheries agreement on the basis of the exclusive economic zone (EEZ) regime, as stipulated in the Convention. In 1997, the two governments reached a new agreement, building on the experience that began in the 1950s, to jointly administer disputed zones. China and Japan continued to negotiate for another three years until they were able to reach agreement on fishing quotas and fishing regulations in each other's EEZ in 2000.[23]

The geographical proximity of China and Japan tells us that disputes over fishing rights cannot be counted as issues of 'low politics', as access to and restrictions from certain areas have direct military and hence security implications. Given the traditional Japanese insistence on the domestic cultural significance of protecting Japanese practices in maritime fishing, including whaling, it would not be unimaginable for the government of Japan to choose to turn fishing disputes into a major security issue in its relations with China. For China as well, the sound-bite polemics of sovereignty being of utmost importance, as evidenced in the first of China's 'five principles of peaceful co-existence', also offered a ready reason for the government of China to treat its fishing disputes as one of 'high politics' should it choose to do so.

The Japanese-held Senkaku (Diaoyu in Chinese) Islands and adjacent waters have been a source of dispute between postwar China and Japan.[24] Viewed from the perspective of international law and norms, there is ambiguity in international declarations dealing with the end of the Second World War in East Asia (i.e., what Japan was surrendering to China). The San Francisco Peace Treaty between the United States and Japan in 1951 did not specify whether or not the United States, which occupied Okinawa until 1972, regarded the disputed areas as part of Japan's Okinawa prefecture.[25] Neither the Chinese nor the Japanese government has shown an inclination to submit the dispute to international legal bodies for final settlement. Then, China and Japan have only their own versions of history to justify their respective claims.

This sovereignty dispute has, since the end of the Cold War, continued to be subject to public expression of nationalist sentiments in both China and Japan. Both the Chinese and the Japanese governments face persistent domestic pressure to take strong and decisive measures to end the dispute once and for all. In 1996, when the Japan Youth Association landed on one of the disputed islets to establish a light tower, the act led to an outburst of public protests in China, Taiwan, and Hong Kong. Similar shows of resolve had taken place before, making the territorial dispute a major source of competing Chinese and Japanese nationalism.[26] While it is impossible to ascertain the role of the governments of Japan and China in these public displays of nationalist feeling, it is important to note that thus far both sides have managed to prevent the dispute from escalating. Neither government chose to ride on the back of the nationalistic movements to turn the dispute into a military conflict.

Sovereignty disputes between China and Japan can have another dimension: energy resources. Ever since 1968, when a report by the UN's Economic Commission for Asia and the Far East suggested that there are petroleum deposits under the East China Sea, the Senkaku/Diaoyu dispute has taken on a contemporary and economic significance. The claimants, China, Japan, and Taiwan, reached a *modus vivendi*, and shelved the sovereignty issue for the entire Cold War period. In 1992, China's territorial sea law did list the islands but Japanese government action has since been to seek clarification from China. In the mid-1990s, both China and Japan promulgated EEZs, but they avoided explicitly delimiting the zones' boundaries. Instead, both governments continue to call for negotiations over boundaries where their claims overlap.

Identification of the Senkaku/Diaoyu Islands as an area with potentially huge deposits of oil and gas serves as an important reference point for alarmist warnings about military conflict among the claimants. For example, to Kent Calder, 'a naval arms race among China, Japan, and possibly South Korea sparked by the changing oil equation is the greatest long-term security danger the region faces'.[27] Thus far, as was the case during the Cold War, there have been routine expressions of displeasure from both Beijing and Tokyo over each other's activities in the East China Sea, including investigations of the seabed and exploration for natural gas. Concurrently, there has been also a pattern of conflict avoidance through government-level talks.

In the summer of 2004, world oil prices reached over US$40 per barrel. World oil prices continued to rise subsequently. Both Japan and China are heavily dependent on imported oil and gas to sustain their economic activities. Sino-Japanese disputes over the Senkaku/Diaoyu Islands and their adjacent waters therefore took on an added importance. But diplomatic disputes over China's operation of a new gas field in the East China Sea are only part of picture. China, Japan, and South Korea agreed to cooperate in their negotiations with Middle Eastern oil-exporting countries, which they all heavily depend on for imports. Indeed, reduction of the overall costs of energy supply would reduce the diplomatic and even larger security costs associated with pursuing each country's sovereignty claims in the East China Sea.[28]

There is yet another case pointing to Chinese and Japanese willingness to avoid conflict. In 2002, Japan sunk a North Korean boat suspected of spying and illegally landing in Japan. The sinking took place on the Chinese side of the EEZ but Japan still decided to raise the sunken vessel. China demanded talks and Japan obliged. In an ironic way, the raised vessel, which later was publicly displayed in Tokyo, serves as an important artifact with which Japan can paint North Korea as a present and tangible threat. By extension, Japan's defense policies, partly justified in terms of an imminent threat from North Korea,[29] are not necessarily in China's interest because North Korea is frequently seen as an ally of China. When we apply that line of reasoning, it would have been in China's interest not to let Japan have the chance of gaining political capital from the North Korean boat incident.

Straight realist IR reasoning alone cannot satisfactorily account for the pattern of conflict avoidance between China and Japan over their territorial sovereignty disputes. In a similar vein, realist IR theories are insufficient to explain China's change of policy when it chose to subscribe to the Code of Conduct on South China Sea, an initiative proposed by the Southeast Asian claimants and endorsed by ASEAN as a group (on the South China Sea in regional community building, see Chapter 6).

Power balancing in East Asia

As we wrote in the introductory chapter, the United States remains the single actor that predominates in the security landscape of East Asia. A vast amount of realist literature has been devoted to reminding each of the various post-Cold War US administrations that it must continue to commit resources and leadership for the purpose of preserving the regional security structure it created during the Cold War, lest it risk seeing its own interests and values sacrificed and the region returning to anarchy.[30]

After the terrorist attacks on New York and Washington in 2001, the Bush administration's focus on its 'war on terror' led some realists to point out that traditional US interests in East Asia deserve attention too. For example, James Auer and Robyn Lim argue that the United States continues to need maritime power and nuclear weapons to ensure security in the western Pacific.[31] Micool Brooke more pointedly argues that the United States must side with its allies to maintain their positions amid the evolving security dynamics in the region, which may in material terms lead to a new balance of power.[32] Such arguments were applied throughout the Cold War era, too. The fact is that the United States may have had shifting priorities in pursuing its defense and diplomatic policies worldwide, but there has been no lessening of US predominance in East Asian security. In other words, the thrust of the argument is that the United States must provide for a balance of power within the East Asian region, which, again, is what precisely what the United States has been doing for the past half century, without showing any particular change in orientation!

Nor has US predominance been seriously challenged. As Peter van Ness observed about post-Cold War China and Japan:[33]

> Each of the two countries [Japan and China] has the capabilities to reject dependency on the US, but neither is even close to doing so, because Japan's leaders can no more conceive of a world without the US security commitment than China can consider opting out of the global capitalist market and returning to the Maoist economic strategy of self-reliance.

There is yet a more critical point to the durability of the US-dominated security structure for the East Asian region. The security alliance between the United States and Japan, since its inception, has always had a function of deterring adventures on the part of China in East Asia, albeit that the overwhelming threat to Japan during the Cold War era was posed by the Soviet Union. The logic of balancing, then, would lead one to think that China would work to weaken the US–Japanese alliance. That has not happened. As James Przystup pointed out in 1999:[34]

> During the cold war, Beijing followed a two-track approach to the U.S.–Japan alliance – formal and principled opposition with informal acceptance and tolerance. For China, the alliance served as a key factor in Asia's regional security equation, in large part by constraining Japan.

This pattern has not changed in the post-Cold War era. Viewed from the Chinese perspective, the US–Japanese alliance serves to restrain Japan from making unilateral use of its military power overseas (that is, without US approval or backing).[35] If anything, China paid a high price for its military exercises in the Taiwan Straits in 1995 and again in 1996. Those exercises can be viewed as a Chinese challenge to the US-dominated maritime sphere of influence in East Asia. Arguably, a division of spheres of influence between China and the United States in the Cold War era is what has kept East Asia at peace. China is the dominant power in continental East Asia while the United States holds primacy over maritime East Asia. Geographically, Taiwan sits right in the middle of the chain of maritime East Asian countries, from Japan in the northeast to Indonesia in the Southeast.[36] The process of strengthening the US–Japanese alliance may have begun years before but the Taiwan Straits crisis certainly served to help resolve Japanese domestic debates in favor of a strengthening of the US-Japanese alliance. Japan's consequent participation in the theater missile defense system has added to the risks of provoking further threatening behavior by China against Taiwan.

In addition, post-Cold War China made no attempt to act as a counter-balance to the United States by approaching Japan as a possible partner. As a matter of fact, given the political dimension of Sino-Japanese relations since the end of the Cold War, it would not have been possible for China even to attempt to do so. Regular exchanges of high-level contacts between the Chinese and Japanese defense establishments did not begin until 1985 and have been sporadic since. Bilateral confidence-building measures, such as exchange visits between the Chinese and Japanese navies, have routinely been held hostage to diplomatic disputes between Beijing and Tokyo over the Japanese government's handling of such history-related issues as visits to the Yasukuni Shrine by a serving Japanese prime minister.[37]

The evolution of strategic relations between the United States and China is such that the two have not got and, given the Taiwan issue in particular and US concerns about a rising China in general, will not get for quite some time to come, strategically closer to each other for the purpose of balancing against Japan. Declarations by US president Bill Clinton and his Chinese counterpart Jiang Zemin about moving the relationship between the two countries on a path of 'partnership' in late 1997 and Clinton's 'Japan passing' gesture of not taking in Tokyo during a visit to East Asia in the summer of 1998 do not really add up to much. Japanese concerns about US Asia policies, vividly captured in the expressions 'Japan bashing' (1980s), 'Japan passing' (1990s) and 'Japan nothing' (since the 1990s), are overstated when viewed in a comparative context of how the United States has pursued its ties with China and Japan. As John Ikenberry observes, growing concerns about the Bush administration's preference for unilateral actions on international issues not withstanding, 'the U.S.–Japan alliance remains the organizational center of the region'.[38]

In contrast, even with the turn toward cooperation between the United States and China after the 11 September 2001 terrorist attacks, strategic relations between the two countries remain tentative.[39] Gone is the 'golden age of the US–China–Japan triangle' during the second half of the Cold War,[40] now that the Soviet Union has collapsed (the rationale of the three countries collaborating to balance against Russia is weak, if not gone).

What then is the possibility of power balancing within the region? According to Lowell Dittmer:[41]

> East Asia consists of four great powers (China, Japan, Russia, and the US), three middle powers (Taiwan and North and South Korea), and a subregional bloc (ASEAN), which is too large (with some five hundred million people) to be a middle power and too fractious to be considered a great one.... During the high cold war the Asia–Pacific region was split, cleaving the four great

powers two against two, while the medium powers received patronage and extended deterrence assurances from their respective patrons (South Korea and Taiwan from the U.S., North Korea from China and the Soviet Union).

Along with the end of the Cold War, China dropped shared communist/ socialist ideology as a factor in its pursuit of ties with the rest of Asia. In fact, of the 'strategic partnerships' China has identified in East Asia, none is with a state that has continued to be governed by a communist/ socialist party.[42] Even before North Korea escalated the tension over its nuclear programs by leaving the Non-Proliferation Treaty altogether, China's pursuit of a relationship with North Korea was more a matter of convenience than a determined strategic decision to become a joint factor balancing against the United States and its allies in the region.[43]

ASEAN may not neatly fit into a conventional IR conceptualization of power status, but it has played a unique role in socializing the major powers into a club for addressing security issues. Both China and Japan have participated in the annual ARF exercise since its inception. For Japan, the pressure for it to be more proactive in defense matters came in the immediate wake of the collapse of the Soviet Union.[44] Since then, Japan has also demonstrated a discernible interest in approaching the management of regional security by being part of what ASEAN has advocated since the founding of the ARF: community building, not power balancing.[45] Likewise, the ARF has also succeeded in socializing China into a habit of conflict avoidance.

In short, what we have witnessed since the end of the Cold War is a persistent pattern of conflict avoidance, not the anarchy–self-help balancing prescription realist IR theorization directs us to predict.[46] This is not to say that inter-state war will not occur. History is not short of surprise military engagements by East Asian countries with each other. Our point here is that well over a decade of conflict avoidance, on top of deepening market integration, provides more than a glimmer of hope for peace and stability in East Asia in the future. In any case, the evolution of post-Cold War history in East Asia has caught realists short in their predictions. Moreover, East Asian regionalism is not mainly derived from state efforts: market influences and private business networks contribute a great deal to the regional community-building process. With the decline and distraction of the US hegemonic role in East Asia, the underlying dynamics of East Asian community building must be viewed from perspectives other than the standard realist prescriptions.

What can liberalists explain?

International relations theorization under the rubric of 'liberalism' consists of three key streams. Commercial liberalism promotes the idea of free trade and commerce across Westphalian nation-state boundaries. Economic interdependence, it is assumed, will reduce incentives for states to use force and will raise the cost of war. Republican liberalism endorses the spread of democracy, and it is hoped that when a state becomes more accountable to its citizenry, its military elites will find it difficult to highjack public opinion to gain support to start a war. Regulatory or institutional liberalism seeks to promote the rule of law and to develop international institutions and practices that ameliorate the security dilemma among states.[47] According to Stephen Krasner, institutions are 'sets of implicit and explicit principles, norms, rules and decision-making procedures around which actors' expectations converge in a given area of international relations'.[48] Institutions can identify legitimate and illegitimate behavior, and thereby help to prevent conflicts, uphold existing harmonious bilateral or multilateral relationships, and ensure a fair and open economic environment. Thus, East Asian regionalism can be explained by interest-driven institutions and rational choices of behavior. The increasing importance of APEC in the early 1990s, for instance, promoted regional cooperation by providing a consultative platform, reducing the transaction costs of cooperation, and increasing trust.[49] Although interest-based regionalism largely occurred in the economic arena, more regional interactions strengthen mutual trust and confidence, and hence lessen prospective security conflicts.

The history of US–East Asian relations from the early twentieth century demonstrates the explanatory power of the commercial and republican streams of liberalist thinking. As Thomas Christensen observed, the United States launched major campaigns to impose a liberalist vision on Asia in 1919, 1945–48 and after 1991, as part of its project to create a world order in the American image.[50] Though a rare exception, there is also characterization of US behaviors in East Asia as those of 'sentimental imperialists'.[51] Such a critique perhaps results more from frustration with the perceived US decline as a world economic power in the 1980s. It is more commonplace, however, for analysts to lament that US policies toward East Asia are insufficiently coherent and realistic (in the sense of befitting changing realities on the receiving end).[52] Such a state of affairs is indeed a natural outcome of the many facets of US foreign policy measures toward China and other East Asian countries. In many ways, what David Shambaugh observed about the United States' 'missionary complex' in its century-old interactions with China is true of US relationships with virtually all countries and societies in the East Asian geographical region. This missionary complex stems from several impulses: commercial (to modernize), religious (to achieve conversion to Christianity), educational (to mold teaching and research), cultural (to impart American values), and strategic (to affect a country's behavior in world affairs).[53] Liberalist theorization argues for a coherent agenda but competing domestic actors and interests in the United States make it unavoidable for the US government to end up being incoherent in pursuing peacetime political and economic ties with East Asian countries.

Recognition of the gap between liberalist theorization and inconsistency (aside from its security commitment, that is) in US policies toward East Asian countries is important for at least two reasons. First, the United States as a market has been instrumental to the success of the export-led growth strategies of East Asian countries. When the United States moved to create NAFTA, there immediately emerged a call from East Asia for NAFTA to function not as an exclusive club but instead to be made open to Asian participation. 'The choice made over NAFTA will determine whether we have a world defined by opportunity and brought closer by trade – or a world divided by jealous cartels, founded on fear and driven further apart by protectionism.'[54] The formal institutional arrangement of NAFTA has not opened to East Asia, with the exception of the bilateral free trade agreement the United States and Singapore signed in 2003. Instead, even for C. Fred Bergsten, a prominent US figure in the eminent experts group behind the creation of the APEC forum, the United States at the turn of the century saw the beginning of discussions for a free trade agreement among China, Japan, and South Korea as 'a world-shaking development', and one that is not necessarily in America's interest.[55] Indeed, commercial liberalist thinking runs into particular difficulties when it is used for making sense of how the post-Cold War United States has balanced pursuit of its own wealth (and power) against using its market influence to bind itself with East Asia more closely. As Richard Feinberg points out, the way the US government has utilized the asymmetries of market power has sought to reflect multiple interests: commercial and diplomatic, tactical and strategic. There is an explicit political agenda in the US approach, contrary to the WTO's apolitical universalism in establishing the General Agreement on Tariffs and Trade (GATT), in dealing with bilateral and regional free trade arrangements.[56]

Second, what liberalist theorists see as a desirable development is not what always what a government in East Asia sees as an ideal choice. For example, the most outstanding success in US efforts to transform East Asian polities in the liberalist image is, arguably, Japan.[57] But postwar Japan, which has embraced the liberalist ideals in domestic politics, has also demonstrated a pattern of commercial liberalism in its foreign policy orientation. A liberalist window of opportunity came for Japan in the summer of 1989, with the Tiananmen Square incident in China. Japan was in a position to conduct economic diplomacy with China along the lines suggested in republican liberalism. But it did not readily join with the United States in choosing to link normal trading rights with the promotion of positive political change in China. The election of Bill Clinton as president of the United States promised to narrow the gap between the US administration and Congress in linking trade with human rights in China. But the human rights–trade linkage for China was not seen by Japan as a welcome development.[58] Even when Japan did choose economic sanctions (more specifically, suspension of development aid to China) as an instrument in dealing with China, it did so rather reluctantly. As a matter of fact, Japan took the lead among G7 nations to end China's post-Tiananmen diplomatic isolation.[59] Besides, Japan's application of economic sanctions to China can be more convincingly explained by employing the realist notion of security, in that Japan would not want to see China armed with a more potent nuclear arsenal.[60]

More to the point is that the mixing of commercial and republican liberalism has a weak following in the East Asian context for a much simpler yet permanently powerful reason: geography. The geographical proximity of the East Asian countries under study in our book means that before any government decides to promote 'democratic peace' in dealing with a neighboring country, it will have to calculate the potential costs more carefully before preparing to reap its potential benefits. A case in point is how Japan handled the illegal migrants arriving in Okinawa from China in a rusted boat that had departed from China's Hainan island to the east of Vietnam in the wake of the 1989 Tiananmen Square incident. The migrants asked for political asylum, citing political oppression back home. The Japanese government ruled out the possibility of granting them political refugee status. Instead, it turned to growing unemployment pressure in China and its possible explosive impact on Japan by entering into governmental-level agreements with China to organize the importation of laborers made surplus in China's reform process. This policy choice was a virtue because Japan itself is suffering from a labor shortage in the low-skilled sectors of the economy, particularly in the remote areas of the country.[61] Similarly, because China shares a 2,000 km common border with Myanmar, it would be difficult for China to apply economic sanctions on that military regime, even under a scenario of a fully democratic Chinese polity. The point here is that it is much easier to pursue the ideals of republican liberalism in the United States than it is among East Asian countries. In a similar vein, one should not ignore the cultural and racial commonalities among European countries when it comes to evaluating the appeal of republican liberalist ideals for policy making.

In a similar vein, republican liberalist theories run into difficulties when it comes to thinking about diplomacy among ASEAN countries. Since its formation, ASEAN has followed the principle of non-interference in a member state's domestic affairs; indeed, this is enshrined in its charter. From a liberalist perspective, republican and institutional, 'non-interference' is precisely what has failed the organization in the sense of making it a vehicle for the formation and spread of democratic values. On the other hand, an argument can be made that virtually all ASEAN states face criticism from 'the West' for not being democratic enough. A possible exception is the Philippines, which successfully overthrew the Marcos regime through non-violent means. But the post-Marcos era has been marked by persistent political instability and economic and social malaise, making it a rather unappealing example to follow. In that sense, for ASEAN governments to stay away from practicing republican liberalist principles on each other amounts to a kind of resistance to outside interference as well.[62]

So, the republican stream in liberalist IR theorization is limited in its explanatory power when it comes to making sense of East Asian political economy. The collapse of the Soviet communist government did not lead to a collapse of similar regimes in East Asia. In contrast, China and Vietnam embarked on revolutionary change only in the realm of economic management. Political change – in the direction of democratization, as liberalists hope – in these two countries was evolutionary at best. The result, as Robert Scalapino observed, is some form of authoritarian pluralism, not democracy.[63] Largely because East Asia at the end of the Cold War was so different from Europe in terms of the staying power of political parties formally embracing communism, there was no shortage of dire predictions for change in the region. For example, Norman Graham insisted that even when one looks at variables favored by liberalists, East Asia appears dangerous, certainly more so than Europe.[64]

Comparison with Europe provides the most potent source of empirical evidence relating to the level of institutional rigor in the various regional arrangements in East Asia as well. In the area of security, there is no NATO in Asia. Part of the explanation is that the United States did not choose to create an equivalent of NATO for Asia in the wake of the Second World War, in spite of its efforts in the formation and management of SEATO. As Christopher Hemmer and Peter Katzenstein point out, around the same time the United States created NATO in Europe, it viewed Southeast Asia as an alien community, far from the kind of community it considered worthy of nurturing and protecting by building a regional security organization.[65] In East Asia, when the Cold War ended, or, more specifically, when Sino-Soviet confrontation and the Vietnamese occupation of Cambodia began to end, the United States was still searching for an appropriate long-term strategy for dealing with China.[66] The outbreak of political unrest in China in the summer of 1989, symbolized by the Tiananmen Square incident, gave further impetus to continuing debates within the American academic and policy communities about how best to deal with China. Realists and liberalists alike still ponder over the question of whether engagement or containment, or a combination of both, better serves the interests of the US and its allies in East Asia. While the United States and China are becoming ever more interdependent in the areas of trade, investment, and finance, although retaining their mutual suspicions of each other's military orientations, the moment for the United States to create a NATO in Asia has not yet come, if indeed it ever will.

Today, the justification for a NATO-like regional security organization is even harder to find. There is no country in East Asia that can serve as a target like the Soviet Union did before and during the Cold War. To Jason Shaplen and James Laney, the difficulties in getting North Korea to stop its nuclear weapons program arguably provide one rationale for building a regional security community in the Northeast Asian region, in part as a strategy to manage 'China's emergence as a power broker in the region'.[67] But North Korea, nuclearized or not, is hardly a candidate for a Soviet-type adversary for those states actively involved in reaching a negotiated solution to the North Korean nuclear program – China, Japan, the United States, Russia, and South Korea. In essence, then, the kind of community Shaplen and Laney advocate amounts to little more than multilateral confidence building. The lack of an enemy that all the members in a security organization share in identifying and investing to confront renders arguments for a NATO-type security organization an extremely weak one.

In 1994, ASEAN established a regular security dialogue mechanism by elevating its post-ministerial meeting to the ARF. This was the first attempt in East Asia to create a regional security organization. The record of the ARF, however, limits claims for its success as an instrument for effective conflict resolution in the region.[68] The South China Sea disputes served as a key background for its creation[69] but nevertheless the ARF has avoided taking on the South China Sea issue. Deference to China's sensitivities is only part of the explanation for the criticism that the ARF is 'built on sand'.[70] The way the United States has treated the ARF since its inauguration also provides a partial explanation for the state of affairs the organization is in. As Evelyn Goh's study makes clear, US participation in the ARF is only a supplement to its engagement strategy with post-Cold War China. For containment and deterrence, the United States continues to rely on its bilateral alliance structure in the region. In addition, because the ARF cannot deal with the core security challenges for the entire East Asian region such as the South China Sea, its importance in the US strategy remains limited.[71]

It is true that the ARF, the largest formal regional security mechanism, does not have the kind of legal nature of NATO and other regional organizations that Europe has. The ARF does not even have its own operational headquarters. With twenty-five members, including Australia, China, Japan, the United States, and the EU, the ARF can be said to be not so regional after all. Nevertheless, it has succeeded in socializing China, the country with which ASEAN member states have unresolved traditional security issues over the South China Sea. In this it has been so successful that China has seen the value of using the ARF format to launch an ARF security policy conference.[72] Certainly the ARF is not institutionally as rigorous as NATO, but its ends – socializing a Cold War era adversary and post-Cold War challenge into full dialogue and confidence building – do provide solid justification for its means.

The more successful part of multilateral diplomacy in post-Cold War East Asia is in the economic realm. ASEAN took the lead in the region by launching AFTA in 1992. In the wake of the Asian financial crisis, ASEAN decided to accelerate the pace of liberalization. By European standards,

AFTA could have achieved more progress in promoting intra-member trade.[73] Nonetheless, AFTA provided a useful platform for Japan and China to engage the Southeast Asian region when the two decided to. Southeast Asia is very diverse in levels of economic development, government policy commitments to trade and investment liberalization, and capacities for investing in infrastructure that can facilitate the movement of traded goods. China and Japan have, over the years, through bilateral and multi-lateral arrangements (such as the UN Development Program and the ADB), provided financial and technical assistance to Southeast Asian countries. AFTA, in terms of creating linkages with the Chinese and Japanese econo-mies, has been useful in the sense that it has fostered a habit of multilateral consultations, which has made it easier and more meaningful for China and Japan to engage the Southeast Asian economies through the formation of free trade arrangements in the region. Granted, there is a general aversion to the use of legal instruments at the regional level to achieve the kind of economic regionalization seen in Europe and North America.[74] However, given the complex political relationships between China, Japan, and Southeast Asian countries in the modern age, it should not be surprising that, thus far, regional economic institutions in East Asia have proceeded more along the lines of dialogue rather than the creation of supranational legal instruments. In other words, institutional liberalist insights do not augur well for evaluating the track record in regional economic institution building in East Asia.

Liberalism comprises a large body of argument. Our review has necess-arily been selective. The point we highlight is that liberalist theoretical insights, when applied to analyzing the political–economic interactions between countries in East Asia, run into the same kind of problems realist arguments present us with. The logical reasoning in liberalist IR thought often guides researchers to seek to determine how far a gap still exists between East Asia and Europe, whose historical and contemporary experi-ences informed those theoretical insights in the first place. What liberalist thinking fails to take into sufficient account is, among other things, the selectivity in US policies toward the region. This observation should not be taken to be 'bashing' the United States, or the West more generally. We do, on the other hand, bring to the fore how the role the United States has played in interacting with China, Japan, and Southeast Asia in the post-Cold War era both contributes to and complicates the evolution of regionalism in the East Asian region.

What can constructivism explain?

Constructivist IR theories are quite diverse. In general terms, construc-tivist approaches emphasize the impact of ideas on definitions of interests and policy choices. They pay close attention to the prevailing discourse(s) in society because discourse reflects and shapes beliefs and interests, and establishes accepted norms of behavior. Different strands of constructivism share a common theme: the capacity of discourse to shape how political actors define themselves and their interests, and thus modify their behavior.

When applied to the study of post-Cold War security for China, Japan, and Southeast Asian countries, constructivist IR insights direct research attention to the formation of distinctive and competing identities as vehicles for achieving legitimacy and security. The central question constructivist IR thinking has attempted to address concerns how China, Japan, and Southeast Asian countries have interacted with each other to manage intra-regional cooperation.

As a matter of factual evidence, it is fairly clear that post-Cold War China, Japan, and Southeast Asian countries have thus far, as institutional liberalist IR thinking laments, failed to create a regional institution that has a binding power comparable to that of similar organizations in Europe and North America, in spite of the economic dynamism seen during the same period. In the economic sphere, a noticeable exception is that East Asian economies since 1999 have finally caught up with the trend of utilizing bilateral preferential trade agreements as an instrument for competing in the global economy. However, as John Ravenhill has documented, the practice of economic 'liberalization without political pain' that has characterized the rush in East Asia to establish bilateral preferential trade agreements does not promise much in terms of promoting overall trade or economic growth.[75] In the area of security, as we outlined above, the ASEAN lead in forming a regional security community has by now spread to encompass the whole of maritime East Asia, with the formal admission of North Korea as a participant in 2000. Yet, few expect the ASEAN secretariat, which also administers the ASEAN dialogue meetings with China and Japan, to be the first place to call when a critical regional security issue arises. Decisions about recognizing East Timor's independent status and the subsequent nation-building project were made in the UN headquarters in New York. It was Australia that took the lead to challenge Indonesia's hold on the territory, and ASEAN as a group was unable to come up with a forceful collective position other than accepting the momentous change.[76]

Constructivist IR thinking about the history of ASEAN, the ARF mechanism it organizes, and the 'ASEAN +' formula of dialogues falls into two camps. The supportive or optimistic camp argues that there is an 'ASEAN way' to security cooperation in Southeast Asia and beyond. To Jose Almonte, a principal architect of the security (ARF), political (ASEAN and ASEAN +), and economic (APEC) formulas, in the post-Cold War world 'Asian leaders will have to nurture cooperative habits to enable the Asia–Pacific region to replace the regional stability now enforced by US arms with the unforced stability of a Pacific community'.[77] This can be possible because 'maintaining peace through the workings of regional organizations – providing increasingly close rules, norms and procedures to bind states together cooperatively – offers a way of transcending a national-interest concept which separates ethics from practicality'. Almonte further envisions a 'Pax Pacificana' as a future direction of change: 'a pluralistic community of equal and sovereign states, each with its own identity but also with a sense of common destiny'.[78]

Constructivism became prominent as a research approach to Southeast Asian security in the 1990s. As Richard Higgott pointed out in 1994, 'Even the most sophisticated and conceptually oriented policy analyses of contemporary development and change in the Asia–Pacific region ignore the significance of underlying ideational questions'.[79] Since then, a large amount of literature has been devoted to debating the explanatory power of constructivism for understanding the evolution of ASEAN, the ARF, and the 'ASEAN way' of diplomacy. Supporters of the constructivist approach insist that the idea of a regional identity, which is created and reinforced through a continuous process of exchange of minds between both government leaders and social elites ('track two diplomacy'), has sustained the peace in Southeast Asia. Furthermore, 'talking shops' though they might have been, the multifaceted exchanges ASEAN has organized since its formation in 1967 has fostered the implementation of the kind of diplomatic frequency and regularity seen in European and North American paths to regionalization. The difference such exercises have made, then, is that, after decades of pressure-free consultations, a shared regional identity has emerged, which in turn will be difficult to break down.[80]

The key problem with the constructivist insistence on the importance of ideas is that it commits the same error as structural realism's insistence on the formation of a new balance of power: it leaves aside the question of the timing of when idea/identity-inspired change takes place. Indeed, as Lorraine Elliott's investigation of how ASEAN handled environmental degradation in Southeast Asia in the mid-1990s informs us, if the promotion of the notion of a shared destiny failed to lead to ASEAN taking collective action over a non-military challenge, then we have good evidence to conclude that there is more rhetoric than reality in a regional identity.[81] Tobias Nischalke goes even further, by flatly calling 'the 'ASEAN way' to community building 'a myth'. 'As an international actor, ASEAN has constituted a community of convenience based on functional considerations rather than a community of shared visions.'[82]

If skeptics about the role of identity are correct, then how do we make sense of the fact that China, which the very creation of ASEAN was meant to garner collective power in order to confront, in fact became an object for ASEAN to socialize? Why did Beijing collaborate with Tokyo, and vice versa, to work with ASEAN on policy initiatives that contravene the preferences of Washington?

At issue here is how much weight IR research assigns to discourse in our identification of a national, regional identity. Claims about the emergence of a unique Asian security discourse are a good case in point. Often pitted against hardcore self-interested comments made by US government officials, an Asian security discourse is supposed to build confidence and trust, to address security concerns, and to ensure that individual nation-state's arms programs (with the exception of those of China and North Korea) need not be viewed with alarm.[83]

If the constructivist approach thrives on exposing the limits of realist and liberalist thinking it also leaves itself exposed, in that claims about the formation of identity often result from selective identification of rhetoric in order to justify policy choices in times of crisis.

The construction of a neighborly community

Our review of the literature on post-Cold War international relations between China, Japan, and Southeast Asian countries, though far from comprehensive, confirms the need to take more than a single approach to researching the subject matter. Indeed, a 'strict formulation of realism, liberalism and constructivism sacrifices explanatory power in the interest of analytical purity'.[84] This point is becoming obvious in more and more studies of Asia–Pacific international relations, particularly in the post-Cold War era.[85]

In the rest of this book, we practice what Peter Katzenstein advocates as 'analytical eclecticism' or a problem-driven approach to the neighborly community-building process in East Asia. Among other advantages, a problem-driven approach 'sidesteps often bitter, repetitive, and inherently inconclusive paradigmatic debates'.[86] David Kang dismisses this approach as one 'that includes a touch of realism, a dash of constructivism, and a pinch of liberalism'.[87] But the complexities of the relationships between the three parties we study, whose evolution indeed makes *the* difference between stability and instability, growth and decline in the entire western Pacific and beyond, justify borrowing insights from all available research perspectives and paradigms where applicable.

Instead, a problem-driven approach allows us to see the dynamics more heuristically. What we claim is that our approach offers a better account of how the situation – by identifying selective issues of region-wide significance – has evolved thus far, by taking into consideration the identity, interests, and institutional norms in inter-state interactions between China, Japan, and Southeast Asian countries since the Cold War's end. What we do not claim is that our analysis yields any definitive predictions. If the past serves as any guide, the future will be full of surprises in this peaceful yet volatile region.

As a matter of overall conceptualization, we maintain that what post-Cold War China, Japan, and Southeast Asian countries have sought to advance is a neighborly community, and that this community-building process is quite different from those seen in Europe and North America. As we stated in Chapter 1, a neighborly community can be understood by using the common-sense analogy of households in a village. By way of everyday interactions, one household reminds the rest of the value of being taken seriously and thus proceeds with the hope that conflict will not be necessary. Conflicts may break out, however, and we do not pretend to be able to specify the conditions under which they will or will not.

Notes

1 Kenneth N. Waltz, *Theory of International Politics*, Reading, MA: Addison-Wesley, 1979, p. 73.
2 Aaron L. Friedberg, 'Ripe for Rivalry: prospects for peace in a multipolar Asia', *International Security*, 18:3 (1993), pp. 5–33.
3 Richard K. Betts, 'Wealth, Power and Instability: East Asia and the United States after the Cold War', *International Security* 18:3 (1993), p. 34.
4 Sorpong Peou, 'Withering Realism? A review of recent security studies on the Asia–Pacific region', *Pacific Affairs*, 75:4 (2002), pp. 575–84.
5 Kenneth Waltz, 'Structural Realism after the Cold War', *International Security*, 25:1 (2000), p. 30.
6 Friedberg, 'Ripe for Rivalry', p. 27.
7 David C. Kang, 'Getting Asia Wrong: the need for new analytical frameworks', *International Security*, 27:4 (2003), pp. 57–85.
8 For a good discussion, see Randall L. Schweller, 'Managing the Rise of Great Powers: history and theory', in Alastair Iain Johnston and Robert Ross (eds), *Engaging China: the management of an emerging power*, New York: Routledge, 2001, pp. 1–31.
9 Robert Gilpin, 'Where Does Japan Fit In?', *Millennium: a Journal of International Affairs*, 18:3 (1989), pp. 329–42.
10 Christopher Layne, 'Less is More: realistic foreign policies for East Asia', *National Interest*, 43 (1996), pp. 64–77.
11 Gilbert Rozman, 'Japan's Quest for Great Power Identity', *Orbis*, 46:1 (2002), pp. 73–91.
12 Debates about China's status in the international system are numerous. For example, see Samuel S. Kim, 'China as a Great Power', *Current History*, 96 (1997), pp. 246–51.
13 For a presentation of the Chinese view and one that challenges it, see: Liping Xia, 'China: a responsible great power', *Journal of Contemporary China*, 10:26 (2001), pp. 17–25; and Bates Gill, 'Discussion of "China: a responsible great power"', *Journal of Contemporary China*, 10:26 (2001), pp. 27–32.
14 Gilbert Rozman, 'China's Quest for Great Power Identity', *Orbis*, 12:3 (1998), pp. 383–402; and Yong Deng and Thomas G. Moore, 'China Views Globalization: toward a new great-power politics?', *Washington Quarterly*, 27:3 (2004), pp. 117–36.

15 Aaron L. Friedberg, 'The Future of U.S.–China relations: is conflict inevitable?', *International Security*, 32:2 (2005), pp. 7–45.

16 Waltz, 'Structural Realism After the Cold War', p. 73.

17 Nadhavathna Krishnamra, 'Regionalism and Subregionalism: the ASEAN experience', in Fu-Kuo Lui and Philippe Regnier (eds), *Regionalism in East Asia: paradigm shifting?*, London: Routledge Curzon, 2003, p. 85.

18 Donald Crone, 'Does Hegemony Matter? The reorganization of the Pacific political economy', *World Politics*, 45:4 (1993), p. 521.

19 Kang, 'Getting Asia Wrong', pp. 57–85.

20 Sheldon W. Simon, 'Introduction', in Sheldon W. Simon (ed.), *The Many Faces of Asian Security*, New York: Rowman and Littlefield, 2001, p. 3.

21 Tiejun Zhang, 'Self-Identity Construction of the Present China', *Comparative Strategy*, 23:3 (2004), pp. 281–301. The author is affiliated with the government-financed Shanghai Institute of International Studies.

22 Pang Zhongying, 'China's Changing Attitude to UN Peacekeeping', *International Peacekeeping*, 12:1 (2005), pp. 87–104; and Allen Carlson, 'Helping to Keep the Peace (Albeit Reluctantly): China's recent stance on sovereignty and multilateral intervention', *Pacific Affairs*, 77:1 (2004), pp. 9–28.

23 Between Japan and South Korea and between China and South Korea as well, there was an identical process of conflict resolution. Sun Pyo Kim, 'The UN Convention on the Law of the Sea and New Fisheries Agreements in North East Asia', *Marine Policy*, 27 (2003), pp. 97–109.

24 Taiwan also claims sovereignty over the same area.

25 Kimie Hara, '50 years from San Francisco: re-examining the peace treaty and Japan's territorial problems', *Pacific Affairs*, 74:3 (2001), pp. 375–380. See also Jean-Marc F. Blanchard, 'The U.S. Role in the Sino-Japanese Dispute over the Diaoyu (Senkaku) Islands, 1945–1971', *China Quarterly*, 161 (2000), pp. 95–123.

26 Phil Deans, 'Contending Nationalisms and the Diaoyutai/Senkaku Dispute', *Security Dialogue*, 31:1 (2000), pp. 119–31.

27 Kent Calder, 'Asia's Empty Tank', *Foreign Affairs*, 75:2 (1996), p. 60.

28 Mariko Sanchanta, 'Gas Provokes Japanese Clash', *Financial Times*, 7 July 2004, p. 10.

29 On post-Cold War Japan's pursuit of relations with North Korea amidst complexities in Japan's relations with the Korean peninsula, see Christopher W. Hughes, 'Japan–North Korea Relations from the North–South Summit to the Koizumi–Kim Summit', *Asia Pacific Review*, 9:2 (2002), pp. 61–78.

30 Betts, 'Wealth, Power and Instability'.

31 James E. Auer and Robyn Lim, 'The Maritime Basis of American Security in East Asia', *Naval War College Review*, 54:1 (2002), pp. 39–58.

32 Micool Brooke, 'Balancing Act', *Armed Forces Journal International*, March 2002, pp. 38–43.

33 Peter van Ness, 'Hegemony, not Anarchy: why China and Japan are not balancing US unipolar power', *International Relations of the Asia–Pacific*, 2:1 (2002), p. 133.

34 James Przystup, 'China, Japan, and the United States', in Michael J. Green and Patrick M. Cronin (eds), *The U.S.–Japan Alliance: past, present, and future*, Chicago: Council on Foreign Relations, 1999, p. 34.

35 Paul Midford, 'China Views the Revised US–Japan Defense Guidelines: popping the cork?', *International Relations of the Asia–Pacific*, 4:1 (2004), pp. 113–45.

36 Robert S. Ross, 'The U.S.–China Peace: great power politics, spheres of influence, and the peace of East Asia', *Journal of East Asian Studies*, 3 (2003), pp. 351–75.

37 Testimony to the extremely tentative nature of military ties between China and Japan is that there is no separate treatment of how China and Japan are engaging each other in the comprehensive book by Greg Austin and Stuart Harris, *Japan and Greater China: political economy and military power in the Asian century*, Honolulu: University of Hawaii Press, 2001.

38 G. John Ikenberry, 'America and East Asia', *Asian Studies (Journal of the Japan Association for Asian Studies)*, 50:2 (2004), p. 13.

39 David Lampton (ed.), *Same Bed, Different Dreams: managing U.S.–China relations, 1989–2000*, Berkeley, CA: University of California Press, 2001.

40 Ezra F. Vogel, Yuan Ming and Tanaka Akihiko, *The Golden Age of the U.S.–China–Japan Triangle, 1972–1989*, Cambridge, MA: Harvard University Press, 2002.

41 Lowell Dittmer, 'East Asia in the "New Era" in World Politics', *World Politics*, 55:1 (2002), pp. 63–4.

42 Tomoyuki Kojima, 'China's "Omnidirectional Diplomacy": cooperation with all, emphasis on major powers', *Asia–Pacific Review*, 8:2 (2001), pp. 81–95.

43 You Ji, 'China and North Korea: a fragile relationship of strategic convenience', *Journal of Contemporary China*, 28 (2001), pp. 387–98.

44 Murray Savle, 'Defending Japan in a Changing World: getting defensive about defense', *The Journal*, 29:5 (1992), pp. 10–19.

45 G. John Ikenberry and Jitsuo Tsuchiyama, 'Between Balance of Power and Community: the future of multilateral security co-operation in the Asia–Pacific', *International Relations of the Asia–Pacific*, 2:1 (2002), pp. 69–94.

46 John Ikenberry and Jitsuo Tsuchiyama (*ibid.*) argue that the logic behind US and Japanese approaches to regional security lies in a more inclusive and cooperative regional order. But for years to come the Asia–Pacific will be a region that will exist somewhere between a balance of power and a community-based security order.

47 Martin Griffiths and Terry O'Callaghan, *International Relations: the key concepts*, London: Routledge, 2002, pp. 180–2.

48 Stephen Krasner, 'Introduction', in Stephen Krasner (ed.), *International Regime*, Ithaca, NY: Cornell University Press, 1983, p. ii.

49 Andrew Elerk, 'APEC Beyond Bogor: an open economic association in the Asia–Pacific region', *Asia Pacific Economic Literature*, 9:1 (1995), pp. 183–223.

50 Thomas J. Christensen, 'China, the U.S.–Japan Alliance, and the Social Dilemma in East Asia', *International Security*, 23:4 (1999), pp. 32–80. See also Roger Buckley, *The United States in the Asia–Pacific Since 1945*, Cambridge: Cambridge University Press, 2002; and Bernard K. Gordon, *New Directions for American Policy in Asia*, London: Routledge, 1990.

51 Mark Borthwick, *Pacific Century: the emergence of modern Pacific Asia*, Boulder, CO: Westview Press, 1992, pp. 363–9.

52 For example, Norman D. Palmer, 'United States Policy in East Asia', *Current History*, 88:537 (1989), pp. 161–6; and Bernard K. Gordon, 'The Asia–Pacific Rim: success at a price', *Foreign Affairs*, 70:1 (1990), pp. 142–59.

53 David Shambaugh, 'The United States and China: cooperation or confrontation?', *Current History*, 96:611 (1997), p. 242.

54 'Building Bloc: let's bring NAFTA across the Pacific,' *Far Eastern Economic Review*, 157:22 (1994), p. 5.

55 C. Fred Bergsten, 'America's Two-Front Economic Conflict', *Foreign Affairs*, 80:2 (2001), p. 19.

56 Richard E. Feinberg, 'The Political Economy of United States' Free Trade Arrangements', *World Economy*, 26:7 (2003), pp. 1019–40.

57 This is true in spite of the fact that the postwar Philippines is by far closest to the United States in the formal organization of power.

58 James McGregor, *et al.*, 'Major Powers Ponder Change in the U.S.: China, Russia, Japan view Clinton with wariness but see possible benefits', *Wall Street Journal*, 5 November 1992, p. A.9.

59 Michael J. Green and Benjamin L. Self, 'Japan's Changing China Policy: from commercial liberalism to reluctant Realism', *Survival*, 38:2 (1996), pp. 35–58.

60 Saori N. Karata, 'Why Japan Suspend Aid to China? Japan's foreign aid decision-making and sources of aid sanction', *Social Science Japan Journal*, 4 (2001), pp. 39–58.

61 Daojiong Zha, 'Chinese Migrant Workers in Japan: policies, institutions, and civil society', in Pal Nyiri and Igor Saveliev (eds), *Globalising Chinese Migration: trends in Europe and Asia*, London: Ashgate, 2002, pp. 129–57.

62 Bob Catley, 'Hegemonic America: the arrogance of power', *Contemporary Southeast Asia*, 21:2 (1999), pp. 157–75.

63 Robert A. Scalapino, 'The End of Communism in Asia: what next?', *Current History*, 375 (1995), pp. 16–22.

64 Norman A. Graham, 'China and the Future of Security Cooperation and Conflict in Asia', *Journal of Asian and African Studies*, 33:1 (1998), pp. 94–113.

65 Christopher Hemmer and Peter J. Katzenstein, 'Why Is There No NATO in Asia? Collective identity, regionalism, and the origins of multilateralism', *International Organization*, 56:3 (2002), pp. 575–607.

66 A concise introduction to the dynamics in bilateral relations between the United States and China is provided by Michael Schaller, *The United States and China in the Twentieth Century*, New York: Oxford University Press, 1990.

67 Jason T. Shaplen and James Laney, 'China Trades Its Way to Power.' *New York Times*, 12 July 2004, p. A.19.

68 Nicholas Khoo, 'Deconstructing the ASEAN Security Community: a review essay', *International Relations of the Asia Pacific*, 4:1(2004), pp. 35–46.

69 G. S. Hearns and W. G. Stormont, 'Managing Potential Conflicts in the South China Sea', *Marine Policy*, 20:2 (1996), pp. 177–81.

70 Robyn Lim, 'The ASEAN Regional Forum: building on sand', *Contemporary Southeast Asia*, 20:20 (1998), pp. 115–36.

71 Evelyn Goh, 'The ASEAN Regional Forum in United States East Asian Strategy', *Pacific Review*, 17:1 (2004), pp. 47–69.

72 Michael Vatikiotis, 'A Diplomatic Offensive', *Far Eastern Economic Review*, 167:31 (2004), pp. 28–30.

73 'Asia: more effort needed; free trade in South-East Asia', *The Economist*, 372:8386 (2004), pp. 52–3.

74 Miles Kahler, 'Legalization as Strategy: the Asia–Pacific case', *International Organization*, 54:3 (2000), pp. 549–71.

75 John Ravenhill, 'The New Bilateralism in the Asia Pacific', *Third World Quarterly*, 24:2 (2003), pp. 299–317. See also John Ravenhill, 'A Three Bloc World? The new East Asian regionalism', *International Relations of the Asia–Pacific*, 2:2 (2002), pp. 167–95.

76 Alan Dupont, 'ASEAN's Response to the East Timor Crisis', *Australian Journal of International Affairs*, 54:2 (2000), pp. 168–70.

77 Jose T. Almonte, 'Ensuring Security the "ASEAN Way"', *Survival*, 39:4 (1997), p. 80.

78 *Ibid.*, p. 90.

79 Richard Higgott, 'Ideas, Policy Networks and Policy Coordination in the Asia–Pacific', *Pacific Review*, 7:4 (1994), p. 368.

80 Sorpong Peou, 'Realism and Constructivism in Southeast Asian Security Studies Today: a review essay', *Pacific Review*, 15:1 (2002), pp. 119–38. See also Nikolas Busse, 'Constructivism and Southeast Asian Security', *Pacific Review*, 12:1 (1999), pp. 39–60; and Amitav Acharya, *The Quest for Identity: international relations of Southeast Asia*, Singapore: Oxford University Press, 2000.

81 Lorraine Elliott, 'ASEAN and Environmental Cooperation: norms, interests and identity', *Pacific Review*, 16:1 (2003), pp. 29–52.

82 Tobias Nischalke, 'Insights from ASEAN's Foreign Policy Co-operation: the "ASEAN way", a real spirit or a phantom?', *Contemporary Southeast Asia*, 22:1 (2000), p. 107. See also Tobias Nischalke, 'Does ASEAN Measure Up: post Cold War diplomacy and the idea of regional community', *Pacific Review*, 15:1 (2002), pp. 89–112.

83 Andrew Mack and Pauline Kerr, 'The Evolving Security Discourse in the Asia–Pacific', *Washington Quarterly*, 18:1 (1995), pp. 123–40.

84 Peter J. Katzenstein and Nobuo Okawara, 'Japan, Asian–Pacific Security and the Case for Analytical Eclecticism', *International Security*, 26:3 (2001), p. 167.

85 An excellent collection of articles employing different theoretical methods is presented by G. John Ikenberry and Michael Mastanduno (eds), *International Relations Theory and the Asia Pacific*, New York: Columbia University Press, 2003.

86 Katzenstein and Okawara, 'Japan, Asian–Pacific Security and the Case for Analytical Eclecticism', p. 183.

87 Kang, 'Getting Asia Wrong', p. 59.

Chapter 3

China and Southeast Asia

The relations between China and ASEAN have developed enormously in the past few decades. To use a Chinese scholar's summary, the relationship started in confrontation (1967 to the mid-1970s), turned to reconciliation (the mid to late 1970s), transformed to cooperation (the 1980s and 1990s) and advanced to partnership (since the late 1990s).[1] After the end of the Cold War, China, as a rising major power, and ASEAN, as an organization of small countries, began to have more common interests in their political and economic relations under the regionalization trend in East Asia. China's growing clout in Southeast Asia and its strategic partnership with ASEAN came just when the Asian financial crisis of 1997 had devastated the Southeast Asian economy, Japan's role was in decline in the 'lost decade', and US military and political power had been stretched thin, as a result of its military operations in Iraq and Central Asia.

To ASEAN countries, the rise of China has presented both an opportunity and a challenge. Yet China's fast-growing economy represents more of an opportunity than a threat, and Beijing's more polished foreign policy confirms that poise. Most Southeast Asian countries like to ride the Chinese wave as far as they can. In their perception, Beijing's main objective in Southeast Asia is to preserve regional stability, as this will be conducive to its domestic economic development. The unease over China's aspirations in the region has become much more muted than a decade ago. Nevertheless, although good neighborliness and mutual trust are official rhetoric in China, there are still enormous complexities in the relationship. ASEAN's inclination to accommodate China is contingent on how Beijing deals with other major powers in East Asia. China's strategic rivalry with the United States and its competition for regional leadership with Japan are likely to put ASEAN in an awkward position. In the longer term, Southeast Asia has to cope with a rising China as it becomes a 'superpower'.[2]

55

China's Southeast Asian policy has gone through significant changes in the past forty years as well.[3] During the Cold War, Beijing's regional policy was more oriented to the big powers and relations with Southeast Asian countries were not a top priority in Chinese foreign policy. However, after Deng Xiaoping's open-door policy and economic reforms in the early 1980s, the role of Southeast Asia in Chinese foreign policy was reassessed. A more regionally focused Chinese foreign strategy after 1989 made Southeast Asia a priority for Beijing's good neighborhood policy. In recent years, to turn the region into a showcase for China's 'peaceful rising' strategy (*He Ping Jue Qi*), the Chinese leadership has become more interested in building good neighborliness and mutual trust with ASEAN states. This policy is evident in China's accession to the ASEAN Treaty of Amity and Cooperation (TAC) and the Joint Declaration on the China–ASEAN Strategic Partnership for Peace and Prosperity in October 2003. To Chinese leaders, 'it is an important component of China's own development strategy to build an amicable, tranquil, and prosperous neighborhood [*Mu Lin, An Li, Fu Lin*] in the [Southeast Asian] region'.[4] Never before has China been so keen to cultivate a deep and comprehensive relationship with ASEAN, or to turn Southeast Asia into 'a good neighbor and a good partner' (*Yu Lin Wei Shan, Yi Lin Wei Ban*). To understand Beijing's rationale and motivation, we first need to look at China's Southeast Asian policy at a very basic level.

Southeast Asia in China's foreign relations

Southeast Asia was known to the Chinese as Nanyang – literally meaning 'South Sea' – through centuries of maritime exploration and trade. Compared with troubles caused by 'barbarians' in the north and north-west, Nanyang was never a security concern to the Chinese empire because of the natural barriers of rugged terrain and its distance from Chinese population centers. The Central Kingdom's early relations with maritime Southeast Asia (Java, Sumatra, Borneo, and Melaka), dating back to the Zhou Dynasty, principally involved trade. The demand for exotic goods from maritime Southeast Asia, especially with growing urban markets during the Tang Dynasty, greatly stimulated Chinese interest in trading with Southeast Asian merchants, and the trade later expanded to the Indian Ocean and Persian Gulf. The expanded trade with maritime Southeast Asia led to the rise of the Malays in trade and shipping, and they became dominant in the region. Thus, during the Tang Dynasty much of the trade was in the hands of non-Chinese merchants and shipping. By the time of the Song Dynasty, however, the advancement in Chinese shipbuilding technology led the Nanyang trade to be done more in Chinese vessels, and Chinese merchants began to establish semi-permanent communities in Southeast Asian trading ports. These communities later grew and became a permanent as well as complicating feature of relations between China and Southeast Asia.

The Southeast Asian kingdoms and principalities ultimately became dependent on international trade, especially trade with China. For this reason, the Southeast Asian kingdoms came to develop official contacts with the Chinese imperial court, through what is known as 'tributary missions'. Over centuries, from the Han to the Ming Dynasties, a 'tributary system' or tributary relations were developed between China and Southeast Asian kingdoms. The earliest known tributary mission to China was in the fourth century from Funan, a kingdom in southeastern Cambodia that waxed and waned.[5] Some of the Southeast Asian rulers dispatched missions in order to legitimize their rule and to raise their status in the eyes of their neighboring rivals. Some were in response to the invitation of the Chinese emperors, who sought exotic products or the gratification of barbarian submission.[6] Regular tributary missions to the court of the Chinese emperor began in the Song Dynasty. For instance, between 756 and 779 three missions from Java were sent to China. In 977 the king of Brunei sent envoys to the court of the Chinese emperor.[7] To the emperor, the tribute signified symbolic submission, rather than the transfer of goods and presents. In fact, the presents the Chinese emperor gave back were even more valuable than those he received. For the rulers of the Southeast Asian kingdoms, the tribute to China was just a polite exchange of gifts – a formality and a courtesy. They recognized China's superior power and status through the tributary missions, and, in return, the Chinese emperor did not send armies to their kingdoms and even provided protection for them. The Chinese emperor was asked for protection from several Southeast Asian kingdoms. In 1408 Brunei asked for his protection when Java, which had saved Brunei from an earlier invasion attempt by the Sulu Kingdom, demanded it to pay tribute. Emperor Yong Le interfered and prevented Java from obliging Brunei to pay tribute. To protect itself from Java's threat, the Srivijaya kingdom sought a similar favor from the Chinese emperor.[8] Thus, China's early relations with maritime Southeast Asia were largely non-threatening and peaceful. Because the Southeast Asian kingdoms paid regular tribute to the Chinese emperor, the Central Kingdom did not see any problems in the relationship, and, instead, the Chinese emperor viewed the relationship as evidence of the moral attraction (*De*) of China.

However, during the Ming Dynasty, emperor Hong Wu and emperor Yong Le reversed the centuries-long government-sponsored maritime trade policy with Southeast Asia, outlawed the junk trade, and managed the tributary trade in a more restrictive way. Yong Le sent his bureaucrats to the southeast kingdoms to streamline his outreach and the tributary system in the region. He even ordered seven great ocean expeditions to maritime Southeast Asia, by Zheng He, from 1405 to 1433. Zheng He's voyages helped to establish orderly conditions for regular maritime trade with Southeast Asia, and extended the tributary system to new countries, stretching to the Indian Ocean. In the eyes of the emperor, forceful intervention and naval expedition were justified to enforce the dictates of the Ming's tributary order and to articulate China's superior place in the world.[9] Yet, the interest in trading with maritime Southeast Asia began to decline, owing to two developments, in China and Southeast Asia. In China, the early seventeenth century saw the Manchurian power emerging in the northeast of the country. As a result, the Ming Dynasty had to shift its attention more to the security threat from the northern frontiers, and moved its capital from Nanjing to Beijing. In Southeast Asia, the Portuguese seizure of Melaka in 1511 marked the violent arrival of Europeans in this part of the world. Although the arrival of Europeans did not immediately disrupt Chinese trade in the region, the Western powers began to impose domination over trade and shipping by force. Trade and tribute, which had existed for centuries in China's relations with maritime Southeast Asia, began to give way to Western primacy and colonization of Southeast Asia.[10] In the following 300 years the whole of Southeast Asia (with the exception of Thailand) was colonized, and the Western powers even began to carve up China after the 1840 Opium War.

Historically, China's policy towards Southeast Asia can be characterized less by the urge to acquire control of adjacent countries, for example by the imposition of client buffer states, than by the concern to deny control of the area to its major superpower adversaries.[11] In fact, as Wang Gungwu, one of the most prominent scholars in the field, argues, the tributary relations did not mean subordination by China of the Southeast Asian kingdoms. China was only one of several entities with which Southeast Asian kingdoms had foreign relations. The Arabs, Persians, and Indians were even more aggressive than the Chinese. The Chinese emperor was content for his superiority to be acknowledged, even if nominally, and did not seek to annex any of these kingdoms.[12] Another leading Sinologist, Lucian Pye, also argues against any dominant Chinese role in Southeast Asia. In his view:

> [from] earliest times the Southeast Asians, living on natural maritime crossroads, conceived of the world as multipolar. Indeed, they were far more sensitive to other civilizations than the Sinic: politically, they modeled their governments after the Hindu concept of the state; in religion, they embraced Buddhism, Islam, and Christianity; and, culturally, they borrowed almost nothing from the Chinese – a fact which has punctured Chinese pretensions of superiority toward Southeast Asians.[13]

Geopolitically, China's development and security in modern times have been influenced more by Northeast Asia than by Southeast Asia. In geopolitical terms China is a Northeast Asian country. But, simply because of its huge size and central location in the Eurasian landmass, China is also an 'insider' in Southeast Asia and it has always viewed Southeast Asia as its 'backyard'. While other major powers (the United States, Japan, and the former Soviet Union) have attempted to project their military power and political influence from a distance, the Chinese leadership has always considered Southeast Asia a vital region at the periphery and a legitimate sphere of influence. Because of its geographical proximity, China would never allow other major powers to establish an accepted sphere of influence in its 'backyard,' and always stands ready to oppose any emerging hostile powers or 'regional hegemon' that might endanger Chinese security. From the Chinese strategic perspective, Southeast Asia's importance, especially the continental Southeast Asia as opposed to the maritime Southeast Asia, lies in the fact that it is the most receptive region for Chinese influence (some areas actually used to be part of China). Before the advent of European colonial powers, most of these Southeast Asian kingdoms had been China's tributaries. Some parts of what are now Vietnam and Myanmar were actually once part of the Chinese empire and directly ruled by the Chinese emperor. In other areas, the Chinese imperial court was often invited to settle claims between rivals for a local throne. Some of these arrangements had survived until as late as the 1930s.[14]

To understand China's regional policy, one has also to appreciate its security behavior of protecting the Chinese heartland through border defense, and control over a large and long-standing strategic periphery.[15] Historically, China's frequent but limited use of force against foreign entities and the pacification of its periphery was primarily for heartland defense (i.e. the core Han civilization). As a result, the expansion and contraction of periphery control on the northwest, northeast, and southeast frontiers was largely associated with the fluctuation in state capacity and the changing balance of power *vis-à-vis* external powers. China has a strong geopolitical interest in preventing major external powers from consolidating positions near its borders, whether those positions are in Northeast Asia, Southeast Asia, or Central Asia. China's regional security objective was 'defensive' in order to create a buffer against external powers.[16] However, to the outside world, China's defensive motivations can, in fact, result in the establishment of domination over a region. For instance, China's road and dam building in Yunnan and Guangxi Provinces, consolidation of control over the South China Sea, and trade and investment in Southeast Asia might eventually be perceived as China's attempt to dominate the region regardless of its pronounced intentions.

Looking at China's peripheral security environment today, however, it is not difficult to see that the significance of Southeast Asia has been on the rise in recent years. In Beijing's security strategy, Southeast Asia is not a top security concern as long as the risks of conflict in the Taiwan Straits and the Korean peninsula remain. But, while the Korean peninsula remains stable and the danger of Japanese remilitarization under check, China still enjoys a manageable geopolitical order in Northeast Asia. In Central Asia, China has successfully projected its power into the region through the Shanghai Cooperation Organization since the breakup of the Soviet Union. The potential competition with Russia, the rise of political Islam, and a US military presence would not pose any immediate security threat to China. Turning to South Asia, despite China's long friendship with Pakistan, the subcontinent is always dominated by India. As New Delhi and Beijing are warming up, there will be no instantaneous security challenge either. So that leaves Southeast Asia, a region where, historically, Chinese influence has been considerable, in part because so many Chinese people have migrated there over the centuries. Moreover, Southeast Asia is an economically vibrant region with increasing economic contacts with China. To further consolidate China's power base in East Asia, it is obviously tempting for China to bring Southeast Asia more under its influence and to expand its strategic space there. In order to understand why and how ASEAN countries and China have constructed mutually beneficial relations after the Cold War, we first need to trace some Cold War developments.

The Cold War and its legacy

The end of the Second World War ushered in a new age for Southeast Asia and China. A defeated Japan and the withdrawing European powers were supposed to be a good starting point from which both the newly founded People's Republic of China (PRC) and the newly independent Southeast Asian nations could build mutual relations without interference from external powers. Yet, when we look back at this period, we find the relationship between the PRC and Southeast Asia was largely shaped by 'external forces', not the traditional factors reflected in the historical tributary relations. The prevailing external factors were the forces deriving from the Cold War: division in political ideologies, the bipolarity caused by East–West competition, and the penetration of the United States and the Soviet Union into the region. Other indigenous factors, such as territorial disputes and the issue of overseas ethnic Chinese populations, were also hindrances, but they were secondary factors.[17] Therefore, relations between China and Southeast Asia during the Cold War were on the one hand shaped by external factors, and on the other hand affected and complicated by the indigenous issues in the relationship. These issues included: first, how the two sides handled the problem of communist insurgents in their interstate relations; second, how the issue of the overseas Chinese migrants was played out; and third, later on, how territorial disputes in the South China Sea were managed. The solution and management of these issues during the Cold War would have important implications for future Sino-Southeast Asian relations.

When the PRC was founded in 1949, most Southeast Asian states had just been created or were in the process of gaining their independence. This was an unfortunate time for both the PRC and the newly independent Southeast Asian states, as the iron curtain of the Cold War was being drawn from Europe to East Asia. Largely driven by political ideology and the 'leaning to one side' policy with the Soviet-led communist camp, Beijing took a revolutionary view of its policy toward Southeast Asian states. The region was perceived as either those that were hostile to the Chinese revolution or those that were sympathetic to the PRC. As a result of their revolutionary experiences of armed struggle, Chinese leaders felt obliged to help Southeast Asian communist parties in their national liberation movements and armed struggle against colonialism, imperialism, and reactionary regimes. Beijing openly proclaimed its support for and even promoted armed revolts throughout the region; this gave Southeast Asian states concerns about China's export of revolution. Liu Shaoqi, vice-chairman of the Chinese Communist Party, told foreign visitors that 'armed struggle is the main form of struggle for national liberation of many colonies and semi-colonies'.[18] To Chinese leaders, the newly independent Southeast Asian states were still under the control of imperialism and former colonial masters, and armed struggle by local communists was their only route to liberation. To Chinese leaders, there were no 'neutrals' between the capitalist and socialist camp. Southeast Asian states would have to choose one camp or the other, and bandwagoning was not an option.

Meanwhile, Southeast Asian states were divided by the Cold War over how to deal with a communist government in Beijing. While most maritime Southeast Asian states (as well as Thailand) maintained relations with the nationalist government in Taiwan until the 1970s, most continental Southeast Asian states preferred good relations with Beijing.[19] As the former colonial nations, Southeast Asian states faced both domestic and external challenges in their state-building process. For political–ideological reasons, some of them were disappointed by the communist victory on the Chinese mainland. A 'Red China' in the communist camp inspired fear among those nations more associated with the capitalist world and the nationalist regime in Taiwan. For example, the Philippines, Thailand, South Vietnam and, later on, Malaysia belonged to the pro-Western group. They sought security protection from the West through defense treaties and alliances. In contrast, North Vietnam and Laos had close ties with the PRC in their wars of national liberation. Cambodia and Myanmar (or Burma, as it then was), however, endeavored to become neutral states between the capitalist and communist camps, and they sought to have Chinese approval of their neutrality policy by establishing good relations with Beijing. Indonesia, under Sukarno, sought to retain good relations with Beijing but steered clear of any contacts with China after 1965.[20]

The PRC's involvement in the Korean War and the confrontation with the United States across the Taiwan Straits caused further apprehension among the non-communist states in Southeast Asia. In order to have a breakthrough in its diplomatic isolation and win sympathy with those states that did not belong to either of the rival camps, Beijing staged a diplomatic campaign toward Southeast Asia from 1952 to 1955. The campaign involved a new tactic of targeting the moderate 'middle field' countries in Asia and Africa. In 1954 Beijing initiated a series of political and economic offensives in Southeast Asia, including the Bandung conference of 1955, and sought a diplomatic breakthrough with the non-communist states on the basis of the 'five principles of peaceful coexistence' and 'Asian–African solidarity'.[21] With these new policies, Beijing played down its revolutionary aims and worked hard to establish close relations with non-communist governments in the region especially. In order to build up its political prestige and reduce Western influence there, Beijing adopted a more tolerant attitude toward non-aligned countries in the name of the 'Bandung spirit', which promoted peaceful coexistence between communist and non-communist non-aligned countries in Asia and Africa. Premier Zhou Enlai conducted an extremely skillful diplomatic campaign to promote this new policy in Southeast Asia. In June 1954 Zhou visited both India and Burma, where he respectively signed joint communiqués with Nehru and U Nu establishing the 'five principles of peaceful coexistence' in bilateral relations.[22] The five principles later became the symbol and catchword of China's new diplomacy toward Afro-Asian newly independent countries.

While China played an important role in the Geneva conference on Indochina, its role at the Bandung conference in 1955 was even more prominent, thanks to Zhou Enlai's successful diplomacy and the five principles of peaceful coexistence. To push forward the diplomatic campaign among the 'middle field' countries in the region, Zhou Enlai also traveled to North Vietnam, Cambodia, India, Burma, Pakistan, Afghanistan, Nepal, and Ceylon (now Sri Lanka) from 1956 to 1957. These visits helped Beijing to advance a new policy toward these countries, that is, that friendly inter-state relations should not preclude close inter-party relations, even when the particular party was trying to overthrow the government. This new policy deviated from the original line of confrontation and hostility.[23]

Nevertheless, a series of domestic political campaigns and the repercussions of the Sino-Soviet split in the early 1960s stranded Beijing's diplomatic initiatives in Southeast Asia. Although some countries in the region were impressed by China's dual image as a revolutionary force seeking peaceful coexistence, the majority of them remained suspicious of China's real intentions. Although China was successful in developing diplomatic relations with the three non-aligned countries in the region – Burma, Cambodia, and Indonesia (up to 1965) – it had little success in developing contacts with the four countries that were clearly aligned with the West – South Vietnam, Thailand, Malaysia, and the Philippines. All four had pursued a consistent policy of non-contact with Beijing. Indonesia under Suharto, suspicious of a Chinese-sponsored revolt, severed all relations with Beijing after 30 September 1965. It was not until the end of the Vietnam War and the dramatic strategic changes in the early 1970s that China's relations with these countries saw a breakthrough.

From the mid-1970s, China began to recover from the domestic turmoil of the Cultural Revolution. Internationally, the US defeat in the Vietnam War, the Sino-US rapprochement, and rising Sino-Soviet tensions dramatically changed Beijing's global strategic perception. Beijing's global strategy began to focus on anti-Soviet hegemony and sought an anti-Soviet united front with Washington, Western Europe, Japan, and any Third World countries that were not allies of Moscow (including Southeast Asian states). In China's domestic politics, the fall of the Gang of Four in 1976 began to change the outside world's perception of China's orientation in its foreign policy. The determined direction imposed by the post-Mao leadership toward the 'four modernizations' greatly improved China's image. To the ASEAN states, China was no longer intent on exporting revolution, and, as a matter of fact, Beijing drastically reduced its material aid to various national liberation movements and communist guerrilla groups. These guerrilla forces split into pro-China, pro-Soviet (or pro-Vietnam), or independent factions and gradually died down. Under its new policy, Beijing was committed to not doing anything harmful to Southeast Asian states, and would separate its inter-state relations from its ties with communist parties in the region.

China's improving image, Southeast Asia's growing confidence about China's open-door policy, and the growing attraction of the Chinese market began to pave the way for a new China–Southeast Asian relationship. Beijing's new thinking in foreign relations helped to lessen Southeast Asia's suspicions about Chinese support of communist insurgents in their countries. Beijing's economic reforms demonstrated that China was gradually freeing itself of various ideological restrictions and trying to integrate itself into the existing international system. China was also quite accommodating in supporting the Southeast Asia's demands in international affairs. For example, it was the first country to endorse Sri Lanka's proposal to turn the Indian Ocean into a zone of peace, and the Malaysian proposal for the neutrality of Southeast Asia. Distinguishing itself from the two superpowers, while fully realizing its limited military and economic capabilities, China's support for non-alignment and neutrality served its objectives well. In the field of arms control and disarmament, China's declaration that it would neither be the first to use nuclear weapons nor use them against non-nuclear countries won support from Southeast Asia.

During the Cold War period, Beijing's relations with Southeast Asia were mainly conducted on a bilateral basis, and bilateralism remained the principal thrust of its Southeast Asian policy. The Cambodian problem, however, provided a good opportunity for China to engage ASEAN as a group and to create a multilateral platform to forge common interests in Southeast Asian affairs. After Vietnam's invasion of Cambodia in December 1978, ASEAN, for the first time, took a firm and united stand on the issue, by demanding that Vietnam withdraw from Cambodia. In support of ASEAN's common position, Beijing undertook a firm anti-Soviet and anti-Vietnamese stand and similarly demanded Vietnam's withdrawal from Cambodia. As a show of support, Beijing even waged a limited border war in February 1979, to 'punish' Hanoi, which greatly boosted relations between China and ASEAN. What motivated Beijing's harsh policy toward Vietnam was its tough anti-Soviet global strategy. By signing a Sino-Japanese peace and friendship treaty in August 1978, and establishing formal diplomatic relations with the United States in December 1978, Beijing further associated itself with the Western anti-Soviet united front. ASEAN's confidence in China was strengthened by this new Chinese foreign policy posture and the perception that China had formed a pseudo-alliance with the United States and Japan to check Soviet global expansionism.[24] In its relations with Southeast Asia, the Chinese leadership also promised: to strictly follow the five principles of peaceful coexistence in inter-state relations; to uphold the principle of opposing hegemonism under all circumstances; to maintain the principles of equality and mutual benefit as well as joint development; and to follow the principles of independence and self-reliance, mutual respect, close cooperation, and mutual support in bilateral relations.[25] Such principles were vague and lacked substance, but they spoke to the hearts of ASEAN states, which championed the 'ASEAN way' of diplomacy.

The Tiananmen Square incident in June 1989 injected new impetus into Sino-ASEAN relations. The sanctions imposed by Western countries following the incident and the collapse of the Soviet and East European communist regimes left China facing international isolation. Chinese leaders had to adjust their foreign policy, and one of their new initiatives was a more Asia-oriented foreign policy, with Southeast Asia as a major focus. While most Western countries reacted adversely to the Tiananmen Square incident, the majority of Third World countries, including neighboring Southeast Asian countries, considered it China's internal affair and thought other countries should not involve themselves. The ASEAN principle of non-interference in another country's domestic affairs was certainly appreciated by the Chinese leadership. China's diplomatic initiatives in Southeast Asia secured satisfactory results within two or three years. For example, in August 1990 China normalized relations with Indonesia, and, as expected, just two months later it established diplomatic relations with Singapore. The normalization of Sino-Vietnamese relations was achieved in 1991, and this was followed by a visit to Vietnam by the Chinese premier in December 1992 and by the start of border negotiations between the two countries.

While the external powers were no longer major impediments by the end of the 1980s, the traditional problems were also on the way to being resolved, or at least effectively managed. Although Chinese support of communist insurgents was basically ended by the middle of the 1980s, the issue of the overseas Chinese migrants in Southeast Asia remained a lingering problem. They have been a critical factor determining the perceptions and policies of both China and Southeast Asian states. More than their absolute numbers might suggest, these ethnic Chinese have played a vital economic and commercial role in Southeast Asian countries, though to what extent has varied from state of state and from time to time. Malaysia, whose population is 30 percent ethnic Chinese, Thailand, with 12 percent ethnic Chinese, and Indonesia, where ethnic Chinese people constitute more than 5 percent of the population, are all sensitive to how Beijing sees their ethnic populations. Indonesia was one of the first Southeast Asian countries to befriend China during the 1950s and 1960s, but suspended its diplomatic ties with China in October 1967 when president Suharto claimed the ethnic Chinese connection endangered his country's security.[26] Throughout the past few decades, there have been allegations of China sponsoring local communist parties and even involving them in various surveillance tasks that go against the fundamental interests of their host countries. Because their dual citizenship allows them to avoid assimilating into local socio-political cultures, and because of their prosperity and the rise of China, ethnic Chinese populations in Southeast Asia have on occasion been the target of the local population's rage, and this has caused tension between China and its near neighbors. Although Beijing abandoned the policy of allowing dual citizenship in the mid-1950s, the older generation of ethnic Chinese people in Southeast Asia still had problems assimilating into local societies, partially because of various discriminatory policies against them in these countries. The ethnic Chinese generally prefer to maintain ties with their families back in China and continue to send back remittances. Chinese leaders have often appealed to them through the concept of 'motherland'. After the open-door policy from the late 1970s, China's patronage of overseas Chinese populations helped to attract a large amount of foreign direct investment from them: in fact this source accounted for some 60 percent of the foreign direct investment China received in the 1980s and 1990s.

However, as time passes and bilateral relations between China and Southeast Asia improve, Southeast Asian countries have become more confident in managing their ethnic Chinese minorities in their societies. Most of the ethnic Chinese, especially the younger generation, have assimilated into local society. They are no longer considered a major security threat from inside these states. The Chinese government has also facilitated the assimilation of ethnic Chinese into local societies. Therefore this issue was no longer a major problem by the 1990s. Most Southeast

Asian states came to terms with Beijing on the issue, including Indonesia. Yet, Indonesia was not the last state to resume its diplomatic relationship with Beijing. Singaporean prime minister Lee Kwan Yew visited China as early as 1976, and he reached an understanding with Chinese leaders that Singapore would normalize its relations with China, but the official recognition would not take place until Indonesia had resumed official ties with China. So Indonesia and Singapore were the last ASEAN states that restored diplomatic relations with Beijing.

The South China Sea dispute, compared with other bilateral problems, remains a more difficult problem for both China and ASEAN countries.[27] If not handled appropriately, the problem could be very damaging to relations. The territorial dispute over the Spratly Islands is a more prominent problem afflicting China and four ASEAN claimant states, namely Vietnam, the Philippines, Malaysia, and Brunei. These claimants to all or part of the Spratlys have in recent years attempted to quietly shore up their ability to enforce their claims to these islands, and part of their defense modernization is linked to contingency planning on the Spratlys. The dispute came to a head in February 1995, when China encroached on the Philippines-claimed Mischief Reef in the Spratlys. That incident gave Manila an incentive to expand its defense budget and to get other major powers involved in the South China Sea dispute. Vietnam's approach in dealing with China over the Spratlys is to enlist a Western third party on the side of its claims. Hanoi awarded an oil exploration contract in 1994 to Mobil Oil for exploration in the overlapping Vietnamese and Chinese claims near the Spratlys. Although each of these countries has displayed a different attitude toward territorial and maritime disputes with China, Beijing is concerned with the possibility of their taking a collective stand on the issue and making the dispute more confrontational. But thanks to the mixed influence of various factors, the South China Sea dispute has not developed into a single critical issue that has evoked a major crisis since the Mischief Reef incident. Both Beijing and ASEAN began to seek ways of reducing tension.[28]

After the Cold War: toward good neighborliness

The end of the Cold War and the disintegration of the Soviet Union created new parameters for the development of the relationship between China and Southeast Asia. Since then, China has taken a very friendly and sophisticated, bilateral and multilateral, approach toward Southeast Asian countries and ASEAN. While economic diplomacy and trade relations have been the main driver in promoting good neighborliness, Beijing's successful conduct of constructive diplomacy, participating in regional multilateral forums, and declining to press its claims over the South China Sea have also played an important role in building mutual trust between the two sides. Southeast Asian countries generally show little fear of Chinese political and economic overtures. Beijing appears to have made progress in persuading the region that a stronger China will not seek hegemony. The improvement in the relationship is partly a function of the changing geopolitical environment in East Asia, ranging from the US 'war on terror' to the North Korean nuclear crisis. But it is also due to China's effort to be taken seriously as a responsible big power in world politics, especially after: its decision not to devalue the renminbi during the Asian financial crisis; its accession to the WTO; and its being chosen as the host for the 2008 Olympics.

Four factors contributed to the new episode in the relationship between China and Southeast Asia. First, Southeast Asian states' perception of China's role in the region has gradually changed since 1989. The disappearance of ideological barriers, China's rise as a major power in East Asia and its integration into the regional economy, the end of bipolarity, and the uncertainties surrounding the United States' future role in Southeast Asia all influenced Southeast Asian countries' perception of China's role in the region.[29] Although most ASEAN states still have lingering suspicions of China's future intentions in Southeast Asia and prefer a residual US presence in the region, the promise of economic cooperation with China seems to outweigh their security fears, at least in the short term.

Second, economic links have become the powerful driving force behind friendlier relations. The fast-growing Chinese economy has created plenty of opportunities for Southeast Asia, and these states cannot afford not to take advantage of the Chinese market. Built on this, both Beijing and Southeast Asia have managed to turn strong economic ties into more convergent and mutually beneficial, rather than divergent, forces in developing their political relations.

Third, while bilateralism still anchors Beijing's relations with most Southeast Asian states, the emergence of multilateralism in Beijing's policy and ASEAN's role as a collective body in more proactive engagement with China has also significantly boosted Sino-Southeast Asian relations. When the Chinese foreign minister, Qian Qichen, was first invited to the twenty-fourth ASEAN ministerial meeting in July 1991 by the Malaysian host, both ASEAN and China created a new mode of interaction to further cultivate their relations. Following that, China became ASEAN's regular dialogue partner in 1992 and an inaugural member of the ARF in multilateral regional security dialogues. By incorporating China within the security-oriented ARF, ASEAN appeared to indicate its consensus on China's future security role in the region and on the need to engage China, rather than to contain or isolate it. To China, active involvement in these multilateral forums not only indicated its recognition of a more salient role played by ASEAN, but also its interest in further developing relations with Southeast Asia through multilateral avenues. As Cui Tiankai, director-general of the

Department of Asian Affairs of the Chinese Ministry of Foreign Affairs, stated, 'China puts equal emphasis on bilateral relations and regional cooperation, making them the two pillars of China Asian policy'.[30] The more institutionalized Sino-ASEAN interactions of recent years have helped to shape more cordial and comprehensive Chinese relations with Southeast Asian countries. Underlying the new cordiality was not only the prospect of mutually beneficial economic relations but also China's greater willingness to engage in ASEAN's multilateral processes and institutions.

Fourth, but not least, Beijing's new regional strategy since the end of the Cold War, characterized by its 'good neighborhood' policy, was a significant factor in improving relationships. After the Tiananmen Square incident, Beijing began to pursue a more region-focused foreign strategy, to prevent its international isolation, and Southeast Asia was one of the target regions for a good neighborhood policy. To turn the region into a showcase for China's 'peaceful rising' strategy (*He Ping Jue Qi*), Chinese leaders have become more interested in building good neighborliness and mutual trust with the ASEAN countries. The developments in China–ASEAN good neighborliness and partnership after the Cold War can broadly be seen in three areas: multilateral engagement and building political trust; economic and functional cooperation; and bilateral relations and good neighborliness.

(1) Multilateral engagement and building political trust

China's involvement in the ASEAN-led multilateral dialogues has gone through several stages, from being passive, to more positive, and to pro-active.[31] The first phase (1991–96) was a passive and more reserved Chinese participation in the ASEAN-driven multilateral process. The first China–ASEAN official dialogues were initiated in July 1991, when Qian Qichen was invited to attend the ASEAN Post-Ministerial Conference (PMC) as a consultative partner. This was a significant event, since, until 1990, some ASEAN member states did not even have formal diplomatic ties with China. At the twenty-fourth ASEAN ministerial meeting, in Kuala Lumpur, Qian Qichen expressed China's interest in strengthening its cooperation with ASEAN. This was received warmly by ASEAN and a series of milestones have followed. ASEAN has been eager to engage China on political and security issues in the region. This was, despite past mistrust and animosity between the two parties, largely a product of China's support for communist parties in ASEAN countries. For its part, China has been receptive to ASEAN initiatives. Hence developments on political and economic issues need to be carefully watched, particularly those relating to potential areas of friction or conflict in the South China Sea. Beijing did not respond enthusiastically to the proposal to establish a multilateral security platform in the Asia–Pacific region, which was developed into the ARF in 1994. Beijing was concerned with the possibility that the security forum might make China vulnerable to multilateral pressure or might allow others to team up against China on territorial issues. It was also worried that the Taiwan issue would be included in discussion, and that the ARF might be used by Washington to interfere in China's internal affairs. To ward off any possible negative development, the Chinese side agreed only to hold annual consultations with ASEAN on political and security issues at the level of senior officials. However, in spite of these concerns, Beijing decided to attend the ARF in 1994, which was held after the annual ASEAN consultation with its dialogue partners. Chinese participation in the ARF did not mean enthusiastic support; it was more a cautious move to guard against any possible institutional development that might jeopardize China's national interests. Beijing was reluctant to see the ARF being developed into an institutionalized security structure along the lines of the Conference (from 1995 the Organization) for Security and Co-operation in Europe.[32]

The second stage of Chinese involvement in the ASEAN-driven multilateral dialogues was from 1996 to 2000. Since China was accorded full 'dialogue partner' status at the twenty-ninth ASEAN ministerial meeting, in July 1996 in Jakarta, cooperation between ASEAN and China has been broadened and deepened. Through its experiences in the ARF and other ASEAN-led multilateral dialogues, like the China–ASEAN senior officials consultation, Beijing moved up on the learning curve. It came to realize that multilateral dialogue may not necessarily be harmful to China's national interests. Rather, these multilateral platforms could be used to promote its own foreign policy agenda. China became more active participating in the ARF and grew used to the 'ASEAN way' of dialogue. As suggested by Rosemary Foot, China became more comfortable because it does not need to form coalitions of supporters and there would be little chance of forming an anti-China alliance in the ARF.[33] China actually used the ARF to propose its 'new security concept' to dampen down any perception of the 'China threat'. The Chinese delegates emphasized that the new concept of security and threat did not mean traditional security and terrorism, and should also incorporate non-traditional security, ranging from pollution to drug trafficking. Getting more comfortable with the process, China began to openly state it would consistently support ASEAN's status as the leading participant in the ARF process.[34]

From year 2000 up to the present, Beijing has become more proactive in participating and promoting multilateral dialogues and cooperation between China and ASEAN. The relationship between them has been elevated to a higher plane with the adoption of the Joint Declaration on Strategic Partnership for Peace and Prosperity. The multilateral dialogues and institutional building with ASEAN have become an important platform from which China has been able to push the relationship forward. China has entered into a number of agreements with ASEAN in the area of political and security cooperation. These include the Joint Declaration of

ASEAN and China on Cooperation in the Field of Non-Traditional Security Issues and the Declaration on the Conduct of Parties in the South China Sea, concluded at the ASEAN–China summit in 2002 in Phnom Penh, Cambodia. China was the first dialogue partner to accede to the TAC, at the ASEAN–China summit in October 2003 in Bali, Indonesia. China has expressed its willingness to work with ASEAN for its early accession to the Protocol to the Treaty on a Southeast Asia Nuclear Weapons-Free Zone (SEANWFZ). As a follow-up to the Code of Conduct declaration, ASEAN and China convened a series of senior officials' meetings. In the field of non-traditional security issues, ASEAN and China signed a memorandum of understanding on Cooperation in the Field of Non-traditional Security Issues in January 2004 in Bangkok to implement the Joint Declaration in the Field of Non-Traditional Security Issues. In this regard, ASEAN and China have successfully implemented all activities based on the 2004 annual plan to implement the memorandum.[35]

In order to improve contacts and communications and promote dialogue on ASEAN–China cooperation and regional and international topics of common interest and concern, both sides agreed to increase regular high-level bilateral visits and interactions. Among the already established dialogue mechanisms, the two sides agreed to strengthen the role of the ASEAN–China senior officials consultation in assisting the ASEAN–China summit, and to use the ASEAN–China ministerial meeting to provide guidance and strategic direction to further enhance ASEAN–China dialogue relations and cooperation. The ASEAN–China joint cooperation committee meeting, the ASEAN–China Working Group on Development Cooperation, and the senior economic officials–Ministry of Commerce of China consultations in monitoring, coordinating, and reviewing ASEAN–China dialogue relations will be further strengthened. These dialogue mechanisms will help to improve coordination and communication at various levels and sectors of functional cooperation, ranging from foreign affairs, economics, transport, customs, youth, and prosecutors-general, to ensure timely and effective implementation of decisions and initiatives taken at the ASEAN–China summit and related ministerial and senior officials' meetings.

(2) Economic and functional cooperation[36]

China has been actively reaching out to Southeast Asia in economic cooperation. In November 2002, the ASEAN leaders and the Chinese premier, Zhu Rongji, signed the Framework Agreement on Comprehensive Economic Cooperation. It provides for an ASEAN–China Free Trade Area (ACFTA) by the year 2010 for the old ASEAN members (Brunei, Indonesia, Malaysia, the Philippines, Singapore, and Thailand), and by 2015 for the newer ASEAN members (Cambodia, Laos, Myanmar, and Vietnam). Through the ACFTA, China has gone ahead of its rival Japan in setting the stage for regional economic integration. Southeast Asian countries have traditionally followed Japan's lead, in the 'flying geese' pattern of economic development. The ACFTA agreement to some extent has formed the economic pillar of their relations, while the code of conduct in the South China Sea declaration constitutes their political pillar.

Over recent years, economic and trade cooperation between ASEAN and China has grown rapidly. The total value of China–ASEAN trade was US$78.2 billion in 2003, comprising US$47.3 billion in ASEAN exports to China and US$30.9 billion in imports to ASEAN from China.[37] These exports and imports had increased by 51.7 percent and 31.2 percent, respectively, from the previous year. The trade value in 2004 increased 35 percent from the previous year, reaching US$105.88 billion.[38] In 2005 the total China–ASEAN trade value reached US$130.3 billion, a 23 percent increase from 2004,[39] with China's imports at US$75.0 billion and exports at US$55.3 billion.[40] ASEAN is now China's fifth largest export market and third largest source of imports. At the ASEAN–China summit in 2003, a target of US$100 billion in two-way annual trade by 2005 was envisaged and it was achieved in 2004, one year ahead of the target. The negotiations over the tariff reduction/elimination schedules and the Trade in Goods and Dispute Settlement Mechanism Agreements were concluded in Beijing in October 2004. The two sides signed the Trade in Goods Agreement and the Dispute Settlement Mechanism Agreement at the ASEAN–China summit in November 2004 in Vientiane.

As for other areas of functional cooperation, ASEAN and China agreed at the ASEAN–China summit on 6 November 2001 in Brunei to focus on five priority areas in the early part of the twenty-first century. These five priority areas are: agriculture, information and communications technology, human resource development, the Mekong River Basin development, and two-way investment. In order to strengthen cooperation in the five agreed priority areas, ASEAN and China signed a memorandum of understanding on a Medium- and Long-Term Plan for Agricultural Cooperation in November 2002 in Phnom Penh and another on Cooperation in Information and Communications Technology in October 2003 at the Bali summit. In order to promote networking and cooperation between governments, business associations, academic institutions, and corporations, a regular ASEAN–China trade exposition was opened in Nanning, China, in May 2005.[41]

ASEAN and China are working closely in implementing the Greater Mekong River area development programs and projects within various frameworks, such as the Greater Mekong Sub-region, ASEAN Mekong Basin Development Cooperation and the Mekong River Commission. China has contributed US$5 million to help regulate some sections of the navigation channel within the territories of Laos and Myanmar.

In the area of public health, in May 2003 China pledged RMB10 million in support of ASEAN–China cooperation on the prevention and control of severe acute respiratory syndrome (SARS). In March 2004 China also established the China–ASEAN Fund for Public Health, which would be utilized for funding cooperative measures to prevent and control cross-border infectious diseases such as SARS and avian influenza.[42] ASEAN and China were tentatively expected to establish an ASEAN–China health ministers' meeting by 2005.

In the field of transport, ASEAN and China signed a memorandum of understanding on transport cooperation at the sidelines of the ASEAN–China summit in November 2004 in Vientiane. The purpose of the memorandum was to strengthen transport cooperation in a more integrated manner, as well as to lay a solid foundation for medium- to long-term collaboration to support the ACFTA. The other functional cooperation areas include cultural exchanges, tourism, and youth.

In terms of funding functional cooperation, the Chinese government has pledged to contribute US$5 million to the ASEAN–China Cooperation Fund for five years (2005–10) to implement the various activities and projects agreed by the two sides. This is additional to its *ad hoc* contributions committed to such disasters as SARS and the tsunami in Southeast Asia.

The depth and width of today's partnership between China and ASEAN reflects deep commitment on both sides. For the Chinese side, Beijing found it is not just in ASEAN's interest but also in its own interest to promote development, rejuvenation, peace, and stability in Southeast Asia. That explains why China wants to be 'a good neighbor and a good partner' with ASEAN, and to intensify regional cooperation and dialogue, bilateral and multilateral. In recent years, economic and trade cooperation between China and ASEAN has become both deep and comprehensive. As mentioned above, ASEAN has become China's fifth largest trading partner and bilateral trade has grown at more than 20 percent annually since 1990. ASEAN's share of China's total trade rose from 5.9 percent in 1990 to 9.2 percent in 2003. For ASEAN, the unease over China's aspirations in the region is now much more muted than it was a decade ago.

(3) Bilateral relations and good neighborliness

China has traditionally attached great importance to bilateralism in its conduct of foreign policy, including with Southeast Asia. China's formal relationship with ASEAN started only in 1991, but its bilateral relations with countries in that region date back much earlier. After the Cold War Beijing continued its bilateral diplomacy, but used its bilateral ties to build a platform on which to promote relations with ASEAN as a group and broader cooperation at the regional level.

Continental (as opposed to maritime) Southeast Asia and China are geographically proximate, culturally contiguous, and historically linked. From the national security perspective, the Chinese policy-makers tend to consider continental Southeast Asian states as part of China's immediate security parameter and its 'soft underbelly' *vis-à-vis* maritime Southeast Asian states. Traditionally, their economy has been more dependent on China than that of maritime Southeast Asia. For a long time Beijing has tended to pay more attention to any developments in continental Southeast Asia than to maritime Southeast Asia because of their impacts on China's southern provinces as well as the country's overall economic development.[43]

Since Thailand is a key player in ASEAN and one of the first three countries that established formal diplomatic relations with China in the 1970s, its relationship with China has received special attention from Beijing. During the financial crisis from 1997, Beijing provided financial aid to allow Bangkok to retain its currency peg with the US dollar. Thailand was the first ASEAN country to enjoy the 'early harvest' from China within the ongoing China–ASEAN free trade process. In 1999 Thailand was the first ASEAN state to sign a bilateral framework agreement on strategic partnership and cooperation with China. In return, Bangkok also used its influence in the ASEAN diplomatic collective to help Beijing establish and promote ties within ASEAN.

There has been significant progress in the Sino-Malaysian relationship since the early 1990s. Malaysian leaders have vigorously defended the non-interference principle and criticized Western human rights diplomacy, and in this have echoed Beijing. In the case of Singapore, the post-Cold War period also saw a deepening of the economic partnership with China and an institutionalization of political ties. China's relations with the Philippines and Indonesia, from time to time, have been plagued by the Spratlys issue and the issue of the Chinese ethnic population, but bilateral economic ties and political trust have become much stronger in recent years.[44]

Vietnam, Laos, Cambodia, and Myanmar are so-called 'new ASEAN' states. Their level of economic development, social and political structures, and shared historical experiences are all quite different from those of the 'old' ASEAN members (Brunei, Indonesia, Malaysia, the Philippines, Singapore and Thailand – the ASEAN-6). Traditionally, China has had great sympathy with the new ASEAN states. Since they have a common border with China (except Cambodia), they have occupied a special place in Chinese foreign relations and Beijing's strategic engagement with ASEAN. After the Cold War, in order to reduce their apprehension of China's role in the region, Beijing worked hard to develop a sound political understanding with them that China would not support rebellious and anti-regime forces in their countries, under the 'good neighborliness' policy. While retaining good relations with Myanmar's military regime, Beijing normalized relations with Laos, Vietnam, and Cambodia in 1988, 1991, and 1994, respectively.[45] Through a series of negotiations, China and Vietnam reached an agreement on their 2,636 km land boundary in December 1999, and committed themselves to continue negotiation on a legally binding boundary between the two countries in the Gulf of Tonkin. In dealing with the 'new' ASEAN member states, Beijing has skillfully used its economic leverage to achieve its political and strategic objectives. China was generous in offering debt reduction, the building of trans-border railways, and other trade benefits to them. China's positive contribution to the Greater Mekong River project closely links the economic development in Yunnan and Guanxi Provinces with continental Southeast Asia. This has not just boosted sub-regional economic integration and cooperation, but also promoted China's overall relations with ASEAN.

Nevertheless, the rise of China is both an opportunity and a challenge for the ASEAN states. Although China's fast-growing economy represents more of an opportunity than a threat and Beijing's more polished foreign policy has reconfirmed that in recent years, ASEAN as a grouping of small countries cannot afford to discount the potential risks brought about by the rise of China in the region. We now turn our discussion to how ASEAN has responded to that rise.

ASEAN and the 'rise of China'

ASEAN does not seem to have had a clear and coherent strategy in coping with the rise of China in the region. As a group of small states geographically straddling a big power like China, an inescapable consequence is that the big power can exert an excessive influence over the small ones. This has long been the experience of Southeast Asian countries, and the ASEAN states are keenly aware that the rise of China is not without negative consequences – actual as well as potential. Though the term 'China threat' has not been used in government documents in recent years, ASEAN officials have turned to highlighting some 'concerns', 'problems,' or 'challenges' when they discuss the strategic dimension of relations with China. It is understandable that the fundamental parameters such as geographical proximity to China and the huge imbalance between ASEAN and China in terms of population, territorial size, economic strength, and military capabilities worry them when they consider long-term relations with Beijing. No doubt the growing Chinese economic and military power has served to reinforce historical fears of China as a hegemon. Among these fears are concerns over how China may behave as a great power during and after its 'peaceful rise', where its defense modernization program will go, and how Beijing will resolve its territorial disputes in the South China Sea.[46]

China's defense modernization and its growing ability to project military force throughout the region worries ASEAN states, especially those that have territorial disputes with China in the South China Sea. Despite rhetoric and confidence-building measures, the 'China threat' will not go away easily. It could be a significant obstacle to the Chinese leadership's aspiration of presenting China as a peaceful and responsible power to the world, and this is the case especially where there is a lack of shared values with Southeast Asian countries and China's process of making foreign policy is not very transparent. Moreover, the lack of mutual trust is a crucial problem for Beijing if it wishes to establish its credibility and reputation among Southeast Asian states, particularly when faced with unpredictable events like SARS and financial crisis.

Although Chinese leaders have tried hard to bolster China's image and credibility in the region, a notable example being in the Asian financial crisis of 1997, Beijing still struggles with an image and credibility problem in the region, and it may take a long time to overcome this. The lack of transparency in China's political system can sometimes make the problem more intractable. China's remarkable economic growth since the 1980s and Beijing's increasingly global orientation have generated a new Chinese activism in Southeast Asia. While Chinese economic activism is always welcomed by Southeast Asia, the Chinese military buildup and growing capability for long-range power projection remain a big concern for ASEAN states.[47] China's dependence on imported oil will increase substantially, and much of this oil will be shipped through Southeast Asian sea lanes.[48] Given China's territorial and maritime claims in the South China Sea, through which about 25 percent of the world's shipping passes, the ASEAN states' long-term suspicion and uncertainty over Beijing's strategic intention will not be readily assuaged. Although Beijing has softened its stand on the sovereignty claims over the entire South China Sea as well as the Spratly and Paracel Islands by proposing simply to shelve the dispute and to concentrate on joint development in the region, the Chinese navy is steadily improving its ability to project force throughout the South China Sea. Without profound changes in China's political system and an effective regional security institution in place, there would be relatively few political or legal constraints on China's use of force, or at least coercion, to pursue its interests.[49]

ASEAN members have differing perceptions of the threat posed by China's growing military power. For example, Singapore apparently sees a need to encourage Washington to maintain a sizable military presence in the Southeast Asian region as a hedge both against rising Chinese military power and against any political unrest spilling over from its neighbors. In January 1998, the Singaporean government announced that it would give US aircraft carriers and other warships access to its new Changi naval base. In the Malaysian view, the Singaporean move was an obvious violation of the ASEAN commitment to the region remaining a 'zone of peace, freedom and neutrality'. Malaysian prime minister Mahathir indicated later that he did not want an increased US military presence because it would cause anxiety throughout the region. The Philippines has a similar view to Singapore, especially after the Mischief Reef incident in February

1995. Manila and Washington had signed a legal framework for resuming military ties (the Visiting Forces Agreement), which was later ratified by the Philippine Senate in May 1999.

There is, though, no single preferred and unified strategy for ASEAN to adopt in dealing with the rise of China. ASEAN states have different views about the prospects for a 'peacefully rising China' and particularly on the extent to which the Chinese military could be a threat. While they have generally rejected more hawkish assessments, they do not want to treat China as a totally benign big power in their neighborhood either.[50] This complicated mindset is reflected in their policy that they want to 'ride the Chinese wave' as best they can, while taking a more even-handed approach toward the rise of China, acknowledging that there are both benefits and costs for Southeast Asia.

There is more concurrence between the ASEAN states over China's economic development. They recognize that China's strategic prioritization of economic development has necessitated changes in Beijing's foreign policy interest and conduct. China's main objective in Southeast Asia has changed to preserving regional peace and stability, as this will be conducive to its domestic economic development and regime stability. China's more pragmatic foreign policy emphasizes cooperative economic relations with its Asian neighbors as well as the Western world. It is in their interest to support China's integration into the regional and world economy. This is not only because it will enhance China's internal stability but also because it will create valuable economic opportunities for ASEAN states in the huge Chinese markets.

For this reason, ASEAN as a whole and individual ASEAN states all recognize the potential benefits and uncertainties associated with China's military modernization as well as with the evolution of the Chinese political and economic system. However, none of them wants to sacrifice or constrain nearer-term opportunities for the longer-run uncertainty. They view the growth of Chinese military power with caution, even if Beijing's present military capabilities do not yet pose a comprehensive or compelling threat to regional security.[51] Therefore, they follow a stratagem of hoping for the best but preparing for the worst. They have proactively engaged China in multilateral dialogues and agreements with the hope of seeing China more fully enmeshed in multilateral institutions and of providing Beijing with clear incentives and opportunities to curb the unilateral exercise of its power. Despite the different views among its members, ASEAN has come to a common stand that engagement is the only realistic policy to pursue. Engagement requires ASEAN to develop and deepen its economic and political linkages with China, thereby weaving the PRC into a complex web of interdependence. ASEAN leaders hope that by engaging China in a security dialogue at both bilateral and multilateral levels, their security concerns *vis-à-vis* their big neighbor can be substantially mitigated.

Meanwhile, most ASEAN states have sought to place their bilateral relations with China on a more practicable basis. None seeks to provoke the Chinese leadership, nor seeks a relationship that is unduly dependent on Beijing, given China's sheer size and strategic weight in regional politics. Each of them tailors its China policy in relation to its own particular political and security needs. While the overall mix does not represent a strategic solution for ASEAN's long-term relations with China, maintaining an array of capabilities and policy instruments is deemed prudent and realistic in addressing an uncertain future.[52] For some ASEAN states, the realist engagement with China must have a military–security dimension that addresses the long-term concern over China's growing military power.[53] The ASEAN-6 states, for instance, realizing their own limited ability to 'balance' China militarily, identified the need to maintain defense links with external powers – primarily the United States, but also the United Kingdom, Australia, and New Zealand – as a prudent hedge against a more assertive or even aggressive China. Although they have played down these links for fear of antagonizing Beijing, their strategy is referred to as 'engagement with insurance'. Chinese leaders obviously understand why the ASEAN-6 have taken this position, and Beijing has not been critical on this count because these states have at least not gone as far as joining with the Western powers in talking of 'containing' China.[54]

Today, there seem to be more factors which could unite China and Southeast Asia than could divide them. Economics is most assuredly the driving force of the relationship. China's spectacular economic growth is providing innumerable opportunities to the countries of Southeast Asia, which have significantly stepped up their trade and investment links with China. Moreover, this has come at a time when Japan's economy has been experiencing structural problems, leaving it in the trough of the economic cycle. In Southeast Asia, therefore, there is a widespread perception that China will be the new engine of growth for the entire region, displacing Japan, which had played that role for the previous thirty years or more. The allure of substantial economic benefits arising out of China's developmental boom has even impelled those Southeast Asian states which were previously cool towards Beijing, such as the Philippines and Indonesia, to exploit the long-term possibilities inherent in China's rapid modernization. Some scholars even believe that ASEAN states use the free trade agreement with China as a catalyst to accelerate their own integration within the framework of AFTA.[55]

Therefore, pragmatism is the defining feature in ASEAN's relations with China, and it has become even more evident in light of certain problems in their overall relations, which both sides are willing to downplay so as to secure mutual benefits. On human rights issues, ASEAN and China have even forged a common stand, and one that has much encouraged Chinese leaders. In the ASEAN PMC with its dialogue partners in July 1997, the differences between ASEAN member states and their Western dialogue partners were considerable. The Malaysian representative requested a review of the UN Declaration on Human Rights, and the move was firmly supported by Indonesia, the Philippines, and China. The US and the EU naturally opposed the review. To Western diplomats, the dialogue became a harsh exchange contrasting Asian and Western values, beliefs, and political systems. On a similar plane, ASEAN took a common stand in objecting to the EU's boycott of Myanmar's participation at the Asia–Europe meeting held in Europe, and the ASEAN members on the UN Commission on Human Rights objected to Western countries' attempt to censure China's human rights record at its annual sessions. The Commission's voting record shows that Japan was the only Asian country to vote against China's no-action motion, while South Korea and the Philippines abstained and the other nine Asian countries (Bangladesh, Bhutan, China, India, Indonesia, Malaysia, Nepal, Pakistan, and Sri Lanka) all supported China's motion.

The SARS epidemic was another showcase for the type of pragmatic cooperation that facilitates mutual benefits and trust. The epidemic could have been a severe setback to relations between China and ASEAN but it turned out instead to be beneficial in this regard. Since the Asian financial crisis, Beijing has campaigned to be seen as Southeast Asia's most reliable, responsible partner. Yet, in February 2003, when SARS began to spread in Guangdong Province in China, Beijing's delays in facing up to the disease and its refusal to promptly cooperate with international health authorities clearly accelerated the spread of SARS to China's southern neighbors. From the initial appearance of the disease in the ASEAN region until early May, ASEAN countries faced the prospect that – beyond the immediate health consequences for their populations – the epidemic might send their economies into prolonged recession. Despite their anger, however, ASEAN governments used quiet persuasion rather than open criticism to steer Beijing toward the multilateral cooperation necessary to deal with the disease. As it turned out, the effect of SARS on trade and tourism was short-lived. By the middle of 2003 the disease had been contained, and the Southeast Asian economy recovered more quickly than expected.

In hoping for the best and preparing for the worst, most of the ASEAN states have found that the US military presence in the region serves as an invaluable deterrence and reassurance for their security. This is because of the weakness of individual ASEAN states and the lack of an effective collective defense *vis-à-vis* China at the collective level. Since gaining independence, Southeast Asian states have learned to maintain a dynamic balance between the major powers in the region. To them, China's emergence as a major regional power could intensify US–China competition in Southeast Asia and increase the potential for armed conflict. The United States is currently the dominant extra-regional power in Southeast Asia. Some of the ASEAN countries continue to rely on US military forces to guarantee regional stability and security, and to balance China's growing power. Washington and Beijing have very different concepts of how security should be organized in the Asia–Pacific region and these competing visions could clash in Southeast Asia.[56] The current US policy interests in Southeast Asia are largely related to the global 'war on terror'. To ASEAN states, Washington seems to have no sense of Southeast Asia as a foreign policy priority, and this is in stark contrast to the Chinese policy, in which a sense of priority regarding the region is clear. In socializing with ASEAN, Beijing and Washington demonstrate very different styles of diplomacy. Washington has little patience with the perceived 'chaos' and 'messiness' of politics in Southeast Asia. Thus, it is difficult to sell to US policy-makers and constituents the importance of investing time and energy to cultivate relationships with the region, despite the fact that nurturing such relationships – through frequent and regular contact and meetings – is the basis of building trust and confidence. Beijing, in contrast, has adopted new diplomatic tactics that are proving very successful. Chinese leaders have spent plenty of political, economic, and diplomatic resources cultivating relations with ASEAN, patiently and effectively. Beijing has a long-term goal of strategic partnership in mind.

Conclusion

China's post-Cold War policy toward Southeast Asia has been soft and sophisticated, using a combination of both bilateral and multilateral approaches. From Beijing's perspective, the good neighbor policy is an important component of China's peaceful rising strategy in the region. As a senior Chinese diplomatic official argues, as the 'China threat theory' still haunts the region from time to time and people still have a sense of uncertainty about China's future development; China's good neighborliness policy would facilitate a fair and friendlier understanding of what China is doing and what it intends to do. In the same vein, China's rise can be realized only with the understanding and support of Asian nations.[57]

Beijing's growing influence is keenly felt in Southeast Asia. While there is no consensus among ASEAN states about the impact of the rise of China, most of them have preferred to 'ride the Chinese wave' as best they can. There are clear signs that the unease and apprehension over the rise of China are in decline or have at least become more muted. Pragmatism is the defining feature of ASEAN's relations with China, and this has become even more evident in light of certain problems in overall relations, which both sides are willing to downplay so as to secure mutual benefits. China's activism in the region is likely to continue, including its participation in multilateral diplomacy, regional free trade initiatives and growing trade relations, the signing of numerous cooperative agreements, and an

increasing number of high-level visits to the region. These will greatly help
the multilayered construction of the neighborly community in East Asia.

Notes

1 Han Feng, 'ASEAN's Relations with Big Powers', in Samuel C. Y. Ku (ed.),
   Southeast Asia in the New Century: an Asian perspective, Kaohsiung: Center for
   Southeast Asian Studies, National Sun Yat-Sen University, 2002, pp. 221–2.
   Han Feng is the assistant director of the Institute of Asia–Pacific Studies at the
   Chinese Academy of Social Sciences, Beijing.
2 For a good discussion on this issue, see Institute of Southeast Asian Studies,
   Developing ASEAN–China Relations: realities and prospects, a brief report on the
   ASEAN–China forum, Singapore: Institute of Southeast Asian Studies, 2004.
3 For good discussion on China's Southeast Asian policy and China–Southeast
   Asian relations, see, among other works: Joyce K. Kallgren, Sopiee Noordin and
   Soedjati Djiwandono (eds), *ASEAN and China: an evolving relationship*, Berkeley,
   CA: University of California Institute of East Asian Studies, 1988; Kwei-Bo
   Huang, *The Association of South East Asian Nations' Confidence and Security
   Building with the People's Republic of China*, Maryland Series in Contemporary
   Asian Studies No. 6, Baltimore, MD: School of Law, University of Maryland,
   2000; Wang Gungwu, *China and Southeast Asia: myths, threats and culture*,
   East Asian Institute Occasional Paper No. 13, Singapore: World Scientific
   and Singapore University Press, 1999; Theresa C. Carino (ed.), *China–ASEAN
   Relations: regional security and cooperation*, Quezon City: Philippine–China
   Development Resource Center, 1998; Liselotte Odgaard, *Maritime Security
   Between China and Southeast Asia: conflict and cooperation in the making of regional
   order*, Aldershot: Ashgate, 2002; and Ho Khai Leong and Samuel C. Y. Ku
   (eds), *China and Southeast Asia: global changes and regional challenges*, Singapore:
   Institute of Southeast Asian Studies, 2005.
4 Chinese premier Wen Jiabao's speech, 'China's Development and Asia's
   Rejuvenation', given at the ASEAN Business and Investment Summit, Bali,
   Indonesia, 7 October 2003.
5 Martin Stuart-Fox, *A Short History of China and Southeast Asia: tribute, trade and
   influence*, St Leonards: Allen and Unwin, 2003, pp. 29–30.
6 *Ibid.*, p. 31.
7 Ma Jinqiang, Zhu Zhenmin and Zhang Guangping, *Dangdai Dongnanya Guoji
   Guanxi* [Modern Southeast Asian International Relations], Beijing: Shijie Zhishi
   Chubanshe, 2000, p. 2.
8 See Wang Gungwu, 'Early Ming Relations with Southeast Asia: a background
   essay', in John K. Fairbank (ed.), *The Chinese World Order: traditional China's
   foreign relations*, Cambridge, MA: Harvard University Press, 1968.
9 *Ibid.*, p. 48.
10 Ma Jinqiang *et al.*, *Dangdai Dongnanya Guoji Guanxi*, pp. 11–21.
11 Michael Yahuda, *Towards the End of Isolationism: China's foreign policy after Mao*,
   London: Macmillan, 1983, p. 219.
12 Wang Gungwu, 'Early Ming Relations with Southeast Asia', pp. 48–9.

13 Lucian W. Pye, 'China and Southeast Asia', in Robert A. Scalapino and Jusuf Wanandi (eds), *Economic, Political, and Security Issues in Southeast Asia in the 1980s*, Berkeley, CA: University of California Institute of East Asian Studies, 1982, p. 157.

14 Wang Gungwu, 'Early Ming Relations with Southeast Asia', pp. 48–9.

15 The most systematic treatment of this issue can be found in Michael D. Swain and Ashley J. Tellis, *Interpreting China's Grand Strategy*, Santa Monica, CA: RAND, 2000, chapter 3, pp. 21–95.

16 *Ibid.*, p. 22.

17 Discussion in this section is drawn from Ma Jinqiang *et al.*, *Dangdai Dongnanya Guoji Guanxi*, chapters 4, 5, and 6, pp. 79–159.

18 Lucian W. Pye, 'The China Factor in Southeast Asia', in Richard H. Solomon (ed.), *The China Factor: Sino-American relations and the global scene*, Englewood Cliffs, NJ: Prentice-Hall, 1981, pp. 219–20.

19 For discussion on this period of China Southeast Asian policy, see, for example, Chen Qiaozhi *et al.*, *Lengzhan Hou Dongmeng Guojia dui Hua Zhengce Yanjiu* [A Study of ASEAN States' Policy Toward China After the Cold War], Beijing: China Social Sciences Publisher, 2001, pp. 2–9.

20 For good discussion on relations between China and Southeast Asia in this period, see, for example, Melvin Gurtov, *China and Southeast Asia: the politics of survival*, Lexington, MA: Heath Lexington Books, 1971.

21 See also, for example, Jay Taylor, *China and Southeast Asia: Peking's relations with revolutionary movements*, New York: Praeger, 1976, pp. 194–5.

22 The five principles were: mutual respect of sovereignty and territorial integrity; non-aggression; not interfering in the other's internal affairs; equality and mutual benefits; and peaceful coexistence. They first appeared in an agreement between China and India on Tibet affairs in April 1954, and later were reconfirmed in Sino-Indian and Sino-Burmese joint communiqués in June 1954.

23 See also Chen Qiaozhi *et al.*, *Lengzhan Hou Dongmeng Guojia dui Hua Zhengce Yanjiu*, pp. 2–12.

24 *Ibid.*, p.12.

25 Premier Li Peng summarized these principles of the China–ASEAN relationship when he visited Thailand in November 1988.

26 Jay Taylor, *China and Southeast Asia*, p. 83.

27 Chapter 6 provides more detailed discussion of this issue.

28 For a good discussion on the South China Sea dispute, see, for example: Mark J. Valencia, *China and the South China Sea Disputes*, Adelphi Paper No. 298, London: Oxford University Press, 1995; Bob Catley and Makmur Keliat, *Spratlys: the disputes in the South China Sea*, Aldershot: Ashgate, 1997; and Liselotte Odgaard, *Maritime Security Between China and Southeast Asia*.

29 Chen Qiaozhi *et al.*, *Lengzhan Hou Dongmeng Guojia dui Hua Zhengce Yanjiu*, p. 22.

30 Cui Tiankai, *Regional Integration in Asia and China's Policy*, China–ASEAN Project Occasional Paper No. 12, Centre of Asian Studies, University of Hong Kong, 2005, p. 9.

31 A good analysis of China's participation in ASEAN-driven multilateral institutional dialogues can be found in Cheng-Chwee Kuik, 'Multilateralism in China's ASEAN Policy: its evolution, characteristics, and aspiration', *Contemporary*

Southeast Asia, 27:1 (2005), pp. 102–22; and James K. Chin and Nicholas Thomas (eds), *China and ASEAN: changing political and strategic ties*, Centre of Asian Studies, University of Hong Kong, 2005. Discussion in this section, and on China's participation in the ARF in Chapter 5, has benefited a great deal from these two works.

32 See Cheng-Chwee Kuik, 'Multilateralism in China's ASEAN Policy', pp. 105–8, and Cheng-Chwee Kuik, 'China's Participation in the ASEAN Regional Forum (ARF): the exogenous and endogenous effects of international institutions', in James K. Chin and Nicholas Thomas (eds), *China and ASEAN: changing political and strategic ties*, Centre of Asian Studies, University of Hong Kong, 2005, pp. 147–51.

33 Rosemary Foot, 'China in the ASEAN Regional Forum: organizational processes and domestic modes of thought', *Asian Survey*, 38:5 (1998), p. 435.

34 Dr Liu Xuecheng, Senior Research Fellow at the China Institute of International Studies, was actively involved in China's participation in the ARF. See his paper 'Strengthening Cooperation in ARF: a Chinese view', given to the first ASEAN–China Forum, 23–24 June 2004, in Singapore. The conference papers and discussion were later summarized and published by the Institute of Southeast Asian Studies as *Developing ASEAN–China Relations: Realities and Prospects* in 2004.

35 See the ASEAN Secretariat website, www.aseansec.org/5874.htm (last accessed April 2006).

36 See Chapters 5 and 7 for more detailed discussion.

37 Data from the PRC Ministry of Commerce's website, at http://english.mofcom.gov.cn/aarticle/statistic/ie/200402/20040200182458.html (last accessed July 2006). The import and export data are drawn from the same source at http://english.mofcom.gov.cn/aarticle/statistic/ie/200402/20040200182458.html (last accessed July 2006), and http://english.mofcom.gov.cn/aarticle/statistic/ie/200402/20040200183706.html (last accessed July 2006), respectively.

38 *Ibid.*, http://english.mofcom.gov.cn/aarticle/statistic/ie/200503/20050300023721.html (last accessed July 2006).

39 *Ibid.*, http://english.mofcom.gov.cn/aarticle/statistic/ie/200603/20060301722237.html (last accessed July 2006).

40 *Ibid.*, http://english.mofcom.gov.cn/aarticle/statistic/ie/200603/20060301722415.html (last accessed July 2006) and http://english.mofcom.gov.cn/aarticle/statistic/ie/200603/20060301722356.html (last accessed July 2006).

41 For more detailed discussion of functional cooperation, see the Plan of Action to Implement the Joint Declaration on ASEAN–China Strategic Partnership for Peace and Prosperity, adopted in Vientiane, Laos, on 27 November 2004, available on the ASEAN website, www.aseansec.org/16805.htm (last accessed July 2006).

42 For more details, see Wang Xinsheng and Yu Changsheng, *Zhongguo Dongmeng Quyu Hezuo yu Gonggong Zhili* [Sino-ASEAN Regional Cooperation and Public Governance], Beijing: China Social Sciences Publisher, 2005, chapters 2 and 3, pp. 36–114.

43 Li Yiping, 'Lengzhan Hou Zhongguo yu Dongmeng Guojia Guanxi Tanxi' [An Analysis of Post-Cold War China–ASEAN State-to-State Relations], *Proceedings*

of 2004 China Association of Southeast Asian Studies Annual Conference, retrieved from Tsinghua Tongfang Optical Disc Databank, p. 6.

44 For more detailed discussion, see Chen Qiaozhi *et al.*, *Lengzhan Hou Dongmeng Guojia dui Hua Zhengce Yanjiu*, chapters 2–9, pp. 61–375.

45 S. D. Muni, *China's Strategic Engagement with the New ASEAN*, IDSS Monograph No. 2, Singapore: Institute of Defense and Strategic Studies, 2002, pp. 30–9.

46 Although Chinese leaders stopped using the expression 'peaceful rise' and used instead 'peaceful development' because the word 'rise' could be interpreted negatively, the implications, for ASEAN states, are the same.

47 For an interesting discussion of the bifurcated nature of Chinese policy in Southeast Asia, see Wayne Bert, 'Chinese Policies and U.S. Interests in Southeast Asia', *Asian Survey*, 33:3 (1993).

48 Most of China's oil imports come through the Strait of Malacca. In Southeast Asia, the China National Petroleum Corporation and the China National Offshore Oil Corporation hold minority shares in offshore production ventures and exploration blocks in the Strait of Malacca and the Java Sea as well.

49 Jonathan D. Pollack, 'Designing a New American Security Strategy for Asia', in James Shinn (ed.), *Weaving the Net: conditional engagement with China*, New York: Council on Foreign Relations, 1996, p. 118.

50 Institute of Southeast Asian Studies, *Developing ASEAN–China Relations*, p. 4.

51 See, for example, Karl W. Eikenberry, 'China's Challenge to Asia–Pacific Regional Stability', in Richard J. Ellings and Sheldon W. Simon (eds), *Southeast Asian Security in the New Millennium*, Armonk, NY: M. E. Sharpe, 1996, pp. 89–122.

52 For a good discussion of ASEAN countries' security dilemmas, see Alan Collins, *The Security Dilemmas of Southeast Asia*, London: Macmillan/St Martin's Press, 2000, chapter 4, pp. 89–132.

53 See Malcolm Chalmers, *Confidence Building in South-East Asia*, Boulder, CO: Westview Press, 1996, pp. 44–5.

54 Joseph Chinyong Liow, 'Balancing, Bandwagoning, or Hedging? Strategic and security patterns in Malaysia's relations with China, 1981–2003', in Ho Khai Leong and Samuel C.Y. Ku (eds), *China and Southeast Asia: global changes and regional challenges*, Singapore: Institute of Southeast Asian Studies, 2005, pp. 296–7.

55 Vincent Wei-cheng Wang, 'The Logic of China–ASEAN FTA: economic state-craft of peaceful ascendancy', in Ho Khai Leong and Samuel C.Y. Ku (eds), *China and Southeast Asia: global changes and regional challenges*, Singapore: Institute of Southeast Asian Studies, 2005, p. 35.

56 See, for example, Wayne Bert, *The United States, China and Southeast Asian Security: a changing of the guard?*, London: Palgrave, 2003.

57 Cui Tiankai, *Regional Integration in Asia and China's Policy*, p. 11.

Chapter 4

Japan and Southeast Asia

The evolution of postwar Japan's foreign relations with Southeast Asia has received extensive study.[1] A general theme portrays Japan working to overcome the legacy of colonialism and to circumvent the international structural barriers imposed on it by the Cold War bipolarity. According to this view, the 'separation of economics from politics' (*seikei bunri* in Japanese) has been the key operational mode the Japanese government has employed when interacting both with individual Southeast Asian countries and with ASEAN as a group. Furthermore, although after the Cold War Japan has used economic aid as an instrument to influence human rights change in Southeast Asia, the thrust of Japan's approach to Southeast Asia has remained more visible in the realm of trade and regional economic development.[2]

Four dimensions of postwar Japan's interest in Southeast Asia are of particular interest. First, to maintain the structure of its international trade and investment, Japan depends on less developed countries as a source of raw materials and as a market for Japanese products. Southeast Asia holds particular importance for Japan in this respect, owing to its geographical proximity. Second, the international shipping lanes through the Southeast Asian region are crucial for the Japanese economy, if for no other reason than that they ensure a smooth flow of Middle Eastern oil to Japan. Third, Southeast Asia serves as a showcase for Japanese commitment to narrowing the development gap between rich and poor countries. This philosophy has come to be known as the 'flying geese' model, with Japan at the head and Southeast Asian economies emulating Japan's industrialization process. Finally, Japan recognizes that the security and stability of the region are vital for its own security.[3]

Slowly but surely in the post-Cold War era, Southeast Asia has grown in strategic importance for Japan. This became marked in 2003, when Japan launched a series of programs to commemorate fifty years of Japanese exchange with Southeast Asian countries and thirty years of relations with ASEAN as a group. The commemoration peaked with a Japan–ASEAN summit held in Tokyo.[4] Commenting on the summit, Soeya Yoshihide offers the following observation:

> Actually, no one recognizes the importance of Japan's role better than Southeast Asian countries, which appear to have braced themselves to work closely with China. We often hear members of the Association of Southeast Asian Nations (ASEAN) say they want Japan to seriously tackle East Asian policy, *even if it does so to counter China*. This is a sign of ASEAN countries' inclination to maintain a balance, and one that shows their trust in Japan through three decades of close dealings with it since the 1970s.[5] (Emphasis added)

In this chapter we review the evolution of postwar relations between Japan and Southeast Asia. We pay particular attention to two issues. How did Japan attempt to integrate Southeast Asia into its projects for East Asian regionalism? And how did the role of China function as the impetus for Japanese diplomacy toward Southeast Asia? Out of this exercise we hope to shed light on complexities of East Asian community building by focusing on Japan's relations with Southeast Asia.

Sense of community shattered: Japan and Southeast Asia, 1945–74

In the immediate aftermath of the Second World War, Japan was isolated from the rest of East Asia in economic, security, and political affairs. The 1952 San Francisco peace treaty obliged Japan to provide war reparations to its former colonies. Yet, because Japan was excluded from the de-colonization process and the national independence movements throughout Southeast Asia, in reality it had the task of rebuilding relations with the newly independent states in all fields of diplomacy.

The primary reason for imperial Japan waging war against China and Southeast Asian countries at the same time was to gain access to oil and other essential raw materials, to fuel its military machine and wartime economy on the domestic front.[6] By the war's end, Japan could no longer tap into Chinese markets for raw materials. In order to rebuild its war-torn economy, Japan had no choice but to turn again to Southeast Asia. It began by settling the war reparations issue with Burma in 1954, while joining the Colombo Plan for Cooperative Economic Development in South and Southeast Asia and SEATO in the same year. These acts demonstrated Japan's commitment to international efforts to develop individual economies in the region and to preventing the spread of communism. It ought to be noted, however, that Japan was allowed to play a bigger role on the economic front than in the regional security sphere, owing to its recent militaristic past, the problematic nature of SEATO itself notwithstanding.

Southeast Asia was a complex area in the emerging Cold War geopolitical structure. Amidst the superpower competition for influence, newly independent countries, especially Indonesia, took the lead in presenting an image of collaborative defiance of former colonizers and of strategic neutrality in the emerging global bipolar power structure. In 1955, Indonesia hosted the Bandung conference, bringing China and India to the same forum, to demonstrate Asian and African solidarity by hoisting the flag of anti-colonialism. China participated and used the occasion to project itself as an actor with a benign foreign policy orientation (see Chapter 3).

Japan was allied with the United States, but nevertheless sent a delegation to the Bandung conference. As a matter of fact, it was Pakistan, which identified itself with the 'free' (i.e., pro-American) world, that invited Japan, as a counterweight against India, which was forging political solidarity with China. Takasaki Tatsunosuke, the principal Japanese delegate to the conference, did not represent the mainstream of the Japanese political arena, but was particularly well suited to articulating a recognition of Japan's historical responsibilities and their implications for Japan's future relations with its Asian neighbors. Indeed, it was Takasaki who spearheaded the officially unofficial trade arrangements between Japan and China in the 1960s. Understandably, Japan's participation in the Bandung conference did not generate a lasting impact on political ties with newly independent countries during the Cold War. Nor did the non-aligned movement, which in part grew out of the Bandung exercise, feature Japan as a prominent member.

Nevertheless, as Iokibe Makoto notes, Japanese representation at the Bandung conference was meaningful for two reasons. First, the conference was a useful forum in which Japan could demonstrate its 'positioning as a member of Asia'. Second, Japan's participation served a function in its relationship with the United States. The United States reportedly noted Japan's 'moderating influence' in the demonstration of Asian–African solidarity.[7] Miyagi Daizo goes further, by identifying the Bandung conference as marking Japan's political return to Asia, albeit in the usual postwar Japanese style of acting only after careful calculation of any likely effect on Japan's relations with the United States.[8]

Japan in the late 1950s did have a vision for its relationship with Southeast Asia. The vision centered upon Japan providing economic leadership for Southeast Asia. In 1957, Japanese prime minister Kishi Nobusuke raised the possibility of creating a 'Southeast Asia Development Fund', on the condition that the United States made a significant financial contribution to it. The proposed Fund was meant to promote the industrial development of Southeast Asia. The US government reacted coldly to this initiative. Kishi presented the same notion on his two trips to Southeast

Asia, but on neither occasion was support from Southeast Asian countries forthcoming.[9] Kishi's proposal was premature. Over the issue of war reparations alone, Japan by 1957 had reached agreement only with Burma and the Philippines, along with the settlement of 'special yen problems' with Thailand. It took another two years for Japan to completely settle war reparations with Indonesia, Laos, Cambodia, and South Vietnam.

But Kishi's proposition did represent the Japanese government's wish to move from reparation diplomacy to a comprehensive strategy for re-establishing ties with the Southeast Asian markets. As Suehiro Akira carefully documents, the Kishi government, building on the Yoshida government's efforts, worked out a policy trinity of war reparation payments, economic development, and economic cooperation with Southeast Asia. Even without US participation or approval, the Japanese government went on to establish an economic cooperation department in the economic affairs bureau of its Ministry of Foreign Affairs in April 1959, one month before it signed an agreement with South Vietnam on war reparations, the last such agreement Japan had to sign. Between 1961 and 1962, Japan established the Overseas Economic Cooperation Fund to serve as a fund provider, the Overseas Technical Cooperation Agency to solicit professionals to partake in Japanese economic assistance projects, and the government-sponsored Institute for Developing Economics to provide research support.[10] These projects, then, equaled an offer to provide leadership in rebuilding the war-torn Southeast Asian economies, by incorporating Southeast Asia into Japan's own economic reconstruction and development programs.

In 1966, Japan tried to provide policy leadership to Southeast Asia by organizing the first Ministerial Conference on Economic Development in Southeast Asia (MCEDSEA). The principal goal of this conference was to disburse Japanese aid in exchange for general support from its Southeast Asian neighbors for Japanese foreign policy, 'But the Southeast Asian states did not like dealing with Japan through MCEDSEA',[11] which stopped meeting in 1975. Also, in 1966, with the United States being a key founding member as well, Japan supported the launching of the ADB.[12] Japan has since held the chair of the ADB, the major regional financial institution serving the developing member economies in Asia. In a sense, the ADB provided a useful venue for Japan to bypass the political difficulties of bilaterally dealing with Southeast Asian countries while gaining the economic benefits it wanted from Southeast Asian markets.

There is another dimension to Japan's approach to regional cooperation in the 1960s. The strategy was to associate Japan with the United States as a means for promoting economic integration in East Asia. This was achieved through the creation of a forum based on the level of development already achieved. Japan was to act as an advocate and spokesperson for Southeast Asian interests. In the 1960s, Southeast Asian states still belonged to the category of 'developing countries'. In contrast, after over a decade of economic reconstruction and industrialization, Japan was recognized as a developed economy through its entry to the Organization for Economic Cooperation and Development (OECD) in 1964. A more visible indication of Japan's return to the international community was its successful hosting of the 1964 Summer Olympics in Tokyo.

Against this background, Japanese economist Kojima Kiyoshi proposed a Pacific Free Trade Area (PAFTA) between the United States, Canada, Japan, Australia, and New Zealand. The proposal was based on the notion that countries with similar levels of development were ready to launch an institutional mechanism to coordinate policies as a means for economic integration. Southeast Asian countries were supposed to create an integrated area of their own, which would then be associated with PAFTA.[13] In 1968, with the backing of the Japanese foreign minister, Miki Takeo, Kojima and his colleagues began to organize conferences in Tokyo to discuss the idea of PAFTA among economists from the above-mentioned countries. From 1969 onwards, the annual conferences also began to involve economists from other Asian countries. Although the idea did not materialize in policy, the conferences became a powerful lobby for disseminating Japanese visions of Asian and Pacific economic cooperation.[14]

From the early 1970s, Japan's pursuit of *seikei bunri* with Southeast Asian countries ran into a considerable amount of political difficulty. After nearly two decades of interactions in the areas of aid, trade, and investment, there grew increasing fears of Japan's economic domination in Southeast Asia. After all, beginning with its war reparations programs and continuing with its development aid programs, including those through the ADB, Japanese economic aid was characterized by strict conditions and tied loans, and heavily favored the immediate business interests of Japanese companies. With memories of the war still fresh, the prevailing public image of Japan in Southeast Asia was of an exploitative economic animal.[15]

As a result, boycotts of Japanese goods took place in Thailand. Malaysia lodged a complaint about Japanese production and export of synthetic rubber. Anti-Japanese demonstrations took place in universities in a number of Southeast Asian countries.[16] In January 1974, prime minister Tanaka Kakuei visited Indonesia, Malaysia, the Philippines, Singapore, and Thailand, all members of ASEAN. 'Anti-Tanaka' riots broke out. The riots in Jakarta were especially violent. Indonesia had been a principal aid recipient of Japan and a key Southeast Asian supplier of oil, gas, and other natural resources to Japan. While in aggregate the Indonesian economy received a boost as a result of the first Middle East oil crisis, Suharto's 'New Order', and especially the widening inequality in Indonesian society, was generating increasing popular resentment. Indonesian students used the Tanaka visit to demonstrate against Suharto's rule and against the presence of foreign investment capital, both in general but also that from Japan in particular. Nevertheless, the 'anti-Tanaka riots' left no mistaking the fact that Japan had failed to cultivate positive feelings in Southeast Asian societies. After all, measured in material terms, Southeast Asia in the 1960s became 'something approaching a Japanese hinterland – whether measured in terms of trade, investment and assistance, or the number of people brought to Japan each year from Southeast Asia for training and education'.[17] Measured in trade volumes alone, by 1964, Japan had replaced the United States as the first or second most important export destination for virtually all Southeast Asian countries.

The timing of the 'anti-Tanaka riots' was particularly challenging for Japanese foreign policy in East Asia. In 1974, the US withdrawal of troops from Vietnam was well in sight, opening up a new set of strategic and political dynamics in continental Southeast Asia. Stability within the region was of direct concern to the maritime Southeast Asian states organized into the ASEAN grouping, which by extension would affect Japanese economic interests in ASEAN member states. Japan's alliance with the United States came under strain, too, because of the two 'Nixon shocks' in the summer of 1971. On 15 July 1971, US president Richard Nixon gave his Japanese counterpart prime minister Sato Eisaku only a few minutes' notice before announcing his official trip to China in February 1972. Yet Sato had repeatedly championed anti-communism, together with a steadfast policy of no recognition of the PRC as the sole representative government of China, as a hallmark of his administration. This dramatic development cast doubt on how seriously the United States took its most important ally in the western Pacific. Precisely one month later, the Nixon administration announced its decision to de-link the US dollar from the value of gold, in addition to applying a 10 percent surcharge on all imports into the US market, thus seriously hurting the Japanese government's economic policies, which were centered upon adherence to US currency policies.[18]

Then, in 1974, Australia became the first dialogue partner of ASEAN, while Australia's pledge of economic support for ASEAN was a mere US$5 million.[19] The message to Japan was clear: its financial contributions to Southeast Asian countries had failed to pay much in the way of political or diplomatic dividends.

The Chinese market had been a key source of raw materials for Japan before and during the Second World War. After the war, Japan pursued a unique version of economic diplomacy with China by circumventing its commitments to the US-led economic blockade against China and allowing those Japanese corporations sympathetic to China's isolation from the capitalist world economy to conduct 'private trade' between the two countries. The aim was, again, to gain access to raw materials in China and prepare for full re-entry into the Chinese market once the political and diplomatic opportunities presented themselves.[20]

From the early 1950s to the late 1960s, Japan's political relations with China and Southeast Asia proceeded along separate paths. The key international actors that affected Japan's pursuit of ties with China were the United States and the Soviet Union, not ASEAN countries individually or collectively. In the early 1970s, however, China became a significant factor for Japan to contend with in its relations with Southeast Asia. In 1973, the first oil crisis broke out in the Middle East. US allies in Southeast Asia, such as the Philippines and Thailand, were seriously affected. In the same year, China emerged on the world market as an oil exporter. China began to export oil to Thailand in 1973 and to the Philippines a year later. Furthermore, China offered its Southeast Asian oil-importing countries 'friendship prices' (i.e., below the world market average). With Japanese oil companies, which also began importing oil from China, speculating that China would be able to replace the Middle East as an oil supplier, China became a highly attractive neighbor.[21]

China was also becoming an important player in Southeast Asia on the geopolitical and diplomatic/political front. During the Vietnam War, Japan had firmly supported the United States while China actively supported Ho Chi Min, leading the Vietnamese resistance. Now that the United States was withdrawing from Vietnam, how China would henceforth interact with Southeast Asian countries was unclear. In addition, for hundreds of years, the ethnic Chinese business networks in Southeast Asian economies had been instrumental in the operation of Southeast Asian economies. The US withdrawal from Vietnam and the Sino-US rapprochement opened new sources of uncertainty in China's relations with Southeast Asian states, including over the ethnic Chinese connection. Should China return to its policy of soliciting support, both financial and political, from the ethnic Chinese communities in Southeast Asian countries, the potential societal instability would not be conducive to Japan's cultivation of a favorable business environment.

Concerning Japan's bilateral relationship with China, Sato's successor, Tanaka Kakuei, managed to use domestic sentiments questioning the United States' sincerity toward Japan to overcome domestic opposition and travel to Beijing in September 1972. On that visit, Japan and China established formal diplomatic relations, a full six years ahead of the United States. Japan and China also moved to open a full trading relationship, taking advantage of the officially unofficial bilateral trade ties since the 1950s (with a short interval from 1958 to 1961).[22] However, in 1972 China was still going through the turbulence of the Cultural Revolution. This meant that Japan could not expect a favorable investment climate in China any time soon. For Japan, uncertainty over its ties with Southeast Asian countries and domestic uncertainty in China were indeed an ominous combination.

In short, from the 1950s to the early 1970s, Japan did succeed in reaching a reconciliation with Southeast Asian countries in a legal sense, by agreeing war reparations with all the Southeast Asian governments.

Japan also succeeded in returning to Southeast Asian markets and began to assert a leadership role through the provision of bilateral development aid and its chair of the ADB. But Japan failed to integrate itself institutionally with Southeast Asia. The so-called 'anti-Tanaka riots' served as a powerful reminder of the political challenges ahead for Japanese diplomacy toward its Southeast Asian neighbors. Although Japan did establish formal diplomatic ties with China, Chinese foreign policy orientation showed no sign of either jointly working with Japan toward regional integration or emulating Japan to become a regional leader. In short, by the mid-1970s, the political–economic situation in the East Asian region was too volatile for any vision of regional community building to materialize.

Getting along and doing well: Japan and Southeast Asia from the 1970s to the 1980s

After the 'anti-Tanaka riots', Japan moved to more formally engage ASEAN by holding regularized government-level forums. In line with the idea of Japanese and Southeast Asian economies moving in tandem in a 'flying geese' pattern, such forums were organized with the goal of facilitating the two-way movement of capital, products, and human resources. The first such effort, focused on the rubber trade, was established in February 1974 but was replaced by the Japan–ASEAN forum in March 1977. In June of the same year the first ASEAN–Japan business people's meeting was held. Subsequently, along with government-to-government exchanges, Japan and Southeast Asian countries established numerous networks among the business, academic, journalistic, and cultural communities. Networking, often of an informal and *ad hoc* nature, became the standard Japanese approach to exercising leadership in interaction with Southeast Asian states and societies.

A major Japanese diplomatic initiative came in August 1977. Prime minister Fukuda Takeo's visit to the then five ASEAN member states (Indonesia, Malaysia, the Philippines, Singapore, and Thailand – ASEAN-5) coincided with the second ASEAN summit meeting. Before Fukuda's trip, ASEAN entered into dialogue relationships with Australia (1974), New Zealand (1975), Canada (February 1977), and the European Community (April 1977). An ASEAN–USA dialogue was due to be held in September 1977. ASEAN held its first summit meeting in February 1976, which marked a major step in the organization's institutional development toward formal regionalism. Fukuda's trip came at a time when Japan was obviously falling behind in ASEAN's outreach to major world powers and after the regional grouping had declared its geostrategic neutrality in 1971.

It was little surprise that Fukuda chose the Philippines as the country to be the last stop on his ASEAN tour and Manila the place at which to deliver

a major speech to outline Japan's foreign policy approach to Southeast
Asia. In March 1977, ASEAN foreign ministers had met in Manila and
signed an intra-regional trade accord. Philippine president Ferdinand
Marcos suggested to the conference that ASEAN hold a summit conference
with Japan on the utilization of raw materials. Japan and ASEAN, Marcos
said, had 'an equal stake in assuring the continued availability of these raw
materials at quantities which would support the modernization of their
[i.e. ASEAN's] economies'.[23] With the memory of the 'anti-Tanaka riots'
still fresh, Marcos's suggestion could not have been more timely for Japan.

Fukuda's Manila speech came to be known as the 'Fukuda Doctrine' in
Japanese policy toward Southeast Asia. Fukuda summarized it himself as
follows:

> First, Japan, a nation committed to peace, rejects the role of a military power
> and on that basis is resolved to contribute to the peace and prosperity of
> Southeast Asia, and of the world community.
>
> Second, Japan, as a true friend of the countries of Southeast Asia, will
> do its best for consolidating the relationship of mutual confidence and
> trust based on heart-to-heart understanding with these countries, in wide
> ranging fields covering not only political and economic areas but also social
> and cultural areas.
>
> Third, Japan will be an equal partner of ASEAN and its member countries,
> and cooperate positively with them in their own efforts to strengthen their
> solidarity and resilience, together with other nations of like mind outside
> the region, while aiming at fostering a relationship based on mutual under-
> standing with the nations of Indochina, and will thus contribute to the
> building of peace and prosperity throughout Southeast Asia.[24]

Fukuda's expression of seeking 'heart-to-heart understanding' with
Southeast Asian countries became a standard point of reference made
by successive Japanese prime ministers on their tours of Southeast Asian
countries. From a Japanese perspective, two other 'Doctrines' (as set out in
Takeshita Noboru's speech in December 1987 in Manila and Hashimoto
Ryutaro's January 1997 speech in Singapore) all highlight the wisdom
of Fukuda's 1977 speech and express a willingness to foster solidarity
with ASEAN.[25] Koizumi Junichiro's January 2002 speech in Singapore
reaffirmed the 'fundamental concepts of the "Fukuda Speech"'.[26]

As Sudo Sueo observes, in the second half of the 1970s Japan had to
deal with four major changes while pursuing its relations with Southeast
Asia: the end of the Vietnam war; 'the US withdrawal from the region'; 'the
rise of China as a major political power'; and 'the ever-increasing Soviet
influence in the region'.[27] About the only factor over which Japan had
complete control was the Japanese market, which had by the mid-1970s
firmly established itself as the leader in East Asia's economic growth. The
evolution of superpower politics and its implications for relations between
Japan and Southeast Asian have been treated elsewhere.[28] In line with the

focus in this book, we now turn to China as a factor influencing Japan's relations with Southeast Asia.

In postwar Japanese foreign policy, the notion of comprehensive security received official backing under the Ohira Masayoshi administration. Among other things, pursuit of comprehensive security implies securing adequate food and industrial material supply, and steering military and political resources accordingly.[29] Conclusion of a peace treaty with China in 1978 made it possible for Japan to fully approach China as a new source of diversification in energy imports. Japan had begun to import oil from China in 1973, the year after formal diplomatic relations were established. As part of its 'four modernizations' drive, China made oil and coal key commodities for export, in exchange for Japanese technology, plants, construction materials, and machines. Chinese oil exports to Japan stood at one million tons in 1973, quickly rising to four million tons a year later, and reaching seven million tons by 1979, when China embarked on a policy of opening to the entire capitalist world economy.[30] The first long-term trade agreement between China and Japan (signed in 1978) contained numerical targets for Chinese exports of crude oil and coal to Japan. Although crude oil from China represented a small amount of the total Japanese import, wild expectations about Chinese production capacity, combined with enthusiasm in some quarters of the Japanese business community for rapid expansion of trade with China, added to the 'China boom' of positive public feelings. To a certain degree, the relationship with China was treated as a special case. The evolution of trade ties between China and Japan during the remainder of the Cold War years was anything but smooth, however.[31] Nonetheless, after China and Japan entered into a formal trade agreement in January 1974, extending to each other 'most favored nation' trading status, the Chinese market was fully available to Japan.

In addition to the growth in trade and investment, questions regarding the extension of ODA to China began to arise at this time. ODA had been a key instrument – managed as a natural follow-up to Japan's war reparations – in Japan's cultivation of Southeast Asian markets. There were debates within Japan about treating ODA for China as part of the Japanese campaign to complete postwar settlements with all its Asian neighbors. But, in the end, the winning side argued that it was in Japan's interest to provide financial support for China's transition out of autarkic socialism.[32] Southeast Asian recipients of Japanese ODA expressed concern about the prospect of China cutting into the Japanese allocation of aid to them. Consequently, the Ohira administration decided to increase the total amount of aid and to make it a condition that ODA to China would not exceed total ODA to Southeast Asian countries.[33]

The emerging tensions between China and Vietnam in the wake of the US withdrawal complicated Japan's wish to assist ASEAN's search for collective power in the face of the Indochina debacle, as was laid out in the third point of the Fukuda Doctrine. Japan did manage to pursue its own ties with the unified Vietnam. Again, the Japanese approach began through economic means. Not only was Japan the most forthcoming donor to Vietnam after the war, but by 1978 the two countries had settled debt problems incurred by the former South Vietnam. 'The way was thus made clear for the strengthening of economic cooperation between the two.'[34]

In the late 1970s, China viewed the Soviet Union as a 'big hegemon' and Vietnam as a 'small hegemon'. In January 1979, in the midst of the Chinese military campaign to 'teach Vietnam a lesson', China's ambassador to Japan reportedly requested Japanese support for the Cambodian Pol Pot regime against Hanoi, as the 1978 Sino-Japanese peace treaty contained an anti-hegemony clause. The request was rejected, but 'Japan began to act on a policy of supporting the Pol Pot regime against Hanoi'.[35] Nor did Japan clearly denounce China's military campaign against Vietnam, which led the Soviet Union to denounce Japan as 'indirectly defending' China.[36]

Concerning the conflict between Vietnam and Cambodia – a key source instability for ASEAN countries which undermined the prospects for regional cooperation – Japanese and Chinese policies turned out to be complementary, in that they both supported Cambodian resistance to the Vietnamese occupation. When the time came for China and the major powers to agree on a resolution to the Cambodia issue, Japan again managed to have a working relationship with all sides concerned.[37]

In the latter years of the Cold War in East Asia, Japan used the 1987 Takeshita Doctrine to make another major declaration to foster 'heart-to-heart understanding' between Japan and Southeast Asian countries. Prime minister Takeshita did more than restate Fukuda's pledge, and addressed current issues. He doubled Japan's pledge of economic aid to US$2 billion as a means of demonstrating Japanese resolve. But unlike in the 1960s, Japan from the 1970s through the 1980s did not propose new schemes to formally institutionalize Southeast Asia in a form comparable to developments elsewhere in the world. Instead, Japan chose networking, of an informal and certainly legally non-binding nature, as the key to exercising its leadership. The only semi-governmental regional cooperation organization Japan worked to establish was the Pacific Basin Economic Council, in 1980, which included China, Taiwan, Hong Kong, and nine other non-ASEAN members across the Pacific. But the Council has functioned as a consultative body only.

There could be many explanations for such developments. Regarding economic cooperation through the creation of formal regional trade blocs, Japan chose to cultivate group power by championing the notion of universal trade liberalization, partly as a diplomatic and political instrument for dealing with the persistent and increasingly acrimonious trade disputes with the United States. The 1985 Plaza Accord,[38] which resulted in a sharp appreciation of the Japanese currency, led to a massive outflow of Japanese corporate investment into Southeast Asian markets. Such investments were helpful in ameliorating the perception of Japan as an exploitative 'economic animal' in Southeast Asian societies. In addition, self-help is a repeated theme in Japan's pursuit of relations with its aid recipients. In the 1970s and 1980s, the region's newly industrialized economies (NIEs – South Korea, Singapore, Taiwan, and Hong Kong) presented good role models for all Southeast Asian countries.[39] In other words, the 'flying geese' wisdom clearly seemed to be working well. Against the background of Latin American economies marred in their own 'lost decades', there was general consensus in discussions about the global economic situation of the day that an East Asian model of economic growth and development generated global economic dynamism.[40]

In the realm of security, the much-feared Soviet influence in Southeast Asia turned out to be largely restricted to the conflict between Vietnam and Cambodia. Detente among China, the United States, and the Soviet Union put the Soviet Union's expansive power in East Asia in check. Relations between China and the Soviet Union began to thaw with the formal beginning of normalization talks in 1983. China made the end of Soviet support for Vietnam's occupation of Cambodia the first of its three demands before full normalization of ties with the Soviet Union was possible. When Mikhail Gorbachev came to power in the Soviet Union, the decay of Soviet military power was obvious and his policies of *perestroika* were seen in Japan as an opportunity for the economic reconciliation of the Soviet Union with East Asia.[41]

To summarize, from the 1970s until the Cold War's end in East Asia, Japan managed to have a working relationship with all its East Asian neighbors. Since Japan had firmly established itself as the undisputed leader in East Asian industrialization, and market integration centered on the Japanese economy as the growth engine, it should come as little surprise that Japan did not make East Asian regionalism a centerpiece of its foreign policy. In hindsight, the evolution of regional security dynamics in the wake of the Vietnam War were such that Japan's role in effecting geostrategic changes in the East Asian region had to be limited, as evidenced in the negative and apprehensive reaction (particularly on the part of China) to the Nakasone administration's 1983 decision to raise Japan's defense spending to above 1 percent of gross domestic product. China entered the regional political economy by way of rejoining the capitalist world economy and pursuing a foreign policy independent of superpower rivalry in the early 1980s. But the honeymoon in Sino-Japanese relations was beginning to come to an end. Furthermore, China's political relations with Southeast Asia moved slowly and tentatively. The regional dynamics were such that East Asia just was not ready for any form of regional community building to take place.

Adapting to a rising China: Japan and Southeast Asia in the 1990s

By all measures, 1989 was a watershed year for Japan in terms of the changing external environment in East Asia. ASEAN economies, rather than the NIEs or China, became the most attractive destination for Japanese outbound investment.[42] Vietnam began to withdraw from Cambodia, paving the way for the end, a year later, of ASEAN's policy of isolating Vietnam. Beginning in the mid-1980s, Vietnam began to pursue an external economic policy similar to China's development strategy. Since Vietnam is traditionally the most vibrant economy among the Indochinese states, the stage seemed set for more years of Japanese leadership in the postwar 'flying geese' pattern of growth, with more ASEAN states riding into NIE-hood. More importantly, the collapse of the Japanese bubble economy in 1989 was not expected to be a long-lasting phenomenon.

The regional environment was also changing quickly. China emerged as a more assertive actor in Southeast Asia. For both Japan and ASEAN countries, the Tiananmen Square incident in China powerfully curbed expectations of an economically liberalizing China following the Asian NIEs in political liberalization, and therefore any notion that China might be a candidate for regional integration as well. China, as part of its strategy to work against the diplomatic sanctions imposed by the G7 governments, worked to improve bilateral ties with ASEAN countries by normalizing its diplomatic relationship with Indonesia in 1990, thereby providing an important stimulus for Singapore and Brunei to follow suit. Indeed, Beijing managed to normalize diplomatic ties with Indonesia only after it convinced Jakarta that it would no longer meddle in Indonesian politics over the ethnic Chinese issue.[43] Now that China had normalized relations with all the ASEAN countries, concern shifted to ethnic Chinese populations in Southeast Asia diverting investment to China, taking advantage of the economic ties between Hong Kong, Taiwan, and the Chinese mainland.

Then came a major change in regional security dynamics. Negotiations between the United States and the Philippines over continued access to military bases beyond 1991 were running into formidable resistance from Philippine nationalism. The United States eventually decided to terminate its facilities in 1992. This led to concern that a 'power vacuum' was emerging in Southeast Asia. Other ASEAN states wanted the United States to remain engaged in the region, for fear that China or Japan would seek to fill the perceived power vacuum.[44]

By dispatching emperor Akihito on a trip to Thailand, Malaysia, and Indonesia in September 1991, the Japanese government was preparing for the closure, at least diplomatically, of a difficult chapter in the country's relations with the rest of East Asia. This was the first time a Japanese emperor had visited another Asian country. Although the peoples of those three countries harbor the least resentment toward Japan, the visit was a significant gesture of reconciliation. A year later, the Japanese emperor was sent on a goodwill mission to China. The emperor's visit and the Japanese parliament's 1995 'no war' resolution to mark the fiftieth anniversary of the end of the Second World War turned out to be insufficient to dispel the feelings people in China and Southeast Asia held toward wartime atrocities committed by the Japanese imperial army. Nevertheless, by setting up a compensation fund to address the 'comfort women' lawsuits, the Japanese government clearly meant to put history in the past.[45]

By the 1990s, the overwhelming view in the region was that China was rising or re-emerging.[46] 'China threat' became a popular reference when debating the impact China would have on the region and beyond. China embarked on a series of diplomatic initiatives designed to dissuade its Southeast Asian neighbors from seeing China as a real threat. Viewed from Japan, China's record of diplomacy was a mixed one. To Seiichiro Takagi, 'the friendlier relations Beijing forged with its neighbors were more the result of Beijing's own flexible approach, including consideration for the negative effects of massive economic power'.[47] In other words, it was China that wanted to improve its ties with Southeast Asian countries rather than the other way round. Such comments are reflective of a more pervasive mood in the Japanese assessment of China's relative power in the region:

> Nevertheless, there was no sense of urgency in Japan about the economic threat China was said to pose. It was widely believed that the level of economic development was so different that China was not going to threaten Japan's lead in the immediate future.[48]

As a matter of fact, in 1994, Japan's bilateral trade deficit with China became its largest.

In the realm of regional security, Southeast Asian countries were shocked by the outbreak of the 1995 Mischief Reef incident between China and the Philippines. China occupied the reef, one of many in the disputed Spratly Islands area. The particularly troubling point is that Mischief Reef is closer to the Philippines than China. The Philippines reacted with intense diplomacy to enlist support for its position, including from its treaty ally the United States. But the United States reacted by taking a neutral position on the territorial dispute.[49] Calls came for Japan to play a more active role in demonstrating solidarity with ASEAN *vis-à-vis* China. As the Japanese diplomat Miyagawa Makio wrote, Japan, which saw its defense minister visiting Southeast Asia in 1988 for the first time since the end of the Second World War, was still facing many dilemmas when answering Southeast Asian calls for assistance in the area of security. To Miyagawa, 'to help [Southeast Asian countries] acquire a matured sense of defense and defense capabilities is far more important for the future security of Southeast Asia than to try to fetter their military arsenal', let alone entering into military arrangements.[50] The Mischief Reef incident did serve as a reminder about the complicated post-Cold War regional security environment for Japan. More incidents like it would clearly have unsettled the regional security scene and have had the potential to affect Japanese use of the sea lanes in Southeast Asia.

Japan nevertheless did involve itself in managing security in the Southeast Asian region. In 1992, Japan sent its self-defense forces to Cambodia to participate in the UN peacekeeping project. China's foreign minister reportedly called Japan's mission 'constructive'.[51] Japan's participation in this project resulted in mixed sentiments in the region, as Southeast Asia continued to grapple with Japan's wartime past.[52] But Japan's support for ASEAN's decision to establish the ARF and the decision to include China from the beginning was a positive contribution to confidence-building measures in East Asia.

China's military exercises in the Taiwan Straits in 1995–96 had a profound impact on how Japan and Southeast Asian countries assessed their regional environment. Though unrelated to the crisis in the Taiwan Straits *per se*, Japan responded to China's unambiguous demonstration of its willingness to use force when necessary in relation to the Taiwan issue by suspending its economic aid in 1995 and formally extending its EEZ in the East China Sea area in 1996, thus challenging China's claims to the disputed Senkaku/Diaoyu Islands.[53] US president Bill Clinton's decision to use its naval deployment in waters close to Taiwan reaffirmed the value of the bilateral alliance for Japan. However, there were few instruments available for Japan to unilaterally deal with China. Southeast Asian countries had different assessments of the level of military threat China posed to the region. In addition to enlisting the support of countries outside the region, such as the UK and Australia, Southeast Asian countries were counting on the United States for 'hard power' – balancing against China – and the ARF for 'soft power' – by engaging China in multilateral security dialogue.[54]

Japan was not to appear passive, however. Prime minister Hashimoto Ryutaro traveled to Southeast Asia in January 1997, in spite of mounting challenges in Tokyo, including dealing with an ongoing Japanese hostage crisis in Lima, Peru. As Inoguchi Takashi observes, 'Hashimoto wanted to solidify ties with ASEAN nations as a counterweight to the awesome uncertainties involving Japan's four neighbors: the US, China, the Koreas, and Russia'.[55] Hashimoto's outline of Japan's Southeast Asian policy towards the end of the century included a proposal for Japan to 'have frank dialogues on regional security with each of the ASEAN countries on a bilateral basis'. Although Hashimoto used positive words in reference to China's place in the region, his identification of 'China's further constructive participation in the international community' as a key challenge for both Japan and ASEAN member states leaves little doubt that Japan saw networking with ASEAN countries in the security arena as a means of countering China's military weight.[56]

By far the most significant event that reminded Japan and Southeast Asian countries of China's impact on the region came when the Asian financial crisis broke out in 1997. Four aspects of China's economic diplomacy in reaction to the crisis are noteworthy. First, by making a monetary contribution to the IMF currency stability loans to Thailand and Indonesia, China arguably demonstrated that its reputation as 'a self-serving Group of One both within and outside the multilateral economic institutions' was now unwarranted.[57] Second, after the outbreak of the crisis, whether or not the Chinese government would choose to devalue the renminbi to protect its own trade interests became a subject of daily scrutiny in the regional and global media. China kept its pledge not to devalue its currency, thus removing an important external variable that might have caused another round of competitive devaluation of Southeast Asian currencies, due to the overlap of Chinese and Southeast Asian exports in major international markets. Third, China played a balancing role in the international debate over a regional monetary mechanism for dealing with future currency shocks. This debate involved three proposals: a Japanese proposal for an AMF; the United States' insistence on no change to the IMF mechanism and its philosophy; and ASEAN's warm reception of the AMF proposal. China did not publicly endorse the AMF idea when it was made public in October 1997, but later fully supported the Chiang Mai initiative, a compromise between the US and Japanese proposals. Fourth, China responded to the outbreak of riots in Jakarta, which targeted Indonesians of Chinese descent, by giving priority to regime stability in Indonesia, rather than riding the wave of Chinese nationalism.[58] These acts indicated to Southeast Asian countries that a rising China did not necessarily equal a self-interested powerful neighbor acting unilaterally.

Japan, too, did its part to demonstrate to Southeast Asian countries that it cared about their plight more than did the IMF in general and the United States in particular. Japan also saw the crisis as an opportunity to play a leadership role in the region, not only in pulling the region out of its crisis, but also in creating a stable regional economic environment. Japan did so at a cost to its relations with the United States, which did not want to see Japan working against US interests and preferences for regional integration.[59]

The late 1990s also saw a sea change in the Japanese government's attitude to preferential regional trade agreements. For much of the 1970 and 1980s, Japan's trade policy was based on the GATT and its successor, the WTO, and the principle of unconditional 'most favored nation' treatment. By supporting the creation of the Pacific Basin Economic Council in 1980 and then the APEC forum in 1989, Japan sought to exercise leadership in Southeast Asia by attuning to Southeast Asian preferences while avoiding upsetting US sensitivities. But the 1997 APEC meeting in Vancouver failed to generate much enthusiasm for further synchronized liberalization across the region. The WTO was also encountering difficulties in promoting further liberalization, as evidenced by the aborted launching of the 'millennium round' in Seattle in 1999. Consequently, a race toward bilateral free trade agreements began among APEC members. In 1998, South Korea started to explore the possibility of a bilateral free trade agreement with Japan, but the process has thus far moved very slowly. When Singapore approached Japan with a proposal for a bilateral agreement in 1999, Japan responded favorably, and the Japan–Singapore Economic Agreement for a New Age Partnership was signed in January 2001.[60] Japan seems to be more comfortable than it once was with forging closer economic ties with its Southeast Asian neighbors.

In 2000, China took a cue from the newly emerging trend for free trade agreements in East Asia and announced its decision to negotiate toward such an agreement with the ASEAN states, which had by then expanded to include all the Indochinese states. When China moved, it went one step further than Japan by offering to include agricultural products in the package. In contrast, Japan chose to enter into the bilateral agreement with Singapore but not any other Southeast Asian economy precisely because Singapore does not have much of an agricultural element in its exports. China also competed with Japan for goodwill in ASEAN countries by agreeing to follow AFTA's scheme of liberalization, in addition to offering unilateral concessions to the Indochinese economies.[61]

China's pursuit of economic diplomacy with ASEAN countries caught Japan by surprise. According to Otsuji and Shiraishi:[62]

> Simply put, Japan has remained stagnant, while the Association of Southeast Asian Nations has lost its economic momentum and its cohesion. China, on the other hand, has emerged as a potential superpower thanks to its enormous economic development and its entry into the World Trade Organization. These developments are now widely seen as signaling the shift in the regional center of gravity from ASEAN to China.

In reality, the 'center of gravity' metaphor better captures the momentum ASEAN set off when it established institutional schemes for regional economic cooperation. In the wake of the Asian financial crisis, AFTA widened to include all ten member economies of continental and maritime Southeast Asia. AFTA also decided to accelerate its target date for further liberalization of trade. The AFTA plus China free trade arrangement represents a step toward ASEAN deepening regional economic cooperation. Given the way these negotiations operated, arguably it is China that is following ASEAN, because the operational model remains the common effective protective tariff scheme AFTA created. Also, China followed AFTA's negotiation protocol, which grants a member economy the right individually to decide the pace of trade liberalization. In other words, in terms of diplomacy at least, it is ASEAN that is setting the mode and pace for China to enter into cooperative economic arrangements.

In the wake of China's economic diplomacy toward ASEAN, in 2003 Japan moved to start negotiations with ASEAN toward a free trade agreement, scheduled for completion by 2012. Meanwhile, Japan also began negotiating bilateral agreements with Thailand, the Philippines, and Malaysia in early 2004, aiming to complete such negotiations as soon as possible. In East Asia, then, there is a race between China and Japan and their respective schemes of economic diplomacy with ASEAN.

It should be noted that although the Chinese government has been bolder than Japan in reaching out to ASEAN, and the Chinese market has attracted the more attention both in the region and worldwide, Japan remains more important than China for Southeast Asia in terms of trade and aid. Strategically Japan remains a key balance to a rising China, which has continuing territorial disputes with Southeast Asian countries over the South China Sea. In other words, China may have overtaken Japan in terms of the momentum toward economic integration in East Asia, but it is Japan that is more important than China to Southeast Asian economies.

In contrast to the competitive mode of establishing free trade agreements with Southeast Asian economies, China and Japan have cooperated with each other in facilitating the Chiang Mai initiative, agreed in 2000.[63] Under the initiative, China and Japan (and South Korea as well) entered into bilateral arrangements with Southeast Asian central banks to serve as lenders of first resort when pressure in Southeast Asian financial markets builds up. In March 2002, the central banks of China and Japan signed a currency swap agreement, promising to assist each other in times of financial duress. What we have seen is a web of bilateral assurances of assistance, without having to go through the process of meeting IMF conditions, should another financial crisis emerge in the region.

To sum up, in East Asia, the 'rise of China' is made tangible largely through China's own practices of economic diplomacy toward Southeast Asia. Both Japan and Southeast Asia have chosen to engage China through economic means as the primary means for adapting to China's rise. In the realm of managing regional security, both China and Japan have refrained from enacting new initiatives with Southeast Asia. The ARF, founded by ASEAN, has served as the linchpin for discussing regional security issues, and remains the only mechanism for addressing regional security concerns.

Conclusion: a new Japanese vision for East Asia?

In the mid-1980s, Japan began more rigorously to pursue a leadership role in East Asia. Japan supported the proliferation of an 'Asianist' approach to prosperity and stability, including the creation of APEC, which builds heavily on ASEAN's preference for voluntary liberalization. The security dimension of the China factor entered the regional scene in the mid-1990s.

Japan reacted to the security challenge by strengthening its bilateral alliance with the United States. In February 2005, Japan went a step further by issuing a joint statement with the United States that included peaceful resolution of the Taiwan issue as a common strategic objective. Japan also actively supported ASEAN's use of the ARF as a vehicle for engaging China (and preventing a 'China threat' from actually emerging).

Since the end of the 1990s, China has emerged as a more assertive actor in East Asian economic integration. Also since the late 1990s, the bilateral relationship between China and Japan has experienced formidable difficulties in the political and diplomatic realm. The situation began to worsen in 2001. Dispute over the Japanese prime minister's visit to the controversial Yasukuni Shrine effectively put high-level visits between the two governments on hold, although the annual APEC and ASEAN + 3 meetings provided a platform for Chinese and Japanese leaders to maintain a minimum degree of high-level contact. However, in May 2005 China dramatically cut short its deputy premier's trip to Japan, one that was originally meant to reinstate political diplomacy. China continued with its protest against Japan by refusing to hold bilateral meetings at the side of the November 2005 APEC conference in Busan, South Korea, and by canceling the China–Japan–Korea leaders' meeting at the side of the ASEAN meeting in December.

Their bilateral political differences have not deterred Beijing and Tokyo from taking advantage of multilateral diplomacy in the East Asian region. Over membership of the first EAS meeting, which took place following the December ASEAN + 3 conference, Japan favored having Australia, India, and New Zealand as its members, as a means of checking China's growing influence in Southeast Asia. China 'compromised' on the EAS membership issue by not challenging Japan's demand. At the same time, Japan gave in to China's demand for making ASEAN the driver for the pace of the EAS process.[64] In any case, China and Japan have been unable to narrow their political differences, let alone to begin jointly working to create a platform for integrating ASEAN countries in a manner similar to postwar Germany and France working to integrate continental Europe.

Does Japan's East Asia policy necessitate confrontation with China? Soeya, as quoted at the beginning of this chapter, seems to suggest just this. As indicated above, there is growing evidence that Japan is moving in the direction of a strategic confrontation with China. If so, can Japan succeed in enlisting Southeast Asian backing in that confrontation? Regardless of the frequency and intensity of diplomatic positioning, China has firmly established itself as an important link in the production network of the region. Viewed at the level of market integration, China's rise is a positive factor, in that it contributes to the growth of intra-regional trade. Maintaining sound trade ties with China is as crucial to Japan as it is for the Southeast Asian economies. In other words, orienting its China policy towards confrontation seems unwise for Japan and unwelcome in Southeast Asia.

As a matter of fact, postwar Japan's East Asia policy began with its efforts to heal the wounds of the Second World War for its East Asian neighbors. Difficulties in relations between Japan and China demonstrate that the task is far from over for Japan. However, for China, the miraculous success Japan achieved in rising out of the ashes of the Second World War has established it as the indisputable market leader in the region. This is true in spite of the contrast between China's record of continuous growth for the past two decades and the so-called 'lost decade' Japan experienced after the collapse of its bubble economy. Simply put, Japan still matters in the region.[65] This probably explains why thus far diplomatic difficulties between Beijing and Tokyo have *not* prevented either from sacrificing Southeast Asian preferences for the style and pace of economic cooperation. In an ironic way, Beijing and Tokyo are in a race to win trust and support from Southeast Asian countries.[66]

Specific areas of competition or confrontation may yet arise between China and Japan. Southeast Asian countries continue to cooperate with both China and Japan in ways they see as suitable and beneficial. ASEAN provides the stage for the political leaders of China, Japan, and Southeast Asia to demonstrate that they can be responsible statesmen and stateswomen when it comes to regional cooperative schemes. This makes any grand Japanese strategy of teaming up with Southeast Asia to contain China unwise and difficult, even if it were possible at all. Rhetoric and posturing not withstanding, Japan continues to react to change in the region. A new Japanese vision for East Asia is not yet in place.

Notes

1 See, for example, Ikuo Iwasaki, *Japan and Southeast Asia: a bibliography of historical, economic, and political relations*, Tokyo: Institute of Developing Economies, 1983; Shoko Tanaka, *Post-war Japanese Resource Policies and Strategies: the case of Southeast Asia*, Ithaca, NY: China–Japan Program, Cornell University, 1986; Sueo Sudo, *The Fukuda Doctrine and ASEAN: new dimensions in Japanese foreign policy*, Singapore: Institute of Southeast Asian Studies, 1992; and Sueo Sudo, *The International Relations of Japan and Southeast Asia: forging a new regionalism*, London: Routledge, 2002.

2 For a succinct overview, see Glenn D. Hook, Julie Gilson, Christopher W. Hughes and Hugo Dobson, *Japan's International Relations: politics, economics, and security*, London: Routledge, 2001, pp. 183–91.

3 Kinju Atarashi, 'Japan's Economic Cooperation Policy Towards the ASEAN Countries', *International Affairs*, 61:1 (1985), pp. 109–27.

4 See 'Calendar of ASEAN–Japan Exchange Year 2003 Programmes/Events' on the Japanese Foreign Ministry's website, www.mofa.go.jp/region/asia-paci/asean/year2003/program7.html (last accessed April 2006).

5 Soeya Yoshihide, 'Use Summit to Advance East Asia Strategy', *International Herald Tribune/Asahi Shimbun*, 8 December 2003, p. 8.
6 Nakamura Takafusa, *The Postwar Japanese Economy: its development and structure, 1937–1994*, Tokyo: Tokyo University Press, 1995, pp. 10–14. See also Jonathan Marshall, *To Have and Have Not: Southeast Asian raw materials and the origins of the Pacific War*, Berkeley, CA: University of California Press, 1995.
7 Iokibe Makoto, *The Diplomatic History of Postwar Japan*, Tokyo: Yukihaku Arma, 2002, pp. 92–3.
8 Miyagi Daizo, *Bandung Conference and Japan's Return to Asia: between the U.S. and Asia*, Tokyo: Soshisha, 2001.
9 Iokibe Makoto, *The Diplomatic History of Postwar Japan*, p. 92.
10 Suehiro Akira, 'The Road to Economic Re-entry: Japan's policy toward Southeast Asian development in the 1950s and 1960s', *Social Science Japan Journal*, 2:1 (1999), pp. 85–105.
11 Peter J. Katzenstein, 'Introduction', in Peter J. Katzenstein and Takashi Shiraishi (eds), *Network Power: Japan and Asia*, Ithaca, NY: Cornell University Press, 1997, pp. 16–17.
12 For a complete listing of these events, see the Japanese Ministry of Foreign Affair's website, www.mofa.go.jp/policy/oda/white/2002/part2_09kiseki.html (last accessed April 2006).
13 Pekka Korhonen, 'The Theory of the Flying Geese Pattern of Development and Its Interpretations', *Journal of Peace Research*, 31:1 (1994), p. 105, who quotes Kojima Kiyoshi and Kurimoto Hiroshi, 'A Pacific Economic Community and Asian Developing Countries', in *Report of a JERC International Conference, Measures for Trade Expansion of Developing Countries*, Tokyo: Japan Economic Research Center, 1966, pp. 93–133.
14 Pekka Korhonen, 'The Theory of the Flying Geese Pattern of Development and Its Interpretations', p. 106.
15 Sueo Sudo, *The Fukuda Doctrine and ASEAN*, chapter 2.
16 Narongchai Akrasanee and Apichart Prasert, 'The Evolution of ASEAN–Japan Economic Cooperation', 2003, p. 66. Paper available online at the Japan Center for International Exchange website, www.jcie.or.jp/thinknet/pdfs/asean_narongchai.pdf (last accessed April 2006).
17 Bernard K. Gordon, 'Japan, the United States and Southeast Asia', *Foreign Affairs*, 56:3 (1978), p. 582.
18 On the immediate impact of the 'Nixon shocks' on public sentiments in Japan and on Japan–US relations, see John K. Emmerson and Leonard A. Humphreys, *Will Japan Rearm? A study in attitudes*, Washington, DC: American Enterprise Institute for Public Policy Research, 1973. See also Robert C. Christopher, 'America and Japan: a time for healing', *Foreign Affairs*, 56:4 (1978), pp. 857–66.
19 Australian Government, *ASEAN and Australia: celebrating 30 years* (Canberra: Department of Foreign Affairs and Trade, 2004), p. 5.
20 Li Enmin, *Zhongri Minjian Jingji Waijiao, 1945–1972* [Sino-Japanese Private Economic Diplomacy, 1945–1972], Beijing: Renmin Chubanshe, 1997. See also Zha Daojiong's English language review of Li's book in *Sino-Japanese Studies*, 12:1 (1999), pp. 66–9. For a Japanese study of the same history, see

Soeya Yoshihide, *Japan's Economic Diplomacy with China, 1945–1978*, Oxford: Clarendon Press, 1998.

21 A. Doak Barnett, *China's Economy in Global Perspective*, Washington, DC: Brookings Institution, 1981, pp. 461–6.

22 The suspension of trade resulted from Chinese sensitivities over the burning of Chinese flags hoisted at a trade exhibition fair in Nagasaki in 1958. For a succinct discussion of the politics of the diplomatic relationship between Japan and China, see Tanaka Akihiko, *Nitchu Kankei 1945–1990* [Japan–China relations, 1945–1990], Tokyo: University of Tokyo Press, 1991, pp. 44–60.

23 'ASEAN Trade Pact Signed', Facts on File, *World News Digest*, 5 March 1977.

24 Sudo Sueo, 'The Fukuda Doctrine, August 18, 1977', in *The Fukuda Doctrine and ASEAN*, p. 246.

25 For a detailed presentation of the Japanese scholarly perspective, see Sueo Sudo, *The International Relations of Japan and Southeast Asia*, pp. 34–40.

26 Koizumi Junichiro, *Japan and ASEAN in East Asia: a sincere and open partnership*, 14 January 2002, Singapore. Available online at the ASEAN website, www.aseansec.org/2802.htm (last accessed April 2006).

27 Sudo Sueo, *The Fukuda Doctrine and ASEAN*, p. 92.

28 See, for example, Iwasaki Ikuo, *Japan and Southeast Asia*; Gerald L. Curtis (ed.), *The United States, Japan, and Asia*, New York: W. W. Norton, 1994; Charles Morrison, *Japan, the United States, and a Changing Southeast Asia*, Lanham, MD: University Press of America, 1985.

29 Akaha Tsuneo, 'Japan's Comprehensive Security Policy: a new East Asian environment', *Asian Survey*, 31:4 (1991), pp. 324–40.

30 For a discussion of China–Japan trade in energy products in the 1970s, see A. Doak Barnett, *China's Economy in Global Perspective*, pp. 457–67.

31 Christopher Howe (ed.), *China and Japan: history, trends and prospects*, Oxford: Clarendon Press, 1996.

32 Tanaka Akihiko, *Nitchu Kankei 1945–1990*, pp. 110–13.

33 Tanaka Akihiko, *ASEAN Factor in Japan's China Policy? A case study of Japan's government loans to China, 1979*, Tokyo: University of Tokyo, Department of Social and International Relations, 1988, p. 23.

34 Sudo Sueo, *The Fukuda Doctrine and ASEAN*, p. 96.

35 *Ibid.*, p. 202.

36 British Broadcasting Corporation, 'USSR criticizes Japanese position on PRC–SRV conflict', 8 March 1979.

37 For a comprehensive review of postwar relations between Japan and Vietnam, see Shiraishi Masaya, *Japanese Relations with Vietnam: 1951–1987*, Ithaca, NY: Cornell University Southeast Asia Program, 1990.

38 See full text of the Plaza Accord (an announcement by the ministers of finance and central bank governors of France, Germany, Japan, the United Kingdom, and the United States) at www.g7.utoronto.ca/finance/fm850922.htm (last accessed June 2006).

39 For one useful comparison of development trajectories in Southeast Asia and those in South Korea and Taiwan, see Anne Booth, 'Initial Conditions and Miraculous Growth: why is South East Asia different from Taiwan and South Korea?', *World Development*, 27:2 (1999), pp. 301–21.

40 The best-known celebration of the East Asian model is World Bank, *The East Asian Miracle: economic growth and public policy*, New York: Oxford University Press, 1993.

41 Shimotomai Nobuo, 'The Soviet Union and East Asia: toward economic reconciliation,' *Japan Quarterly*, 35:4 (1988), pp. 390–4.

42 Hoshino Takashi, 'Japanese Investment Shifting to ASEAN', *Tokyo Business Today*, 57:10 (1989), pp. 58–60.

43 For a review of the issue of ethnic Chinese populations in Sino-Indonesian relations, see Leo Suryadinata, 'The Chinese Minority and Sino-Indonesian Diplomatic Normalization', *Journal of Southeast Asian Studies*, 12:1 (1981), pp. 197–206.

44 Michael Vatikiotis, 'Yankee Please Stay', *Far Eastern Economic Review*, 150:50 (1990), pp. 30–1. For an American perspective on changes in the regional geostrategic scene, see Bernard K. Gordon, 'The Asian–Pacific Rim: success at a price', *Foreign Affairs*, 70:1 (1990), pp. 142–59.

45 Chunghee Sarah Soh, 'Japan's National/Asian Women's Fund for "Comfort Women"', *Pacific Affairs*, 76:2 (2003), pp. 209–33.

46 Joseph S. Nye makes a distinction between the two terms in his 'China's Re-emergence and the Future of the Asia–Pacific', *Survival*, 39:4 (1997), pp. 66–8.

47 Seiichiro Takagi, 'China as an "Economic Superpower": its foreign relations in 1993', *Japan Review of International Affairs*, 8:2 (1994), p. 116.

48 Munakata, Naoko, 'The Impact of the Rise of China and Regional Economic Integration in Asia: a Japanese perspective', Statement Before the US–China Economic and Security Review Commission (US Congress) Hearing on China's Growth as a Regional Economic Power: Impacts and Implications, 4 December 2003, p. 1.

49 Zha Daojiong and Mark Valencia, 'Mischief Reef: geopolitical context and implications', *Journal of Contemporary Asia*, 31:1 (2001), pp. 86–103.

50 Miyagawa Makio, 'Japan's Security and Development Policy for Southeast Asia', *Japan Review of International Affairs*, 10:2 (1996), p. 168.

51 Takagi, Seiichiro, 'China as an "Economic Superpower"', p. 109.

52 *Far Eastern Economic Review*, 'The Slowly Rising Sun: what Japan must do to win Asia's trust', 156:21 (1993), p. 5.

53 Michael J. Green and Benjamin L. Self, 'Japan's Changing China Policy: from commercial liberalism to reluctant realism', *Survival*, 38:2 (1996), pp. 35–58.

54 Allen S. Whiting, 'ASEAN Eyes China: the security dimension', *Asian Survey*, 37:4 (1997), pp. 299–322.

55 Inoguchi Takashi, 'Japan Wants New Asian Pals', *Far Eastern Economic Review* 160:6 (1997), p. 28.

56 'Japan's Diplomatic Offensive', *Wall Street Journal*, 24 January 1997, p. A.14. See the full text of Hashimoto's speech appended in Seuo Sudo, *The International Relations of Japan and Southeast Asia*, pp. 133–7.

57 William Feeney, 'China and the Multilateral Economic Institutions', in Samuel S. Kim (ed.), *China and the World: Chinese foreign policy in the post-Cold War era*, Boulder, CO: Westview Press, 1994, p. 247.

58 Zha Daojiong, 'China and the May 1998 Riots of Indonesia: exploring the issues', *Pacific Review*, 13:4 (2000), pp. 557–75.

59 Ellis Krauss, 'The US, Japan, and Trade Liberalization: from bilateralism to regional multilateralism to regionalism', *Pacific Review*, 16:3 (2003), pp. 307–29.

60 Naoko Munakata, *Evolution of Japan's Policy Toward Economic Integration*, Center for Northeast Asian Policy Studies, Washington, DC: Brookings Institution. Archived at www.brookings.edu/fp/cnaps/papers/2001_munakata.pdf (last accessed June 2006).

61 Zha Daojiong, 'The Politics of China–ASEAN Economic Relations: assessing the move towards a free trade area', in Kanishka Jayasuriya (ed.), *Asian Regional Governance: crisis and change*, London: Routledge Curzon, 2004, pp. 232–52.

62 Otsuji Yoshihiro and Shiraishi Takashi, 'Building Closer Ties with ASEAN', *Japan Echo*, 29:2 (2002), p. 8.

63 For a technical description of the Chiang Mai initiative, see Worapot Manupipatpong, 'The ASEAN Surveillance Process and the East Asian Monetary Fund', *ASEAN Economic Bulletin*, 19:1 (2002), pp. 111–21.

64 The authors are thankful to Professor Qin Yaqing of the Chinese Foreign Affairs University for sharing these insights.

65 Arthur Stockwin, 'Why Japan Still Matters', *Japan Forum*, 15:3 (2003), pp. 345–60.

66 Zha Daojiong, 'Zhongri Guanxi yu Dongya Hezuo' [Sino-Japanese Relations and East Asian Cooperation], *Riben Xuekan* [Japan Studies], 89 (October 2005), pp. 8–22.

Chapter 5

Engaging China and Japan the 'ASEAN way'

This chapter focuses on how ASEAN has engaged China and Japan through the 'ASEAN way' of diplomacy in regional dialogues and community building. Founded in 1967, ASEAN was then mainly charged with dealing with internal security concerns and economic development. However, ASEAN later found itself facing a tough mission in managing its relations with external big powers. In order to maintain a stable external environment for its growth, ASEAN, as a group of relatively weak states, has to seek a unique way engaging external powerful states. During the Cold War, ASEAN's original five states (ASEAN-5) tried to limit external powers' intervention in the region as much as they sought to involve them for political, security, and economic purposes. A Zone of Peace, Freedom and Neutrality (ZOPFAN) was proposed but was not successful. After the Cold War, a more mature and confident ASEAN began to explore different ways, formal and informal, to engage major external powers, with the expectation that ASEAN would thereby be able to disseminate its basic concepts and norms in maintaining regional order and stability. ASEAN leaders have been innovative in devising a set of ASEAN-sponsored dialogue mechanisms and platforms to engage external powers in the region, such as the ARF, ASEAN + 1, ASEAN + 3, and the latest format, ASEAN + 3 + 3, as conceived in the first EAS. Using this unique way of diplomacy, ASEAN confidently and successfully expanded its dialogue and cooperation mechanisms to three Northeast Asian countries (China, Japan, and South Korea) after the Asian financial crisis of 1997. More importantly, the emerging ASEAN + 1 and ASEAN + 3 processes help to cultivate closer economic and political ties between Southeast and Northeast Asia, and contribute to a longer-term prospect of building an East Asian-only or larger regional grouping. Based on this ASEAN + x model, ASEAN has put itself at the center of the regional community-building process.

In this chapter we discuss why and how ASEAN has engaged China and Japan in regional community building through the 'ASEAN way' of diplomacy. In engaging with China and Japan, ASEAN states have adopted a combination of individual and collective policies aimed at influencing Beijing's and Tokyo's regional behavior. ASEAN's message for these two Northeast Asian powers is balanced and nuanced. They want to engage them and influence their behavior through dialogues and consensus building, as well as to take full advantage of their economic development. They do not want to become the victim of a Sino-Japanese power rivalry in East Asia. They want to engage them for regional community building, to maintain a good regional atmosphere, and to lock them into a regional multilateral institution-building process in which ASEAN is in the driver's seat. The ASEAN + 3 forum has also become a good platform on which Beijing and Tokyo can engage with each other outside the framework of formal bilateral relations and so can avoid being left behind in regional community building. This 'ASEAN way' of diplomacy is an interesting phenomenon in contemporary international relations.

The 'ASEAN way' of engagement: origin and rationale

From its very inception, the challenges facing ASEAN were not just internal but external as well. With boundaries fixed by colonial rulers, cultural and religious differences, and ongoing regional wars, how a group of diversified small states could glue themselves together was a big test for the organization. To explain ASEAN's success, we have to start with some fundamental principles and beliefs the founding members had conceived for this organization.

The objectives for ASEAN when it was established in 1967 were broad. The Bangkok Declaration, which established the organization, lists seven aims and purposes of the Association:

1 to accelerate economic, social, and cultural development in the region through joint endeavors;
2 to promote regional peace and stability;
3 to promote cooperation and mutual assistance in the economic, social, cultural, technical, scientific, and administrative fields;
4 to provide assistance to each other in the form of training and research facilities in the aforementioned fields;
5 to collaborate more effectively in agriculture and industry, to expand trade, to improve transportation and communication facilities, and to raise the living standards of the peoples;
6 to promote Southeast Asian studies;
7 to maintain close and beneficial relations with international and regional institutions with similar aims and purposes.[1]

Box 5.1 ASEAN basic documents (1967–2005)

- Bangkok Declaration, Bangkok, 8 August 1967
- Zone of Peace, Freedom and Neutrality Declaration (ZOPFAN), Kuala Lumpur, 27 November 1971
- Declaration of ASEAN Concord (Concord I), Bali, 24 February 1976
- Treaty of Amity and Cooperation in Southeast Asia (TAC), Bali, 24 February 1976
- Protocol Amending the Treaty of Amity and Cooperation in Southeast Asia, Manila, 15 December 1987
- Agreement on the Common Effective Preferential Tariff (CEPT) Scheme for the ASEAN Free Trade Area (AFTA), Singapore, 28 January 1992
- Protocol to Amend the Framework Agreement on Enhancing ASEAN Economic Cooperation, Bangkok, 15 December 1995
- Treaty on the Southeast Asia Nuclear Weapon-Free Zone (SEANWFZ), Bangkok, 15 December 1995
- ASEAN Vision 2020, Kuala Lumpur, 15 December 1997
- Second Protocol Amending the Treaty of Amity and Cooperation in Southeast Asia, Manila, 25 July 1998
- Ha Noi Plan of Action, Ha Noi, 15 December 1998
- Declaration on the Conduct of Parties in the South China Sea, Phnom Penh, 4 November 2002
- Declaration of ASEAN Concord II (Concord II), Bali, 7 October 2003

Source: ASEAN Secretariat at www.aseansec.org/145.htm (last accessed April 2006).

These objectives and principles were reaffirmed by the Declaration of ASEAN Concord (also known as Concord I) and the TAC, both adopted at the first summit meeting of the ASEAN leaders, in 1976.

Concord I and TAC, together with other fundamental political documents of ASEAN (see Box 5.1), have set out the normative foundation and overall vision of the organization. Concord I stressed: political stability for each state and for the region as a whole; the establishment of the ZOPFAN; the elimination of poverty, hunger, disease, and illiteracy; assistance relief for member states in distress owing to natural disaster; and the development of an awareness of regional identity and the creation of a strong ASEAN community.[2] As for the TAC, it establishes six specific principles and policies of conflict management in the Southeast Asian region:

1 mutual respect for the independence, sovereignty, equality, territorial integrity, and national identity of all nations;
2 the right of every state to lead its national existence free from external interference, subversion, or coercion;

3 non-interference in the internal affairs of one another;
4 settlement of differences or disputes by peaceful means;
5 renunciation of the threat or use of force;
6 effective cooperation among themselves.

These principles, combined with its diplomacy and institutional mechanisms, constituted the normative foundation of ASEAN's way of avoiding, preventing, or managing conflict within the organization, and, later, were extended to constitute the 'ASEAN way' of engaging external powers diplomatically.[3]

Based on these underlying principles and norms, the 'ASEAN way' of engagement comprises a set of rules or a sub-culture used by the organization to deal with internal conflicts as well as to engage external states. Some scholars argue that the 'ASEAN way' is a distinctly Malay cultural approach to the process of interaction. It emphasizes that a decision must be made through a careful and equal deliberation among participants.[4] Although scholars differ on how exactly the 'ASEAN way' of diplomacy works, and on how effective it is, most of them agree that its major features include informality, consultation, consensus building, and an incremental approach to conflict resolution. Putting aside the issue of how effective it is, the 'ASEAN way' is particularly suited to conflict management and conflict resolution. It is imperative in conflict management that consensus is reached before any official decision is adopted. No matter whether there are shared values, and cultural and religious identity, consensus is a significant procedural rule of the game. To some people, it is a slow process of incremental deliberation, in which an organization moves toward collective decisions based on group thinking. The 'ASEAN way' requires a non-confrontational attitude, a genuine willingness to see the points of view of others, a conscious refrainment from exerting influence or coercion over other member states, and a willingness to be patient and to persevere in reaching consensus. Adherence to these norms produces slow and time-consuming decision making.[5] This distinct ASEAN-styled process of diplomacy is evident in the high frequency of meetings between heads of states and governments, ministers, and senior officials, when they consider political, economic, and social issues. The number of meetings reaches 230–250 annually.[6]

From a constructivist point of view, the 'ASEAN way' is a set of norms, attitudes, principles, and procedural guidelines for multilateral engagement. To retain a collective strategy and group-thinking type of consensus building, it is important for members to share values and to have a common identity. The common identity and the 'ASEAN way' reinforce each other. In a practical sense, the core notion of the 'ASEAN way' rejects legalism and emphasizes socialization and consensus building, which form the nucleus of ASEAN's institution-building strategy in Southeast Asia and the wider Asia–Pacific region.[7] ASEAN has become more confident in relying on the collective process and forging group thinking, and has avoided establishing a central coordinating power, to maintain its unity and to engage other powers.

In sum, the 'ASEAN way' requires each member state to observe some basic norms, including: the principle of seeking agreement and harmony; the principle of sensitivity, politeness, and agreeability; the principle of quiet, private, and elitist diplomacy versus public washing of dirty linen; and the principle of being non-Cartesian, non-legalistic.[8] In addition to these procedural principles, ASEAN's substantive principle of non-interference, enshrined in the TAC, must also be observed. This principle, adopted in the 1976 TAC and reaffirmed in the 1987 Protocol Amending the TAC, was meant to protect ASEAN member states from meddling by states outside the organization, rather than from internal friction. However, over years the non-interference policy came under stress when ASEAN faced internal challenges, such as how to deal with Myanmar's military rulers over human rights issues. As it grew more mature and prosperous, there was a need for ASEAN to move from non-interference to constructive engagement, and then to constructive intervention (in the Myanmar case) in others' internal affairs, as long as there was a consensus for doing so.[9] But ASEAN has to stand firm on upholding its non-intervention principle *vis-à-vis* external big powers.

If the 'ASEAN way' has been successful in managing internal conflict, it is a completely different ball-game when it comes to dealing with external big powers. As a group of weak players, ASEAN's policy toward external powers has always been built on a paradox: on the one hand it wants to ward off external powers, but on the other hand it needs their presence, military and political, in the region. Although the Southeast Asian states wanted to remove themselves from this paradox, they often found they could not do so, especially during the Cold War period.

ASEAN's principle of seeking peace, freedom, and neutrality was initially established by the ZOPFAN Declaration in November 1971. In later years, the scope of ASEAN's goals continued to widen. At the Manila summit in December 1987, ASEAN leaders also called for the establishment of the SEANWFZ. But how feasible these principles were and how ASEAN could abide by the principle of peace, freedom, and neutrality were big questions. To outside observers it was natural to ask whether it was symbolic or substantive, and how ASEAN could translate the ZOPFAN principle into policy during the Cold War. This is a good starting point for us to analyze ASEAN's management of its external relations, and why and how the 'ASEAN way' affected its engagement with external powers after the Cold War.

In the early 1970s ASEAN was facing tremendous challenges from both inside and outside. The Vietnam War reached a critical turning point and internal communist insurgency posed a vital threat to most Southeast Asian states. This was an unsettling time for these states because of the unexpected changes taking place in Southeast Asia. In 1969 the Nixon administration was planning a gradual withdrawal from Vietnam, but then the situation in South Vietnam began to deteriorate after the Tet offensive in early 1968. In order to manage a gradual disengagement from Vietnam, Washington needed to readjust its Southeast Asian as well as its global strategy in facing the challenge from the Soviet Union. Nixon sent his national security adviser, Henry Kissinger, on a secret mission to China in 1971 to explore a US–Chinese rapprochement. Nixon's visit to China in February 1972 created what was a 'strategic triangle' in world politics, and it opened up a new chapter for Southeast Asian politics as well.

The response of ASEAN-5 to the United States' declining role and the changing strategic environment in Southeast Asia was the adoption of the ZOPFAN Declaration at the meeting of foreign ministers in Kuala Lumpur in November 1971. The ZOPFAN Declaration, initiated by Malaysia, attempted to address the changing external environment and an emerging tripolarity in Southeast Asia. It was not a *policy* of non-alignment and neutrality but rather, by way of compromise among the ASEAN members, an expression of a *desire* to make Southeast Asia a 'zone of peace'. In making the proposal, Kuala Lumpur hoped a policy of neutralism and opening diplomatic relations with China would demonstrate to its Malaysian ethnic Chinese population that its legitimacy was endorsed by Beijing. However, it was unlikely that Southeast Asia could become non-aligned and free of external involvement. Indonesia, as the first among equals in ASEAN, rejected Kuala Lumpur's idea of neutrality. Indonesia's argument was nicely articulated by its foreign minister, Adam Malik, in an article in September 1971. Malik argued that regional stability could be achieved only:

> through developing among ourselves an area of internal cohesion and stability, based on indigenous socio-political and economic strength.... In fact, I am convinced that unless the big powers acknowledge and the Southeast Asian nations themselves assume a greater and more direct responsibility in the maintenance of security in the area, no lasting stability can ever be achieved.[10]

The other ASEAN member states had problems with this, because of their security agreements with external powers. For instance, the Philippines did not want to abandon the Manila Pact of 1954 with Washington. Thailand was not willing to adopt non-alignment, as Bangkok was fighting a communist guerrilla insurgency. Singapore was concerned about US disengagement from the region if ASEAN adopted a policy of neutrality and non-alignment.

Thus ASEAN-5 was in disarray at this difficult time. The main problem was that the member states did not like external powers' control of Southeast Asian affairs but they were not in position to limit such influence.

They wanted to be more independent in shaping regional politics, but they could not afford to lose the external powers' involvement in the region. The fact that 'neutrality' did appear in the title of the ZOPFAN Declaration was more a matter of paying lip service to Kuala Lumpur's proposal than an official adoption of a non-alignment and neutrality policy by ASEAN. The neutrality provision was a desirable objective to pursue in the future, rather than ASEAN's position in the early 1970s. On the contrary, the Declaration clearly reiterated Jakarta's preference that the member states strengthen their own internal security through socio-economic development and create a stable region free of external interference. ZOPFAN was regarded as a long-term goal, while the more immediate concern was for ASEAN to assume a primary role in creating a stable region, a Southeast Asia isolated from superpower rivalry in Indochina. In principle, the 1967 Bangkok Declaration affirmed the sovereignty of member states and demanded respect for the UN Charter. However, despite the rhetoric, ASEAN's early years saw heavy intervention in the region by the big powers, and the organization had to find ways to steer away from the Vietnam War in the 1960s and 1970s.

Eventually, Vietnam's invasion of Cambodia in December 1978 provided a good opportunity for ASEAN to play a more assertive and collective role in Southeast Asian affairs. The Soviet-sponsored invasion clearly violated ASEAN's principles of sovereignty and territorial integrity, and thus forced it to take a stand. Throughout the 1980s ASEAN was successful in keeping the Cambodian crisis on the international agenda, in determining that the issue was Vietnam's invasion of Cambodia rather than the overthrow of the Pol Pot regime, and in finding a diplomatic resolution to the conflict. Although an international conference on Kampuchea (as Cambodia was called under Pol Pot) in July 1981, initiated by ASEAN members and under the auspices of the UN secretary-general, failed to produce any substantial progress, it signified ASEAN's leading role in the issue. ASEAN maintained international support for the defeated Khmer Rouge regime in retention of its UN seat and ensured that UN resolutions condemned the Vietnamese invasion rather than Pol Pot's indefensible human rights records.

The Cambodian issue was finally settled at the second Paris conference in October 1991. It was a diplomatic achievement of ASEAN following its consistent and collective stand in the dialogue process with Vietnam, Laos, and the Cambodian parties since July 1988. But the resolution of the Cambodian issue, as everyone understood, would not be possible unless Moscow withdrew its support for Vietnam, and without intervention from the US, China, and the UN. However, the Cambodian experience came as a lesson for ASEAN, in that the resolution of the crisis came from outside the region, and ASEAN itself gained little credit. Southeast Asia is part of the wider East Asian security complex, and it cannot escape therefore from the influence of external powers. ASEAN could not pursue an approach toward external powers based on ZOPFAN principles. Again, ASEAN might have wished to keep the external big powers at arm's length but it could not afford not to have them involved in the region.

The end of the Cold War provided an opportunity to readjust ASEAN's relations with external powers. With the closure of the Subic Bay US naval base in the Philippines in 1992 and Russia largely leaving Cam Ranh Bay in Vietnam around the same time, both Washington and Moscow were reducing their military presence in Southeast Asia. However, ASEAN states quickly realized the need to renew their defense ties with Washington. Despite Malaysia's criticism, Singapore was the first to sign an agreement with Washington, in November 1990, which allowed the relocation of some of the US aircraft and personnel from Subic Bay. Singapore has long been an advocate of a US military presence in Asia, first as a balance against the Soviet Union, and now as a balance against China. In the 1990 agreement, Singapore allows US naval vessels access to the Sembawang naval base, and for a US logistics coordinating unit to be based in Singapore. In January 1998 Singapore announced that it would further facilitate the US military presence by allowing US naval vessels, including aircraft carriers, access to the Changi naval base upon its completion. The Philippines and Thailand have had close security links with Washington since 1951, when both countries signed mutual defense treaties with Washington and allowed the presence of US bases. These bases were removed from Thailand in 1977 and from the Philippines in 1992. However, Thailand continues to hold annual exercises with the United States, and the Philippines concluded a Visiting Forces Agreement that allowed US–Philippine exercises to resume after the closure of the Subic Bay base.

Malaysia and Indonesia were somewhat ambivalent about the US military during the Cold War, but the rise of China seems to have convinced them of the merits of a US military presence. Beginning in 1997, US warships began making regular port calls to Malaysia for the first time, and the Malaysian defense minister said the region needed a continued US military presence. Malaysia began to hold joint military exercises with the US and made available to the US its maintenance facilities at Subang airport and Lumut naval yard. The strongest opponent of external involvement in the region, Indonesia, has offered Washington its ship-repair facilities at Surabaya. Indonesia has also begun to allow port calls by US vessels in the past few years. Even Vietnam seems to be acknowledging the benefits of a US naval presence in Southeast Asia, and is interested in exploring a 'nascent military relationship', such as allowing US naval ships to visit the Cam Ranh Bay naval base. Both Singapore and Malaysia are also parties to the 1971 Five Power Defense Arrangement with the UK, Australia, and New Zealand. Indonesia is not a member of the Arrangement, but it has moved closer to the organization by forging defense links with Australia. In December 1995 Australia and Indonesia signed a security treaty calling for consultations in response to external threats to either country. The agreement was short on detail, but was generally reckoned to be aimed at China, having been signed in the wake of China's occupation of the Mischief Reef. For ASEAN states, it is not only desirable to have a US military presence, but it is unrealistic for them to avoid security and defense ties with external powers. They consider their defense links with Western powers as insurance or a hedging strategy against the rise of China, in case their engagement fails and Beijing pursues regional hegemony or a more expansionist policy in the South China Sea. Although there are differences over human rights issues with Washington, the ASEAN states consider the United States a largely benign power, which makes no territorial demands in Southeast Asia and has vested interests in maintaining stability and freedom of navigation.

While the ASEAN states do want to maintain a defense relationship with the Western powers, there are however limits to this policy. According to ASEAN officials, member governments want the United States to be 'on tap, but not on top'.[11] This means they do not want to see a heavy US military deployment in Southeast Asia, which would run counter to the 1967 Bangkok Declaration and the 1971 ZOPFAN Declaration, but, rather, a limited US presence in the region. The policy of engagement with insurance is not without its risks. The ASEAN states on the one hand want defense links with Western powers, but on the other hand they do not want the links to be so strong that Beijing perceives it as containment against the rise of China. The ASEAN states thus have to strike a fine balance between their security needs and their engagement with China. That was why, after the Cold War, ASEAN began to pursue a more active engagement strategy with China and other Northeast Asian powers in the 'ASEAN way' of engagement – to avoid being passively affected by the big power rivalry, as happened during the Cold War period.

ASEAN's engagement with the wider region

After the Cold War, ASEAN began to change its official position of insulating Southeast Asia from external powers' influence to one of actively engaging them. Since the early 1990s ASEAN has therefore adopted a higher profile in the wider Asia–Pacific region through active engagement with external powers (the United States, Russia, Japan, China, Canada, South Korea, Australia, New Zealand, and the EU). This ASEAN way of networking has led it to initiate and engage in an economic platform (APEC), a security forum (the ARF), an intercontinental forum with Europe (the Asia Europe Meeting, ASEM), and an East Asian regional forum (the ASEAN + 3 process) to deal with big powers more confidently in the post-Cold War era.

Several reasons explain why ASEAN has become more positive in engaging with the wider region since the end of the Cold War. First, the disappearance of bipolarity created more room for small states to play a role in international politics. Second, the drive for economic primacy redefined national interest and foreign strategies, which made it possible for states to engage in regional economic cooperation and even regional institution building. Third, ASEAN's own development and expansion made it more confident in standing as the principal organization representing the interests of the whole of Southeast Asia. To be in a better position still to engage other major powers, ASEAN has intensified its efforts toward internal integration since the end of the Cold War, and the pace of integration has been picking up, especially since the 1997 Asian financial crisis. The AFTA was launched in 1992, and it officially came into effect on 1 January 2002. To narrow the gap between the old ASEAN members and the newcomers (Cambodia, Laos, Myanmar, and Vietnam), the Initiative for ASEAN Integration (IAI) was put into action in 1999. ASEAN leaders also committed themselves to building an ASEAN Community by the year 2020, at the Bali summit in October 2003 (ASEAN Concord II). The envisioned Community will rest on the three pillars: the ASEAN Economic Community, the ASEAN Security Community, and the ASEAN Socio-cultural Community.[12] A unified and strong ASEAN would be able to shape and set the regional agenda more proactively.

ASEAN's external relations are built on a three-layered structure. At the bilateral level, ASEAN has engaged with its 'dialogue partners', which include Australia, Canada, China, the EU, India, Japan, South Korea, New Zealand, Russia, and the United States. Spinning off from this ASEAN + 1 mechanism is the '+ 3' multilateral dialogue with three Northeast Asian states (China, Japan, and South Korea), and this ASEAN + 3 dialogue has constituted an emerging intra-regional platform in East Asia since 1997. The third level of external engagement is inter-regional, which includes participating in the activities of APEC, ASEM, and the East Asia–Latin America Forum, and contacts with regional inter-governmental organizations such as the Economic Cooperation Organization, the Gulf Cooperation Council, the Rio Group, the South Asian Association for Regional Cooperation, the Southern African Development Community, the Andean Group, the South Pacific Forum, the Shanghai Cooperation Organization, and some UN affiliated programs.[13]

ASEAN's engagement efforts, as evidenced by AFTA, APEC, ARF, ASEM, and the 'ASEAN +' mechanisms, are still unfolding and have greatly contributed to building cooperative ties with states in East Asia and beyond. Being the primary driver in setting political, economic, and security agendas, ASEAN seeks to play a pivotal role in the regional and international community, and to advance its common interests on a larger platform. The ASEAN-style codes of conduct promote dialogue with big powers in a multilateral way, rather than through unilateral or bilateral action. ASEAN believes security is achievable only in concert with the big powers, rather than of through its own (unilateral) policy. This 'ASEAN way' of engagement and cooperative security strategy has become a trademark of ASEAN's role in today's world politics.

A good illustration of the ASEAN style of consensus-based decision making, in a multilateral regional forum, is APEC. In their consensus-based decision making, APEC and ASEAN complement each other, although this has frustrated the efforts of the United States and other countries to speed up the process of trade liberalization. Many APEC members, such as the United States, Japan, and Australia, have been ASEAN's dialogue partners for several years, and there is a history of cooperation on many levels between ASEAN and APEC. Some have feared that ASEAN might be swallowed up by APEC, but so far the concern has not materialized, with the ASEAN countries being able to develop their own schedule for trade liberalization via AFTA. Moreover, ASEAN leaders have been able to play key roles within the APEC framework; prime examples include the establishment of the APEC Secretariat in Singapore, the adoption of the Bogor Declaration, and the Manila Action Plan for APEC.

Another showcase for the 'ASEAN way' of engagement is the ARF, established in Bangkok in 1994. The ARF was initiated and established by ASEAN for discussion of international security issues and regional conflict management in the Asia–Pacific region. Initially the ARF was a rather small group, composed of ASEAN and its dialogue partners (Japan, China, the United States, and the EU), meeting annually at the ministerial level as an informal consultative body. It is a brand new security dialogue platform, with nineteen dialogue partners in 1994: Indonesia, Singapore, Brunei, the Philippines, Thailand, Malaysia, Vietnam, Cambodia, Papua New Guinea, Laos, China, Japan, South Korea, Russia, the United States, Canada, Australia, New Zealand, and the EU. India and Myanmar became members of the ARF at the third ministerial meeting in 1996, Mongolia was admitted at the fifth ministerial meeting in 1998, and North Korea was admitted at the seventh in 2000. The ARF now has twenty-five members.[14] The ARF was designed to be an original vehicle for preventive diplomacy in the Asia–Pacific region, and is a natural choice to lead conflict resolution in the region. Different from APEC, whose agenda is more on regional trade liberalization, the security-oriented ARF dialogues cast doubt on whether the 'ASEAN way' can be effective in large and more diverse security forums in the Asia–Pacific region. Some scholars charge that ASEAN has been painfully slow in reacting to regional financial crisis and regional security problems (e.g., in East Timor), and that the informal dialogue and the lack of infrastructure have little substance.[15]

The ASEAN states have always been realistic enough to know that they cannot escape the dynamics of competition between the big powers but they can manage it, whether between the US and the Soviet Union during the Cold War or between China, the US, and Japan in the post-Cold War years. Therefore, in searching for regional order and stability, ASEAN states have individually or as a group pursued a pragmatic strategy to optimize economic relations with the big powers while reducing or hedging against security risks. Economic interdependence and security dialogues, they believe, will help to lessen any security threat, but security dialogues are not sufficient in themselves to remove it. Engaging with a rising China will help to tie Beijing into cooperative undertakings in the region. But the rationale of a balance of power is also needed when they engage with China: they need to keep the US and other powers involved, albeit at arm's length, to balance or hedge against China should the engagement strategy fail.[16]

For ASEAN states, the rise of China will come with security risks as well as economic risks. They know it. China is a reality they have to face, and the best way for ASEAN to deal with it is to engage China and to bring other big powers (Japan, the US, India, and even Russia) in to balance the 'rise of China'. In engaging China through trade and multilateral security dialogue, ASEAN states recognize that a US strategic presence is crucial as a stabilizing force. Several ASEAN states, notably Singapore and Thailand, have offered extensive base facilities and logistic support to US forces and concluded bilateral military agreements with Washington. They have openly voiced their concern that the US should remain fully engaged in Asia. ASEAN states also want to see Japan play a bigger political and security role in the region, to complement its economic stature, and have encouraged a more active Japanese role in UN peacekeeping and regional efforts to fight piracy, smuggling, and environmental damage. The creation of the ARF in 1994 as a security 'talking shop' to engage the big powers is a good example of how ASEAN states have acknowledged the fact that their security cannot be isolated from events in the wider Asia–Pacific region.

There is no doubt that ASEAN has successfully made itself the principal architect of an ASEAN-ized regional security dialogue process. ASEAN believes none of the big powers, neither China nor the US and Japan, given their mutual distrust and prevailing rivalry, could be in a position to define a new regional order acceptable to all other states after the Cold War. Japan, although it has been the predominant source of foreign investment in Southeast Asia, is not viewed as being able to assume such a prominent managerial role in East Asian security because of its lack of repentance for the past.[17] ASEAN has sought to engage all the big powers by a cooperative security approach to achieve a balance of power among them. Cooperative security is the pursuit of security with adversaries as well as allies. It is an inclusive approach that seeks dialogue and consultation among like-minded states as well as those with different perspectives on regional security problems. By convening different arrangements for regional dialogue, ASEAN hopes to promote norms of acceptable conduct that will reduce uncertainty about others' intentions, constrain their actions, and prevent any of them from achieving hegemony. Through the annual ARF meetings, ASEAN leaders believe that ASEAN's records in enhancing regional security by processes of dialogue, conciliation, conflict management, and in the building of national resilience have strengthened its credentials as the primary driving force in establishing a new regional order.[18]

Engaging China the 'ASEAN way'

ASEAN and China have come a long way in building stable and mutually beneficial relations since the end of the Cold War. There have been remarkable advances in economic, political, and security cooperation. More institutionalized dialogue was initiated only in July 1991, when Beijing began to attend the ASEAN PMC as a consultative partner. This was significant as, until 1990, some ASEAN members did not even have formal diplomatic ties with China. Chinese foreign minister Qian Qichen was invited to the twenty-fourth ASEAN ministerial meeting, in Kuala Lumpur in July 1991, as a guest of Malaysia, and he expressed China's interest in strengthening cooperation. This was received warmly by ASEAN and a series of milestones have followed:

- China became a formal member of the ARF upon its launch in July 1994, and ASEAN and China agreed to have consultations on political and security issues of common concern.
- China become a full dialogue partner of ASEAN in July 1996, and attended the PMC for the first time with that status.
- China participated in the ASEAN + 3 summit upon its inauguration in July 1997.
- China and ASEAN signed the Declaration on the Conduct of Parties in the South China Sea in November 2002.
- China and ASEAN signed the ASEAN–China Framework Agreement on Comprehensive Economic Cooperation in November 2002.
- China was the first dialogue partner to accede to the TAC, in October 2003.

The ASEAN–China summit has become an annual event since the first informal meeting in Kuala Lumpur in 1997. This has provided a framework within which the two sides can discuss economic as well as political and security issues of common concern. It is apparent that ASEAN has sought to be the driving force behind the ARF and ASEAN + 3 processes. The Southeast Asian countries not only have sought to lead the process, but also to engage with China over some of the most difficult security issues facing them. By engaging China, they generally want to achieve three objectives.

First, engagement and dialogue are expected to increase China's stake in regional peace and stability. There are different views on how to manage

120

the problems associated with the rise of China. Some contend that if China achieves greatness via the economic route, its political and diplomatic influence will be sufficient enough to shape the future course of the region, removing the need for China to assert itself militarily. Others believe that, on the contrary, China wants it all: economic greatness and territorial aggrandizement through force of arms. For analysts, the first perspective seems to have greater validity in the near and medium term, while the second view may well have resonance over the longer term. The ASEAN states are no doubt aware of both possible outcomes. They have adopted a strategy of buying as much time as possible for the region, while enjoying the benefits of Chinese economic growth, before the medium term begins the transition to the longer term. For them, the rubric of economics can help to keep China benign, and burgeoning trade and investment linkages have their obvious benefits to the economies of both the ASEAN states and China. Such linkages also have an indirect security element, insofar as increasing interdependence has the effect of giving Beijing a stake in the peace and stability of the region.

Second, ASEAN wants to ensure that the notion of the 'China threat' does not become a self-fulfilling prophecy, by maintaining good relations with Beijing. The ASEAN states have not been publicly critical of Chinese security policy. This kind of statecraft has more to do with the enlightened self-interests of ASEAN member states than any suggestions of doctrinaire inclinations. As Singapore's senior minister Lee Kuan Yew has put it: 'Small Asian nations are too prudent to express their fears [about China] publicly'.[19] Mahathir bin Mohamad, the former Malaysian prime minister, often criticized those observers who have engaged in inflating threats to East Asian security, and thereby souring the atmosphere. In May 1996, for instance, he assailed 'undeterred balance-of-power enthusiasts' for exaggerating threats to regional stability and consequently deliberately minimizing 'what Asia has been able to accomplish over the last generation'.[20] In March 1996, when Beijing conducted military exercises and missile testing in the Taiwan Straits in reaction to the visit to the United States of the Taiwanese president, Lee Teng-hui, Southeast Asian countries were largely muted in their response to Beijing's military actions, no matter how egregious they seemed. The apparent reason was that they accepted that Taiwan was a domestic Chinese issue and did not feel that it was their place to be seen interfering in the domestic affairs of another country – an avowed ASEAN principle of long standing. The Southeast Asian states are only too aware of the proximity of growing Chinese power and, being pragmatic, they have apparently decided that the best course of action is to reconcile themselves to that fact and to accommodate China's rise. To some extent, this 'ASEAN way' of response fits very well with Beijing's preferred style of diplomacy.

The third of ASEAN's long-term objectives in engaging Beijing is to lock China into regional multilateral institutions, which will not only moderate but also gradually transform Chinese regional behavior. As Michael Leifer observed in 1996, when ASEAN and its dialogue partners convened at the Singapore PMC in May 1993, the balance of power factor was very much in mind, with China identified as a potential hegemon. But the objective of the ARF exercise was not necessarily to contain China. Indeed, it was hoped that the economic incentive would serve to bring about the constructive engagement which has become part of regional rhetoric.[21] By bringing China into a security framework, ASEAN countries hope that Beijing will then operate within that framework, taking cognizance of the interests and sensitivities of other ARF members; in other words, they hope to lock China into a constraining multilateral arrangement.[22] While this scheme appeared initially to be sound, subsequent events suggested that the Chinese were not prepared to be 'constrained' or 'engaged' on the terms set by ASEAN.[23]

China's encroachment on the Philippines-claimed Mischief Reef, which came to light in February 1995, was a disquieting case from the ASEAN perspective. It was disquieting because, hitherto, in enforcing its claims to the Spratly Islands, China had always tended to encroach on Vietnamese-held islets in the chain, deliberately avoiding the ASEAN claimants – Malaysia, the Philippines, and Brunei. The Mischief Reef incident changed all that, and indicated that Beijing, possibly with a view to the impending ASEAN membership of Vietnam in July 1995, was no longer going to make a distinction between the various Spratly claimants. This apparent Chinese policy change caught the ASEAN states completely by surprise. After the initial surprise, ASEAN seemed resolved to take a unified stand against China. Senior officials of the grouping, meeting their Chinese counterparts in April 1995 in Hangzhou, China, told the Chinese that Beijing's actions in the South China Sea were very serious and that it should cease building military structures on disputed islands.[24] Now it was Beijing's turn to be surprised at the turn of events – namely a unified stand by ASEAN. This stand on the Spratly Islands issue seemed to draw a more conciliatory tone from China at the August 1995 ARF meeting in Brunei, at which Chinese foreign minister Qian Qichen gave the clear impression that Beijing was now willing to discuss the Spratly issue multilaterally with ASEAN, and to accept UNCLOS as a basis for negotiations to resolve the dispute. The foreign minister's remarks were widely applauded by other ARF governments. His remarks, however, seemed to ring hollow when Chinese Foreign Ministry spokesman Shen Guofang reasserted Beijing's old position affirming China's sovereignty over the islands and contending that the ARF was not an appropriate place to discuss what he characterized as a 'bilateral' issue.

Some observers in Southeast Asia have called this the 'three steps forward, two steps back' approach, whereby China would advance into the South China Sea and when confronted by expressions of regional disquiet would give the impression of being conciliatory, then, when the dust had settled, it would make a further advance into the area. The logical result of an apparent Chinese minuet – 'three steps forwards, two steps back' – is one of steady and inexorable advance. There seems to be a general appreciation of this fact on the part of governments of every ASEAN country, though they are unlikely to articulate it publicly, again because they do not want regional atmosphere to get murky and the 'China threat' to become a self-fulfilling prophecy.

In the near to medium term, the states of Southeast Asia will most likely adopt a suitably deferential stance in relations with their large northern neighbor. China is expected to exert a greater economic, cultural, and diplomatic influence in what it considers its 'backyard' over the coming decade. Beyond the near to medium term, however, things are less clear. Nothing in the ASEAN experience suggests that the grouping subscribes to any inflexible principles. In the conduct of their international relations, the ASEAN states have been agnostic, and they will likely give China substantial freedom of action so long as it does not lead to a situation of conflict or to Chinese interference in the sovereign rights and affairs of member states. Should those lines be crossed, however, it is likely that ASEAN deference to China would be put aside, in favor of a stronger and united stand. The question that naturally arises is whether by that time China's strength would have grown to such proportions that ASEAN, as a collective entity, would be unable to stem China's ability to dictate terms. The answer to this question is likely to become clearer a decade from now. Until then, a mix of pragmatism, adroit diplomacy, internal cohesion, and expanding military capabilities will be the predominant ASEAN approach in its relations with China or any other aspiring major power in the Asia–Pacific region.

For Beijing, China and ASEAN are geographically close to each other, historically linked with each other, culturally contiguous to each other, and have forged close ties since ancient times. Although some ASEAN countries used to have a very deep apprehension of and even hostility to China, Sino-ASEAN relations returned to normal after the Cold War. China and ASEAN countries should adopt a forward-looking attitude, and China is committed to developing its partnership of good neighborliness and mutual trust with ASEAN. In 1996, China became a full ASEAN dialogue partner, no longer merely a consultative dialogue partner. One year later, in December 1997, president Jiang Zemin and ASEAN leaders held their first summit and issued the Joint Declaration on China–ASEAN Cooperation Toward the Twenty-First Century, in which they announced their decision to establish a forward-looking partnership of good neighborliness and mutual trust. Between 1998 and 2000, China and the ASEAN countries signed a bilateral framework document, and issued an action plan for twenty-first-century cooperation. In November 2002, at the sixth China–ASEAN summit, the heads of all eleven governments signed the Declaration on the

Conduct of Parties in the South China Sea.[25] This was a breakthrough for Beijing and ASEAN, in showing their strong commitment to resolving their territorial and jurisdictional disputes by peaceful means, and to promoting a peaceful, friendly, and harmonious environment in the South China Sea. Had there not been the political trust built on in previous engagement, all these achievements would have been unthinkable.

The case of the ARF and China

From the ASEAN perspective, economic interdependence and security dialogues should help to lessen the security threat of a rising China, by linking Beijing into cooperative undertakings. But security dialogue is not sufficient in itself to reduce the threat. ASEAN has to keep the US and other powers involved in regional security dialogue and build a multilateral security system to constrain China. The ARF is a good example of ASEAN's engagement policy with China. In this case we can clearly see that the social milieu has been created inside formally weak institutions. The familiarity, consensus building, consultation, and non-coercive argumentation, and the avoidance of legalistic solutions, all make the process itself a critical variable in explaining the mutual benefit of cooperation between ASEAN and big powers.[26]

The idea of engaging external major powers through an ASEAN-driven forum was discussed at the first post-Cold War ASEAN summit, in Singapore in January 1992. ASEAN leaders at the summit agreed to 'intensify its external dialogues in political and security matters using the ASEAN Post-Ministerial Conferences (PMC)'.[27] In May 1993, after the first round of dialogue with its PMC dialogue partners, the ASEAN chair of the meeting stated: 'The continuing presence of the United States, as well as stable relationships among the United States, Japan, and China and other states of the region would contribute to regional stability'.[28] The ARF was launched in 1994 as the first ever region-wide security forum in the Asia–Pacific based on ASEAN's cooperative security approach. There had been similar calls for regional political dialogue before, such as Soviet president Mikhail Gorbachev's proposal at Vladivostok in 1987 for a Pacific version of the Conference on Security Cooperation in Asia. But ASEAN leaders were concerned about the organization losing its relevance in regional affairs and becoming a 'pawn' in big power politics. They insisted that ASEAN must retain its role in setting dialogue agendas – making sure that Western states would not raise human rights issues, and not becoming marginalized in any regional security dialogue. The use of the PMC framework provided ASEAN with the advantage of having a controlling influence over the agenda, and placed ASEAN at the center of the process. As Singaporean foreign minister Shanmugam Jayakumar indicated, 'For

ASEAN, the issue now is not how to avoid entanglement in big power conflict. It is how to maintain a stable balance of the major powers at a time of immense fluidity.'[29] Some scholars think the ARF enables Southeast Asian states to ASEAN-ize regional security dialogue by engaging external powers in a more institutionalized way.[30]

From the very beginning, ASEAN has played a leading role in organizing and setting the agenda for the ARF process. The ARF seeks to promote and establish a regional security order that could accommodate its members' diverse political and security interests through a three-stage dialogue process: stage 1 is to promote confidence-building measures; stage 2 is to develop preventive diplomacy; and stage 3 is to elaborate approaches to conflict. In so doing, the ARF process has to adopt a gradual, evolutionary approach, with decision making by consensus and movement 'at a pace comfortable to all its members in order to achieve its long-term objectives'.[31] The evolution from stage to stage is accomplished via a two-track process, with track I mainly involving government officials, and track II involving academics and non-governmental specialists.[32] Through candid and frank discussion among dialogue partners, the ARF process encourages greater transparency, mutual trust, and understanding of each other's concerns and positions. Since it is impossible to move the ARF forward without a high degree of mutual understanding and trust among dialogue parties, the process focuses on confidence building as its main thrust. At the fourth ARF, ministers agreed to set up an Intersessional Support Group on Confidence Building Measures, to identify areas in the overlap between confidence building and preventive diplomacy, and ways and means of addressing them (though with a focus on confidence building). In addressing the issue of overlap, a common understanding on a working concept of preventive diplomacy and the principles governing its practice was reached, to provide a common basis on which to explore this overlap and to enhance confidence in the process. Pursuant to this, the ministers at the sixth ARF, in Singapore, instructed the Intersessional Support Group to explore the overlap between confidence-building measures and preventive diplomacy, but focusing *inter alia* on the development of the concepts and principles of the latter.

In the ARF process, preventive diplomacy is a core concept for multi-lateral security discussion. Essentially, preventive diplomacy involves preventing disputes or conflicts between states from emerging, or if they have emerged then to stop them from escalating into armed confrontation, or at least to stop such disputes or conflicts spreading. A range of measures to use in preventing crises were introduced and discussed at the ARF. These included the following:

1 *Confidence-building measures* refer to efforts in building mutual trust and confidence between states. The successful application of preventive diplomacy has to be built upon continuous efforts to maintain and

enhance trust and confidence. Without a high degree of trust before a crisis emerges, it is unlikely that preventive diplomacy in the later stages of any conflict can be carried out.

2 *Norm building* refers to nurturing accepted codes of conduct or norms of behavior among Asian–Pacific states. Codes of conduct enhance predictability and strengthen cooperative behavior, while norm building increases trust between states in the region. ASEAN uses its organizing role in the ARF process to introduce norms and codes of conduct consistent with those in the TAC and the UN Charter.

3 *Enhancing channels of communication* encourages open and direct communications among ARF participants and it helps to promote transparency, with a view to avoiding misperception or misunderstanding. Such channels advance information sharing and allow for early warnings.

Drawn mainly from discussions in the Council for Security Cooperation in the Asia-Pacific (CSCAP), eight principles of preventive diplomacy were adopted in the ARF process, which include diplomacy, non-coerciveness, trust, confidence, consultation, and consensus.

Beijing was at first suspicious but then became more comfortable with the ARF process as it became more involved in it. China's skepticism in the early years of the ARF (from 1994 to 1996) was largely due to its concern that this multilateral mechanism might eventually be dominated by Western powers, and that ASEAN might use the forum to internationalize the Spratly issue.[33] Beijing's attitude gradually changed after 1997, as China began to deepen and widen its participation in international multilateral forums, and even started its own multilateral endeavor – the Shanghai Five process – in 1996. Chinese diplomats began to have more positive views of the ARF because it is an open forum for ASEAN-style dialogue and consensus. It is driven by ASEAN, not controlled by Western powers.[34] Since then, Beijing has sent delegates to regular meetings at ministerial, senior official and working levels each year. Having been formed three years earlier than ASEAN + 1 and ASEAN + 3, the ARF has become a major regional multilateral platform, on which Beijing and other ARF parties can discuss regional and international security issues, and engage in mutual trust building through dialogue. In order to handle the rapidly increasing portfolio of ARF and other regional activities, a new division, the Regional Cooperation Division (*Diqu Hezuo Chu*), was set up in the Department of Asian Affairs of the Chinese Foreign Ministry.[35]

China was particularly pleased when, at the second ARF ministerial meeting, all parties agreed the ARF process should be evolutionary, taking place in the three broad stages outlined above (the promotion of confidence-building measures, the development of preventive diplomacy, and the elaboration of approaches to conflicts).[36] It is in this forum that China and ASEAN have gradually decreased their suspicion and apprehensions, and built confidence and mutual trust, and this has paved the way for the 10 + 1 and 10 + 3 formats. Ever since its formation, the two sides have worked closely with each other in helping the ARF process move forward smoothly. As Chinese officials state, China has all along supported ASEAN's leading role in the ARF, and will continue to do so in future.

Western commentators tend to portray the ARF as a 'talking shop', but Chinese officials seem to appreciate it for that very reason. For Beijing, the ARF has undertaken changes, particularly after 11 September 2001, and there have been more concrete results from the talking shop. According to the assessment of a Chinese diplomat who has participated in the process, there have been several major achievements in recent years that have kept Beijing interested.[37]

First, the ARF made useful exploratory endeavors to increase mutual understanding and confidence among its participants, and to step up regional security dialogue and cooperation. It became more focused on the issues that have potential impacts on regional security, and produced the 'Chairman's Statement of Fighting Against Terrorism' and the 'ARF Statement on a Measure Against Terrorist Financing'. The ARF has implemented nearly eighty confidence-building measures and, among them, China has hosted seven ARF projects.[38] Although there have been no substantive agreements, the ARF has organized discussions of disaster relief, peacekeeping, national defense and security policy, preventive diplomacy, transnational crimes, and anti-terrorism measures, which China believes instrumental to regional security.

Second, the eighth ARF ministerial meeting adopted three papers: the 'ARF Concept and Principles of Preventive Diplomacy'; 'Enhanced Role of the ARF Chair'; and the 'Terms of Reference for the ARF Experts/Eminent Persons'. Further, in July 2002, the ARF ministerial meeting adopted 'Stock-taking of the ARF Process', and decided to form a new Intersessional Support Group on international terrorism and transnational crimes. Again, short of any formal agreement, Beijing is happy to see more detailed dialogue and discussion on a wider range of security issues, and the dialogue proceeds at a pace controlled by ASEAN. In their speeches to the ARF, the Chinese delegates even argued for the broadening of the discussion and the involvement of security and defense officials in the process, a multilateral military-to-military dialogue. They proposed that the ASEAN Secretariat be assigned to assist the ARF chair in coordinating the ARF's work, and to give new impetus to the ARF's future development.[39]

The third reason why Beijing has become more comfortable with the ARF process is that the 'ASEAN way' of norms, practice, and principles is being employed in the ARF. These norms, practice, and principles, as discussed above, include adopting decision by consensus, consultation, and an incremental approach to solving disagreements, moving at a pace comfortable to all, and not meddling in each other's internal affairs.

These norms and principles, the Chinese strongly believe, should guide the progress not only of the ARF, but also serve as a reference and role model for other regional organizations.

The fourth reason why Beijing is more interested in the ARF process is that it provides a useful venue and platform for bilateral meetings, particularly for those who have no diplomatic relations or for whom meeting would be difficult otherwise. When the North Korea joined the ARF in 2000, its bilateral meetings with the United States and Japan during the seventh ARF ministerial meeting drew international attention. China also took advantage of the ARF to conduct bilateral meetings, and one of the important ones was the Sino-US meeting at the foreign minister level at the side of the ARF in 2001, which represented the initial high-level contact after the EP-3 spy plane incident in April of that year. As the ARF admits more members, it will provide more opportunities for bilateral meetings within a multilateral platform.

In general, Beijing has become more comfortable with the ARF mainly because it is, as ASEAN countries maintain, a process, not an organization. Given the complexity of its membership, it is quite natural that there are different views in the ARF, but, in one Chinese diplomat's words, 'If we shared the same views in everything, it would be not necessary for the ARF to exist today'.[40] Since the main purpose of the ARF is to provide an avenue for all participants to exchange views and ideas, both China and ASEAN feel it is useful to engage in this cooperative security forum, to address regional common concerns. Before the 'Stock-taking of the ARF Process' was adopted, there had been some dissatisfaction. Some Western participating states proposed that the current ARF chair be changed and a co-chair be introduced. The argument was that the ARF should move on to the second of its three stages – the development of preventive diplomacy. To them, the ARF should be institutionalized as an organization for resolving regional conflicts. These states even mapped out a road plan for the ARF's institutionalization. The Chinese took ASEAN's side by strongly objecting to these proposals. In China's view, the ARF should continue to develop at a pace that is comfortable to all participants, and to continue to take decisions by consensus, with the confidence-building measures remaining the key to the ARF process. Beijing also supports ASEAN's continued exercise of its leading role in the ARF process, and believes that no decision should be made on moving on to the development of preventive diplomacy until a consensus is reached on this. This position is appreciated by ASEAN. Many Western observers think that, since China wants the process to move at a slower pace than other members, China has *de facto* control over the discussion and implementation of each stage.[41] However, besides being more accustomed to the procedural rules, any such apparent control arises simply because Beijing has learned from the process and has begun to play a more positive role in the ARF.[42]

Considering the changing security environment in East Asia, the Chinese delegation agreed to and subsequently supported the expansion of the dialogue agenda to include more non-traditional security issues. Indeed, the Chinese believe the ARF should be more focused on the non-traditional security issues, especially since such issues have become real security threats in the region. Being transnational or even trans-regional in nature, most of these issues are difficult for one or even a few countries to deal with. In July 2001, the Chinese delegation proposed that the ARF should highlight its dialogue and cooperation on non-traditional security issues. Like many countries in the region, China believes multilateral cooperation is the only way to tackle them. As for technical matters, the Chinese delegation argued that the ARF should encourage its advisers – 'experts and eminent persons' – to undertake an in-depth study of those issues and to identify the prioritized topics for ARF dialogue.

Following its accession to ASEAN's 1976 TAC in June 2003, Chinese foreign minister Li Zhaoxing formally proposed that the ARF establish a new Security Policy Conference, whose participants would be primarily military personnel, to draft a new 'concept paper' or pact among ARF dialogue partners on promoting peace, stability, and prosperity in Southeast Asia. The agenda at the ARF Phnom Penh meeting was dominated by anti-terrorism, North Korea's nuclear challenge, and mounting disgust with Myanmar's ruling junta. China therefore succeeded in gaining significant attention for its own priorities by aligning itself with Southeast Asian delegations.

The proposed ARF Security Policy Conference was part of Beijing's strategy to promote its 'new security concept' to the world. Different from the traditional security conception, the 'new security concept' emphasizes giving equal attention to the security concerns of each country, and guaranteeing security for all through united action, rather than seeking 'absolute security for oneself and threaten[ing] other parties' security'. ASEAN members welcomed China's proposal and agreed that a concept paper would be circulated 'in due course'. In order to show Beijing's sincerity, Li Zhaoxing also pledged to seek to get China's accession to the TAC ratified quickly. ASEAN opened the treaty to outside accession in 2000, and China's accession helped to induce other major powers to follow the suit.

China's proposal to codify its 'new security concept' in an international agreement is a significant move, given Beijing's traditional attitude to international security treaties. It may intend the move as a parallel security step to the free trade agreement that promises to integrate the region's economies. In the near term, a Security Policy Conference of military officers from the twenty-five ARF countries is something of a gamble for Beijing, given that the United States has well established, enduring military-to-military relations with most of the ARF states, including five formal allies. Several US defense treaty partners, especially Australia and

Japan, can be expected to resist any efforts to introduce a new security pact that suggests that bilateral treaties should be replaced by a region-wide collective security organization. On the other hand, China is likely playing this initiative long. The themes of China's 'new security concept' of the mid-1990s, echoing generalized principles such as non-interference and renunciation of the threat or use of force, will be difficult for a number of Southeast Asian governments to oppose. Among other things, the principles resemble articles in ASEAN's own TAC, to which Beijing has already acceded (though not yet ratified). However, looking to future contingencies in the region, such principles could be considered by the United States and its allies as dangerous limits on freedom of military action.

ASEAN's engagement with Japan

Compared with its engagement with Beijing, ASEAN's engagement with Tokyo has a longer history, with more institutionalized dialogue addressing more economic issues of mutual concern than political problems. In response to the declining US role in the region after the Vietnam War and rising anti-Japanese feeling in Southeast Asia, Tokyo began to take up more active diplomacy toward the region, in addition to its strong economic regional role. The turning point for this diplomatic activism was the Fukuda Doctrine of 1977. Prime minister Takeo Fukuda was a highly esteemed foreign policy leader as well as a politician. His Asia-centered diplomacy and foreign policies were an attempt to challenge the then prevalent notion of Japan being 'an economic giant but political pygmy', and to make a difference to Japan's relations with this part of the world. In a major policy speech in August 1977 Fukuda articulated what were called three principles of Japan's Southeast Asian policy:

1 Japan rejects the role of a military power and is resolved to contribute to the peace and prosperity of Southeast Asia;
2 Japan will do its best to consolidate the relationship of mutual confidence and trust, based on a 'heart-to-heart' understanding;
3 Japan will be an equal partner of ASEAN and its members states, will cooperate positively with them to foster a relationship based on mutual understanding with Indochina countries, and will contribute to the building of peace and prosperity throughout Southeast Asia.

Following in Fukuda's footsteps, Japanese prime ministers and foreign ministers have made frequent visits to Southeast Asia since then. According to Japanese scholars:

> the ASEAN connection has become the *sine qua non* of Japan's international position. This commitment has to be consistently carried out since it is the

only official commitment ever promulgated by the Japanese government except for its important relations with the United States.[43]

Initiated by Japanese foreign minister Sunao Sonoda, a political get-together between Japan and ASEAN states was institutionalized in June 1978, with the intention of later expanding to include the US, Canada, Australia, New Zealand, and the European Community. Although we cannot determine whether this proposal led to the institutionalization of the ASEAN PMC in 1993, Tokyo was active in initiating it as early as the 1970s. In the early meetings of Japanese and ASEAN foreign ministers, the focus was on the relevance of Japan's economic aid to Hanoi as a stabilizing factor in the region. While Japan argued that aid was its political leverage, ASEAN warned of the danger of strengthening the Vietnamese communist regime. In 1980 the dispute was settled in ASEAN's favor, but Tokyo maintained its political dialogue with Hanoi. At the third meeting of foreign ministers, in June 1981, Japan disclosed its 'comprehensive political settlement' of the Cambodian problem and offered support for ASEAN's proposal for an international conference on it. In engaging Japan, ASEAN not only solicited Tokyo's political support on the settlement of the Indochina problem, but also secured more economic assistance for the region. For Tokyo, Southeast Asia became an arena in which Japan tried to transform its image as a 'political pygmy'. A good example of this was Japan's 'Partnership with a Global Perspective' proposal by foreign minister Tadashi Kuranari in June 1987.

In parallel with the political dialogue, meetings of ASEAN and Japanese economic ministers were also held, from November 1979. Early on, these meetings took place with the foreign ministers. They covered a wide range of issues, from trade, investment, and transfer of technology, to development assistance, as well as the world economic situation. But the involvement of the economic ministers in these meetings was largely symbolic, and they were dominated by the foreign ministers. Meetings of the economic ministers did not become more substantial until 1992, when both sides agreed to hold the first annual meeting between the Japanese Ministry of International Trade and Industry and ASEAN economic ministers, in Manila in October of that year. In the midst of the Asian financial crisis five years later, ASEAN and Japan agreed to upgrade their economic relations.

ASEAN's interest in engaging Tokyo was mainly due to its economic ties with Japan. After the appreciation of the Japanese yen in 1985, Japanese businesses began to relocate their manufacturing bases to Southeast Asian countries on a massive scale. This came with a dramatic increase in Japan's imports from Southeast Asia and the region's exports to Japan (especially from the founding ASEAN states). In the bilateral dialogue, Tokyo appeared to approach regionalism more from a commercial point of view – improving infrastructure, emphasizing local goods and services, and providing ODA.

From the 1970s to the early 1990s, Tokyo's thinking on regionalism was largely anchored in the Asia–Pacific framework. Japanese leaders had always believed there was a need to keep the United States engaged in East Asia, in part to reassure Washington and the rest of Asia about its own postwar intentions. For this reason, Japan was instrumental in forming the ADB in the 1960s and promoting Asia–Pacific dialogue through the APEC process in the late 1980s.

Dialogue between ASEAN and Japan in the 1980s and up to the mid-1990s was largely about economic issues and less about regional economic cooperation, because Tokyo at that time enjoyed *de facto* economic leadership in East Asia. With its primary economic position in the region, there was no sense of an economic or political rivalry for leadership. However, after the Asian financial crisis, Tokyo began to feel strong competition from China in regional economic and even political leadership in the region. China's decision not to devalue its currency during the crisis and Tokyo's economic recession and its downward drifting currency made ASEAN turn more to Beijing, instead of Tokyo, for economic help. While Japan's trade with the rest of East Asia now remains steady, China's trade with Asian countries grows rapidly. For example, China now makes up 20 percent of South Korea's foreign trade, is Hong Kong and Taiwan's largest trading partner, and has overtaken the United States as the country taking the largest share of Japan's exports. Since the early 1990s China has taken a greater share of Asian trade with countries outside the Asian region. Thus, China became the driving force behind Japan's increasing interest in regional integration and community building. Although Japan's idea of establishing the AMF in 1998 was quickly dismissed by Washington, Tokyo came up with the Miyazawa initiative for more bilateral financial aid at times of economic crisis. Japan's growing interest in regional integration and community building can also be seen in its willingness to engage in and launch the ASEAN + 3 process in 1998 and the Chiang Mai initiative in 2000.

ASEAN + 3 and community building

Although ASEAN is still apprehensive about a powerful rising China and suspicious of the benefit of Japan's involvement in the region, its economic relations with these Northeast Asian powers are becoming more positive and also more significant. The pressure from economic globalization has called for an answer on where East Asian regionalism is headed. Growing economic regionalization in East Asia has shown that the natural direction is toward a combination of north–south regionalism. ASEAN has seen an increasing need to extend toward Northeast Asia, and Northeast Asian states (including South Korea) agree that they cannot afford to miss out on regional cooperation and integration. At this juncture the ASEAN + 3 process began, during the peak of the Asian financial crisis, in December 1997. At ASEAN's second informal summit, in Kuala Lumpur in December 1997, Chinese, Japanese, and South Korean leaders were invited to meet with ASEAN counterparts to discuss regional economic and financial problems as well as issues of common interest. Thus, the ASEAN + 3 (or 10 + 3)[44] process was born.

There is no doubt that economic integration is the primary driving force for the community-building process in East Asia. Yet, the beginning of the ASEAN + 3 process in 1997 showed an important step toward the institutionalization of regional dialogue on issues beyond those of an economic nature. The ASEAN + 1 dialogue preceding the foundation of the ASEAN + 3 process was more substantive on issues of political, economic, and security-related issues. However, it is the ASEAN + 3 process that has created a bridge between Northeast and Southeast Asia on a regional platform for all. This regional platform not only promotes East Asian dialogue but also can serve as a buffer between the two Northeast Asian big powers (China and Japan) within an ASEAN-driven arrangement.

The ASEAN + 3 process is a set of complex meeting/dialogue mechanisms of cooperation, molded ASEAN-style consultations. Dialogue is at various levels on a wide range of issues. The ASEAN + 3 process as a big umbrella includes three separate 10 + 1 meetings between ASEAN leaders and their counterparts from the three Northeast Asian countries. Within each 10 + 1 framework, there are one 10 + 1 annual summit, three ministerial meetings (foreign, economic, and transport ministers) and six 'working parallel mechanisms'. For instance, within the China–ASEAN dialogue framework, there are six levels of meeting: ASEAN–China Senior Officials Political Consultations;[45] the ASEAN–China Joint Cooperation Committee;[46] the China–ASEAN Joint Committee on Economic and Trade Cooperation; the China–ASEAN Joint Committee on Science and Technology;[47] the ASEAN Committee in Beijing;[48] and the China–ASEAN Trade Council.[49] At the ASEAN + 3 level, there are six ministerial meetings (foreign, finance, economic, labor, agriculture and forestry, and tourism), which report to the 10 + 3 summit. At the same time, within the framework of 10 + 3, China, Japan, and South Korea have also established an informal '+ 3' summit meeting, five ministerial meetings (foreign, finance, economic, environmental protection, and intellectual property), and cooperation among economic research institutes of the three countries. This '+ 3' platform was difficult to attain. It would not have been possible if there had been no ASEAN + 3 process. Heavily influenced by the ASEAN consultation culture, the ASEAN + 3 process has created an integral regional dialogue mechanism in which ASEAN maintains political leverage.

After 1997, the ASEAN + 3 process began to gain momentum in terms of networking and socializing its member states. The early ASEAN + 1 and

ASEAN + 3 summits were more symbolic than substantive achievements. Yet, when Chinese premier Zhu Rongji proposed to sign a free trade agreement with ASEAN in 2001, Beijing's initiative generated more substantive dialogue in the forum, and it also spurred the other two Northeast Asian states to follow suit. As China–ASEAN dialogue has moved to cover a wide range of issues, from agriculture, telecommunication, Mekong sub-regional cooperation, and human resources, to non-traditional security, both Japan and South Korea have also put more efforts into substantive cooperation with ASEAN.

Now let us turn to some of the more concrete examples of progress that has resulted from ASEAN + 3 functional cooperation.

ASEAN–China Free Trade Area (ACFTA)

The idea of forming the ACFTA was first put forward by Chinese leaders in 1999. One year later, the two sides formed an expert group to conduct a feasibility study of the idea. The group undertook extensive study of this initiative for almost one year, and presented a report to the ASEAN–China summit in 2001 with the recommendation of establishing the ACFTA by 2010. The ASEAN–China Framework Agreement on Comprehensive Economic Cooperation was signed at the 2002 ASEAN–China summit. The goal is to create a win–win large-scale free trade area for both China and ASEAN. It is estimated that it will become the third largest market in the world, with a population of 1.7 billion, a gross domestic product of US$2 trillion and two-way trade valued at US$1.23 trillion. Negotiations on the modalities for tariff reduction and elimination schedules, which started in 2002, resulted in the Trade in Goods Agreement and Dispute Settlement Mechanism Agreement, which were completed in Beijing in October 2004. ASEAN and China signed these two Agreements in November 2004 in Vientiane.

It is recognized that effort to accelerate the establishment of the ACFTA serves the common interests of China and ASEAN, for the earlier it is in place, the sooner China opens its market to ASEAN, and the two sides can benefit from it. It will not only forge closer China–ASEAN economic cooperation, but also help the overall development of East Asian cooperation. The two sides are committed to the success of their negotiations. And China has assured ASEAN that ASEAN will gain more than China.

'Early harvest' programs

In order to speed up the process of establishing the ACFTA, opening up the agricultural market through the 'early harvest' programs gave great impetus to the negotiations. Agricultural cooperation was one of the five priority areas in the negotiations. In November 2002, ASEAN and China signed a memorandum of understanding entitled Medium- and Long-Term Plan of Agricultural Cooperation, which allowed some categories of agricultural products into the Chinese market. Meanwhile, Chinese premier Zhu Ronji suggested in 2002 that cooperation over information technology be reached at an earlier date than had been set, and a memorandum of understanding entitled Cooperation in Information and Communications Technology (ICT) was signed on 8 October 2003 at the Bali summit.

Greater Mekong River area

There have been two summits on the Greater Mekong Sub-region and the six parties involved adopted the Joint Greater Mekong Sub-region Summit Declaration and the Development Matrix. The development of the Mekong Sub-region is not only a key area for cooperation between China and ASEAN, but also an important element in the ASEAN integration process. ASEAN has made infrastructure, human resources development, information and communication technologies, and regional economic integration the four priorities of the 'Initiative of ASEAN Integration'. Therefore, it is necessary for China to support ASEAN integration in these four fields. So far, China has published the Country Report on China's Participation in Greater Mekong Sub-region Cooperation, which defines its plans and key projects for Chinese participation in the program. China has also signed a framework agreement with Laos on its provision of US$30 million in interest-free loans and grants to improve the Laos section of the Kunming–Bangkok road. China will also make funds available for the comprehensive renovation and construction of the Kunming–Hekou railway in support of an early connection of the pan-Asian railway. China has exchanged letters with Cambodia, Laos, and Myanmar to provide zero tariff treatment for the majority of their exports to China from 1 January 2004. China is willing to consider sponsoring the Inland Waterway Improvement Project in Cambodia, Laos, Myanmar, and Vietnam, and other projects with funds from the China–ASEAN Cooperation Fund.[50]

ASEAN–Japan Comprehensive Economic Partnership

At a separate summit, ASEAN and Japan signed the Joint Declaration on a Comprehensive Economic Partnership, which envisions a 'partnership, with elements of a free-trade area' to be implemented within ten years. Japan is already using the model of its bilateral agreement with Singapore in discussions with Thailand, the Philippines, and Vietnam, which were expected to provide the basis for a Japan–ASEAN framework agreement in 2006. In contrast to Japan and China, South Korea has not pursued its own economic arrangement with ASEAN, and appears not to be minded to do so. Prime minister Kim Suk-soo suggested that while South Korea was interested in establishing a free trade zone in East Asia, any deal would have to be a medium- or long-term one, due to domestic concerns about agricultural and marine imports from Southeast Asia. Seoul remains active with ASEAN, however, having established the South Korea–ASEAN fund of about US$2 million aimed at Cambodia, Laos, Myanmar, and Vietnam. Just before the summit, South Korea inaugurated a high-technology training center in Phnom Penh as part of its APEC commitment to reduce the digital divide.

Cooperation in non-traditional security areas

Terrorism and other non-traditional security issues have become increasingly salient. The 11 September 2001 attacks in the United States and a series of terrorist incidents in Indonesia and the Philippines have made both sides feel it imperative that countries in the region join in dealing with non-traditional security threats. There is growing consensus between China and ASEAN in this regard. Now China and ASEAN are exploring new ways and means of cooperating over security issues, in particular the non-traditional security issues, such as transnational crime. In November 2002, the two sides signed the Joint Declaration of ASEAN and China on Cooperation in the Field of Non-Traditional Security Issues.[51] Both will accordingly focus on the prevention of terrorism, drug smuggling, and illegal immigration, through information sharing, personnel exchanges and training, enhancing capabilities, and providing legal assistance in cracking down on transnational crime. Just as China and ASEAN are cooperating well in combating drugs, cooperation in cracking down on terrorism and other transnational crime is expected to be smooth as well.[52] In the political and security field, ASEAN and China signed the Declaration on the Conduct of Parties in the South China Sea at the same summit. China also expressed interest in acceding to the ASEAN TAC, and to working toward signing the SEANWFZ.

East Asian free trade area

At the 2003 summit, ASEAN leaders endorsed a plan to transform the region into a giant free trade zone by 2020, with several urging a faster pace if they are to keep up with the rest of the world. According to ASEAN secretary-general Ong Keng Yong, the Association is working on free trade agreements to be completed with China in 2010, India in 2011, and Japan in 2012, and is also considering advancing the 2020 deadline set by the APEC summit in 1994.[53] If completed on schedule, that would indeed be a tremendous achievement in regional integration and community building.

At its inception, the ASEAN + 3 process focused on economic issues, beginning with financial cooperation. In 1999, the third ASEAN + 3

summit issued the Joint Statement on East Asia Cooperation, which identified its future direction and eight key areas of cooperation, ranging from the
economic, social, and political to the security fields. The *Final Report of the
East Asia Study Group*[54] then mapped out the future for ASEAN + 3 cooperation. The Initiative for Development in East Asia ministerial meeting held in
Tokyo promoted ASEAN + 3 cooperation in the development field. Since the
turn of the century, the ASEAN + 3 cooperation mechanism has matured
and become more pragmatic. Because the world is witnessing increasing
globalization, East Asia's development cannot be achieved in isolation.
ASEAN + 3 cooperation should continue to maintain its open nature, and
to establish relations with other regional organizations, such as the APEC,
the ASEM and others. In the long run, as mapped out in the East Asia
Study Group's report, ASEAN + 3 cooperation will pursue the evolution of
the ASEAN + 3 summit into an East Asian summit and the formation of
the East Asia free trade area.

Conclusion

Facing the opportunities and challenges brought about by economic
globalization, East Asian states did not passively wait for outside help:
they took action to organize themselves in meeting the challenges. As the
Malaysian prime minister Mahathir bin Mohamad said, 'Asia must assert
itself. It must not just follow. Indeed Asia can be an equal partner with
the other groups in the world, the European Union and the NAFTA.'[55] In
comparison with Europe, North America, and Latin America, East Asia as
a region has been a late-comer in engaging itself in regional integration
and community building. Yet, after the Asian financial crisis of 1997, East
Asian states really geared up their regional cooperation so as to keep up
with the times and develop appropriate frameworks for regional integration and institution building.

The regional multilateral cooperation frameworks, ASEAN + 3 and
ASEAN + 1, have given momentum to the building of an East Asian-
only grouping in the region since the Asian financial crisis. This vision
of regionalism is quite different from that based on an APEC-wide
Asia–Pacific grouping. Although an East Asian-only community could be
supplementary to and coexist with APEC and other regional multilateral
organizations, the formation of a unique composite and multilayered
regional cooperation framework will best serve the interests of East Asian
states and suit the characteristics of the region. At this important juncture,
it would be far-sighted for ASEAN, China, and Japan to join closer together
and make an even greater contribution to regional multilateral cooperation. This would be conducive to peace, development, prosperity, and
stability in Asia, and that of the world as well. In this endeavor, ASEAN

is in the driver's seat, leading the community-building process through its engagement with China and Japan, while the big powers are on the back seat, following ASEAN's lead.

Notes

1 Bangkok Declaration, Thailand, 8 August 1967. For the full text, see www. aseansec.org/1212.htm (last accessed April 2006).
2 Declaration of ASEAN Concord, Indonesia, 24 February 1976. For the full text, see www.aseansec.org/1216.htm (last accessed April 2006).
3 Kamarulzaman Askandar, Jacob Bercovitch and Mikio Oishi, 'The ASEAN Way of Conflict Management: old patterns and new trends', *Asian Journal of Political Sciences*, 10:2 (2002), p. 22.
4 See, for example, Philips Jusario Vermonte, 'China–ASEAN Strategic Relations: a view from Jakarta', in James K. Chin and Nicholas Thomas (eds), *China and ASEAN: changing political and strategic ties*, Hong Kong: Centre of Asian Studies, University of Hong Kong, 2005, p. 95.
5 Hussin Mutalib, 'At Thirty, ASEAN Looks to Challenges in the New Millennium', *Contemporary Southeast Asia*, 19:1 (1997), p. 79.
6 Kusuma Snitwongse, 'Thirty Years of ASEAN: achievements through political cooperation', *Pacific Review*, 11:2 (1998), p. 184.
7 Amitav Acharya, *Regionalism and Multilateralism*, Singapore: Times Academic Press, 2002, p. 247.
8 Hadi Soesastro (ed.), *ASEAN in a Changed Regional and International Political Economy*, Jakarta: Centre for Strategic and International Studies, 1995, pp. iii–ix.
9 See Amitav Acharya, *Regionalism and Multilateralism*, chapter 9, 'Sovereignty, Non-intervention and Regionalism', pp. 228–37.
10 Adam Malik, 'Southeast Asia: Towards an Asian Asia', *Far East Economic Review*, 25 September 1971, p. 31.
11 Quoted in 'Mahathir Assails Stability Threats', *International Herald Tribune*, 18–19 May 1996, p. 4.
12 For details of the ASEAN Community, see Concord II, issued on 7 October 2003 in Bali, Indonesia. For the full text, see www.aseansec.org/15159.htm (last accessed April 2006).
13 For more information, see the ASEAN Secretariat website, www.aseansec.org/64.htm (last accessed April 2006). To support the conduct of ASEAN's external relations, ASEAN has established committees composed of heads of diplomatic missions in the following capitals: Brussels, London, Paris, Washington, DC, Tokyo, Canberra, Ottawa, Wellington, Geneva, Seoul, New Delhi, New York, Beijing, Moscow, and Islamabad.
14 Pakistan joined the ARF in 2004 as its twenty-fourth member, and East Timor in 2005 as the forum's twenty-fifth member.
15 Anthony L. Smith, 'ASEAN's Ninth Summit: solidifying regional cohesion, advancing external linkages', *Contemporary Southeast Asia*, 26:3 (2004), p. 420. For a related discussion, also see Markus Hund, 'From "Neighbourhood

Watch Group" to Community?', *Australian Journal of International Affairs*, 56:1, pp. 99–122.

16 For a good discussion of this issue, see Ralf Emmers, *Cooperative Security and the Balance of Power in ASEAN and the AEF*, London: Routledge Curzon, 2003, chapter 5.

17 On relations between ASEAN and Japan, see, for instance, Lee Poh Ping, 'ASEAN and the Japanese Role in Southeast Asia', in Alison Broinowski (ed.), *ASEAN into the 1990s*, London: Macmillan, 1990, pp. 162–83.

18 Jürgen Haacke, 'Collective Foreign and Security Policy: the emergence of an ASEANized regional order in East Asia?' paper presented at the International Studies Association annual meeting, March 1998. Available online at www.ciaonet.org/conf/haj02 (last accessed June 2006).

19 Barry Wain, 'Beijing and Hanoi Play with Fire in South China Sea', *Asian Wall Street Journal*, 20 July 1994, p. 5.

20 Quoted in 'Mahathir Assails Stability Threats', *International Herald Tribune*, 18–19 May 1996, p. 4.

21 Michael Leifer, 'Truth about the Balance of Power', in *Structure*, Singapore: Institute of Southeast Asian Studies, 1996, pp. 50–1.

22 Gerald Segal, 'East Asia and the "Constrainment" of China', *International Security*, 20:4 (1996), p. 123.

23 Larry M. Wortzel, 'China Pursues Traditional Great-Power Status', *Orbis*, 38:2 (1994), p. 165.

24 'ASEAN United on Spratlys Issue in Talks with Beijing, Says Manila', *Straits Times*, 6 April 1995, p. 14.

25 This was adopted at the Sixth China–ASEAN summit, in Phnom Penh, 4 November 2002.

26 Amita Acharya, 'Ideas, Identity and Institution-Building: from the ASEAN way to the Asia–Pacific way', *Pacific Review*, 10:3 (1997).

27 Jeannie Henderson, *Reassessing ASEAN*, Adelphi Paper No. 328, London: International Institute for Strategic Studies, 1999, p. 26.

28 Quoted from Michael Leifer, *The ASEAN Regional Forum*, Adelphi Paper No. 302, London: International Institute for Strategic Studies, 1996, p. 20.

29 Ralf Emmers, 'The Influence of the Balance of Power Factor Within the ASEAN Regional Forum', *Contemporary Southeast Asia*, 23:2 (2001), pp. 276–7.

30 Jürgen Haacke, 'Collective Foreign and Security Policy'.

31 Quoted from 'ASEAN Regional Forum (ARF) Concept and Principles of Preventive Diplomacy', on the English-language homepage of the Chinese Ministry of Foreign Affairs, at www.fmprc.gov.cn/eng/wjb/zzjg/gjs/gjzzyhy/2612/t15316.htm (last accessed April 2006).

32 See Simon S. C. Tay, with Obood Talib, 'The ASEAN Regional Forum: preparing for preventive diplomacy', *Contemporary Southeast Asia*, 19:3 (1997), pp. 252–68; and Sheldon W. Simon, 'Evaluating Track II Approaches to Security Diplomacy in the Asia–Pacific: the CSCAP experience', *Pacific Review*, 15:2 (2002), pp. 167–200.

33 Kuik Cheng-Chwee, 'Multilateralism in China's ASEAN Policy: its evolution, characteristics, and aspiration', *Contemporary Southeast Asia*, 27:1 (2005), pp. 105–8; and Kuik Cheng-Chwee, 'China's Participation in the ASEAN Regional Forum (ARF): the exogenous and endogenous effects of international

institutions', in James K. Chin and Nicholas Thomas (eds), *China and ASEAN: changing political and strategic ties*, Centre of Asian Studies, University of Hong Kong, 2005, pp. 147–51.

34 ASEAN members chair and coordinate the ARF annual meetings in rotation each year.

35 Kuik Cheng-Chwee, 'China's Participation in the ASEAN Regional Forum (ARF)', pp. 150–1.

36 This was decided by the Second ARF Ministerial Meeting held in Bandar Seri Begawan, Brunei, 1 August 1995.

37 See Wang Jianqun, *Forging Closer China–ASEAN Cooperation at the Regional Multilateral Arena*, China–ASEAN Occasional Paper Series No. 2, Centre of Asian Studies, University of Hong Kong, 2003.

38 China hosted the following ARF confidence-building projects: (1) co-hosting with the Philippines the ARF Intersessional Support Group meeting in Beijing, 6–8 March 1997; (2) the ARF Symposium on Tropical Hygiene and Prevention and Treatment of Tropical Infectious Diseases in Beijing, 25–27 November 1998; (3) the ARF Professional Training Program on China's Security Policy in Beijing, 10–19 October 1999; (4) the fourth ARF Meeting of Heads of Defense Colleges and Institutions in Beijing, 6–8 September 2000; (5) establishment of the ARF Regional Maritime Information Center in Tianjin, 2000; (6) the Seminar on Defense Conversion in Beijing, September 2001; and (7) the ARF Seminar on Military Logistics Outsourcing Support, in Beijing, 25–27 September 2002.

39 Wang Jianqun, *Forging Closer China–ASEAN Cooperation at the Regional Multilateral Arena*.

40 *Ibid.*

41 For example, see Rosemary Foot, 'China in the ASEAN Regional Forum: organizational processes and domestic mode of thought', *Asian Survey*, 38:5 (1998), p. 432.

42 Alastair Iain Johnston did a good study of China's participation in the ARF as an example of the effect of socialization in international institutions. See his chapter 'Socialization in International Institutions: the ASEAN way and international relations theory', in G. John Ikenberry and Michael Mastanduno (eds), *International Relations Theory and the Asia–Pacific*, New York: Columbia University Press, 2003, pp. 107–62.

43 Sueo Sudo, *The International Relations of Japan and South East Asia: forging a new regionalism*, London: Routledge, 2002, p. 55.

44 It used to be 9 + 3, but changed to 10 + 3 when Cambodia joined ASEAN in April 1999.

45 It started in 1995, when it was called simply Political Consultation, but adopted the present name at the fourth round of consultation meetings. At the time of writing, eight rounds of consultation meetings had been held.

46 The ASEAN–China Joint Cooperation Committee was formed in February 1997 in Beijing. It is aimed at promoting and coordinating bilateral cooperation in the fields of human resources development, personnel, and cultural exchanges between China and ASEAN. It is supported by the China–ASEAN Cooperation Fund, to which China contributed a total amount of US$5.7 million.

47 The China–ASEAN Joint Committee on Economic and Trade Cooperation and

the China–ASEAN Joint Committee on Science and Technology were both established in July 1994.

48 The ASEAN Committee in Beijing was established by the then ASEAN heads of missions in Beijing in 1996. It now consists of ten ASEAN ambassadors in Beijing and the chairperson rotates every half a year.

49 The Council was established in 2001.

50 These were the six new proposals made by China at the sixth China–ASEAN summit, in November 2002.

51 For the full text of the Joint Declaration of ASEAN and China on Cooperation in the Field of Non-Traditional Security Issues, signed at the ASEAN–China summit in Phnom Penh on 4 November 2002, see the ASEAN Secretariat website, at www.aseansec.org/13185.htm (last accessed April 2006).

52 Amitav Acharya, 'China's charm offensive in Southeast Asia', *International Herald Tribute*, 8 November 2003.

53 Achmad Sukarsono and Gde Anugrah Arka, 'SE Asian Leaders Sign Plan for Free Trade Bloc', Reuters, 7 October, 2003.

54 The East Asia Study Group's report provides some visionary views of community building in East Asia. Its recommendations are in two categories. First, it proposes seventeen short-term measures for the ASEAN + 3 process, such as forming an East Asia Business Council, establishing an East Asian Investment Information Network, and concrete measures for cooperation in human resources development, infrastructure, information technology, non-traditional security, and healthcare. Second, it suggests nine medium-term and long-term measures: the formation of an East Asian Free Trade Area; promotion of investment by small and medium-sized enterprises; the establishment of an East Asia Investment Area; the establishment of a regional financing facility; the pursuit of a more closely coordinated regional exchange rate mechanism; the pursuit of the evolution of the ASEAN + 3 summit into an East Asian summit; the promotion of closer regional marine environmental cooperation for the entire region; building a framework for energy policies and strategies, and action plans; and working closely with non-governmental organizations over policy consultation and coordination to encourage civic participation and state–civil society partnership in tackling social problems. For a full text of the report, see www.aseansec.org/viewpdf.asp?file=/pdf/easg.pdf (last accessed June 2006).

55 This was stated by the Malaysian prime minister in a speech entitled 'The Future of Asia', given on 9 June 2000, in Tokyo.

Chapter 6

Managing security challenges: the South China Sea

This chapter focuses on how China, Japan, and Southeast Asian countries have dealt with the South China Sea as a regional security challenge since the end of the Cold War. Apart from the Taiwan Straits, the South China Sea is arguably the outstanding if not the sole challenge that directly impacts on political–economic relations among all the East Asian states. This is true because the United States has by and large kept its hegemonic order in East Asia, an order that is set to last for several more decades, while alternatives to that order are either not desirable or unattainable.[1] With the United Sates providing the regional security order, China, Japan, and Southeast Asian countries have an opportunity to demonstrate to each other the kind of neighborhood they would like to foster for themselves through their interactions over utilization of the South China Sea for their own economic and diplomatic purposes. In standard IR terminology, space is left for China, Japan, and Southeast Asian countries to deal with the South China Sea as a 'low politics' issue on a daily basis.

The geographical and geostrategic positions the South China Sea occupies make it a constant security dilemma for virtually all powers in the Asia–Pacific region. Indeed, studies of security issues related to the South China Sea have generated a life of their own. Examination of the South China Sea as an issue in the international system suggests it can be treated as an indicator of the shifting balance of power between China and the United States, with US allies playing a supportive role. However, for the East Asian states, peace or war over the South China Sea is a much more direct challenge that transcends the conceptual divide between traditional and non-traditional security in IR research.[2]

First, the suggestions that the South China Sea may hold reserves of oil, gas, and mineral resources have been made since the late 1960s. Japan's reliance on offshore energy supplies, which dates back to the Second World

142

War, and China's dependence on imported oil and gas supplies since the early 1990s have kept alive speculations about intra-regional rivalry for control of the South China Sea as a potential site of energy production, and this rivalry would only add to their rivalry for influence in shaping the sub-regional order.

Second, related to the unsettled sovereignty disputes over the South China Sea, the Straits of Malacca (between Malaysia and Indonesia) in particular and the South China Sea in general are becoming all the more critical for maritime commercial shipping between Northeast Asian and Middle Eastern and European markets. Since the end of the Cold War, the increase in the incidence and in the technological sophistication of attacks on cargo ships and oil tankers has led to maritime piracy again becoming a serious concern. However, differences in legal rights and jurisdictional responsibilities for dealing with maritime piracy have prevented the emergence of a cooperative regime among the coastal East Asian states. These differences, meanwhile, leave room for China and Japan, the two big powers, to project their respective security interests toward Southeast Asian states in a more general sense.

In this chapter, we examine post-Cold War intra-regional diplomacy over three issue areas associated with the South China Sea as a security question for China, Japan, and Southeast Asian countries: the territorial sovereignty disputes, the South China Sea and East Asian energy supply, and Southeast Asian maritime piracy.

The territorial sovereignty disputes

Putting the Southeast China Sea in perspective

There is no agreed history of the actual sovereignty of the South China Sea. A country's legitimacy in making sovereignty claims is often based on descriptions of continuous occupation or utilization. But immediately the difficulty arises of evaluating evidence presented from one national perspective. Each nation involved will go as far back in history as possible to find evidence to support its claim. Ancient references written in indigenous East Asian languages are often imprecise and conflicting in naming the islets, rocks, and other features. Many of the rocks and islets are in fact regularly submerged by the tides. All the parties involved in the South China Sea territorial disputes (China, Vietnam, Malaysia, Indonesia, Brunei, and Taiwan) can produce a wealth of literature to support their claims. But the first matter to resolve is often the names of islets and other features. This leads to disagreement over whose evidence is more historically accurate and by implication more credible. It then becomes evident that reliance on a historical approach to discussing the South China Sea disputes is highly problematic.[3]

143

Related to the difficulty of impartiality in taking a historical approach is the political acceptability – to the claimant – of recommendations based on international law. UNCLOS was finally agreed in 1982 and entered into force in 1994. All the South China Sea claimants (except Taiwan, which is not a member of the UN) have ratified UNCLOS. UNCLOS allows the delimitation of a twelve-mile sovereign zone and a 200-mile EEZ (nautical miles). But dispute then arises over the baseline for such delimitation. Each claimant's use of a baseline has to be accepted by the other claimants for a legal solution to be workable. Stein Tonnesson has proposed an alternative utilization of the UNCLOS principles. In his view, the claimant states could jointly delimit a twelve-mile zone around each of the disputed islands and then agree to disagree about those zones. That would make it possible to divide the rest of the South China Sea in an equitable way, based on distance from the shores of the surrounding countries. To Tonnesson, such a division might also give the region an opportunity to develop a capacity for managing resources and protecting the marine environment.[4] Indeed, there is no shortage of proposals to preserve regional public goods. However, since international law grants a state the right to choose whether or not to use international legal instruments such as the International Court of Justice as the body of final arbitration, the prospect of reaching an impartial, optimal solution for all claimants still remains in each claimant state's hands. In other words, an international legal approach swings right back to international politics.

A third and perhaps most prolific approach to analyzing the South China Sea disputes is to situate them within the international and regional political–security dynamics. This approach views events and trends on the basis of changes in the international system and in the balance of power, global and regional. At the risk of oversimplification, it sees post-Cold War Southeast Asia as free from clear and imminent threats to the region's security: there is no war, there are no openly defined adversaries among the ten ASEAN states, and intra-regional boundary disputes appear manageable. Except for the South China Sea, that is. Furthermore, with the scaling down of the US military presence in Southeast Asia in the early 1990s, China has emerged as the likely candidate to be the dominant power in the region. But Japan, in spite of the pervasive perception of its decline, still matters. Furthermore, Japan is the only candidate within the region to counterbalance China's influence.[5]

Then the question arises of how to arrive at a definitive conclusion about China's intentions regarding the South China Sea. Studies like Eric Hyer's, which have used China's past behaviors in territorial settlements to predict benign Chinese behavior, were proved premature when the Mischief Reef incident (discussed below) erupted in 1995.[6] China's recent record in settling territorial disputes has not been consistent, either. Since the end of the Cold War, China has held fast to its sovereignty claims in the South

China Sea. In contrast, throughout the 1990s, China moved to resolve a number of territorial disputes with its neighbors, including Kazakhstan, Kyrgyzstan, Laos, Russia, Tajikistan, and Vietnam. More to the point is that:

> in most of these agreements, China received only 50 percent or less of the contested territory; for example, in resolving a long-standing dispute over the Pamir Mountains, which Tajikistan inherited from the Soviet Union, China accepted only 1,000 of the contested 28,000 square kilometers.[7]

Obviously, over territorial disputes, China has thus far treated its Southeast Asian neighbors differently, in opting for negotiated solutions with its neighbors over land disputes but refusing to compromise over maritime claims. As we maintained in the introductory chapter to this book, it is not our purpose to offer definitive explanations for the state of affairs in the post-Cold War evolution of relations between China, Japan, and Southeast Asia. Instead, we try to shed light on how interactions between these major players have prevented the South China Sea disputes from being turned into a military conflict.

Post-Cold War China and the South China Sea disputes

In February 1995, the Philippines announced that it had discovered Chinese built structures on Mischief Reef (Meijijiao in Chinese and Panganiban in Filipino). China's immediate reaction to the Philippine protest was that these were merely temporary shelters for Chinese fishermen who frequent the disputed waters as part of their traditional fishing grounds. The Philippines destroyed some of the Chinese markers of territorial ownership on Mischief Reef but left the structure intact. Then, the Philippines intensified its arrests of Chinese fishermen in the wider contested Spratly Island waters.

Internationally, knowledge of the Mischief Reef incident spread three messages about China's pursuit of its relations with other claimants in the South China Sea in particular and in the entire Southeast Asian region in general. First, China was conducting a 'creeping invasion' of a small and weak neighbor. Second, China's occupation of the Mischief Reef served to validate the prophecy of an economically growing and militarily strengthening China posing a threat to its Southeast Asian neighbors. Third, the Philippines had signaled its resolve to stand up to a belligerent big power in the same geographical neighborhood. The totality of these messages was that, over the South China Sea disputes, China had to be put in check.

China responded to the Philippines' campaigns for international sympathy by offering to negotiate a solution. Bilateral negotiations ended with the issuing of a joint statement in August 1995. The statement said that, pending resolution of the dispute, the two sides agreed to abide by a six-point code of conduct in the area. Those six points are in many ways identical to the ASEAN declaration on the South China Sea, issued in July 1992. In addition to emphasizing the need to resolve all sovereignty and jurisdictional issues pertaining to the South China Sea without resort to force, China and the Philippines 'agreed to keep an open-minded attitude on the constructive initiatives and proposals of regional states to pursue multilateral cooperation in the South China Sea at the appropriate time'.[8]

Although China stood by its long-held position of working bilaterally with Southeast Asian claimants, its joint statement with the Philippines seemed to indicate acceptance of a role for ASEAN to mediate in its bilateral dispute with the Philippines. This can be viewed as a departure from China's steadfast position on managing its disputes with Southeast Asian claimants within a strictly bilateral format. In addition, the joint statement echoes the Bangkok Declaration by promising to work toward promoting first bilateral and then multilateral cooperation in fields such as protection of the marine environment, safety of navigation, scientific marine research, disaster mitigation and control, search and rescue operations, meteorology, and maritime pollution control. These are issues that affect the interests of all countries in Southeast Asia.

In short, China and the Philippines managed to temporarily shelve the dispute by enlarging the areas they promised to join in working on. In addition, the statement made it possible for the Philippines to claim moral solidarity with fellow ASEAN members and for China to indicate its intent to take ASEAN's collective power seriously.

In November 1996, China's president visited the Philippines and repeated the other long-standing Chinese offer over the resolution of the entire South China Sea dispute: joint development. But the Philippines took advantage of renewed US interest in strengthening its bilateral military ties by proposing to have the Spratlys disputes included on the agenda of its defense meeting with the United States. The stalemate continued, with the Philippines continuing to keep the issue alive by raising international awareness about Chinese occupation of Mischief Reef and asserting its sovereignty by routinely arresting Chinese fishermen operating in the Scarborough Shoal area, a rich fishing ground easily reachable from China's Hainan Province.[9]

In late 1997, the Chinese foreign minister used the occasion of his participation in an event in Kuala Lumpur celebrating the thirtieth anniversary of the establishment of ASEAN to unveil, for the first time, China's 'new security concept'.[10] Among other things, the 'new security concept' rejects alliance, particularly alliance directed at the interests of a third party, as an instrument for achieving regional security. It pledges consultation and cooperation as the desirable approach to China's international relations. Obviously, China was cashing in on the goodwill it had fostered

146

with Southeast Asian countries over its handling of the Asian financial crisis that past summer. Indeed, as discussed in Chapter 3, the regional financial crisis of 1997 proved to be the turning point in China's inter-actions with Southeast Asia.

The Sino-Philippine dispute over Mischief Reef erupted anew in October 1998, when the Philippines announced its discovery that China had been fortifying and expanding the structures built in 1995. The two govern-ments again went into negotiations. China rejected the Philippine demand that it dismantle the structures. The Philippines responded by taking the issue onto the international stage, calling for ASEAN to support its position and asking the UN to allow the Philippines to seek Security Council arbitra-tion as the last resort. China, as expected, rejected UN involvement.

In 1998, however, over the Mischief Reef dispute *per se*, the Philippines stood alone. During that year's ASEAN summit in Hanoi, in spite of the Philippines' request for its inclusion, ASEAN avoided dealing in public with the dispute. In addition, the US Clinton administration continued to abide by the United States' Cold War practice of not taking a position over territorial disputes between its Asian treaty allies and their neighbors. In spite of the Philippine senate's final approval in 1999 of a visiting forces agreement, which allowed for the return of US military personnel to the Philippines, the Clinton administration stayed clear of the Mischief Reef dispute between China and the Philippines.

China and the Philippines have in fact managed not to let the Mischief Reef incident stand in the way of bilateral high-level diplomacy. As is customary in Chinese diplomacy, exchange of visits by heads of state is one way to foster a positive political atmosphere. That atmosphere, in turn, is necessary for amicably dealing with specific but difficult issues. From 1996 to 2005, the Philippines had four different presidents and each traveled to China at least once while in office. China reciprocated by sending its prime minister and president to the Philippines on four occasions. In 1999 the two countries established an annual consultation mechanism at the vice-ministerial level, for the purpose of confidence building. Defense ministers of the two countries also exchanged visits. In April 1998 the Philippines agreed to host a port call by a Chinese navy fleet.[11] Then, in May 2005, China and the Philippines held their first bilateral defense talks and agreed to hold such meetings annually and to exchange military personnel for training. China also agreed to open five military training slots for Philippine military personnel.[12] In other words, the two governments showed that, in spite of the difficulties over the Mischief Reef, they were still able to have a working relationship with each other.

The Philippines, meanwhile, continued to exercise its soft power of constraining China in the South China Sea. Its main approach was to push for the establishment of a regional code of conduct for China to agree with ASEAN as a group. The notion of such a code had first emerged in 1991, at the second Indonesia-led informal Workshop on Managing Potential Conflicts in the South China Sea. Beginning in 1992, the Philippines led the effort to achieve consensus among ASEAN states over the drafting of such a code. Within ASEAN, the Philippines, Malaysia, and Indonesia held different positions on the geographical coverage of the code, and the role of third parties (i.e., in addition to China) in enforcing the code, among other things. In addition, Vietnam, a key party to the dispute, did not become an ASEAN member until 1995.[13] Nonetheless, when China's president Jiang Zemin visited Manila in November 1996, the first Chinese head of state to do so since bilateral diplomatic ties were restored in 1975, Philippine president Fidel Ramos raised the issue of the code of conduct with him.[14]

China's response was initially lukewarm to the Philippine push for China to join negotiations over the draft regional code of conduct. It responded by insisting that a joint statement between Chinese and ASEAN heads of state in December 1997 in Kuala Lumpur would be sufficient. Throughout the Philippines-led ASEAN process of negotiating a joint code of conduct, China was adamantly opposed to inclusion of the code as a topic for discussion in the ARF, which has such non-claimants as the United States, Japan, and Australia.

Finally, in July 1999, China dropped its opposition and agreed to begin negotiating over the code of conduct in the ASEAN–China PMC meeting. The reason behind China's change of attitude may be threefold. First, ASEAN no longer insisted on involving external members as parties to the code. Second, in 1999, China had completed negotiations with Vietnam over the demarcation of their land borders, and the two countries had agreed to settle disputes over maritime borders in the Gulf of Tonkin a year later. This made Vietnam an active supporter of an ASEAN–China code of conduct in the South China Sea.[15] Third, Thailand, which is not a direct party to the South China Sea territorial dispute, began to play a mediating role between China and ASEAN claimants.[16] With the Indonesian economy devastated by the financial crisis of 1997 and Indonesian domestic politics in disarray, Thailand's activism filled a significant void in ASEAN efforts to tie China to a code of conduct. With Thai–Vietnamese disputes over the Gulf of Thailand settled, Thai leadership was more easily accepted among ASEAN states as well.

After two years of negotiation, from 2000 to 2001, which saw China offering its own draft of the code, China and ASEAN agreed a code of conduct. In November 2002 the foreign ministers of China and ASEAN states signed the China–ASEAN Declaration on the Conduct of Parties in the South China Sea. This Declaration represents significant progress in managing the maritime territorial disputes between China and Southeast Asian claimants, and by extension in China's overall relationships with all ASEAN states. It has become a standard object of reference by Chinese officials and diplomats in the multiple forums for consultation between China and ASEAN.

It ought to be noted, however, the 2002 Declaration does not seem to have deterred the claimants, China, Vietnam, and the Philippines in particular, from continuing with economic development projects in the disputed waters. It has since become routine for the three governments to accuse each other of violating the code but to defend their own actions as being within either the continental shelf or their EEZ.

In short, over the South China Sea territorial disputes, China has changed from reacting defensively to ASEAN to being viewed as a willing party to the 'ASEAN way' of diplomacy. How the future evolves remains to be seen.

Japan and the South China Sea territorial disputes

Japan is not a direct party to the South China Sea territorial disputes, but it has played both a historical and a contemporary role in their resolution. Japan's military expansion in the 1930s triggered a dispute with France over the Spratly and Paracel Islands. The South China Sea was a 'Japanese lake' from 1942 to 1945. After its defeat in the Second World War, along with the 1952 San Francisco Peace Treaty, Japan formally lost its claims to occupied territories, including Formosa (Taiwan), the Pescadores, and the Spratly Islands. Neither the San Francisco Peace Treaty nor the US return of Okinawa to Japan in the 1970s resolved Japan's territorial disputes with Russia, South Korea, and China/Taiwan.[17] Postwar Japan has since been preoccupied with dealing with those territorial disputes.

After the end of the Cold War, as a part of its attempt to raise its international profile, Japan has encouraged discussion of the South China Sea territorial disputes under the ARF, the Indonesian-led informal workshop, and other informal regional security forums. After the Mischief Reef incident, Japan, at the request of the Philippines, urged China to resolve the dispute peacefully at a bilateral vice-ministerial meeting in Beijing in March 1995. The Japanese press reported that high-ranking Japanese leaders, including the prime minister, had raised the Mischief Reef issue at a number of meetings with their Chinese counterparts.[18] However, Japan is not a party to the Indonesian informal workshop. China has traditionally opposed letting the ARF be turned into a forum to deal with the South China Sea issue. In other words, direct Japanese influence over the evolution of the South China Sea territorial disputes is rather limited. The South China Sea, at the level of sovereignty disputes, has remained a part of Japan's 'China problem' in its overall diplomacy.

Conclusion

It is possible to summarize the post-Cold War evolution of regional diplomacy over the South China Sea territorial disputes as follows. First and most obvious is that, contrary to theoretical predictions about a military clash being inevitable, China and other South China Sea claimants have managed to find a formula for peaceful coexistence. Second, China's turn to ASEAN to deal with difficult problems was probably the single most important factor in the overall peace in the region since the end of the Cold War. Finally, if the recent past can be relied on as an indicator, future peace perhaps relies on closer cooperation among all the East Asian states on fronts other than the territorial disputes *per se*. In other words, by letting the disputes stand for as long as possible while they cooperate on other less contentious issues, East Asian governments have a chance of preserving the fragile regional peace.

The South China Sea and East Asian energy supply

For much of the Cold War era and thereafter, how East Asian countries have satisfied their individual demands for energy has been a constant subject for discussion in relation to regional security. With continued speculation regarding the existence of exploitable oil and gas reserves in the South China Sea, the territorial disputes take on an additional dimension: energy supply security.

The logic behind the sustained interest is straightforward. At the market level, Japan, the Philippines, South Korea, Singapore, and Taiwan are established importers of oil and gas. They could each benefit from tapping into the South China Sea as an alternative source of supply in order to reduce their dependence on the Middle East. Individually or collectively, these East Asian nations have only a limited if any role to play in maintaining stability in the volatile Middle Eastern region. Domestic demands for oil and gas in Brunei, Indonesia, and Malaysia are rising and their reserves are diminishing. Together with Vietnam, these Southeast Asian countries are expected to become net importers of oil between 2010 and 2015. Then there is China, which became a net importer of oil in 1993 and has since been searching for suppliers worldwide, including in the Middle East and Southeast Asia.

At the level of regional security, China, the Philippines, Vietnam, Malaysia, Brunei, and Taiwan not only lay claim to all or part of the Spratly and Paracel archipelagos and their surrounding maritime space, but also have a military presence on one or more islands. A military clash between any pair of them over energy reserves would cause significant damage to the political and economic welfare of the entire region, given the web of economic interdependence that has emerged since the end of the Second World War.

The literature on the South China Sea in East Asian countries' search for secure energy supplies ranges from the alarmist to the cautionary and to the legalistic. But before we go further in examining the matter in relation to the complex process of the countries seeking to foster a stable neighborhood in the post-Cold War era, it is important to bear in mind the following:

> Whenever the term 'Spratly Islands' is mentioned in the news it is almost inevitably preceded by the words 'reputedly oil rich'. Estimates of the hydro-carbon resource potential of the Spratlys area vary wildly up to a staggering 30 billion tons of oil. The great range in estimates stems largely from insufficient data.
>
> While there is almost certainly oil and gas in the Spratly Islands area, whether there is enough, and of the required quality to justify exploitation is another matter.[19]

Energy in intra-regional politics: before the Cold War's end

In the colonial era, competition for control of oil fields in today's Indonesia and Myanmar was a direct cause of war between Japan and the Netherlands and France. From the end of the Second World War until the first inter-national oil crisis of 1973, the South China Sea proper and its coastal states did not feature prominently in oil supply security for East Asia. Japan did return to develop oil and gas in Southeast Asia but used economic aid and investment as the key instrument for entering into long-term oil supply arrangements with Indonesia, Brunei, and smaller Southeast Asian producers. The arrangement was mutually beneficial to both Southeast Asian states and Japan, although in Thailand and Indonesia there were public protests against Japanese exploitation of natural resources in the early 1970s. But the fact of the matter was that the Southeast Asian econ-omies had to rely on the Japanese market for investment capital and export in order to transform themselves from resource-based to manufactures-driven exporters. Meanwhile, such protests served as a reminder for Japan to strictly practice its promised separation of economics from politics in dealing with the Southeast Asian region collectively and bilaterally.

The first oil crisis brought China into the East Asian energy supply security landscape. China took advantage of the Japanese search for secure sources of supply outside the Middle East by offering to sell crude oil to Japan. The first shipment of Chinese crude oil reached Japan in 1973, one year after the two countries established diplomatic ties. Although the amount of Chinese oil sold to Japan was initially small, the fact that China and Japan agreed to include Chinese oil for Japanese industrial plants in their first trade agreement in 1978 provides testimony to the mutual benefits of the arrangement. In 1973, China also began selling oil to Vietnam, Thailand, and the Philippines. Thailand and the Philippines were targets of the Arab oil embargo because of their support for US military operations in the Middle East. Wild expectations of China replacing the Middle East to meet its Asian neighbors' demand for oil soon dissipated. But Beijing's timely helping hand, in spite of its political undertones, was useful to the region.[20]

For China, the first oil crisis served as a strategic opportunity to move its foreign economic policy orientation from *yibiandao* ('leaning to one side', that is, toward the Soviet and communist bloc) to *yitiaoxian* ('walking one line'). The 'line' refers to China's attempt to create a channel for East–West trade and geostrategic cooperation by economically linking up with Japan, US allies in Asia, and, later, Western European countries. Indeed, against the background of the Cold War, China's role in East Asian energy supply security was seen as China competing with the Soviet Union for influence.[21] In the United States, which had begun the process of a strategic rapprochement with China, there was some concern that China was boosting its influence in East Asia by meeting its neighboring states' hopes of receiving major oil shipments. But there was no alarm, in part because the Chinese oil industry was very little understood.[22]

In the early 1970s China had reached a surplus in oil supply. With a low industry base, there were few expectations of China going offshore to explore for oil in order to meet its domestic needs, or to trade oil for technology and equipment with other countries. It was generally understood that China was under no pressure to obtain oil from the continental shelf beyond its territorial jurisdiction. More importantly, China was still going through its Cultural Revolution, amid a chaotic and prolonged leadership struggle. China's foreign policy priority was to win as many supporters in its neighborhood as possible, particularly given the fact that China had recently gained the diplomatic success of unseating Taiwan from the UN (in 1972). In short, China's presence in the East Asian energy supply scene was treated as benign and even welcome.

For much of the 1970s, the Yellow Sea and East China Sea dominated international attention as a 'time bomb' ready to explode. Since the end of the Second World War, China, Japan, South Korea, and Taiwan have had a long and complex history of disputes over equitable utilization of fisheries and other natural resources in the seas geographically linking them. In the late 1950s, China entered into bilateral arrangements with Japan to avoid clashes in fisheries in the Yellow Sea. But between China and South Korea there was no joint fisheries management regime similar to the Sino-Japanese arrangement. Finally, enmity between China and Taiwan prevented any meaningful regional consultations over the East China Sea and Yellow Sea.

Additionally, in 1968, the Committee for Coordination of Joint Prospecting for Mineral Resources in Asian Offshore Areas under the UN Economic Commission for Asia and the Far East conducted the first geological survey of the Yellow Sea and East China Sea. The Committee's 1969 report suggested that large hydrocarbon deposits might exist in the waters off the Senkaku/Diaoyu Islands. This report had the unintended consequence of intensifying the maritime boundary disputes in Northeast Asia.[23] Complicating the regional scene was the fact that when China, by way of assuming its seat in the UN in 1972, began to be an active participant in the negotiations over the UN law of the sea, it adopted a strategy of mixing promotion of its own national interests with projecting itself as a supporter of Third World causes against the two superpowers.[24] These and other developments meant that the East China Sea and Yellow Sea appeared to be much more volatile than the South China Sea was.

China began to conduct its own search for offshore oil and gas in 1960. From 1979 onward, China opened itself to international collaboration, Japan included, for exploration in all the seas along its coast. In 1982, Chinese and Japanese oil operators found oil in the Bohai Bay region in the Yellow Sea. Although the size of the reserve was not significant, it was important because it showed that China and Japan did not have to focus on the disputed Senkaku/Diaoyu Islands area as a source of oil or gas supply.

Sino-Japanese tensions over maritime sovereignty were kept in check throughout much of the 1970s largely because Chinese sales of oil to Japan kept rising, in spite of the meager three percentage points of the Chinese share of Japan's total oil imports on the eve of the second oil crisis in 1979. Japan responded to this second crisis by pursuing a multifaceted energy policy, focusing on conservation and increasing its domestic refinery capacities for the purpose of weathering the sudden price rises for light crude oil in the world market. In addition, economic logic bound China and Japan in the area of coal, a dying industry in Japan. China needed Japanese capital for the development of its coalmines and for the transportation infrastructure to export coal to Japan.[25] Against this background, Japan chose not to pursue exploration for oil and gas in the East China Sea.

By way of establishing the China National Offshore Oil Corporation in 1982, China formalized its industry regime for offshore oil exploration and development, including through joint ventures with international oil companies. This strategy worked well, in part because it played into the international oil industry's thirst for new discoveries around the globe. By the mid-1980s, China had signed contracts with over a dozen foreign oil companies in virtually all the continental shelf areas accessible and deemed commercially worthwhile.

In the Southeast Asian context, for much of the Cold War period, China had energy-related disputes mainly with Vietnam. Before the fall of Saigon and the US withdrawal from Vietnam, both China and Vietnam had carried out military actions to emphasize their territorial claims in the South China Sea. But those clashes were not treated as a source of regional instability in the larger Cold War context. Immediately after the end of the war in Vietnam, Vietnam raised the issue of sovereignty over the Paracel and Spratly archipelagoes in the South China Sea with China. Vietnam demanded that China recognize its claims to the South China Sea when the secretary-general of the Communist Party of Vietnam visited China in September 1975. The visit ended without the usual joint communiqué.[26]

Following the fall of the Soviet Union, Vietnam adopted the same strategy as China had to solidify its claims to resources in its own zoning of the Vietnamese continental shelf by offering joint exploration and development contracts to international oil companies. By 1992, Vietnam had signed contracts with companies based in the UK, France, Norway, the Netherlands, Indonesia, Japan, and South Korea. There was also speculation that Vietnam was holding one block 'in reserve for U.S. companies to enter bidding, pending easing of U.S. trade sanctions against Vietnam'.[27]

In short, before the end of the Cold War, China and Japan had managed to avoid military conflict over potential energy deposits under the East China Sea through developing energy reserves on the Chinese continent for use by Japan. Military positioning did take place, however, between China and Vietnam over sovereignty claims in the South China Sea, but, by involving international oil companies, both China and Vietnam raised the stakes for venturing into energy-related military clashes over the sea.

The difference the year 1992 made

The year 1992 was arguably the single most eventful one for East Asian energy security. Iraq's invasion of Kuwait and the ensuing first Gulf War reminded Japan yet again of the vulnerability of its Middle Eastern oil supply in particular and of the international system in general. Other East Asian countries likewise felt the impact but it was the potential for Japan and China to compete in gaining increased amounts of oil and gas from the maritime states of Southeast Asia that was more worrisome. By 1992, China seemed to have recovered from a period of retrenchment back to autarkic socialism, as was symbolized by Deng Xiaoping's call for deeper engagement in the international economic system on his tour of southern China. A newly accelerated Chinese economy was bound to place more pressure on the international energy markets. A year later, China's own oil import statistics confirmed the country's status as a net oil importer.

The South China Sea formally became in embroiled in the question of East Asia's energy supply security in February 1992, when China passed a territorial waters law. For decades China had maintained the most sweeping claims to the entire South China Sea region but its passage of a territorial waters law increased international concern.[28] Enactment of the law would bring, for the first time, China into direct conflict with the Philippines, which had overlapping claims with China, Vietnam, and Malaysia in the Spratly region. International reaction to the Chinese law was in part rooted in sympathy for the Philippines: it had been a long US ally and was becoming more vulnerable due to the pending closure of US bases in that country. Indeed, the Chinese territorial waters law provided the impetus for a new separate stream of research into the political and strategic implications of the territorial disputes in the region: China and the 'oil-rich' Spratly disputes.[29] Andrew Tanzer's characterization of the Spratly area as 'Asia's next flash point' has since become a standard reference.[30]

Still in 1992, a major dispute between China and Vietnam emerged over drilling rights in the Paracel region. In May that year, the China National Offshore Oil Corporation signed a cooperation contract with Crestone Energy Coporation, headquartered in Denver in the United States, to jointly explore a block in Wan'an Bei. Although exploration was not expected to get under way until late 1994, Vietnam demanded that China rescind its contract with Crestone. The Crestone dispute attracted international attention for two reasons. First, China reportedly pledged that its navy would defend drilling operations against possible Vietnamese attacks. Second, a spokeswoman for the US State Department confirmed that a US embassy official had attended the Crestone contract signing ceremony in Beijing. But 'she stressed the official's presence should not be interpreted as support for Chinese territorial claims in the South China Sea and said the embassy had no role in the matter'.[31] The Sino-Vietnamese dispute therefore assumed wider implications. On the one hand, it showed that Vietnam and the United States were having continuing difficulty in normalizing bilateral diplomatic relations. On the other hand, the Clinton administration had difficulties of its own in dealing with China, and the school of thought favoring a containment strategy toward China was gaining ground. In other words, the Crestone incident served as a timely reminder of the volatile nature of oil and gas exploration in the South China Sea.

The Philippines also became a part of the unfolding drama, although in the Spratly archipelago area. With foreign assistance, the Philippines had developed a nascent oil and gas industry, although on balance that country has always been reliant on imported oil and gas to meet its energy demands. In June 1992, the Oklahoma-based *Oil and Gas Journal* published a detailed report by two scientists who worked for the Manila-based Trans-Asia Oil and Mineral Development Corporation. In spite of the tentative tone in the majority of the map-dotted text describing the geological formations in the West Batangas basin, the article, 'published with the permission of the Office of Energy Affairs, Philippines', concluded that 'in view of these positive attributes, the basin is considered to have promising potential for significant hydrocarbon accumulation and, therefore, merits exploratory drilling'.[32] This helped to whet the excitement about the 'oil-rich Spratly area'.

Oil exploration is a capital-intensive and high-risk business. It is customary for oil companies to publicize their tentative findings, partly as a strategy to attract investment capital to fund further exploration. Regarding the actual oil and gas potential of the South China Sea, a lack of data about the geology of the area and ambiguity in the geographical coverage of the surveys makes corroboration difficult. A further uncertainty is whether any find would meet the engineering, economic, environmental, and legal criteria that major oil companies apply as part of a pre-investment analysis. Over the years, China and the Philippines have made the most optimistic predictions about oil and gas reserves in the South China Sea. No independent third party has ever conducted a geological survey of the entire area. As an infrequently cited author cautions, much of the 'oil-rich Spratly' talk risks being more a fiction than science.[33]

Nonetheless, the research community that focuses on the international political and security implications of the search for oil and gas often has to live with inconclusive industry data. For the claimants and other interested parties as well, the risk of concluding that the South China Sea has no oil and gas is equally high. This explains the continued interest in the South China Sea in East Asian countries' search for energy supply security.

A tentative beginning for joint development

China first declared its basic policy orientation toward managing disputed territorial waters in 1978, when Deng Xiaoping proposed to Japan the notion of 'shelving disputes, conducting joint development' over the Senkaku/Diaoyu Islands and their adjacent waters. The same stance was repeatedly offered as way to pacify complaints from Southeast Asia about China over the South China Sea.

In early September 2004, China and the Philippines announced an agreement on a three-year project by their state oil companies, Philippine National Oil Company and the China National Offshore Oil Corporation, to gather data on petroleum resources in parts of the South China Sea. The project would include collecting, processing, and analyzing seismic data, including in the disputed Spratly area. Under the arrangement, China and the Philippines will share the estimated $7 million cost of collecting and analyzing the data. The project will not address the territorial claims.

Announcement of the joint project represents a significant yet tentative step toward actual joint development. Neither China nor the Philippines made the joint project a highlight of Philippine president Gloria Macapagal Arroyo's trip to Beijing:

> Manila emphasized that the agreement to pursue 'co-operative scientific research' did not mark any change in the sovereignty claims of the two sides in the area, while China's foreign ministry did not mention it in an official report of Mrs Macapagal's visit.[34]

There is no public information about which side, China or the Philippines, initiated discussions about the joint project. One possible reason for the low-key announcement was that for the joint project to lead to joint exploration and development would require a change to the 1987 Philippine constitution, which requires national control of all exploration and exploitation of natural resources in Filipino territory. And the joint study keeps intact separate and competing Chinese and Filipino positions on territorial sovereignty over the same waters.

Another possible reason is that although Arroyo did not make the outstanding Mischief Reef dispute between the two countries a topic for discussion on her 2004 trip to Beijing, press reports in Manila revealed that the Philippines had not yielded on its position over territorial sovereignty claims. As with Arroyo's 2001 trip to China, the Philippine side's choice of not raising the Mischief Reef issue was tactical. Philippine officials are quoted as saying that 'unless [China's] President Jiang brings it up, the President herself will seize the chances to reiterate the Philippines' original request for China to dismantle its facility in the Mischief Reef or turn over the same to the Philippine government'. At the very least, the Philippines would want China to agree to joint use of the structures on Mischief Reef.[35]

Meanwhile, the announcement of the Sino-Philippine joint project brought complaints from Vietnam, which claimed that both China and the Philippines had violated the code of conduct in the South China Sea signed between ASEAN and China in 2002.[36] As a matter of fact, Vietnam did not appear to be the only party concerned about the implications of a joint seismic study between China and the Philippines. At an ASEAN meeting in Manila in late September 2004, the Philippine foreign affairs under-secretary for policy, Sonia Brady, was quoted as saying that:

> I told them that we are not violating the 2002 declaration on the conduct of parties to the South China Sea when we signed that agreement. I explained to them that the agreement is just for a joint research to determine the presence of oil, gas, and other mineral deposits and not actual drilling.[37]

In any case, the Sino-Philippine joint project apparently did not lead to concrete action, as there is little information about its development.

Then, in March 2005, the state-owned Vietnam Oil and Gas Corporation joined its Chinese and Philippine counterparts in announcing the launch of a tripartite joint seismic survey of the Spratly Islands.[38] Likewise, there has been little information how the three-way cooperative scheme is progressing.

It must be noted, however, that joint development is seldom easy. As Choon-ho Park observes:

> Joint development of ocean resources is an attractive idea insofar as it appears to obviate the need for settling complex boundary disputes. In reality, of course, joint development merely postpones the difficult allocation problem to the time when actual resources are in hand, ready to be divided among the joint venturers.[39]

For the time being, it does appear, however, that China, the Philippines, and Vietnam have taken a significant diplomatic step toward turning the

South China Sea issue from one of diplomatic friction (and possible military conflict) to one of cooperation. However tentative the steps taken, it is too early to be so skeptical as to write off the scheme. Even if the announcement of the tripartite seismic study comes to little in the end, it sets an important precedent for conflict management in the future.

Maritime piracy in the South China Sea

Living with the Straits of Malacca

Throughout history, the sea lanes in Southeast Asia have been essential for keeping open the flow of trade between the Indian Ocean and the South China Sea, continuing on further west to Africa, the Middle East, and Europe, and further east to continental China, Japan, Korea, and the Americas. After the end of the Second World War, Northeast Asian countries began to rely more and more heavily on Middle Eastern oil to fuel their industrialization. The Southeast Asian sea lanes therefore assumed a strategic role for Northeast Asian countries. In addition, the Indonesian archipelago and Malaysia are significant sources of industrial supply for Northeast Asian countries. The sea lanes also offer Southeast Asian countries an opportunity to be part of the global flow of trade.

It follows that the Southeast Asian sea lanes, the Straits of Malacca in particular, face the challenge of being turned from a gateway into a choking point if the coastal states seek to enforce aspects of their national sovereignty or if there is military deployment by external states for geostrategic reasons. States geographically external to the region have long fought for control and influence over the use of the sea lanes. From the end of the Second World War through to the collapse of the Soviet Union, potential threats to the Straits of Malacca included:

1 failure to confront problems of safety of navigation through the straits;
2 coastal states' attempts to control freedom of passage for reasons of national security;
3 naval deployment by an extra-regional power, intended to interrupt passage through the straits;
4 violent piracy, particularly that directed at oil tankers;
5 contention among the neighboring countries regarding overlapping maritime claims.[40]

Few of these threats can be dealt with effectively by relying on resources indigenous to those nation-sates with sovereign rights over the Straits alone. As a matter of fact, it is the very lack of indigenous resources that has allowed the direct involvement of external states.

158

Over the course of the past half century, the Straits of Malacca have weathered such threats and played a key role in the ever increasing global and regional commerce. This is true in spite of continued traffic congestion, hazardous cargos, and pollution in the Straits. The Straits' coastal states have not attempted to put in place an embargo against external countries using the Straits and indeed cannot afford to do so, given their reliance on continuous external trade and inward investment. Although overlapping maritime claims among the coastal states remain, Indonesia and Malaysia actually have set a precedent for peacefully reaching a permanent settlement by mutually agreeing to use the International Court of Justice for final arbitration. In short, there are few reasons for either exaggerating the threats to the Straits of Malacca and other sea lanes in Southeast Asia or downplaying the potential for the coastal states to keep them under effective control.[41] What is truly required, then, is international collaboration with the coastal states to deal with the technical challenges to maintaining the safety of the Straits.

Along with the collapse of the Soviet Union went concern over super-power competition for a naval presence in the region, and the associated risks of the Straits of Malacca and other sea lanes closing. Since the end of the Cold War, the United States has kept its 'hub and spoke' design for maintaining the security order in the western Pacific. Formal military ties, though short of treaty alliance arrangements, between the United States and the Philippines, Thailand, and Singapore provide a policy guarantee that the United States will militarily protect the sea lanes when necessary. China is often cited as a potential challenger to the regional hegemony of the United States. However, the gap between China and the United States in naval power in Southeast Asia is wide and it would take decades for China to narrow that gap.

The above discussion leads us to focus on maritime piracy as the day-to-day security issue in the area for China, Japan, and Southeast Asian states. Indeed, the United States traditionally treats maritime piracy in Southeast Asia a 'low politics' issue. In spite of a renewed awareness of piracy as a security challenge after the end of the Cold War, well into the late 1990s several US agencies continued to monitor the situation and the Maritime Administration 'periodically issues advisories to all U.S. flag merchant ships regarding piratical incidents in certain areas of the world, including Southeast Asia'.[42] Even against the background of heightened media reporting of the increase in incidents of piracy toward the end of the 1990s, policy recommendations published by the conservative Heritage Foundation were restricted to encouraging international institutions as well as Southeast Asian states themselves to be more effective. The only proactive steps were taken by the United States Coast Guard, a non-military entity, when it trained foreign maritime authorities to fight piracy.[43]

In the wake of the 11 September 2001 terrorist attacks on the United States, and more particularly after an attack on a US military ship off Yemen in 2002, sea-borne terrorism against US military installations worldwide became an issue of heightened concern. US media reports began to associate maritime piracy in Southeast Asia with terrorism. But specialists were quick to point out the lack of wisdom in having the two phenomena conflated. Instead, it was recommended that the United States provide assistance in the building of indigenous capacity for the enforcement of law and order.[44]

The coastal states of the Straits of Malacca do not welcome a proactive military role by the United States to fight maritime piracy in the area, either. In March 2004 admiral Thomas Fargo of the United States Pacific Command suggested options included the use of high-speed vessels to conduct effective interdictions in Southeast Asian sea lanes. The reaction from Malaysia, Singapore, and Indonesia was negative. Instead, the three states prefer technical assistance rather than a direct role for the United States. There has been no initiative from the United States specifically targeting maritime piracy in Southeast Asia.[45]

General challenges in dealing with maritime piracy

In Asia, maritime piracy is a phenomenon as ancient as the history of the region's sea-borne trade. For much of the second half of the twentieth century, the issue of piracy was essentially sidelined by the ideological struggle between the two superpowers. With the end of superpower conflict and of the perceived constraint on regional security, piracy in Southeast Asia once again emerged as a prominent security problem.

The task of combating piracy in Southeast Asia, including in the narrow sea lane of the Straits of Malacca, is made politically sensitive by several factors. First, the very definition of a piratical act varies according to which international organization is compiling the data. The International Maritime Bureau (IMB) defines it more broadly than does the UN International Maritime Organization (IMO). The IMO definition gives priority to the location of an attack – the high seas – while the IMB focuses more on the intent to commit theft. Either of these definitions in turn has to be reconciled with domestic legislation by sovereign states before the offenders can be effectively dealt with by law. In short, a state's sovereign right is at stake.

Second, it is widely acknowledged that the statistical incidence reveals only a portion of actual attacks. Shipping companies, insurance companies, port authorities, and their governments have competing and even opposing vested interests in seeing an attack reported to the IMB's Piracy Reporting Center in Kuala Lumpur, Malaysia. Besides, the Center was created only in 1992, which severely limits making historical comparisons. The true scale of the problem, which generates much motivation for government action, remains unknown.

Third (and closely related to the second factor) is the task of committing the resources necessary for preventing piracy, as well as for locating the perpetrators and punishing them. As is also seen with such trans-border crimes as drug trafficking, there is no easy agreement over which party ought to be doing what in order to tackle a particular trans-border problem. Because national independence in Southeast Asia is a relatively recent development, it is easier for those states from which the perpetrators originate to ignore the problem, especially when the target of an attack is an entity outside the country or region.

Finally, the globalization of the international shipping industry poses a challenge for intra-regional cooperation based on the nation-state as the unit. Cost reduction by ship-owners leads to confusion between the flag flown by a passing vessel and its actual ownership. A ship on a transnational mission is often international in crew membership as well as in cargo ownership. Such a state of affairs makes dealing with the consequences of piracy a time-consuming and costly process, even when political resolve is not an issue.[46]

In short, piracy has become one of those issues that do require regional coordination and cooperation, but it could easily affect the goodwill of states within the region. Below we examine how China and Japan have interacted with Southeast Asian states over the challenge of maritime piracy.

Post-Cold War China and Southeast Asian piracy

In the early 1990s, China became associated with the rapid increase in piracy in Southeast Asian waters. In 1994, the Chinese government launched a year-long countrywide campaign against smuggling and other crimes that were beginning to affect the Chinese market's attraction to foreign investment capital. Toward the end of that year, Chinese law enforcement authorities claimed victory in prosecuting over 21,000 cases of cross-border smuggling.[47]

While the Chinese government's intention was to curb the illegal inflow of foreign-made products, ranging from cigarettes to second-hand automobiles, some of the activities of the Chinese maritime law enforcement agencies apparently went beyond international norms. The IMB began to identify an emerging triangle of piracy in the South China Sea: Hong Kong, Luzon in the Philippines, and China's Hainan Island. This triangle was described as having replaced the Straits of Malacca as the world's most notorious zone for piracy.

With corroboration of these findings by law enforcement authorities in Hong Kong, the UN IMO's safety committee chair traveled to Beijing in March 1994, specifically to ask the Chinese authorities to put an end to unlawful seizure of goods and to put in place full-scale inspection of ships, in Hong Kong waters and even the high seas, by Chinese naval and coast guard personnel. Such acts had received wide publicity in the international and regional media. Media reports accused China of conducting state-sponsored piracy. China justified some cargo seizures as a means to stop what it called 'illegal shipping' near the disputed islands in the South China Sea. China also denied that it was condoning piracy by Chinese entities, including its own military units, but acknowledged that rogue elements in the country's anti-smuggling drive might have acted out of personal greed. When in April 1994 the central government of China rescinded the right of local authorities to issue identification numbers to boats and established a centralized system of control for boat numbering, international complaints apparently had begun to bear positive results.[48]

It is not our purpose here to delve into the actual role China played in the spate of maritime incidents in the Southeast Asian and East Asian waters. Events in 1994 led to speculation that China was taking advantage of the less frequent Russian and US naval movements in the region to fill a post-Cold War vacuum. After all, China was one of the earliest signatory states to UNCLOS, which was set to take effect toward the end of 1994.

In May 1996, China ratified UNCLOS and issued its new baselines concerning the South China Sea territorial dispute. China's ratification of the law, coupled with the Chinese foreign minister's expression of China's willingness to have the issue discussed at the level of technical experts during the twenty-eighth ASEAN ministerial meeting in July that year, rekindled ASEAN's hope for a peaceful resolution of the South China Sea territorial disputes. A meeting of minds among China and ASEAN states over the interpretation of the law of the sea would help cooperation over combating maritime piracy as well.

The outbreak of the Asian financial crisis in 1997 changed the priority in regional diplomacy. Maritime piracy fell from prominence in China–ASEAN interactions, in spite of the IBM reports of yet another wave of incidents after 1998.

In 1998, China began to take more forceful unilateral action to deal with maritime piracy. Two main factors contributed to this new resolve. First, from the mid-1990s there were an increasing number of reports that international agencies had tracked to Chinese ports vessels missing on the high seas. The Chinese legal system was cast in a negative light when courts simply demanded that some of those vessels leave port. There were even occasions when Chinese courts decided to auction the confiscated vessels to Chinese bidders simply because it was too troublesome to iden-tify the vessels' legal owners. As a result, China decided to strengthen its legal regime against those pirated foreign vessels that ended up in China.[49] Second, more and more Chinese vessels were targeted by pirates who had formed an international syndicate involving Chinese, Indonesian, Thai, and other Southeast Asian offenders. In southern China, smuggling and piracy threatened to disrupt oil distribution. As a result, China began to give priority to law and order, leaving to one side its traditional sensitivity over a pirate's nationality. The best-known case was in 1999, when a Chinese court changed its previous practice of expelling foreign nationals convicted of piracy and sentenced to death a team of pirates, including an Indonesian national. That team had seized the Hong Kong-based *Chang Sheng* cargo ship and taken it to a port in southern China.[50]

In 2002, China and ASEAN signed the Joint Declaration on Cooperation in the Field of Non-Traditional Security Issues. Those issues included trafficking in illegal drugs, people smuggling (including trafficking in women and children), maritime piracy, terrorism, arms smuggling, money laundering, international economic crime, and cyber crime.

In short, since the mid-1990s, maritime piracy shifted from being an issue that threatened to isolate China further from its Southeast Asian neighbors to one that became a cause for regional cooperation. China and ASEAN countries have a long way to go to control piracy, but China has demonstrated to its ASEAN neighbors that it is making an effort and that it is indeed willing to joint with its ASEAN neighbors in dealing with regional challenges.

Post-Cold War Japan and Southeast Asian piracy

By virtue of its history and degree of dependence on international seaborne trade, Japan has always had a high stake in keeping the Southeast Asian sea lanes, the Straits of Malacca in particular, free from navigational hazards, including pirate attacks. One of the most memorable reminders to Japan of navigational safety in the Straits came in January 1975. The 24,000-ton Japanese oil tanker *Showa-maru* ran aground just outside of the port of Singapore, on its way back from the Persian Gulf, and leaked 3,600 kilolitres of crude oil, causing damage costing $17.8 million. It then becomes understandable that, since 1970, Japan has been the largest financial and technical contributor to hydrographic surveys around the Malacca and Singapore Straits and to the installation of navigational aids in the area.[51]

For much of the period since the Second World War, Japan constrained its policy role in combating maritime piracy in Southeast Asia to the provision of financial and technical assistance to coastal states in the region. However, the persistence of the problem lends credibility to the argument that Southeast Asian states have not acted adequately to address the issue. Furthermore, given Japan's own economic stake as well as its close association with major powers in the world, Japan is in the best position to garner a more forceful international response to maritime piracy in Southeast

Asia.[52] In other words, Japan was caught between respecting the coastal states' sovereignty and being accused of free-riding on Southeast Asian states for keeping the sea lanes free of piracy.

As a matter of fact, until the late 1990s, when maritime piracy in Southeast Asia was gaining attention in the media, the Japanese government's policy response remained low key. Illustrative in this regard is the following news report in the *Daily Yomiuri* in December 1998:

> The Japanese Shipowners Association encourages exchanges of information as part of its system of safeguards. But the Transport Ministry said that, even if a Japanese-registered ship is attacked or seized by pirates, the government can do nothing except to seek the strengthening of sea patrols through diplomatic channels.[53]

Part of the reason for the low-key response up until then might have been the low number of casualties involving Japanese nationals. The news report quoted above mentioned four piracy incidents in 1994 and one in 1997 involving Japanese ships and that 'there were no reports of Japanese casualties'. The Japanese Ministry of Transport lists three Japanese nationals as being directly affected in the 182 pirate attacks on 'ships related to Japan' from 1989 through to 2002.[54] This method of accounting, however, has to be put in perspective. The method refers to three categories of ships: those registered under Japanese law, those owned by Japanese companies, and those with Japanese crew.

Then, in November 1999, Japan drastically changed its policy orientation toward dealing with maritime piracy in Southeast Asia. Prime minister Keizo Obuchi proposed to the ASEAN + 3 summit in Manila the creation of a 'regional coast guard body', which would have the Japanese coast guard patrolling the sea lanes of Southeast Asia in ways that were to be specified if the proposal met with agreement from Japan's East Asian neighbors.

Japan packaged its proposal by indicating that it had made the turn-around in policy upon the suggestion of Indonesia. In 1999 Indonesia, still recovering from financial crisis, was often identified as ineffective in preventing piracy. Although this background to the Japanese proposal was not clearly collaborated by Indonesia, it served as a good indication of its delicate nature. After all, Southeast Asia was not truly ready for a Japanese security role in its waters, despite the theoretical wish to have Japan counterbalancing China.[55]

China joined the ASEAN + 3 meeting that discussed regional anti-piracy measures in Singapore in March 2000. The meeting was meant to be a preparatory step for the Regional Conference on Combating Piracy and Armed Robbery Against Ships, in Tokyo a month later. Japan had envisioned the adoption at the Singapore meeting of a declaration on the establishment of a regional anti-piracy body, but the Chinese delegation presented a point-by-point rebuttal of Japan's draft declaration.[56] By early 2001, the Japanese government admitted that its initiatives had run into difficulty in winning acceptance around the region.[57]

China's opposition to any proposal for that would legitimize a para-military role for Japan in Southeast Asia is yet another symptom of the difficulties in bilateral relations between Japan and China. Indeed, Chinese academics have been quick to associate Japan's regional anti-piracy initiatives with the ongoing political campaign in Japan to revise domestic legislation to allow the Japanese defense forces to assume more active roles domestically and in the region. The conclusion, as expected, is that Japan is simply using the maritime piracy problem in Southeast Asia as a pretext for returning militarily to the region.[58]

Japan, on the other hand, continued with its push to establish a regional anti-piracy mechanism. Prime minister Junichiro Koizumi's proposal to the 2001 ASEAN + 3 summit in Brunei called for the establishment of an information-sharing center in the region. The Koizumi proposal marked a significant withdrawal from the Obuchi proposal of 1999: Japan no longer proposed having its own coast guard patrolling Southeast Asian waters, unilaterally or in tandem with the coastal states. Instead, the newly proposed center would be linked online to coast guard authorities of the sixteen participating countries (the ASEAN + 3 states, and Bangladesh, India, and Sri Lanka). After two years of negotiations, the Regional Cooperation Agreement on Combating Piracy and Armed Robbery Against Ships in Asia was signed in Tokyo in November 2004.[59] The idea behind this information center is that it will allow the often cumbersome diplomatic channels to bypassed, to ensure a quick response time.

It should be noted that for Japan, maritime piracy in Southeast Asia is usually presented as one of a long list of threats, including illegal entry to Japan from the ocean, North Korean spy ships operating in Japanese waters, and the discarding of defunct vessels along the Japanese shoreline.[60] Such a conceptual approach often leads to an overtly military–strategic undertone in Japan's approach to dealing with piracy before it reaches Japanese shores. As John F. Bradford points out, various domestic political interests in Japan saw piracy in Southeast Asia as an opportunity to push forward a larger regional security agenda.[61] Instead of responding to maritime piracy in the region as a technical issue, China and Japan seem to have taken advantage of the persistence of piracy incidents and made the issue a source of competition for regional influence.

In short, maritime piracy ought to be an issue over which cooperation among China, Japan, and Southeast Asian states, the coastal states of Malaysia, Indonesia, and Singapore in particular, can yield significant results. But proposals to jointly deal with the matter by attempting to stop a piratical act wherever it takes place have been become embroiled with the wider intra-regional geopolitical dynamics. East Asian governments continue to grope for a region-wide mechanism for dealing with the challenge pirates present. The benefits of socializing with each other probably outweighs the difficulties of not being able to find any easy resolution to the problem.

Conclusion

After the end of the Cold War, the South China Sea initially appeared to be a likely source of intra-regional military conflict. China's 1995 occupation of the Mischief Reef and Philippine actions in response cast a shadow over the region's security landscape. But China and the Philippines managed to contain the dispute; other ASEAN states chose not to inflame the situation, and eventually succeeded in socializing China through the joint declaration on a code of conduct in the South China Sea. Among all the claimants, there has been no relenting on individual claims. Yet a parallel development has also taken place: cooperation on less contentious issues.

The capacity of the South China Sea to satisfy East Asian countries' energy supply has yet to be tested. The announced tripartite seismic survey by China, the Philippines, and Vietnam does open a window of opportunity for joint development, particularly if technologically recoverable and commercially exploitable reserves can be found in the areas beyond the three countries' respective claims to the continental shelf. In an ironic way, international law actual helps to sustain the political nature of the energy dimension of the South China Sea disputes. Perhaps deepening levels of interdependence among the claimants and other states in the region are the surest guarantee against military adventures.

Maritime piracy in the Southeast Asian sea lanes, the Straits of Malacca in particular, affects the welfare of the states in the region more directly than it does other parties around the world. However, the establishment of a genuinely effective regional regime for combating such criminal acts has proved difficult. Both China and Japan need the support of Southeast Asian states for their respective aspirations to build up their regional influence. This fact provides an assurance against any unilateral Chinese or Japanese attempts to force Southeast Asian states to accept their respective security agendas by citing maritime piracy as a cause (or an excuse).

Out of the case studies presented in this chapter, it is possible to conclude that non-traditional security issues are often treated in the same mode as traditional security issues. Diplomacy takes precedence over substantive cooperation. However, by relying on the lowest common denominator – diplomacy – as the solution, states in East Asia have a greater opportunity to keep the peace (no matter how fragile) in the region. What we have seen is a mixed pattern of cooperation and deterrence. It is difficult to envision a drastic change to the status quo in the foreseeable future.

Notes

1 John Ikenberry, 'American Hegemony and East Asian Order', *Australian Journal of International Affairs*, 58:3 (2003), pp. 353–67.
2 For a discussion of the conceptual problems in research literature on the South China Sea, see Zha Daojiong, 'Security in the South China Sea', *Alternatives: Global, Local, Political*, 26:1 (2001), pp. 33–52.
3 Stein Tonnesson, 'Why Are the Disputes in the South China Sea so Intractable? A Historical Approach', *Asian Journal of Social Science*, 30:3 (2002), pp. 570–601.
4 Stein Tonnesson, 'China and the South China Sea: a peace proposal', *Security Dialogue*, 31:3 (2000), pp. 307–26.
5 Mark Beeson, 'Japan and Southeast Asia: the lineaments of quasi-hegemony', in Gary Rodan, Kevin Hewson and Richard Robinson (eds), *The Political Economy of Southeast Asia: conflicts, crises, and change*, London: Oxford University Press, 2001, p. 283.
6 Eric Hyer, 'The South China Sea Disputes: implications of China's earlier territorial settlements', *Pacific Affairs*, 68:1 (1995), pp. 34–54.
7 Evan S. Medeiros and M. Taylor Fravel, 'China's New Diplomacy', *Foreign Affairs*, 82:6 (2003), p. 25.
8 Zha Daojiong and Mark Valencia, 'Mischief Reef: geopolitical context and implications', *Journal of Contemporary Asia*, 31:1 (2001), pp. 86–103. The full text of the Sino-Philippine joint statement is reproduced on page 100 of that article.
9 For a study of Hainan Province's management of its maritime fishing industry, the cause of Sino-Philippine disputes over fishing rights, see Zha Daojiong, 'Localizing the South China Sea Problem: the case of China's Hainan', *Pacific Review*, 14:4 (2001), pp. 575–98.
10 'Qian Qichen Unveils New Security Concept at Event Celebrating 30th Anniversary of ASEAN', *Renmin Ribao*, 16 December 1997, p. 6.
11 For an in-depth discussion of this and other acts of Chinese military diplomacy, see Kenneth W. Allen, 'China's Foreign Military Relations with Asia–Pacific', *Journal of Contemporary China*, 10:29 (2001), pp. 645–62.
12 AFP and Carina I. Roncesvalles, 'RP and China to Hold Annual Defense Talks, Swap of Cadets', *Business World* (Manila), 24 May 2005.
13 Christopher Chung, *The Spratly Islands Disputes: decision units and domestic politics*, PhD Thesis, University of New South Wales, Australia, 2004, pp. 313–31.
14 Leotes Marie T. Lugo, 'Ramos Meets with China's Jiang', *Business World* (Manila), 27 November 1996.
15 Nguyen Hong Thao, 'Vietnam and the Code of Conduct for the South China Sea', *Ocean Development and International Law*, 32:2 (2001), pp. 105–30.
16 Kriangsak Kittichaisaree, 'A Code of Conduct for Human and Regional Security Around the South China Sea', *Ocean Development and International Law*, 32:2 (2001), pp. 131–47.
17 Hara Kimie, '50 Years from San Francisco: re-examining the peace treaty and Japan's territorial problems', *Pacific Affairs*, 74:3 (2001), pp. 361–83.
18 Lam Peng Er, 'Japan and the Spratlys Dispute: aspirations and limitations', *Asian Survey*, 36:10 (1996), pp. 1005–6.

19 'A Code of Conduct for the South China Sea?', *Jane's Intelligence Review*, 20 October 2000. Available online at www.janes.com/security/international_security/news/jir/jir001027_1_n.shtml (last accessed April 2006).

20 For a good account of these developments, see A. Doak Barnett, *China's Economy in Global Perspective*, Washington, DC: Brookings Institution, 1981, pp. 460–9.

21 Arthur Jay Klinghoffer, 'Sino-Soviet Relations and the Politics of Oil', *Asian Survey*, 16:6 (1976), pp. 540–52.

22 Choon-ho Park and Jerome Alan Cohen, 'The Politics of China's Oil Weapon', *Foreign Policy*, 20 (fall 1975), p. 49.

23 Choon-ho Park, *East Asia and the Law of the Sea*, Seoul: Seoul National University Press, 1983.

24 Menno T. Kamminga, 'Building "Railroads on the Sea": China's attitude towards maritime law', *China Quarterly*, 59 (1974), pp. 544–58.

25 Eguchi, Yujiro, 'Japanese Energy Policy', *International Affairs*, 56:2 (1980), pp. 263–79.

26 Ramses Amer, 'Sino-Vietnamese Normalization in the Light of the Crisis of the Late 1970s', *Pacific Affairs*, 67:3 (1994), p. 358.

27 'Vietnam Steps Up Offshore E&D Push', *Oil and Gas Journal*, 90:25 (1992), p. 38.

28 For an in-depth analysis of the 1992 Chinese law, see Liyu Wang and Peter H. Pearse, 'The New Legal Regime for China's Territorial Sea', *Ocean Development and International Law*, 25 (1994), pp. 431–42.

29 For one of the earliest research articles on the subject, see John W. Garver, 'China's Push Through the South China Sea: the interaction of bureaucratic and national interests', *China Quarterly*, 132 (1992), pp. 999–1028.

30 Andrew Tanzer, 'Asia's Next Flash Point?', *Forbes*, 150:10 (1992), pp. 96–8.

31 'Territorial Disputes Simmer in Areas of South China Sea', *Oil and Gas Journal*, 90:28 (1992), p. 20.

32 Benjamin S. Austria and Raymundo A. Reyes Jr, 'Possibilities of W. Bantagas Basin in Philippines South China Sea', *Oil and Gas Journal*, 90:23 (1992), p. 80.

33 Clive Schofield, 'The "Oil Rich Spratlys": myth or reality?', paper presented to the Human and Regional Security Around the South China Sea Conference, University of Oslo, Oslo, Norway, 2–4 June 2000.

34 Mure Dickie and Roel Landingin, 'Oil Pact Marks New Approach to Disputes by China', *Financial Times* (Japanese edition), 3 September 2004, p. 6.

35 Norman P. Aquino, 'GMA Kicks Off China Visit', *Business World* (Manila), 30 October 2001, p. 1.

36 'Vietnam Objects to Spratlys Deal', *Energy Compass*, 16 September 2004, p. 1.

37 'RP–China Spratlys Study', *Business World* (Manila), 21 September 1994, p. 1.

38 'Three State Firms Plan Joint Oil Survey of Disputed Spratlys', *Wall Street Journal*, 15 March 2005, p. 1.

39 Choon-ho Park, *East Asia and the Law of the Sea*, p. 14.

40 Michael Leifer, 'The Security of Sea-Lanes in Southeast Asia', *Survival*, 25:1 (1983), p. 16.

41 Hamzah Ahmad, *The Straits of Malacca: a profile*, Kuala Lumpur: Pelanduk Publications and Maritime Institute of Malaysia, 1997.

42 Peter Chalk, 'Contemporary Maritime Piracy in Southeast Asia', *Studies in Conflict and Terrorism*, 21:1 (1998), p. 102.

43 Dana R. Dillon, 'Piracy in Asia: a growing barrier to maritime trade', *Heritage Foundation Backgrounder*, 1379 (22 June 2000), pp. 1–5.

44 Adam J. Young and Mark J. Valencia, 'Conflation of Piracy and Terrorism in Southeast Asia: rectitude and utility', *Contemporary Southeast Asia*, 25:2 (2003), pp. 269–83.

45 Barry Wain, 'Strait Talk', *Far Eastern Economic Review*, 167:16 (2004), p. 17.

46 For an update on these and other issues, see Derek Johnson and Mark Valencia (eds), *Piracy in Southeast Asia: status, issues and responses*, Singapore: Institute of Southeast Asian Studies, 2005.

47 'Over 21,000 Smuggling Cases Prosecuted This Year', *Renmin Ribao*, 28 December 1994, p. 2.

48 Information in this and the previous paragraphs is based on the following news reports: 'Mainland Piracy Documented', Central News Agency (Taiwan), 7 April 1994; 'Pirate Attacks Rising Sharply, Warns UN Body', *South China Morning Post*, 26 July 1995; 'China Denies Piracy Reports', 17 March 1994, UPI.

49 Zou Keyuan, 'Piracy at Sea and China's Response', *Lloyd's Maritime and Commercial Law Quarterly*, autumn 2000, pp. 364–82.

50 P. T. Bangsberg, 'China Sentences 13 to Death in Hijacking Case', *Journal of Commerce*, 23 December 1999, p. 14.

51 Akaha Tsuneo, 'Japan's Response to Threats of Shipping Disruptions in Southeast Asia and the Middle East', *Pacific Affairs*, 59:2 (1986), pp. 266–7.

52 Ger Teitler, 'Piracy in Southeast Asia: a historical comparison'. Paper available online at www.marecentre.nl/mast/documents/GerTeitler.pdf (last accessed April 2006).

53 Ishida Kakuya, 'Piracy Seen Increasing in Strait of Malacca', *Daily Yomiuri*, 29 December 1998, p. 2.

54 See table listed on the Japanese Shipowners' Association's official website, at www.jsanet.or.jp/data/index.html (last accessed April 2006).

55 Nayan Chanda, 'Foot in the Water', *Far Eastern Economic Review*, 163:10 (2000), pp. 28–9.

56 An Xiaohui, 'Xinjiapo "Haidao Duice Huiyi" Jishi' [Report on the 'Measures Against Piracy at Sea Conference' in Singapore], *Renmin Gong'an* [People's Public Security], December 2000, pp. 11–12.

57 Ministry of Foreign Affairs, Japan, 'Present State of the Piracy Problem and Japan's Efforts', December 2001. Available online at www.mofa.go.jp/policy/piracy/problem0112.html (last accessed April 2006).

58 Xu Ke, 'Dongnanya de Haidao Wenti yu Yatai Diqu Anquan' [The Southeast Asian Piracy Problem and Security in the Asia Pacific], *Dangdai Yatai* [Cotemporary Asia Pacific], March 2002, pp. 46–51.

59 The full text of this agreement can be seen on the website of the Japanese Ministry of Foreign Affairs, at www.mofa.go.jp/mofaj/gaiko/kaiyo/pdfs/kyotei_s.pdf (last accessed April 2006).

60 Yamada Yoshihiko, *Umi no Terrorism* [Terrorism from the Seas], Tokyo: PHP Research Institute, 2003.

61 John F. Bradford, 'Japanese Anti-Piracy Initiatives in Southeast Asia: policy formulation and the coastal states' responses', *Contemporary Southeast Asia*, 26:3 (2004), pp. 480–504.

Chapter 7

Economic diplomacy and the ASEAN + 3 process

This chapter examines the economic diplomacy engaged in by China, Japan, and Southeast Asian states in relation to the formation of a regional economic community to deal with bilateral problems and to meet economic development challenges that have faced the entire region in the wake of the financial crisis of 1997. In the previous chapters, diplomacy has largely been considered in the context of political and security relations. In this chapter, it is considered within the regional economic context. We focus on how East Asian states, Southeast and Northeast, have managed to forge common interests and to develop strategies for building a neighborly community through economic cooperation, following a period of economic difficulties from 1997.

The process of East Asian economic integration and regional institution building is full of twists and turns. The changing regional balance of power – the rise of China and the relative decline of Japan – has led to different visions of future regional community building. Relations between China and Japan, the two strongest candidates for regional leadership, are strained. At the regional level it is economic diplomacy and ASEAN's initiatives that have played a pivotal role in regional community building. Economic diplomacy has prevented Sino-Japanese political tensions from hindering their economic relations and their participation in the regional multilateral platforms. It is of interest to examine how the trio have interacted with one another on the regional multilateral platforms, principally the ASEAN + 3 process, and how that process has begun on to move the states on a course toward an Asian community through trade liberalization schemes and other mechanisms of regional integration.

170

The idea of the East Asian Economic Caucus (EAEC) and the Asian financial crisis

Two US scholars recently raised a seemly simple but profound question: 'Why is there no NATO in Asia?'[1] If we answer the question from the logic of hegemonic stability theory, the answer is simple: the US hegemonic power built NATO in Europe, but it did not build institutions in Asia. Yet, as the two scholars who raised the question suggested, the hegemonic stability theorists missed the point and the difficulties in East Asian institution building have more to do with the weakness of regional collective identity and sources of regionalism in East Asia.

The concept of East Asia as a region is a relatively new one. There was no coherent conceptual framework for the 'region' of East Asia until the Malaysian prime minister Mahathir bin Mohamad first put forward the abortive idea of an 'East Asian Economic Group' (EAEG) in 1990. As originally conceived, the EAEG would comprise the six ASEAN members plus Japan, South Korea, China, Hong Kong, Chinese Taipei, and Vietnam. In his view, the more developed countries in East Asia (i.e., Southeast Asia and Northeast Asia) should do more in consultation and cooperation to help lesser-developed economies in the region to overcome difficulties, and to help transitional economies such as Cambodia, Laos, and Vietnam with reform and reconstruction. The idea was discussed in several ASEAN ministerial meetings, PMCs, and a special meeting of senior economic officials in Bandung, 15–16 March 1991. At the opening of the twenty-third meeting of ASEAN economic ministers, Mahathir stressed the need to work together with other East Asian countries through the formation of the EAEG, because he believed ASEAN countries alone were not strong enough to make a difference in world trade. He argued the EAEG would be GATT-consistent and would not be a trade bloc against third parties. The EAEG would strengthen rather than being detrimental to ASEAN's cohesiveness. At the fourth ASEAN summit, in Singapore in January 1992, ASEAN leaders endorsed the proposal by using the East Asian Economic Caucus (EAEC), instead of the EAEG, as part of ASEAN's efforts to establish and strengthen cooperation with other countries and regional economic organizations, as well as APEC. Later, under the direction of the ASEAN secretary-general, the EAEC was to become a 'caucus within APEC', rather than an ASEAN body.[2]

The idea of the 'caucus within APEC' was to some extent the seed for an East Asian economic community. The EAEC would function independently, not as a mechanism of APEC. Rather, it would discuss not only APEC issues but also issues of its own concern, according to its own agenda and work program. The EAEC idea pointed at a future integrated East Asian community, one that would join Southeast Asian countries and their Northeast Asian counterparts while excluding membership from the outside region.

Politically, however, an East Asian-only economic grouping was, though not impossible, not realistic at a time when APEC was attracting all the attention in the region. To most international politics observers, the EAEC was merely an illusion. As a matter of fact, it was strongly opposed by Washington, and was treated with indifference even by the major East Asian countries. However, over fifteen years after the idea of the EAEC was first mooted, it is now increasingly becoming a reality – though again back within the ASEAN + 3 process. The impetus for the rise of East Asian regionalism or the turning point that changed most East Asian countries' attitude toward regionalism was the Asian financial crisis of 1997.

Why did the Asian financial crisis provide such a powerful impetus for the EAEC? To answer this question, we have to come back to how fragile most East Asian economies and their financial systems were before 1997. Ronnie C. Chan, a Hong Kong business tycoon and president of the Hang Lung Development Corporation, argued that most East Asian economies must face two tests: first, how healthy are their economic and financial structures; and second, how well do their governments and private sector manage their financial affairs? Some East Asian economies like Hong Kong and Singapore pass both tests, while others like Japan, Taiwan, and mainland China fail the structural test but nevertheless manage their affairs acceptably. China is also helped by the fact that its financial market is not open to the outside world. South Korea, Indonesia, Thailand, Malaysia, and the Philippines fail both tests, as proven by the economic turmoil during the Asian financial crisis.[3]

During those economically difficult times, East Asian states, especially ASEAN states, learned a hard lesson. The financial crisis devastated the regional economy as well as the world market. But policy-makers in Washington seemed more concerned with the financial situation in Mexico, their poor southern neighbor, than with Southeast Asian economies. The lukewarm support of Washington, and the faulty and harsh rescue packages offered by the IMF all made East Asian leaders realize how vulnerable their economies were in the face of a regional financial crisis, and how unreliable was the help offered by the United States and the international financial institutions. The East Asian leaders began to appreciate the significance of regional cooperation for coping with future regional economic problems. This was because they considered the US and IMF much less helpful than expected and the conditions of the IMF rescue packages unpalatable.

The inaction of APEC at this critical juncture was also a big disappointment to East Asian states. APEC encompasses the biggest and some of the most dynamic economies in the world, and has established the ambitious goal of trade liberalization of all its developed members by 2010 and of its developing members by 2020. This trade liberalization is seen as a major driver for the flow of investment, goods, service, and technology in the Asia–Pacific region. However, the APEC process does not purport to forge a common political identity; nor is it intended to establish a sense of common security. In contrast to the institutionally based integration process in Europe, APEC has consciously avoided heavy institutionalization and has accepted diversity among its participants. Similarly, in contrast to the hegemon-led and legally tuned market integration in North America, East Asian states are happy that APEC has kept the United States' hegemonic tendencies in check within the organization. They are comfortable with a slow, deliberate process of consensus-based decision making, and implementation is based on what is known as 'concerted unilateralism', without formal legal enforcement. This pragmatism makes it difficult for APEC to identify common interests beyond trade liberalization, and it was why APEC failed to take a common stand on the 1997 financial crisis in East Asia. Instead, APEC confined itself to an expression of concern for the East Asian countries affected by the financial crisis. This made East Asian members feel APEC was largely irrelevant in the face of a future regional economic crisis.

The economies of Southeast Asian states and ASEAN as a whole were hit hard and much weakened by the financial crisis. The difficulties in the ASEAN states prompted their leaders to turn to Northeast Asia. At the same time, Northeast Asian countries were seeking ways to exploit the evolution of the ASEAN free trade area. As more than half of East Asian countries' foreign trade was intra-regional and roughly two-thirds of their foreign investment also came from within the region, it made sense to seek more intra-regional, rather inter-regional, economic cooperation and integration. From the ASEAN perspective, approaching Northeast Asia through the ASEAN + 3 process would be an important means to strengthen ASEAN's status and relevance, and to locate sources of economic support and cooperation from within Asia.

If Mahathir's EAEG idea should get credit for East Asian regionalism, he should get even more credit for hosting and facilitating the first ASEAN + 3 summit, which was more far-reaching in historical terms. By 1996, Japan, South Korea, and China had all become formal dialogue partners of ASEAN. As ASEAN was preparing its annual summit with the Japanese prime minister Ryutaro Hashimoto in 1997, a new idea of inviting the Chinese and South Korean leaders to join the ASEAN–Japanese summit was initiated and endorsed. On 16 December 1997, Mahathir played host to the historic inaugural ASEAN + 3 summit, which was convened back to back with the second ASEAN informal summit and the three successive ASEAN + 1 summits with the Chinese, Japanese, and South Korean leaders in Kula Lumpur. In the aftermath of the Asian financial crisis, East Asian leaders and elites began to realize that creating a new Asian political bloc that excluded the 'white' nations in East Asia, based on Mahathir's idea of the EAEG, would be a sensible move. The first ASEAN + 3 summit was an important breakthrough in regional community building, and, in the eyes of ASEAN leaders, what was more important was that the earlier opposition from Washington had finally been overcome.

The new momentum to East Asian regional cooperation

The Asian financial crisis was the catalyst for the formation of the ASEAN + 3 process. As Toyoo Gyohten, president of the Institute for International Monetary Affairs, observed:

> the [Asian] crisis raised an issue of great importance that needs to be tackled by East Asia as a whole ... that is whether it is necessary for East Asia, like America and Europe to strengthen its regional cooperative ties.... East Asia has no mechanism for coping with its own problem.[4]

For ASEAN states, the crisis underscored the benefits of establishing formal economic links with the more developed economies in Northeast Asia as a means of averting any possible future crisis. Despite the fact that there was APEC, the inability of that organization to provide a coherent response to the affected economies created disillusion with this big regional grouping. As a result, it created a new momentum for an East Asian-only regional solution, to hedge against future economic shocks. As the existing mechanisms had proved inadequate in responding to the economic, political, and security challenges, the emergence of ASEAN + 3 – a multilateral institution, albeit at the regional level – highlighted a new direction for East Asian regionalism.

Actually, during the financial crisis, ASEAN had convened several meetings of heads of state, economic and finance ministers, and representatives from the private sectors to work out an ASEAN response. The meetings came up with several measures to address the impact of the financial crisis, as well as recommendations for the direction of future regional cooperation. These measures included:

- a joint call for international support to address problems in international currency trading and international finance;
- a joint appeal to the large economies – the United States, Japan, and the EU – to help resolve the crisis;
- the promotion of trade within Southeast Asia and East Asia using local currencies;
- the establishment of a more effective regional surveillance mechanism of the economic policies and practices of ASEAN members, which was to be facilitated by fuller disclosure of relevant economic data.

Two years after the first informal summit in 1997, the ASEAN + 3 leaders met in Manila in November 1999 and issued a joint statement that outlined the areas of cooperation in the economic, social, political, and security fields. Since then, the ASEAN + 3 process has emerged as a comprehensive framework with a wide range of agendas. It conducts regular meetings not only at the summit level but also at various ministerial levels. ASEAN + 3 has developed through the existing ASEAN institutions and follows the ASEAN modalities of consultation, consensus building, and a rotating ASEAN-led chair. Modeled on ASEAN's organizational culture, the ASEAN + 3 process operates as a loose, informal institution without any treaty or formally binding agreement between the participating states. Instead, it creates a web of relations between the members, and this web has grown quickly since the first meeting of the heads of government.

The ASEAN + 3 process has a much broader framework and agenda than Mahathir's EAEG notion. It involves not only cooperation in trade, investment, and finance, but also consultation on political and security issues. In the last few years non-traditional security issues, ranging from drug trafficking, environment, illegal immigration to SARS and avian flu have also been on the agenda. The areas of consultation and cooperation are still expanding because the process allows its members to raise any issues of common concern at a level and in a mode that is acceptable to every member.

One of the important achievements of the states under the ASEAN + 3 framework was the Chiang Mai initiative in May 2000. The ASEAN + 3 finance ministers agreed in Chiang Mai, Thailand, to set up a regional currency swap arrangement should another financial crisis arise, or simply to guard against international speculation on regional currencies. The Chiang Mai initiative has two main components:

1 an expanded ASEAN swap arrangement;
2 a network of bilateral swap arrangements among ASEAN countries, China, Japan, and South Korea.

The swap arrangement had originally been established among the ASEAN-5 (Indonesia, Malaysia, Philippines, Singapore, and Thailand) in 1997, when it had a total facility of US$100 million. This was increased to US$200 million a year later, and to US$1 billion under the Chiang Mai initiative (and with the inclusion of all ASEAN members). The bilateral swap arrangements, on the other hand, require the Northeast Asian parties to enter into a swap transaction to provide liquidity support (to overcome balance of payment difficulties) for a currency up to a specified amount. As of December 2003, the size of the bilateral arrangements had reached US$35 billion (see Table 7.1). More importantly, the measures outlined under the initiative constitute an important step toward multilateral financial cooperation in the region, and it has the potential to be upgraded to a regional mechanism such as the AMF, which could then be used in the event of a financial crisis.

Building a neighborly community

Table 7.1 Progress in the Chiang Mai initiative (by December 2003)

Bilateral swap arrangement	Currencies	Date of agreement	Amount committed (US$ billion)
Japan–Korea	US dollar/won	4 July 2001	7*
Japan–Thailand	US dollar/baht	30 July 2001	3
Japan–Philippines	US dollar/peso	7 August 2001	3
Japan–Malaysia	US dollar/ringgit	5 October 2001	3.5*
Japan–China	Yen/renminbi	28 March 2002	3
Japan–Singapore	US dollar/Singapore dollar	10 November 2003	1
Japan–Indonesia	US dollar/rupiah	17 February 2003	3
China–Thailand	US dollar/baht	6 December 2001	2
China–Korea	Won/renminbi	24 June 2002	2
China–Malaysia	US dollar /ringgit	9 October 2002	1.5
China–Philippines	RMB/peso	29 August 2003	1
China–Indonesia	US dollar/rupiah	30 December 2003	1
Korea–Thailand	US dollar/baht	25 June 2002	1
Korea–Malaysia	US dollar/ringgit	26 July 2002	1
Korea–Philippines	US dollar/peso	9 August 2002	1
Korea–Indonesia	US dollar/won; or US dollar/rupiah	24 December 2003	1

*The US dollar amount includes the amounts committed under the US$30 billion New Miyazawa initiative of 1998. Within the package, US$5 billion was committed for Korea and US$2.5 billion for Malaysia.

In addition to the Chiang Mai initiative, there has been a series of other initiatives in regional economic cooperation under way since 1997, including the Manila Framework Group established in 1997, the Boao Forum in 2001, and the Asian Bond Market in 2003. All these have reinforced the surge of economic regionalism in East Asia. Still, though, the ASEAN + 3 process serves as the central framework for regional community building.

Under the ASEAN + 3 framework,[5] it is not an exaggeration to say that the small countries from Southeast Asia played the leading role in driving the big powers in Northeast Asia into regional community building in East Asia. This is because, in some way, the ASEAN + 3 process is built on ASEAN's dialogue mechanism with its official dialogue partners, and it was ASEAN's wish to turn it into more formal and institutionalized regional dialogue. For ASEAN, the ARF is more on the political and security side of regional dialogue involving states inside and outside the region, while the 'ASEAN + 3' process is more on the regional political and economic side

176

of community building. Given its pivotal position in the various regional forums, ASEAN has been in the driver's seat, facilitating and initiating regional dialogue. It has played a central role in East Asian community building. To better understand this role, it is now useful for us to examine what motivated ASEAN as a group to initiate dialogue with Northeast Asian states even before 1997.

ASEAN + 3: bridging Southeast and Northeast Asia

The relations of ASEAN as a grouping with Northeast Asia started with its dialogue with Japan in 1973. In August 1977, at the second ASEAN summit, in Kuala Lumpur, ASEAN leaders met with the Japanese prime minister, Takeo Fukuda. Under the so-called 'Fukuda Doctrine', he re-assured them that Japan's policy toward Southeast Asia would give top priority to supporting the development of ASEAN countries. At the third ASEAN summit, in Manila in December 1987, ASEAN leaders met with the new prime minister, Noboru Takeshita. The bilateral dialogue in some way reflected ASEAN's desire to engage with Japan for greater economic cooperation, as well as Japan's wish to deal with Southeast Asia as a group, and to consolidate its position in the region.

Seoul was ASEAN's second dialogue partner from Northeast Asia. ASEAN and South Korea first established their sectoral dialogue relations in November 1989. ASEAN's cooperation was at first confined to trade, investment, and tourism. South Korea was upgraded to full dialogue partnership in July 1991, at the twenty-fourth ASEAN ministerial meeting, in Kuala Lumpur.

At that same meeting, ASEAN's relations with China were started in 1991, when the Chinese foreign minister, Qian Qichen, was invited as guest of the host (Malaysia) to attend the opening ceremony and, more importantly, to meet with ASEAN foreign ministers in an informal consultation session. ASEAN and China quickly found mutual interest in their subsequent contacts and consultations. China became a full dialogue partner at the twenty-ninth ASEAN ministerial meeting, in Jakarta in 1996.

In 1994, China, Japan, and South Korea also joined ASEAN in launching the ARF in Bangkok. In using the 'ASEAN way' to manage Asia–Pacific countries and the EU, the ARF process has been successful in promoting consultation and consensus building, and the ARF has developed at a pace comfortable to all of its participants. The ASEAN + 3 process, on the other hand, has been equally successful in promoting consultation and consensus building in economic affairs, but even more successful in promoting enlightened regionalism and sustainable economic cooperation in East Asia. In that sense, ASEAN has transformed itself from a small sub-regional organization into a major voice for peace, justice, and moderation in the Asia–Pacific region. It is the only regional organization in Asia that provides a political forum in which Asian countries and the world powers can discuss and consider security problems, political issues, and military concerns. The relative peace, security, and stability that ASEAN has helped maintain in Southeast Asia, as well as in the Asia–Pacific region more broadly, have been good for development. They have created a political environment in which rapid and sustained economic growth has become possible. Economic development in turn has brought about social progress and human development.

The ASEAN + 3 process is about more than just economic integration: it is targeted at a much broader vision of East Asian community building. As the 1999 ASEAN + 3 summit's Joint Statement on East Asia Cooperation indicated, the aim is 'to deepen and consolidate collective efforts with a view to advancing mutual understanding, trust, good neighborliness and friendly relations, peace, stability and prosperity in East Asia and the world'.[6] Within this context, the ASEAN + 3 leaders underscored their commitment 'to handling their mutual relations in accordance with the purposes and principles of the UN Charter, the Five Principles of Peaceful Co-existence, the Treaty of Amity and Cooperation in Southeast Asia, and the universally recognized principles of international law'.[7] With these commitments, the ASEAN + 3 leaders agreed to promote closer linkages in East Asia and to translate the growing regional interaction into a more peaceful and stable regional community.

ASEAN's role as the driving force for community building is reflected in its successful diplomacy, bilaterally as well as multilaterally, with China, Japan, and South Korea in forging a common vision of an East Asian community. At the beginning of the ASEAN + 3 process, the emphasis was more on strengthening cooperation between ASEAN and each of those three states, building on their existing dialogue mechanisms. After the three bilateral meetings in the inaugural ASEAN + 3 summit on 16 December 1997, ASEAN and three Northeast Asian leaders issued three separate joint statements on their own forms of bilateral cooperation toward the twenty-first century. The ASEAN–China statement affirmed the commitment to 'promote good-neighborly and friendly relations, increase high-level exchanges, strengthen the mechanism of dialogue and cooperation in all areas to enhance understanding and mutual benefit' and to 'resolve their differences or disputes through peaceful means, without resorting to the threat or use of force'. In the ASEAN–Japan joint statement, ASEAN and Japanese leaders:

> expressed their determination to work together to ensure that future generations would live in peace and stability and that social and economic development would be sustained. With a view to fostering an enhanced partnership, they decided to intensify dialogues and exchanges at all levels.

In the ASEAN–South Koran joint statement, the leaders 'agreed that the stability and prosperity of Northeast and Southeast Asia were inter-linked and it was essential for both sides to work closely together for the mutual benefit of both regions'.

To ASEAN leaders, these three separate joint statements had a common theme: cooperation between ASEAN and each of the three Northeast Asian nations would benefit both sides and would be a foundation for regional cooperation in East Asia. Built on this common theme, ASEAN took the initiative of formulating the common goals for future East Asian community building. At the ASEAN + 3 summit in Hanoi on 16 December 1998, it was agreed that the ASEAN + 3 summit would henceforth be held annually. Another important outcome was a decision to set up the East Asia Vision Group (EAVG), on a proposal by the South Korean president, Kim Dae Jung.

The work carried by the EAVG has become so far the closest to a preliminary constitutional effort to consolidate the ASEAN + 3 process. Under the leadership of a former South Korean foreign minister, Han Sung-joo, who was appointed to chair the EAVG, twenty-six intellectuals (two from each state), in their 'track two' capacities, held several meetings to discuss the vision of East Asian cooperation. The EAVG submitted to the ASEAN + 3 summit in Brunei in 2001 a landmark prospective report entitled *Towards an East Asian Community: region of peace, prosperity and progress.*[8]

At the fourth ASEAN + 3 summit, in Singapore in November 2000, a proposal by president Kim Dae Jung to establish an official East Asia Study Group (EASG) was adopted. The EASG was established in March 2001 and consisted of the secretary-general of ASEAN and senior officials from each of the ASEAN + 3 member states. It was charged with producing for the ASEAN + 3 leaders a more substantive set of recommendations for future action. The EASG submitted its final report to the ASEAN + 3 summit in November 2002. A brief comparison between the EAVG report and the EASG final report is useful here. The EAVG report put forth altogether fifty-seven recommendations in several categories, and twenty-two of them were highlighted in the executive summary of the report, in the following areas:

1 economic cooperation (four recommendations);
2 financial cooperation (three recommendations);
3 political and security cooperation (four recommendations);
4 environmental cooperation (four recommendations);
5 social and cultural cooperation (five recommendations);
6 institutional cooperation (two recommendations).

The EASG report, however, is more focused and practical. Derived from the EAVG's list, the EASG report presented twenty-six recommendations, seventeen of which were short-term measures ready for implementation, while the other nine were medium- to long-term measures.[9] The short-term measures were easier to implement, and included the formation of an East Asia Forum, an East Asia Business Council, and a network of East Asian eminent intellectuals, and the promotion of East Asian studies. The long-term measures included the formation of an East Asia free trade area and the evolution of the ASEAN + 3 summit into an East Asian summit. The EASG report argued that an East Asia summit was both inevitable and necessary, and it proposed the formation of an East Asian Community as well.

ASEAN + 3 leaders in the 2003 Cambodian summit warmly endorsed the outcome of the EASG. The leaders agreed that the evolution of ASEAN + 3 into an East Asian summit, together with institutionalization of other East Asian cooperation mechanisms, would create regular channels of communication and cooperation. The East Asian Community could start with the establishment of an East Asian free trade area as an interim step toward linking existing free trade areas in East Asia.

In retrospect, the rationale of Mahathir's EAEG idea was to form an East Asian pillar to balance the power of North America and Europe, by way of enhancing intraregional trading arrangements and making them attractive to the European and American trading blocs. Mahathir hoped that East Asia, on the basis of its fast-expanding market power, would be able to bargain on equal terms and even alter the rules set by the Western countries. Membership of the EAEG was limited to East Asian countries on the rationale that they have something in common, with regard to both their attitudes to economic development and their culture.

However, it was not culture or attitudes that brought them closer: rather, economic interests have driven collaboration, within the ASEAN + 3 framework. After the 1997 financial crisis and as a result of the global economic slowdown, trade volume between ASEAN and China, Japan, and South Korea declined by 9.1 percent in 2001, to US$185.2 billion. Thus, regional economic integration as a means to promote trade and investment flows was a major task for ASEAN. In the meeting of the ASEAN + 3 economic ministers held in Hanoi in September 2001, ASEAN proposed nine projects to further ASEAN + 3 cooperation. These involved: strengthening the competitiveness of ASEAN small and medium-sized enterprises; a training program on practical technology for environmental protection; an Asian common skill standard for information technology engineers; an Asia e-learning initiative; an ASEAN satellite image archive; an environmental study; and people-to-people information technology transfer. In the 2002 meeting in Brunei, seven more projects were initiated.[10]

Mahathir's EAEG idea suggested a more exclusive form of East Asian regionalism – an Asian-only 'non-white' regional structure – and the ASEAN + 3 framework fits this profile. Within this framework, Malaysia and China are interested in moving East Asian regionalism in a pan Asian direction, while Japan, Singapore, and Indonesia prefer a more inclusive regional association. These differences over direction have not prevented ASEAN + 3 members from drawing up a series of bilateral agreements on free trade areas and closer economic partnership with others. ASEAN has signed bilateral trade arrangements with the United States, the EU, Australia, India, Japan, and China. Among them, the most important ones were the ASEAN–China Framework Agreement on Comprehensive Economic Cooperation, signed on 5 November 2002, and ASEAN's economic partnership with Japan, signed the year after. As China has aggressively pursued a strong China–ASEAN axis within the ASEAN + 3 framework, Japan has sought to balance China's growing power in the region. To some extent, the ASEAN–China free trade agreement has triggered fierce competition between Japan and China in the trilateral relationship.

China's initiative on the ASEAN–China Free Trade Area (ACFTA)

As discussed above, East Asian regionalism began to gain new momentum after the Asian financial crisis in 1997. For example, a proposal for the AMF emerged from the Chiang Mai initiative in 2000, and a similar multilateral financial surveillance mechanism called the Manila Framework was also established. As East Asian countries pushed forward on regional financial cooperation, bilateral initiatives constituted the major driving force for regional integration. Among the bilateral initiatives, the ACFTA was undoubtedly a breakthrough.

China's rapid economic development and growing importance to the region was clearly demonstrated by its leverage and willingness to form free trade areas with its neighbors. In the economic realm, many Southeast Asian countries see China as a threat as well as an opportunity. While on the one hand a more prosperous China might buy more Southeast Asian exports and invest more capital, on the other China absorbs most foreign direct investment in East Asia, leaving less for ASEAN countries and posing tough competition for a wide range of Southeast Asian products. China has been concerned with the danger of deteriorating relations with the United States and the increasing distrust between Tokyo and Beijing. Improvement of China–ASEAN relations therefore assumes increasing significance in China's regional policy; and enhancing mutual interests and interdependence is the best way to erode the ASEAN states' perception of the 'China threat'. The Malaysian prime minister Abduallah Ahmad Badawi stated in 2004, 'China is today a creator of prosperity of the highest order. Political and social linkages are bound to eventually follow suit. It is therefore important to use every opportunity and establish ties.'[11] More importantly, China's rapid development began to serve as an engine of economic growth for the region. During 1995–2002, China–ASEAN trade grew an average of 19 percent annually; in 2002, it reached a record US$54.8 billion – an increase of 31.8 percent from 2001.[12] And in 2003 it topped US$78 billion. From the perspective of Southeast Asia, China's trading patterns are particularly beneficial: Southeast Asia as a whole maintains a trade surplus with China of US$8 billion annually, largely from its enormous exports of raw materials and precision machinery.[13]

In many ways, the establishment of the ACFTA represents a challenge to what can be achieved by mutual engagement. China and the ASEAN countries have expanded and deepened their economic cooperation, and rapid progress has been achieved. In November 2002, China and ASEAN signed the Framework Agreement of Comprehensive Economic Cooperation,[14] launching the process of establishing the ACFTA (the Agreement will serve as its legal basis). In 1975, the bilateral volume of trade between China and ASEAN was only US$523 million. It is gratifying to see that, by 1996, this had reached US$20 billion. Trade between the two sides totaled US$41.6 billion in 2001, which was four times higher than in 1991, making China the sixth and ASEAN the fifth biggest trading partners with each other. From January to August 2002 alone, trade between the two sides reached US$33.29 billion, an increase of 24.4 percent on the corresponding period in the previous year.

The amount of two-way investment has also been rising. ASEAN had become the sixth largest investment source for China by 2000. By 2001, there were 17,972 ASEAN direct-investment projects in China, with a total contract value of US$53.46 billion and monetary investments of US$26.17 billion. In 2000, ASEAN (mainly Singapore, Malaysia, Thailand, Indonesia, and the Philippines) invested in 1,047 new projects in China, up by 15.6 percent from the year before, with US$3.05 billion contracted, up by 3.1 percent. In 2001, ASEAN invested in 1,239 projects, with a total contract value of US$3.37 billion and monetary investments of US$2.98 billion. In the first three quarters of 2002, ASEAN contract investment in China reached US$4.3 billion, and the associated monetary investment US$2.38 billion. By 2001, China had invested in 740 projects in ASEAN countries, with a total investment of US$650 million. In that year, China invested in forty-eight projects, with an investment of US$200 million.[15]

In a parallel development, all ten ASEAN countries have now become official tourist destinations for Chinese citizens. In 2001, the total number of tourists traveling between China and ASEAN countries reached 3.38 million. It was then estimated that this total would be over 4 million in 2002. At the same time, China has been actively pushing for a regional free trade agreement that will encompass Brunei, Indonesia, Malaysia, the Philippines, Singapore, and Thailand in 2010, and incorporate Vietnam, Laos, Myanmar, and Cambodia by 2015. Experts have suggested that once the ACFTA is established in 2010, China's exports to ASEAN will grow by US$10.6 billion, or 55.1 percent, and ASEAN's exports to China will surge by US$13 billion, or 48 percent.[16] The total trade volume will reach US$1.2 trillion.[17] Individual Chinese entrepreneurs are also expanding China's economic reach throughout Laos and Myanmar, where some regions now use only the renminbi and speak Chinese. In some sectors, not surprisingly, China's expansion is not especially welcome: electronics, furniture, motorcycles, and fruit and vegetables are just some of the areas in which Chinese goods have begun to supplant those traditionally produced in Southeast Asia.[18]

While China has made rapid strides in expanding its trade relations with Southeast Asia, not surprisingly its role as a source of investment for the region has been developing much more slowly. Still, it has taken steps to assert itself in this arena as well. It is committing US$100 million in aid and investment to Myanmar, developing Indonesian natural gas reserves, investing in infrastructure in the Philippines, establishing rail and highway links with Cambodia, Thailand, and Singapore, and promising to dredge part of the Mekong River in Laos and Myanmar to make it suitable for commercial navigation. In terms of both development assistance and foreign direct investment, however, China lags far behind the regional leader, Japan. Tokyo is the top aid donor to ASEAN members. In 1997 Japan pledged US$30 billion in assistance to strengthen the economies of the region, and by 2001 was providing 60 percent of the development assistance to the region. In terms of foreign direct investment, China's investment in Southeast Asia in 2003 was US$941 million, about one-fifth of that of Japan. Japanese firms invested almost US$2 billion into ASEAN economies in 2000, US$3.1 billion in 2002, and US$4.8 billion in 2003. The United States is also a critical source of foreign direct investment, at around US$3 billion in 2003.

The ASEAN–China Free Trade Area as economic statecraft?

With the goal of establishing the ACFTA by the year 2010, ASEAN and China completed negotiation on trade of goods, and a mechanism for settling trade disputes by the end of 2005. The next step is to work out an agreement on investment and trade within the service sector. Given the current pace of negotiation, it is likely the goal of the ACFTA will be achieved several years before the target year. What has made the ACFTA process so smooth? What has motivated the two sides?

From a purely economic point of view, a free trade agreement between ASEAN and China makes a lot of sense. All countries involved would gain from the linkage, whereas it would not seriously harm the economic interests of their other trade and investment partners, thereby ensuring unobstructed relationships with the US, the EU, and Japan. Politically, it appears evident that the ACFTA will serve the foreign policy objectives of China, whereas the effects on its domestic economy will contribute to its aim of internal political stability through economic growth. It also appears that the ACFTA will serve both the political and the security interests of ASEAN member states. The ACFTA is not only feasible, but also desirable for both sides.

How can the ACFTA be linked to the AFTA? At the third ASEAN informal summit, in November 1999, the Southeast Asian leaders agreed to readjust their schedule for the AFTA, to push forward the goal of free trade by 2010 for the original six members and by 2015 for the other four members.[19] By January 2002, all products on the 'inclusion list' of the original six members had their tariffs reduced to 0–5 percent, with some exceptions. Vietnam, Laos, Myanmar, and Cambodia were to have a maximum tariff of 0–5 percent by 2003, 2005, 2005, and 2007, respectively. The ACFTA regime will initially have a dual track, that is, with the ASEAN-6 in one track and the newer ASEAN states in the other.[20] The ACFTA Framework Agreement committed the parties to a schedule of free trade in goods by 2010 for ASEAN-6, and by 2015 for the newer ASEAN members. It also contains an asymmetrical phase-in scheme.[21] For China, the average import tariff for industrial products will be 8.9 percent by 2005 and for agricultural products 15 percent by 2004.

The economic benefits the ACFTA is expected to generate can be sorted into four categories: the scale of the economy; economic efficiency; investment prospects; and geopolitical benefits. In relation to the first of these, the ACFTA will create an economic region with 1.7 billion people (the biggest free trade area in the world in terms of population size), a regional gross domestic product of about US$2 trillion, and total trade estimated at US$1.23 trillion.

Second, the ACFTA should increase economic efficiency by removing trade barriers and encouraging specialization in production. A key feature of the Agreement is the non-maintenance of quantitative restrictions and the elimination of non-tariff barriers. The removal of these trade impediments will lower the costs of trade transactions, further increase trade between ASEAN and China, and enhance economic efficiency. As low-cost imports flow from one member to another, specialization in production will ensue, thereby boosting real income in both ASEAN and China as resources flow to sectors where they can more efficiently and productively be utilized.[22]

There is no doubting that the comprehensive commitments made by China in its WTO accession agreement will result in a significantly more liberal and open Chinese economy. The ASEAN countries, for their part, have been unilaterally liberalizing their economies since the 1990s and the process of regional economic liberalization through the AFTA has supplemented this process. However, both ASEAN and China maintain practices that hamper trade and investment flows, while measures stimulating these flows have not been implemented. These barriers have included:

1 *High tariff rates, particularly on some products of export interest to the other region.* Several lines have tariff rates of well over 100 percent. In addition to import duties, some ASEAN countries levy a sales tax on most

imported goods. Average tariffs in China are higher than average 'most favored nation' rates in the WTO members of ASEAN.

2 *Non-tariff barriers, in the form of quotas, licensing requirements and other import control measures.* In addition, corruption, bureaucracy, and lack of coordination between customs and other import-regulating agencies should also be regarded as non-tariff barriers.

3 *Unequal and burdensome standards and norms.* ASEAN countries maintain different regimes with regard to standards, labeling, and certification requirements, whereas the cost, duration, and complexity of permit processes are burdensome. This hampers production for an ASEAN market and has a negative effect on the economies of scale pursued by many industries.

4 *Restrictions on trade in services.* Barriers in the service sector include restrictions on banking licenses, stringent requirements for insurance companies, and limitations on foreign direct investment in sectors considered to be of strategic importance, such as the telecommunications sector.

5 *Absence of investment protection agreements.* This type of agreement promotes and safeguards investment made in another territory.

The third major benefit is expected to come from the improvement of investment prospects within the ACFTA area. The formation of the ACFTA will aid in generating more investments for ASEAN. Not only will more ASEAN and Chinese companies be willing to invest within the integrated market, since market risk and uncertainty will be lowered, but US, European, and Japanese companies, which are interested in making inroads into the Asian market, will also be attracted to invest in the integrated market. On its own, China has been successful in luring investors into its growing economy, for it has the essential investment determinants in place. China's market potential is already well established, and its performance in relation to some indicators of institutional quality and macroeconomic and political stability is better than that of the ASEAN states. And, despite the perceived inadequate legal framework, high inflation, and the pervasiveness of red tape and corruption, foreign investors are looking at the long-term benefits of investing in China more than at the short-term problems. As such, the integration of ASEAN with China could entice more foreign corporations, which each market alone could not otherwise attract. With a larger market, more intense competition, increased investment, and economies of scale, investors will be more inclined to locate in the integrated region.

In terms of ASEAN–China trade structure,[23] the top five ASEAN exports to China in the early 1990s were: oil and fuel; wood; vegetable oils and fats; computers and machinery; and electrical equipment. Collectively, the share of these five products amounted to 75.7 percent of all ASEAN exports to China. By 1999, the order of importance had changed, away from primary commodities and toward manufactured products. Computers and machinery and electrical equipment grew from 12.4 percent to 38.2 percent of ASEAN exports to China. Also, the share of the top five products decreased to 60.3 percent of total exports to China. ASEAN imports from China were always more diversified. In 1993 the top five ASEAN imports from China were computers and machinery, electrical equipment, oil and fuel, cotton, and tobacco. Collectively they made up just under 40 percent of ASEAN imports from China. In 1999, electrical equipment and computers and machinery were still the top imports, but their share had increased to nearly half of all ASEAN imports from China.

The exports where China enjoys the greatest advantage are: base metals and metal articles; textiles and clothing; footwear; vegetable products and prepared foodstuffs; vehicles; stone, cement and ceramics; and miscellaneous manufactured articles. In 2000 they accounted for 38 percent of China's exports to ASEAN and for only 8.8 percent of China's imports from ASEAN. Exports where ASEAN enjoys greatest advantage are mineral products (including mineral fuels), plastics/rubber, wood and wood articles, pulp and paper, and fats and oils. In 2000 they accounted for 42 percent of China's imports from ASEAN, while constituting only 11.6 percent of China's exports to ASEAN. Over the last decade, the strongest growth has occurred in the trade of manufactured products, with trade in computers and machinery and electrical equipment rising the most. The fact that these products were both the leading exports and imports of both ASEAN and China suggests the importance of intra-industry trade. It is important to realize that, in ASEAN as well as in China, foreign enterprises are responsible for a substantial share of the exports in intermediate goods and manufactured end products. Obviously it will be in the interest of intra-industry trade to further decrease import – and export – barriers, making both ASEAN and China (even) more attractive for foreign direct investment.

Taking into account the facts that both ASEAN and China rely on the markets of developed countries to export their excess capacity and that both are major destinations for foreign direct investment from developed countries rather than significant investors in each other, there appears to be ample room for a further expansion of the existing trade and investment relations. A preferential trade agreement would certainly help to stimulate such a development, according to a simulation done by the ASEAN–China Expert Group on Economic Cooperation. The simulation showed the following effects of the ACFTA:[24]

- ASEAN exports to China will expand by 48 percent, while China's exports to ASEAN will rise by 55.1 percent.
- Both ASEAN and China will see a reduction in their trade with other partners. Hence, the overall effect is a modest rise in total exports. Total exports from ASEAN will increase by 1.5 percent, whereas China's total

exports will increase by 2.4 percent. The ACFTA will thus in large part result in trade diversion, rather than an overall expansion of trade. It should be noted that this is not unusual. The same phenomenon has occurred within the EU. Also, Mexico's trade with the US increased significantly after NAFTA went into force, not only in absolute terms, but also as a percentage of its total trade, but to the detriment of Mexico's trade with other main trading partners, including the EU.

- The sectors where bilateral trade expansion will coincide will be textiles and clothing, electrical appliances and machinery, and other manufactures.
- Real gross domestic product will increase for all countries concerned. On the ASEAN side, the biggest winner in absolute terms will be Indonesia (US$2.27 billion), with Vietnam being the winner in relative terms (2.15 percent). The effect on China's gross domestic product will be a modest increase of US$2.21 billion, or 0.27 percent. In absolute terms the negative effects on the economies of the US and Japan will total US$7.05 billion, whereas the collective positive effect on the economies of ASEAN and China will be US$7.61 billion. In relative terms, the effects on the US and Japanese economies will be minimal: for the US –0.04 percent and for Japan –0.09 percent.

Finally, the ACFTA is expected to bring more geopolitical benefits. For China it should further contribute to its increasing prominence in East Asia. The ACFTA should reaffirm China's position as an economic and production hub in Asia. Looking at the rest of Asia from this perspective, the other Asian economic powerhouse, Japan, will probably be marginalized. Although China has at present – and presumably for a substantial period into the future – no interest, no need, and no capability to compete with the United States in world politics and the global economy, the ACFTA should, in the long run, help it to become one of the 'poles' in a multipolar world. It is also important to note that the ACFTA will boost economic growth in those Chinese provinces that share a border with ASEAN states, and that it is instrumental in maintaining regime security for the communist government. Also, since Indonesia is a major exporter of oil and natural gas, the ACFTA will help China to gain access to nearby energy sources and decrease China's dependence on oil imports from the Middle East and other troubled regions.

For geopolitical reasons, Beijing has followed a principle of 'giving more and taking less' (*Duo Yu Shao Qu*) in its economic relations with ASEAN states in recent years. This policy aims at winning over trust by offering more economic benefits. China's decision to form a free trade area with ASEAN was one major step in its diplomacy toward the region, but it is not difficult to see that the ACFTA decision resulted from a largely diplomatic–political imperative on the part of China, after years of studious Chinese efforts to win ASEAN's trust since the end of the Cold War. In terms of economic benefits, the ACFTA would help to increase China's gross domestic product by 0.3 percent, while ASEAN as a whole would receive 1.0 percent contribution to their gross domestic product. However, in proposing the ACFTA, China mainly had two strategic goals in mind: development of its southwestern provinces; and competition with Japan in terms of demonstrating leadership in regional economic affairs.[25] In October 2004 Beijing unilaterally began to provide early tariff benefits on 573 products, including agricultural and manufactured goods, from ASEAN states to the Chinese markets. This 'early harvest' package exemplified the 'giving more and taking less' policy and was perceived by ASEAN states as a big concession by China.[26]

In considering China's motivation, Taiwan's political and economic relations with ASEAN was another factor we cannot neglect. As a major exporter to China, to the extent that Taiwan registers a substantial surplus in its bilateral trade with China,[27] it is in Taiwan's interest to maintain a level playing field. The ACFTA might distort that position, thus increasing the need for Taiwan to enter into a similar sort of arrangement with China. That would push Taiwan toward an economic relationship with China that would (better) resemble an intra-state relationship.

Some ASEAN countries – Brunei, Indonesia, the Philippines, and Vietnam – are or have been involved in territorial disputes with China. Therefore one could wonder whether, from a security perspective, it is in their interest to become economically more dependent on China. On the other hand, ASEAN leaders are also pragmatic. They have undoubtedly recognized that their prospects for economic advancement might have dramatically decreased after the Asian financial crisis of 1997. They must also have recognized that the prospects for China to become the dominant power in Asia, economically, politically, and militarily, are good. As such, they must have perceived that the Chinese market will become increasingly attractive, whereas China's increasing political and military power will be inevitable and therefore something ASEAN will simply have to adjust to. In that perception, 'containment by engagement' becomes the key concept. The conclusion would then be that the ACFTA will be beneficial to the welfare of the ASEAN people and will also address their security concerns.

In theory at least, there is a possibility that ASEAN would have to choose between economic linkage with Japan and economic linkage with China. In practice, however, Japan is still lagging behind China in forming a free trade area with ASEAN. In order not to yield the regional economic leadership role to China and not to miss the boat in the regional drive toward free trade, Tokyo has become more proactive in signing bilateral Economic Partnership Agreements (EPAs) with ASEAN states. Japan signed an EPA with Singapore in 2002, and is negotiating an EPA with Thailand, the Philippines, and Malaysia. At the regional level, Tokyo has proposed to establish an East Asian EPA to counterbalance China's increasing economic influence in the region.[28] If an East Asian free trade area or East Asian EPA ever does indeed emerge, it would be a major step toward regional integration and could offset economic challenges posed by an expanding EU (which also aims to form a free trade area with Russia), by NAFTA, and by a possible future free trade area of the Americas.

Japan's vision of a regional community

Japan's economic ties with ASEAN were much stronger than those between China and ASEAN, and Japan is still ASEAN's largest export market. Skeptics could point to the fact that Japan's trade with ASEAN (more than US$119 billion at December 2003) significantly exceeds that of China, at least at present. However, trends suggest that both China and Japan are offering growing markets for Southeast Asian goods, and are producing more goods desired by Southeast Asian countries. While trade between Japan and ASEAN jumped from US$97.6 billion in 2002 to US$119 billion in 2003, trade between China and ASEAN has grown at a faster pace. This suggests that both Japan and the United States have proceeded far more slowly in developing free trade agreements with regional actors than China. Thus far, the United States has established bilateral free trade agreements only with Singapore and Thailand, and US agricultural subsidies, as well as concerns with most of the poorer countries in Asia over rules on foreign investment, anti-trust regulation, and transparency in government procurement are likely to slow any additional bilateral trade negotiations with the United States.

Recently, Japan has been more aggressive in pursuing its own bilateral free trade agreements, with an eye toward the formation of a regional free trade area in the future. It has signed bilateral free trade agreements with Singapore and Mexico, and was hoping to conclude trade agreements with Thailand, Malaysia, and the Philippines within the next few years. At the ASEAN + 1 level, Japan has actively engaged to form a closer economic partnership in light of China's economic diplomacy in the region.[29] It has also initiated talks with Indonesia. In contrast to China, however, Japan talks less about what a regional free trade agreement will bring to the region, and – perhaps for domestic consumption – more about the overwhelming benefits that it will bring to the Japanese economy, which already runs a trade surplus with the region. The Japanese government believes that a free trade arrangement with ASEAN would add as much as US$18 billion to Japan's gross domestic product and create as many as 260,000 jobs.[30]

Tokyo's imperial vision of leading a 'Great East Asian Co-Prosperity Sphere' never materialized due to its aggression in the Pacific War. Japan has tried to promote a new type of economic regionalism in East Asia, but has encountered strong resistance, owing to its 'historical burden'. On the one hand, the ASEAN + 3 process is not an ideal platform for Japan to play a leading role in the region. On the other hand, it is a regional platform that Japan cannot afford to be left out of. Japan does not want to miss out on regional integration, but, for the Japanese, it is more desirable to have Japanese–US co-leadership in Asia and, economically, it would be best to build the regional economic community on the basis of the 'flying geese' pattern.

Washington's ambivalence

Ever since the US-led allied forces defeated Japanese imperial ambitions in the Asia–Pacific region, Washington has deeply involved itself in East Asia. The US-centered 'hub and spoke' security structure has served as the anchor for regional peace and stability in the Asia–Pacific region. The regionalization of East Asia has been dependent on US power projection in the region. After the occupation of Japan ended, in 1952, the United States decided to maintain a large military presence in many countries in the Asia–Pacific region, which was instrumental in upholding bilateral alliances, largely to contain the advance of Soviet and Chinese-backed communism in the Korean peninsula and Southeast Asia. However, the 'hub and spoke' structure of managing East Asian security and politics was somewhat relaxed after the Cold War, when the Clinton administration joined the security discussions in the ARF with a view of promoting multilateral security institutions in the region.

On the economic front, the Clinton administration had a hands-on policy in upgrading the APEC process to summit level from 1993. The APEC summit is a particularly interesting venue in which to actively promote the idea of open economic regionalism, which itself would lead to greater access to difficult Asian markets and, possibly, to an earlier conclusion of the GATT's Uruguay Round of trade negotiations. However, although the GATT/WTO eventually got going, APEC never went as far as the US wanted. Most Asian states, primarily ASEAN ones, succeeded in keeping APEC as an incremental process led by discussion and cooperation, so it did not become particularly institutionalized or legalistic. Therefore, in the late 1990s the Clinton administration began to downplay APEC and focused more on bilateral negotiations to advance the US free trade agenda with countries in the region. Washington's policy on China's accession to the WTO was a good example of this.

When George W. Bush came to office in January 2001, his neo-conservative foreign policy team demonstrated more interest in geostrategic than in geo-economic issues. They pointed the finger at China as a 'strategic competitor' and at North Korea as a state belonging to the 'axis of evil', with nuclear weapons ambition. The Bush administration showed little interest in APEC, Southeast Asia, or regional multilateral economic cooperation.

After 11 September 2001, the administration became more keen on formulating a unilateral global foreign strategy in favor of intervention and pre-emptive military attacks against selected terrorism-sponsoring states (first seen in Afghanistan and Iraq), and general containment of any possible alliance of external and internal factors that might be working against the United States' self-declared benevolent designs. Evidence on the overall geopolitical result of Bush's unilateralist policies is still inconclusive. After its invasion of Iraq in 2003, the US and its vocal allies have lost much trust around the world, and have strained the transatlantic partnership almost to breaking point. Moreover, Washington has become bogged down in Iraq, Afghanistan, and the broader Middle East region. As a result, it has paid little attention to regional political and economic developments in East Asia. This 'vacuum of attention' has created an opportunity for China to expand its influence in the region. Although Washington has become increasingly concerned with China's rising prominence in Southeast Asia, it does not have any vision or concrete agenda to stop it. Instead, the United States continues to focus on combating those groups labeled as evil terrorists in Southeast Asia, without engaging in any regional political or economic dialogue. As for the emerging ASEAN + 3 process and the prospects of East Asian community building, Washington is taking a wait-and-see approach.[31]

Expanding ASEAN + 3: a new vision of community building?

The ASEAN + 3 process was intended by ASEAN states to bind Southeast Asia more closely with Northeast Asian major powers so as to ensure their own prosperity and greater regional influence. It has become a vehicle for regional community building because both Beijing and Tokyo have so far been happy to let ASEAN take the lead role. Will future community building in East Asia develop within the ASEAN + 3 framework? Where will ASEAN + 3 head? Let us turn to a discussion of the different visions of the future for ASEAN + 3.

First, ASEAN + 3 now faces challenges over how to deepen and widen its course and process. At the ASEAN + 3 meeting of foreign ministers on 25 July 2005, the foreign ministers reaffirmed their commitment to the ASEAN + 3 process and its continued relevance to East Asian regional cooperation. In order to bring greater depth to such cooperation, they agreed to speed up and complete the implementation of all seventeen short-term measures of the EASG by the tenth anniversary of ASEAN + 3 cooperation in 2007. After eight years of cooperative efforts, the ASEAN + 3 process now covers seventeen sectors and has forty-nine mechanisms with which to facilitate and implement cooperation. Besides the sectoral bodies, some non-governmental mechanisms, such as the Network of East Asia Think-Tanks and East Asia Forum, are being considered. The ASEAN + 3 countries consider the implementation of the IAI as well as the Vientiane Action Program as part of their efforts to support the process of ASEAN integration. As for how to push forward regional community building, the foreign ministers agreed that India, Australia, and New Zealand, apart from ASEAN + 3 members, would be invited to attend the first EAS in December 2005. In a very diplomatic way, they stated that 'they welcomed the decision of ASEAN to keep the EAS open, outward-looking and inclusive and for the continued driving seat of ASEAN'.[32] The ASEAN + 3 leaders in their 2004 summit agreed to issue a second Joint Statement on East Asia Cooperation on the tenth anniversary of the ASEAN + 3 process. With this roadmap on deepening and widening ASEAN + 3 cooperation, do we see a new vision of East Asian community building? In the context of the wider Asia–Pacific region there have long existed different visions of regionalism and community building.[33] Discussion of the relationship between APEC and the ASEAN + 3 process led to the elaboration of an 'Asia–Pacific' view and an 'Asianist' view of regional integration, in addition to the continuous debates on the relationship between the wider region and the sub-region, and on the market-driven integration of national economies versus the need for policy coordination to manage its destabilizing consequences. The Asian financial crisis then prompted further discussion of two competing visions or models of regionalism: the EAEC versus APEC.

Malaysia's EAEC model would include only East Asian states, in a loosely structured consultative group. While the other ASEAN countries have not been on the forefront espousing it, they have nevertheless been broadly supportive of the idea. In Mahathir's view, after all, ASEAN would be the nucleus or core of the EAEC. In the 1990s the Clinton administration was consistently against the 'caucus' idea because it would create an 'artificial dividing line down the middle of the Pacific'. Washington knew of course that the so-called 'line' was far from artificial, and its strident opposition to Mahathir's project stemmed from the fact that it would reinforce trends that were already at work. Already, intra-Asian trade made up some 60 percent of East Asia's trade and it was (and is) growing much faster than its trade with other parts of the world. The size of Japan's trade with Asia had outstripped its trade with the US, and Southeast Asia had overtaken the US to become Korea's biggest market. With East Asia becoming both an integrated production base and its own biggest market, the formation of the EAEC would accelerate the lessening market dependence on the US and promote greater political independence. By proposing the first APEC informal summit in Seattle in November 1993, the Clinton administration gave a big push to the Asia–Pacific regionalism based on APEC membership.

However, the race for effective liberalization between AFTA and APEC was largely run without reference to the essential contradiction between the two enterprises. AFTA's objective to become a substitute for more comprehensive liberalization was largely dampened by the financial crisis of 1997. Nevertheless, that crisis prompted ASEAN to turn to Northeast Asia for trade liberalization and economic partnership, and that created an ASEAN united front *vis-à-vis* APEC. Southeast Asia remained economically weak after the crisis, which wiped out ASEAN's institutional strength, although its group identity remained strong. Southeast Asian countries differ significantly and, therefore, their interests vary greatly as well. Nevertheless, there is increased momentum toward the coalescence of a free market in East Asia. Both the Chinese and the Japanese have suggested the establishment of an 'East Asia community', with the creation of an Asian bond market, which could have negative implications for the United States. Its purpose would be to recycle huge Asian surpluses rather than diverting them to US markets. There is also momentum for the creation of an AMF.

The ASEAN + 3 developments have strengthened the sense of an Asia for Asians, and an Asia that does not necessarily involve the United States. While Japan has played a leadership role in developing new currency arrangements, China will likely become an increasingly important force. Throughout Southeast Asia, China's currency, the renminbi, is becoming more widely used. And as China takes steps to make the renminbi convertible, it may well emerge as the dominant regional currency. In contrast, Japan's banking and debt troubles have worn out the Japanese economy, and the yen is becoming 'less suitable' as a vehicle for wider Asian monetary integration.

The reality, then, is that China is assuming a leadership role in the regional economy and aggressively pursuing the ACFTA. Regardless of its motives, China will naturally become economically engaged in the region because it is a neighbor, and this is certain to produce both economic and security gains for the region (including China itself). Yet Japan remains the predominant source of investment, retains a larger trade relationship, and drives the currency negotiations within the region. The United States continues to be Southeast Asia's most important trading partner, but the stagnant level of trade suggests that the US may be finding other markets, such as China, more attractive, and that unless greater attention is paid to contributing to Southeast Asia's continued economic growth, the US will rapidly lose its status as the region's key trading partner.

Conclusion

Since the Asian financial crisis in 1997, progress toward an East Asian neighborly community has picked up pace. It is largely driven by economic and functional cooperation between the ten ASEAN and three Northeast Asian states. ASEAN has provided leadership as well as the institutional framework in the community-building process. The ASEAN-centered 'hub and spoke' structure has helped East Asian states find appropriate frameworks within which to conduct dialogue and to socialize into a regional neighborly community. Based on its robust economic growth, China has become more proactive in participating in and promoting multilateral regional integration and community building.

Looking ahead, a structure of regional economic cooperation is gradually emerging on the basis of the ASEAN + 3 process. There are apparently three concentric circles taking shape in the region. The largest (outside) circle is the ASEAN + 3 free trade area and economic integration, while the ASEAN + 1 grouping constitutes the middle circle, linking the developed and developing economies in the region. At the core should be the '+ 3' cooperation mechanism between China, Japan, and South Korea. However, due to current 'structural problems' in relations between China and Japan, it is reasonable to say the core is the most difficult part of the East Asian community-building process, and there is no prospect of Beijing and Tokyo being able to sort out their problems in the short term.

Notes

1 Christopher Hemmer and Peter J. Katzenstein, 'Why Is There No NATO in Asia? Collective identity, regionalism, and the origin of multilateralism', *International Organization*, 56:3 (2002), pp. 575–607.

2 For more detailed discussion, see Termsak Chalermpalanupap, 'Towards an East Asia Community: the journey has begun', paper presented to the Fifth China–ASEAN Research Institutes Roundtable on Regionalism and Community Building in East Asia, organized by the University of Hong Kong's Centre of Asian Studies, 17–19 October 2002. The author is special assistant to the secretary-general of ASEAN.

3 Ronnie C. Chan, 'Asia's Crisis and China's Response', *PacNet Newsletter*, 27 March 1998.

4 Toyoo Gyohten, 'East Asian Initiative Needed in Crises', cited in *Institute for International Monetary Affairs Newsletters*, No. 4, 1999 (English translation).

5 In the 1997 ASEAN + 3 summit, it was '9 + 3', not '10 + 3', because there were only nine ASEAN members at that time to meet with their Northeast Asian counterparts: Cambodia did not officially become an ASEAN member until April 1999.

6 The ASEAN + 3 summit's Joint Statement on East Asia Cooperation, 28 November 1999, Manila, is available online at www.aseansec.org/5469.htm (last accessed April 2006).

7 *Ibid.*

8 East Asia Vision Group. *Towards an East Asian Community: region of peace, prosperity and progress.* Report submitted on 31 October 2001 to ASEAN + 3, available online at www.aseansec.org/4918.htm (last accessed April 2006).

9 *The Final Report of the East Asia Study Group*, submitted to ASEAN + 3 leaders' meeting in Phnom Penh, Cambodia, on 4 November 2002, available online at www.aseansec.org/viewpdf.asp?file=/pdf/easg.pdf (last accessed June 2006).

10 This was the consultation between the fifth ASEAN economic ministers and the ministers of China, Japan, and South Korea, 14 September 2002, Bandar Seri Begawan, Brunei Darussalam. The new projects included: an East Asia Special Cooperation Initiative; a Comprehensive Action Plan for ASEAN + 3 small and medium-sized enterprises; a seminar on an economic and technological development zone; and promoting the entertainment industry within ASEAN and China, Japan, and South Korea.

11 Quoted by Denis D. Gray, 'Anxiety and Opportunities Mount as Chinese Colossus Exerts Influence on Southeast Asia', Associated Press, 30 March 2004.

12 Bian Shen, 'New Opportunity for China–ASEAN Trade', *Beijing Review*, 1 May 2003, p. 18.

13 Denis D. Gray, 'Anxiety and Opportunities Mount as Chinese Colossus Experts Influence on Southeast Asia'.

14 The Framework Agreement allows five more years for the new ASEAN members to join the ACFTA. The Chinese side has also decided to accord 'most favored nation' status to the three non-WTO members, namely, Vietnam, Laos, and Cambodia.

15 The trade data were provided by the Ministry of Foreign Trade and Economic Cooperation, China.

16 Bian, 'New Opportunity for China–ASEAN Trade', p. 19.

17 Hongmei Shen, 'Knocking Down Asian Trade Barriers', *Beijing Review*, 17 April 2003, p. 42.

18 Denis D. Gray, 'Anxiety and Opportunities Mount as Chinese Colossus Exerts Influence on Southeast Asia'.

19 Brunei Darussalam, Indonesia, Malaysia, Philippines, Singapore and Thailand are the ASEAN old six members.

20 Cambodia, Laos, Myanmar, and Vietnam.

21 Within NAFTA, this was for example the case with Mexico and the US.

22 See Raul L. Cordenillo, 'The Economic Benefits to ASEAN of the ASEAN–China Free Trade Area (ACFTA)', 18 January 2005. The author works in the Studies Unit, Bureau for Economic Integration, ASEAN Secretariat. The report is available online at www.aseansec.org/17310.htm (last accessed April 2006).

23 The following is based upon and partly adapted from *Forging Closer ASEAN–China Economic Relations in the 21st Century*, a report submitted by the ASEAN–China Expert Group on Economic Cooperation in October 2001.

24 *Ibid.* Note that Brunei, Cambodia, Laos, and Myanmar were not included in the simulation.

25 Zha Daojiong, 'The Politics of China–ASEAN Economic Relations: assessing the move toward an FTA', *Asian Perspective*, 26:4 (2002), pp. 53–82.

26 Zaidi Isham Ismail, 'ASEAN, China to Complete Talks by June', *Business Times*, 30 March 2004, p. 2.

27 According to figures from Taiwan's Board of Foreign Trade, trade with Hong Kong and China combined made up 17.1 percent of Taiwan's total trade, registering a surplus of US$23.959 billion.

28 Although Japanese officials have publicly denied the possibility that they regard

China's economic rise as a threat to Japan's interests, the Japanese business community views such events with concern, as it increasingly distorts the Japanese 'flying geese' model of development.

29 The two important documents in Japan–ASEAN economic cooperation are: the Joint Press Statement of the Seventh Consultation Between the ASEAN Economic Ministers and the Minister of International Trade and Industry of Japan, 7 October 2000, and the Joint Press Statement of the Ninth Consultation Between ASEAN Economic Ministers and the Minister of Economy, Trade and Industry of Japan, Bandar Seri Begawan, 13 September 2002.

30 Audrey McAvoy, 'Fearing Rivalry with China, Free Trade Agreements Are Suddenly the Rage in Japan', Associated Press, 2 April 2004.

31 Morton Abramowitz and Stephen Bosworth, 'Adjusting to the New Asia', *Foreign Affairs*, 82:4 (2003), pp. 119–31.

32 See chair's press statement of the sixth ASEAN + 3 foreign ministers meeting, Vientiane, Laos, 27 July 2005. Available online at www.aseansec.org/17601. htm (last accessed April 2006).

33 See, for example, Richard Higgot and Richard Stubbs, 'Competing Conceptions of Economic Regionalism: APEC versus EAEC in the Asia–Pacific', *Review of International Political Economy*, 2:3 (1995), pp. 518–22.

Chapter 8

ASEAN and Sino-Japanese relations

This chapter focuses on ASEAN as a factor in political–economic relations between China and Japan in the post-Cold War era. The evolution of Sino-Japanese relations is a key environmental factor in ASEAN's search for both its own resilience within the Southeast Asian sub-context and its relevance in maintaining stability in the larger East Asian region. Against the background of the gradual decline of the US-centered hegemonic system both internationally and in the East Asian region specifically, Sino-Japanese relations have evolved from a relatively undisturbed pattern of accommodation (from the 1970s up to the end of the 1980s) to a cautious yet increasingly firm pattern of guarding against enlargement of each other's role in regional affairs (in the 1990s) and outright strategic rivalry with the century's turn. In the process, the role of ASEAN has changed from one of little relevance to that of an indispensable stage on which China and Japan seek to demonstrate their respective commitments to regional community building. ASEAN is making China and Japan learn to accommodate each other, particularly over regional issues.

There is an important caveat in framing a discussion about ASEAN as a factor in the evolution of Sino-Japanese relations. Unlike the G7/8, ASEAN's annual meetings do not produce political statements on issues beyond the Southeast Asian region. Neither ASEAN as a group nor individual member states project themselves as actors that can influence the direction of change in bilateral relations between China and Japan. To the contrary, ASEAN has sought only to cope with shifts in Sino-Japanese relations and their impact on regional security and economic welfare. Moreover, ASEAN member states do not move in unison when it comes to pursuing ties with China and Japan. These factors make it difficult – indeed, virtually impossible – for ASEAN to collectively take overt positions when a major dispute between China and Japan arises. But, since the end of the Cold War, both

China and Japan have treated ASEAN as an important platform on which to conduct their regional diplomacies. Coupled with ASEAN's institutionalization of diplomatic engagement with China and Japan, a case can be made that ASEAN is increasingly becoming an indispensable environmental factor affecting the evolution of Sino-Japanese relations.

In this chapter, we first examine the evolution of Sino-Japanese relations since the end of the Cold War. In order to keep our discussion in line with the overall focus of the book, we highlight two issue areas in Sino-Japanese rivalry that impact the interests of Southeast Asian countries: human rights diplomacy, and Taiwan. Then, we examine the utility of ASEAN as a platform for Sino-Japanese diplomacy.

Post-Cold War Sino-Japanese relations: from accommodation to rivalry

Since the end of the Second World War, Sino-Japanese relations have been problematic. During the early phase of the Cold War, Japan adopted policies toward China that differed from those of its key ally, the United States, by allowing officially unofficial trade ties with China in spite of the US comprehensive embargo against China and the US demand for Japan to partake in it. Japan's pursuit of unofficial economic diplomacy with China fitted well, if only partially, with China's desire to drive a wedge between the United States and its key ally in East Asia.[1] In 1972, Japan moved swiftly to normalize full diplomatic ties with China and accommodated China's demand on the Taiwan question more readily than the United States did. But a clash of Chinese and Japanese nationalisms soon began to become a regular feature of daily diplomatic wrangling between the two governments. Throughout the 1970s and 1980s, however, the key feature of Sino-Japanese relations was one of mutual accommodation.[2]

Southeast Asia did feature in Sino-Japanese relations in this period, but only in a limited fashion. In 1978 Deng Xiaoping expressed an interest in low-interest concessionary government loans from Japan, known as ODA. Within Japan, debates arose regarding an acceptable justification for accommodating the Chinese request. Southeast Asian countries became concerned about the possibility of a concurrent decline in Japanese ODA to be dispersed to them. In 1979, the Japanese government justified granting such loans to China on the basis that it was in Japan's self-interest to support China's nascent economic reform. Japan moved to allay Southeast Asian concerns by making the amount of its ODA to China on a par with that to Southeast Asia.[3]

In other words, mutual accommodation between China and Japan was the pattern and Southeast Asian interest was a side factor. But this pattern was to change with the end of the Cold War, first over human rights as an issue of international diplomacy, and then over Taiwan.

Human rights

China's Tiananmen Square incident of 1989 ushered in the rivalry that began to characterize Sino-Japanese relations after the period of accommodation. Most of the G7 governments immediately defined the incident as a serious violation of human rights by the Chinese government against its own citizens, thereby justifying political–diplomatic sanctions by 'like-minded' industrialized states. Japan found itself caught in a dilemma. On the one hand, since the mid-nineteenth century, Japan has thrived on identifying with Western political values and accepting Western political norms in domestic politics. In other words, Japan had benefited from 'getting out of Asia' (the title of an essay written in 1885 by the Japanese sage Fukuzawa Yukichi). Logically, the Tiananmen Square incident presented Japan with a golden opportunity to solidify its status as a major 'Western power'. On the other hand, Japan's geographical proximity to China meant that it was against Japan's self-interest to take full advantage of China's situation. First, Japan had invested heavily to cultivate China as a market, in addition to Southeast Asia, as part of Japan's pursuit of 'comprehensive security'.[4] Second, China had consistently warned of a possible 'revival of Japanese militarism' and had challenged postwar Japan to live up to its moral responsibility over imperial Japan's record of invading its Asian neighbors. China's complaints concentrated on how the Japanese government dealt with its war memorials and commemorations, for example the addition of the names of fourteen class A war criminals sentenced to death by the Tokyo tribunal to the controversial Yasukuni Shrine, as well as on the questionable contents of Japanese high-school history textbooks. Southeast Asian countries have not demonstrated the same severity in criticizing Japan but instead have focused on how Japan has failed to live up to its responsibilities in compensating the survivors of wartime Japanese mistreatment of 'comfort women'. Still, China's complaints about Japan in this respect would strike a chord right across East Asia. At issue is whether or not today's Japan can assume the moral high ground in criticizing its East Asian neighbors over human rights.

Over the war record issue, China traditionally acted as the self-appointed speaker for all those Asian countries that had suffered from Japanese occupation. Although Southeast Asian countries would not engage in the same Chinese practice of criticizing a Japanese prime minister's visit to the controversial Yasukuni Shrine as an endorsement of right-wing Japanese sentiments, and by extension an endorsement of an inclination to revive Japanese militarism, they did not object to China taking issue with Japan over the Yasukuni controversy.[5] In other words, Japan would not necessarily win much sympathy or support from its Asian neighbors by demonstrating total solidarity with the United States and other G7 governments.

The 1989 G7 summit statement condemned the Tiananmen crackdown and called on its members to coordinate in applying diplomatic and

economic sanctions against China. The release of the statement indicated
Japanese consensus with a 'Western' stance on the Tiananmen issue *per
se* and on human rights in China more generally. But Japan also acted to
demonstrate dissent with the other G7 governments.

> Initially Japan emphasized the need to prevent the isolation of China while
> silently taking the same measures as the West. However, when Japanese
> leaders felt assured that China would not be isolated, their concern for Japan's
> own isolation among the Western powers became more important. Japan
> took the unequivocal step of identifying with Western values of democracy
> and human rights at the G-7 Paris Summit in July 1989. After the Summit,
> it expressed its commitment to Western human rights values with increasing
> clarity, while at the same time removing the post-Tiananmen sanctions.[6]

Although Japan acted as a bridge of sorts between China and the rest
of the G7 nations, it soon found that role a difficult one to play in the
larger East Asian context. Beginning in 1990, China launched its own
diplomatic campaign to prevent more widespread diplomatic sanction
at the UN Human Rights Commission and its Sub-commission, which
meets each spring in Geneva. After an interval of twenty-five years, the
UN decided to hold a World Conference on Human Rights in June 1993,
in Vienna. In preparation for the Conference, a regional meeting for
Asia was held in Bangkok in March 1993. China won strong and active
support from Malaysia, Indonesia, and Singapore for its positions. The
thirty-point Bangkok Declaration stated that 'poverty is one of the main
obstacles hindering the full enjoyment of human rights'. It called for the
promotion of human rights through 'co-operation and consensus, and
not through confrontation and the imposition of incompatible values'.
Part of the envisioned strategy was to democratize the UN system so
as 'to respect and ensure a positive, balanced and non-confrontational
approach in addressing and realizing all aspects of human rights'. In
addition, the Declaration: emphasized principles of respect for national
sovereignty and territorial integrity, non-interference in internal affairs
of states, and non-use of human rights as an instrument of political
pressure; reiterated that all countries, large and small, have the right to
determine their political systems; stressed the universality, objectivity, and
non-selectivity of all human rights, and the need to avoid the application
of double standards in their implementation; and recognized that while
human rights are universal in nature, they must be considered in the
context of a dynamic and evolving process of international norm setting.[7]
The Bangkok Declaration contained arguments about human rights that
were identical to the Chinese government's positions.[8] All thirty-nine
countries participating in the regional meeting, including Japan, signed it.
But Japan's delegation issued a 'strong six-point reservation' at the plenary
closing meeting. The statement explained that Japan 'joined the consensus

adopting the declaration with a spirit of cooperation and compromise, but it reserved its views and could not subscribe to several points declared'.[9]

China and its Asian allies in the diplomatic battle over human rights took their fight to the Vienna conference and thereby openly displayed their differences with Japan in its identification with Western, mainly US opposition to cultural relativism.[10] It should be noted, meanwhile, that China's exploitation of differences among East Asian governments over human rights diplomacy did not end with the UN meeting. It has since made a drive to derail US-sponsored UN resolutions criticizing China's human rights practices a centerpiece of its regional diplomacy. In contrast, Japan routinely sided with the United States in the decade-long annual diplomatic exercise until the US dropped its campaign.

The early 1990s saw Southeast Asian countries, Singapore and Malaysia in particular, asserting 'Asian values' as a means of defending themselves against criticism of human rights practices by the United States and the rest of the West.[11] China and its Southeast Asian neighbors formed a united front in arguing against the notion of the universality of human rights and, in particular, against linking assessment of a country's human rights records to access to international markets, including development aid.

Since the 1950s, Japan has been the largest aid donor to China and Southeast Asian countries. In June 1992, Japan adopted a new ODA charter to include 'full attention ... to the situation regarding the securing of basic human rights and freedoms in the recipient country'. Japan suspended ODA to Burma/Myanmar in 1988 when the military junta took control of the government through a coup. It resumed aid to Burma in 1996 and has since played the double role of siding with the United States and European countries in calling for improvement of human rights in Myanmar while at the same time continuing to provide aid.[12]

In the late 1990s, particularly after the Asian financial crisis, human rights became less prominent in everyday diplomacy between the West and China as well as Southeast Asia in general. In 1997 ASEAN expanded its membership to include Myanmar. The fact that there has been no boycott of ASEAN after it granted membership to Myanmar indicates a level of international acceptance of ASEAN's 'flexible engagement' approach. Nonetheless, over the issue of human rights, Japan and China presented sharply contrasting images to Southeast Asia. China has pursued a consistent policy in support of the status quo, while Japan has wavered. Southeast Asian countries rallied behind China over human rights in international diplomacy in the past and may again do so when the international environment changes. By way of demonstrating intra-ASEAN solidarity, ASEAN members have indicated their opposition to the pro-Western dimension in Japan's human rights diplomacy. Thus, the human rights issue has become one aspect of the strategic rivalry between China and Japan, both bilaterally and in regional diplomacy.

Taiwan

Taiwan has been a source of contention in Sino-Japanese relations since the 1895 Treaty of Shimonoseki, which annexed Taiwan to Japan during the Qing Dynasty. For the first two decades of the Cold War, Japan followed the United States in its dealings with Taiwan in international diplomacy. Then, in 1972, Japan created a diplomatic formula for dealing with the Beijing–Taipei rivalry, and extended diplomatic recognition to Beijing but kept intact all aspects of ties with Taipei, except formal diplomatic representation. The Japanese formula soon became a model for the rest of the world to follow and has withstood changes to China's external environment ever since. In a sense, the 1972 formula assisted China at least to maintain the status quo of ensuring no acceptance of Taiwan's sovereignty declaration by the overwhelming majority of member states of the UN.

The end of the Cold War did not alter the nature of the strategic relationship between China and Japan, and the mutual suspicion continued. China's suspicion of Japan was enhanced when Japan changed its post-1972 practice of not making official contact with the Taiwanese government, which could be seen as an upgrading of ties with Taiwan. Such contacts began with a high-ranking official of Taiwan's legislative body in July 1990, and soon became a source of irritation in relations between Beijing and Tokyo. In 1994 Japan proposed to invite the Taiwanese president, Lee Teng-hui, to participate in the opening ceremony of the Asian Games in Hiroshima, thereby setting off the first major post-Cold War diplomatic crisis between Beijing and Tokyo over Taiwan.

The 1995–96 Taiwan Straits crisis, when China conducted repeated live-ammunition military exercises, was a major source of concern throughout East Asia. The US–Japan joint declaration on security, signed in June 1996, and completion of the review of the Guidelines for Defense Cooperation between Japan and the United States a year later, did not originate as a joint Japan–US contingency plan for the Taiwan Straits. However, as Soeya Yoshihide argues:

> Theoretically speaking the revised guidelines can be applied to a Taiwan contingency if it is judged as affecting Japan's own security. The Japanese government has never denied this point, which is in essence what it means when it says that 'situations in the areas surrounding Japan' are a situational concept and not a geographical one.[13]

From a Japanese perspective, as Soeya continues, 'the possibility of Japan taking independent military action in a Taiwan contingency is nil unless it is directly attacked'.[14]

But from a Chinese perspective, even before the Taiwan Straits crisis and the subsequent strengthening of the Japanese–US security alliance, Japan had already begun to pursue its own agenda of reconnecting with Taiwan for political ends.[15] Granted, after the end of the Cold War, Japan was not the only country that upgraded official contacts with Taiwan. But unlike other countries, Japan has to deal with a unique and powerful legacy in Taiwan politics, and by extension China's persistent guard against Japan's role in the political tussle between Beijing and Taipei.

One of the many legacies of Japanese colonial rule in Taiwan is that a generation of the Taiwanese elite were educated in their youth to identify themselves as Japanese rather than Chinese. Ethnic identification has been a major source of societal division in Taiwanese politics, especially after the island embarked on a process of political democratization. The idea of a 'New Taiwanese' is partially informed by the notion that the Nationalist Party was an 'alien regime' in Taiwan. In addition, the Taiwanese were taught to think about their government's relationship with mainland China as a 'special state-to-state' one. The refusal to identify with China therefore strikes at the heart of the ideological core of China's reunification project. Without a shared Chinese cultural/political identity with those living in mainland China on the part of the people living in Taiwan, there can indeed be no unification to speak of.[16]

Japan today enters the scene of politics across the Taiwan Straits because a reorientation of Taiwanese history toward the formation of a non-Chinese identity finds a receptive audience among the right wing in Japanese society. Although scholars differ as to what constitutes the right wing and what actual influence it holds in Japan's China policies, it has been customary for the Chinese government and Chinese scholars to identify the Japanese right wing, as well as the Japanese administration's refusal to sanction right-wing activities, as a destabilizing factor in political relations between Tokyo and Beijing. Indeed, it is commonly understood that the right wing in Japanese politics has played a pivotal role in the high-school history textbook controversies between the two governments since the mid-1980s.[17]

The election victory of the Democratic Progressive Party in Taiwan in 2000 did not help ameliorate Chinese suspicion of Japan seeking to keep Taiwan separate from China. A key policy platform of the party is its opposition to unification with China under Beijing's 'one country, two systems' formula. Many party members would back the argument of the Taiwan Solidarity Union (the most hardcore independence group) that it was Japan that saved China from half a century of imperial Chinese rule. The logic goes, then, that Japanese annexation of Taiwan from Qing Dynasty China marked the real beginning of Taiwanese independence, which was lost again when the Chinese Nationalists under Chiang Kai-sheck moved into Taiwan in 1948.

Sino-Japanese rivalry over the Taiwan issue was escalated in February 2005, when a joint statement from a meeting of US and Japanese defense and foreign affairs ministers identified 'the peaceful resolution of issues concerning the Taiwan Strait' as a 'common strategic objective' for the bilateral alliance between Washington and Tokyo. Although the very phrase itself amounts to little more than stating the obvious, the timing of the statement was not helpful to Beijing's attempt to stabilize dynamics across the Taiwan Straits. Since the late 1980s, there has been a parallel development in cross-Straits dynamics. On the one hand, economic inter-actions have deepened, making the Chinese mainland market indispensable for Taiwan. On the other hand, the net result of Taiwanese democratization is such that there is no easy consensus within Taiwanese society about what to do about unification with China. By the second half of 2004, the Nationalist Party in Taiwan, which does not champion a policy based on a confrontational stance to the mainland, risked being permanently marginalized. Against this background, Beijing worked to reach out to the Nationalists and other opposition forces in Taiwan. In May 2005, Beijing invited the leaders of Taiwan's opposition parties to the mainland and on their tours highlighted the ties that continue to bind the mainland and Taiwan. The visits *per se* were not sufficient to resolve the long-lasting disputes across the Taiwan Straits.[18] But, viewed from the perspective of keeping the region stable, such projects are helpful. Therefore, for Japan to openly take a stance of committing itself to a joint role with the United States in supporting Taiwan cannot do anything other than deepen its strategic rivalry with China.

Taiwan and stability across the Taiwan Straits are important to East Asian security and economic prosperity. In contrast to the post-Cold War Japanese trajectory of incrementally yet firmly supporting Taiwan's separa-tion from the Chinese mainland, Southeast Asian states have chosen to accommodate China. Over the Taiwan Straits crisis of 1995–96, as Allen Whiting reports:

> ASEAN eyes China with concern but not alarm. There is no anticipation of an expansionist China seeking to take over any country by attack, subver-sion, or economic domination. Rather the fear is that territorial disputes can prompt forceful assertiveness by Beijing that will threaten individual claims and disrupt the regional environment for economic growth dependent on trade and investment.[19]

For the purpose of dealing with uncertainties across the Taiwan Straits, ASEAN's approach has been to use its 'soft power', by way of creating the ARF for socializing and constraining China from moving too far down the path of upsetting the status quo in the Taiwan Straits. Indonesia, Singapore, and Thailand in the early 1990s did respond to Taiwan's campaigns to enlarge its international profile, by agreeing to host 'holiday trips' by Lee Teng-hui. But they quickly withdrew the offer after China lodged formal protests. In the process of reacting to the Asian financial crisis of 1997, China raised objections to Taiwan taking advantage of Southeast Asian countries' dire need for outside help by offering financial assistance in exchange for upgraded diplomatic contacts. But China also acted to offer its own assistance to Southeast Asia. Perhaps more to the point is that China, by way of its nuanced reaction to the anti-ethnic Chinese riots in Indonesia, pursued its own version of 'soft power': it had no intention of taking advantage of the plight of Southeast Asian countries by using ethnic Chinese communities as a Trojan horse for interfering in the domestic affairs of Southeast Asia.[20]

In short, Taiwan remains a sore point in Chinese diplomacy both in the region and worldwide. Over the past decade, Japan has reacted by taking advantage of China's growing dependence on securing a stable external environment, and has begun asserting an unambiguous role for itself in cross-Straits relations. In contrast, ASEAN collectively and Southeast Asian countries in general have sought not to arouse Chinese ire over Taiwan.

Sino-Japanese rivalry on the rise

In May 2005, political–diplomatic tensions between China and Japan again attracted international media headlines when China's vice-premier, Wu Yi, abruptly cancelled a meeting with the Japanese prime minister the very day it had been scheduled to take place, reportedly at China's request. The direct cause for the cancellation was that Japan's prime minister, Koizumi Junichiro, had told the Japanese parliament just the day before Wu's arrival that China should 'not interfere' in the issue of his visits to the Yasukuni Shrine. Beijing deemed such a comment as Koizumi rebuffing Chinese the president, Hu Jintao, over a condition for the resumption of high-level diplomatic contacts between Beijing and Tokyo (i.e., that Koizumi would not visit the Shrine again), as Hu had requested while at the Asia–Africa summit in Jakarta, Indonesia, in late April 2005. Japan reacted to Wu's cancellation by accusing China of failing to live up to the minimum standards of international diplomacy.[21] Then, on 17 October 2005, Koizumi made his fifth visit to the Shrine since taking office. The timing of this trip was particularly unfortunate: the morning of the same day saw two Chinese astronauts returning from their space flight. The contrasting image was of Japanese leaders busy marching to the past while Chinese leaders made going into the future a priority.

At the November 2005 APEC meeting in Busan, South Korea, China made a point of not scheduling a bilateral meeting with Japan either at the foreign minister level or between the leaders of the two countries. China and South Korea also cancelled the 2005 three-way leaders' meeting while at the annual ASEAN meeting in Jakarta in December 2005. These events marked an end to the past practice of Chinese and Japanese leaders holding bilateral talks on the edge of multilateral forums. Indeed, with annual meetings of APEC and ASEAN (which had themselves evolved into multi-lateral forums from initially bilateral diplomatic arrangements), Chinese and Japanese leaders have ready forums for holding at least two rounds of bilateral talks each year. China's refusal, since 2002, either to invite the Japanese prime minister to Beijing or to send the Chinese prime minister to Tokyo has become the strongest indicator of the depth of political/diplomatic difficulties between the two governments.

China has a history of protesting against the visit to the Shrine by a Japanese prime minister. Before Koizumi was elected leader of Japan in April 2001, Japanese prime ministers usually refrained from paying public tribute at the Shrine after China's initial protest against prime minister Nakasone Yasuhiro's visit to the Shrine in August 1983. But Koizumi made a trip to the Shrine at least once a year a campaign pledge. He honored his promise by making his first visit on 14 August 2001. On 8 October 2001, he made a one-day trip to Beijing. A spokesman for the Japanese Ministry of Foreign Affairs explained Koizumi's trip in the following manner:

> The visit at this time was motivated by the recent situation between Japan and China, in particular the bilateral relationship which has been a little bit stuck, especially after Prime Minister Koizumi's visit to Yasukuni Shrine last August. In anticipation of the leaders meeting at the APEC Economic Leaders' Meeting in Shanghai [November 2001], Prime Minister Koizumi visited China in order to improve relations between Japan and China. Prime Minister Koizumi visited the Marco Polo Bridge and he also paid a visit to a museum that commemorates the Sino-Japanese War.... Overall, the visit was quite successful in bringing our relationship back on track.[22]

But bilateral diplomatic relations between Beijing and Tokyo were anything but 'back on track'. By the time Koizumi visited Beijing, the most notable issue in the 'little bit stuck' bilateral relationship was the months-long negotiations over Japan's imposition of temporary safeguard measures on imports of agricultural products from China. The measure had been imposed by Koizumi's predecessor, Mori Yoshiro, days before he was to leave office.[23] While Japan has a long history of such disputes with its trading partners, it was the first time that Japan had deviated from its decades-long abidance by principles of multilateral free trade, by applying quantitatively restricted measures on imports into Japan. In the end, China made Japan wait for a compromise until just before China's formal accession to the WTO. WTO membership would allow China to lodge a formal protest against Japan, which would mean prolonging the dispute. Since a good portion of Chinese agricultural exports to Japan resulted from Japanese investors importing their products made in China, domestic pressure in Japan was building up for the Koizumi government to back down. After all, China included competitive Japanese products in the Chinese market among its list of retaliatory measures. Viewed more broadly, Japan's dispute with China over agricultural products has more to do with the continuing process of deindustrialization in Japan. Rationally speaking, Japan has many more options than entering into protective measures against China.[24] However, when China is identified as the main contributing factor to Japan's deindustrialization, the issue becomes more complex and necessarily incurred nationalistic feelings on both sides.

The fragile nature of political relations between China and Japan soon manifested itself in two incidents that originated in North Korea. In December 2002, the Japanese coast guard opened fire on and sank a North Korean boat suspected of illegally landing in Japan. The incident took place within China's EEZ in the East China Sea. China demanded that Japan negotiate with it over terms for raising the boat and Japan found it necessary to oblige. Although the incident was essentially an irritant caused by North Korea, it certainly demonstrated to China Japan's willingness to use force, even in waters close to China.[25] As stated in Chapter 2, the incident ended as an irritant to bilateral ties between China and Japan. Moreover, against a background of increasing Sino-Japanese tensions, it was a diplomatically damaging development. Then, in May 2002, when a small group of North Korean refugees forced themselves into the compound of the Japanese consulate in Shenyang in China, Beijing and Tokyo found themselves unable to cooperate in dealing with a pressing issue that affected the interests of both countries. Instead, it was much easier for politicians and diplomats to utilize the incident to play to nationalistic sentiments in both societies.[26]

In the summer of 2004, Sino-Japanese rivalry erupted over a matter that goes directly to the heart of high politics: territorial disputes in the East China Sea. In addition to complaints about a Chinese submarine accidentally entering Japanese waters, Japan accused China of drilling for natural gas too close to its demarcation of a 'median line', which China does not recognize. At issue is the location of the Chuanxiao gas field, which China first reported to be in operation in 1995.[27]

Under UNCLOS, a coastal country can claim an EEZ extending 200 nautical miles from its shore. Both China and Japan have ratified UNCLOS. In this case, Chinese and Japanese offshore territorial claims overlap in the East China Sea. China claims the disputed ocean territory as its own EEZ, since it is part of China's natural extension of its continental shelf. Japan, on the other hand, claims the disputed ocean territory as its own EEZ, on the basis that it is within 200 nautical miles (370 km) from Japan's coast. The Chunxiao gas field is said to straddle the EEZ areas both countries claim. Diplomats of the two countries entered into several rounds of consultations, but their positions remained far apart.[28]

Although the East China Sea has been a place of territorial dispute between China and Japan since the end of the Second World War, the events of 2004 took on an added significance: China's search for energy security and Japan's perceived attempts to derail Chinese efforts to achieve energy security. Before the Chunxiao dispute arose, and from about 2002, China and Japan had entered into competition for the same Russian source of oil supply.[29] Discussions between Russia and China for a pipeline supply of oil and gas date back to 1994. The contrast between the numerous agreements for pipeline construction signed and the absence of actual action on the Russian part is indicative of the increasingly hollow nature of the Russo-Chinese strategic partnership.[30] Japan apparently prevailed over China because it was willing to finance pipeline construction within Russia.

The Chunxiao dispute, then, is indicative of the seriousness of the Sino-Japanese rivalry for a simple reason: both Chinese and Japanese oil companies operated in the same disputed waters in the early 1980s. Against the background of high oil prices and China's attempts to diversify its energy supply, Japan's protest against Chinese drilling in the East China Sea was the latest acrimonious incident in the difficult political ties between China and Japan.

Sino-Japanese rivalry culminated in China opposing Japan's bid for a seat as a permanent member in the UN Security Council. When Japan had launched a similar bid in 1994 (and failed), China was not at that time actively engaged in denying Japan's quest for recognition as a 'normal country'. In September 2004, China's opposition to the Japanese bid was put on vivid display when Chinese Foreign Ministry spokesman Kong Quan commented on Japan's bid by observing that 'the United Nations is not a board of directors. Its composition cannot be decided according to the financial contributions of its members.'[31] Kong was obviously referring to the fact that Japan pays a much larger share of contributions to the UN than China does. In March 2005, the Chinese government apparently allowed the launching of a massive Internet campaign, which collected millions of signatures, opposing Japan's bid for a permanent seat on the UN Security Council. In early April, street demonstrations against Japan in general and its UN bid in particular broke out across China. Because Japan is experiencing diplomatic difficulties with China and South Korea simultaneously over Koizumi's repeated visits to the Yasukuni Shrine, Japan's failure in its campaign at the sixtieth anniversary meeting of the UN in September 2005 was a foregone conclusion.

Kitaoka Shinichi, a former University of Tokyo professor and the Koizumi government's ambassador tasked with the specific role of winning Japan's UN bid, passionately argues that the societal movements in China were part of a grand Chinese design to deny Japan's quest for normality in international politics. To Kitaoka:

> Japan's record as a peace-loving nation over the past 60 years is unmatched. Our country has not been involved in a single war during that time, and it does not possess weapons of mass destruction. China, on the other hand, has

been involved in several armed conflicts. It possesses nuclear weapons and in fact has a number of missiles aimed at Japan. For such a country to cite the 'fear of resurgent Japanese militarism' is truly ironic.[32]

China's denial of Japan's bid for a permanent seat on the UN Security Council is the single most powerful indication of competition for regional leadership. In spite of China's impressive records of economic growth, against the background of sluggish growth in the Japanese economy, Japan is still by far a much more significant investor, trader, and aid provider than China is to Southeast Asian countries. China's claim for regional leadership rests more on the ideational front: it appoints itself as a speaker for the interests of developing countries in East Asia. Through its conduct of human rights diplomacy since the 1990s, China has demonstrated its willingness to serve as a guardian of East Asian developing countries' political interests in the proverbial East versus West conflict.

It has to be noted, however, that Sino-Japanese rivalry is as real as it is a matter for analytical interpretation. What is real is the worsening of official and public images China and Japan have presented each other since the 1990s.[33] What is also real is that, since 2001, dispute over the history issue has prevented a Japanese prime minister from being invited to China and vice versa. The absence of exchange of high-level contacts reinforces the image of a relationship in disarray and, meanwhile, provides space for more acrimonious rhetoric in both societies about each other. Arguably, difficulties in political–diplomatic relations between Japan and China at the century's turn were a continuation of the pattern of pragmatism amid passion in the 1980s.[34] In the sphere of security, China and Japan continue to stand on guard against each other. An improvement in bilateral security ties hinges as much on efforts between Beijing and Tokyo as it does between Beijing and Washington.[35] Nevertheless, the level of economic interdependence between China and Japan has deepened, parallel to the continuing search for a new paradigm of diplomatic and strategic engagement with each other. Neither history nor theory can provide an assurance that the current stalemate in bilateral diplomacy has to continue.

The ASEAN platform for Sino-Japanese diplomacy

China and Japan enlist ASEAN in regional diplomacy

From 1967, the year ASEAN was founded, to 1975, the year the United States withdrew from Vietnam, ASEAN lived under the shadow of US hegemony. The evolution of political and economic relations between China and Japan was likewise heavily conditioned by relations between China and the United States. The Nixon/Kissinger detente with China therefore created a strategic imperative for Japan to establish diplomatic relations with China in 1972. But Southeast Asia, and the momentum in regional diplomacy

ASEAN symbolized, did not feature much in either Japan's approach to China in the early 1970s, or vice versa.

In 1976, China made friendly overtures to ASEAN member states by closing radio stations based in China that had broadcast propaganda against the governments of Thailand and Malaysia.[36] China's war with Vietnam in 1979 postponed prospects for China and ASEAN to engage each other. The first formal diplomatic engagement between China and ASEAN took place in July 1991, after China had helped to engineer a cease-fire for Cambodia. Malaysia, which was hosting ASEAN's annual PMC, invited the Chinese foreign minister, Qian Qichen, as a guest. It took another five years for diplomatic relations between the two to be institutionalized.

In the mid-1990s, ASEAN began to become a serious factor for both China and Japan in their respective regional diplomacies. In spite of the Japanese emperor's visit to China in 1992 and the Japanese parliament's 'no war' resolution upon the fiftieth anniversary of Japan's surrender, China and Japan failed to reconcile their differences over Japanese commemoration of the Second World War. Worse still, the Taiwan problem was becoming a key variable in political–strategic relations between Beijing and Tokyo as well. The regional strategic environment was therefore becoming more challenging for ASEAN.

As stated at the outset of this chapter, ASEAN has not made amelioration of Sino-Japanese rivalry a key mission. But individual ASEAN state leaders have on various occasions made public their preference for improved Sino-Japanese relations. A case in point was in August 1997, when Goh Chok Tong, Singapore's former prime minister, told the Japanese prime minister, Hashimoto Ryutaro, that Japan should pursue a policy of 'constructive engagement, rather than that of containment' in dealing with China. Goh made such comments shortly before Hashimoto's visit to Beijing to commemorate the twenty-fifth anniversary of the re-establishment of Sino-Japanese relations.[37] The key issue of contention between Beijing and Tokyo was the latter's refusal to rule out Taiwan as a potential crisis area in the ongoing review of US–Japanese defense cooperation. China saw a lack of clarification on joint US–Japanese military operations 'in areas surrounding Japan' as unacceptable.

As a matter of fact, in January 1997, when Hashimoto visited Southeast Asia on the occasion of the thirtieth anniversary of the founding of ASEAN, he indicated that part of the reason for the deepening of Japan–ASEAN ties was to help integrate China into the region. In his major policy speech, Hashimoto made the following observations:

> Now that China has been following a path of modernization through its policy of reform and openness, she takes part in every arena. It is important for the rest of the world to support the policy direction and to enhance wide ranging dialogues and exchanges with the international community. I am convinced that the presence of a politically stable, economically prosperous

China, bound by ties of trust with the rest of the world, would be in everybody's interest in the Asia–Pacific and the world over.[38]

Of the three important speeches by a Japanese prime minister on tour in Southeast Asia (the other two being Fukuda's in 1977 and Takeshita's in 1989), Hashimoto's was the first to make a specific reference to China as an issue in Japan's consideration of ASEAN's role in managing regional affairs.[39] There are two possibilities for understanding the background to Hashimoto's reference. First, in 1996 ASEAN accorded China the status of full dialogue partner. This means that Japan was supporting a policy choice that had already been made. Second, in early 1997, the hand-over of Hong Kong back to Chinese sovereignty was well under way. Relations between China and the United States had yet to be put on a stable basis. It was thus in Japan's interest to enlist ASEAN as part of an effort aimed at increasing the stakes for China to live up to its own rhetoric of pursuing a foreign policy of peace in the region.

By early 1997, it was becoming obvious that China, too, had made institutionalized engagement with ASEAN an integral part of its regional diplomacy. In the wake of the Taiwan Straits crisis of 1995–96, China began to move away from its pretensions of being a global (but isolated) power and toward pursuing its goals by forging closer relations with its immediate neighbors. Southeast Asia became the arena for the Chinese leadership's cultivation of a multipolar world, in addition to the 'Shanghai Five' forum for stabilizing China's northwestern frontier.[40]

Although China and Japan commemorated their twenty-fifth anniversary of full diplomatic ties in 1997, bilateral tensions were on the rise. While other Asian countries quietly commemorated 15 August as the anniversary of the end of the Second World War, China celebrated it for Chinese victory over Japan. In particular, remembrance of the Nanjing Massacre of 1937, committed by the imperial army during its occupation of China, became an issue of contention. Statements by high-ranking Japanese officials that the massacre was a total fabrication by the Chinese did not help cool the controversy. Against this background, China's prime minister, Li Peng, took China's concerns about Japan on his visit to Malaysia. Beijing also led Asian countries in offering tacit support to Cambodia's controversial new government in 1997.[41] Since ASEAN member states were working hard to bring Cambodia into the organization, China's support of stability in Cambodia was a welcome development for ASEAN.

Meanwhile, ASEAN began to pay greater attention to interacting with the other great powers, in addition to China, across the region, for fear of China filling the perceived power vacuum after the United States downgraded its military presence in Southeast Asia. ASEAN also saw the beginning of deteriorating ties between China and Japan as a destabilizing factor.[42] As ASEAN was reaching its own thirtieth anniversary, it saw a changing regional and global environment that demanded that the organization look beyond the Southeast Asian sub-region itself.[43] ASEAN, by way of establishing its dialogue partner arrangement with China and Japan (ASEAN + 1) simultaneously and by involving such outside powers as the United States and Australia in the ARF process, began to play an informal role in making China and Japan see the potential fallout of their bilateral disputes on the rest of the region and, by extension, on their own interests in the region.

In short, by 1997, the stage was set for ASEAN, China, and Japan to begin socializing with each other in diplomatic forums. China and Japan enlisted ASEAN's support against the background of increasing tensions in their bilateral relations. ASEAN stepped into the fray because there was an opportunity for it to demonstrate its resilience in dealing with growing tensions among the larger powers in the wider East Asian region.

ASEAN provides the stage for Sino-Japanese diplomacy

One of the unintended consequences of the Asian financial crisis in the summer of 1997 was that the multilayered diplomatic forums ASEAN initiated to enlist big power support for economic recovery and strategic dialogue became an indispensable venue in which China and Japan could maintain high-level diplomatic contacts. These venues for regional diplomacy include APEC and the ASEAN + 1 and ASEAN + 3 meetings.

Exchange of high-level visits between China and Japan became less frequent after late August 1995, when Japan suspended economic loans to China in protest against China's nuclear tests. Political ties between China and Japan were further strained in 1996, when Japanese right-wing groups landed on the uninhabited Senkaku/Diaoyu Islands and with Hashimoto's visit to the Yasukuni Shrine. Still, when the annual APEC meeting was held in Manila in November, China's president, Jiang Zemin, and the Japanese prime minister held bilateral meetings during their stay. Jiang and Hashimoto tried to mend the strained ties by agreeing during their Manila talks to launch reciprocal visits (Hashimoto to China in 1997 and Jiang to Japan in 1998). Furthermore, as China's drive to join the WTO was experiencing increasing difficulties, Hashimoto expressed Japan's support for China's entry before the UK returned Hong Kong to China, on 1 July 1997.[44]

The agreed exchange of visits did materialize, but relations between the two countries took a turn for the worse. Jiang's official trip to Japan in November, the first by a Chinese head of state, was meant to usher in a new era of 'partnership of friendship and cooperation for peace and development'. The visit did result in a joint declaration on cooperation over a wide range of issues, including setting up a hot line, encouraging youth exchanges, relaxing restrictions on Chinese tourists entering Japan, and environmental conservation.[45] But the two sides failed to reach agreement on political issues because Japan would not agree to include even a single word of apology in relation to the Second World War. Since then, the issue has taken on an exaggerated importance in bilateral diplomacy.

After the Jiang visit to Japan, Japanese domestic demand was growing for its leader not to engage in 'apology diplomacy' toward China. In parallel, the Chinese leadership after the death of Deng Xiaoping found it difficult to appear soft on Japan over the issue. These factors made a repetition of the practice of using a high-level exchange of visits to mend fences increasingly difficult. But neither China nor Japan chose to let the state of affairs in their bilateral diplomatic ties stand in the way of pragmatic diplomacy. The two big powers found ASEAN's annual meetings a useful venue for high-level diplomatic contacts without incurring more domestic criticisms.

At the time of the first China–ASEAN summit, in 1997, China was simply hoping to show itself to be a reliable neighbor. By the time of the sixth ASEAN summit, in Hanoi in December 1998, the ASEAN + 3 format for regional dialogue, involving China, Japan, and South Korea, ASEAN was successfully reminding both China and Japan that there was an alternative to letting deterioration of their bilateral diplomatic ties become a growing concern to smaller powers in the region. The message was simple: if Chinese and Japanese political leaders were unable to meet in each other's capital, there was a venue for them to meet outside.

In May 2000, China invited a team of 5,000 Japanese citizens to Beijing as cultural ambassadors. Behind the fanfare was an indication of a Chinese inclination to return to the 'people to people' diplomacy approach used before the two countries established formal diplomatic ties.[46] Mori Yoshiro became the first Japanese prime minister since the two countries had established formal diplomatic ties in 1972 who did not travel to China while in office (April 2000–April 2001). Yet still, in addition to Chinese premier Zhu Rongji's trip to Japan in October 2000, Zhu and Mori met while at the annual ASEAN summit in Singapore. A major development to come out of the meeting was an agreement to formalize the informal summit among Chinese, Japanese, and South Korean leaders.[47]

Since 2001, there has emerged a pattern in Sino-Japanese diplomacy. On the one hand, there is no exchange of high-level visits to each other's capital. China insists that Japan drop its prime minister's visit to the Yasukuni Shrine as a precondition for a resumption of such contacts. Japan ignores the Chinese demand, and Koizumi made a point of refusing to conduct any 'apology diplomacy' with China, by making public trips to the Shrine at least once a year. On the other hand, China and Japan use the annual APEC and ASEAN informal summits to try to convince each other on the thorny dispute over the Shrine and its relevance to present-day bilateral relations, and by trying to find common ground on issue areas that are less divisive. Such a pattern continued until the November 2005 APEC meeting in South Korea.

Without ASEAN, or more specifically without the diplomatic forums it has created and continues to organize, Sino-Japanese ties might have been worsened even more than they did, and faster. The bilateral meetings between Chinese and Japanese leaders at ASEAN and APEC meetings have not resulted in improved diplomatic bilateral ties, but ASEAN and APEC have at least provided the necessary mechanism for both Chinese and Japanese leaders to regularly reassure each other.

ASEAN becomes the target for competition in Sino-Japanese diplomacy

Against the background of the continuation of difficulties in political diplomacy between Beijing and Tokyo, China and Japan each quickened the pace of their engagement with ASEAN. Furthermore, neither Tokyo nor Beijing allowed difficulties in their bilateral diplomacy to affect relations with ASEAN.

In the wake of the Asian financial crisis, Japan first proposed the establishment of an AMF. That proposal failed, principally because of opposition from the United States.[48] In 1999, when Singapore approached Japan with a proposal to establish a bilateral free trade agreement, Japan quickly agreed. This marks Japan's decision to replace its single-minded pursuit of multilateralism with a blend of both bilateral arrangements, such as free trade agreements, and multilateral ones.

China responded to Japan's move toward deepening economic ties with Singapore, the linchpin in economic integration within ASEAN's regional free trade area, by proposing to form the ACFTA in 2000, negotiations on which formally started in 2001, and signing an agreement on a framework for broad-ranging expansion of economic cooperation, with the ACFTA as the centerpiece, in 2002. In 2002, China also announced its decision to forgive $3 billion of debt owed to it by six of the poor ASEAN member states, thus contributing to ASEAN's effort to narrow intra-regional gaps.[49]

China's move triggered a sense of urgency in Japan to act to enlarge and deepen its own economic integration with the entire ASEAN region. As Akira Kojima observed:

> The day after China sealed its [free trade] agreement with ASEAN, Japan finally agreed to 'begin consultations' with ASEAN in 2003 on an economic cooperation agreement incorporating an FTA. Japan appears to be a step behind China, which has already decided what practical preparations it needs to make in order to implement its agreement with ASEAN. Considering it was Japan's diplomatic efforts that led to the creation in 1997 of the ASEAN + 3 dialogue framework, the objective of which was to avoid isolating China in Asia, it now looks as if China has turned the tables on Japan in terms of forging closer ties with ASEAN.[50]

If the race between China and Japan to establish free trade agreements with ASEAN still represents a competition between Beijing and Tokyo for regional influence, under the ASEAN + 3 framework China and Japan have demonstrated that they can work together on regional economic issues. After the AMF failed to materialize, the ASEAN + 3 countries continued to search for a regional mechanism that could satisfy both demands from the United States for a role by the designated lender of last resort (the IMF and World Bank) and the region's own desire for self-help (see more detailed discussion in Chapter 7).

As part of the implementation of the Chiang Mai initiative, in March 2002 China and Japan signed a bilateral currency swap agreement. Under the accord, the Chinese central bank can procure yen funds up to the equivalent of US$3 billion. Then, in May 2005, China, Japan, and South Korea, the three most influential economies in the East Asian region, agreed to increase the bilateral swap arrangements among them, thus providing a boost for the initiative's prospects.

The Chiang Mai initiative arguably affects the economic welfare of the entire East Asian region. Moreover, China and Japan have demonstrated that they can leave their bilateral differences aside when it comes to providing welfare for their smaller Southeast Asian neighbors.

On regional development issues, China and Japan do have different preferences when it comes to specific international projects involving cooperation in Southeast Asia. A case in point is the utilization of the ADB to finance infrastructure projects in continental Southeast Asia. China prefers to use ADB-funded projects as part of its scheme to upgrade the infrastructure linking southwestern Chinese provinces with localities across the border, whereas Japan sees greater merit in enhancing Southeast Asian countries' capacity for trading with Japan.[51] But Japan has not objected to China playing a larger role, including using the ADB's resources in its own infrastructure projects to improve connections within continental Southeast Asia. China even emulated Japan by financing a regional poverty-reduction fund in March 2005. The fund China donated to the ADB is small (US$20 million) compared with similar funds Japan has set up, but, by designating its fund for the promotion of regional cooperation and poverty reduction in Asia, China has made a political and diplomatic point that, as its economic power grows, China is willing to share its wealth with ASEAN and other ADB members in the same way that Japan has done.

Since the ASEAN + 3 platform was established, it has become customary for ASEAN to enlist the support of China, Japan, and South Korea in efforts to fight such non-traditional security challenges as SARS.[52] China has engaged ASEAN more actively than Japan, in part because the need for China to reassure Southeast Asia is much greater, because China is often both the source and victim of growing non-traditional security challenges in the region. On the other hand, it is significant that Japan has chosen not to let its bilateral difficulties with China adversely affect ASEAN countries' solicitation of support from China, Japan, and South Korea.

In summary, since the mid-1990s, there has emerged a parallel development in East Asian diplomacy. One the one hand, China and Japan have failed to reconcile their differences over the commemoration of the Second World War. Their bilateral relations have entered an era of rivalry. On the other hand, both China and Japan have found ASEAN a necessary framework for promoting regional community building. In the process, the various institutional mechanisms centered on the 'ASEAN way' of diplomacy have served as the alternative means by which China and Japan can pursue the pragmatic aspect of their bilateral diplomacy.

The leadership issue in East Asian community building

With Sino-Japanese relations marred by increasing rivalry, the issue of leadership in East Asian regionalism is becoming more critical. Ideally, reconciliation would be possible between China and Japan, in the same fashion as that between Germany and France in the history of the EU; this would facilitate deeper integration among the East Asian countries under discussion in this book. Unfortunately, that prospect now looks farther off, owing to the structural nature of Sino-Japanese rivalry.

Sino-Japanese rivalry is structural for at least three reasons. First, two decades of sustained Chinese economic growth has enhanced the confidence China has in the country's international role and stature. China's persistent demand for Japan to come to terms with dealing with its war history can and should be interpreted as a show of self-confidence. The Japanese economy, in spite of its decade-long record of sluggish growth, has been instrumental in the growth of the Chinese economy. In 2004, China replaced the United States as Japan's largest trading partner. Meanwhile, Japan has resisted any prospect of letting China go down the path of returning to the China-centered tributary order in East Asia. Building closer ties with ASEAN, and simultaneously living with the slow process of economic regionalization under the ASEAN + 3 framework, become a logical strategy for Japan in preserving its regional influence.[53]

Second, the Taiwan question, which has now emerged as a key rationale for the continuation of the Japan–US security alliance, stands in the way of Sino-Japanese reconciliation at the strategic level. Japan is increasingly bold in making preservation of the status quo across the Taiwan Straits a manifest duty in its security and foreign policies.[54] This new strategic environment for China is entirely opposite to the situation in the early 1970s, when Japan did not hesitate to differ from the United States in dealing with the rivalry between Beijing and Taipei. With China standing guard against Japanese involvement in the evolution of dynamics across the Taiwan Straits, it is unlikely that China will relent in keeping Japan on the defensive, including the strategy of warning the rest of the region of a revival of Japanese militarism.

Third, as China's economic ties with Southeast Asia deepen, the prospect of Japan losing its status as leader in the 'flying geese' formation of East Asian economic development (as Japan's 2001 white paper on international trade warned) is not comforting to Tokyo. Japan's baulking at free trade discussions either bilaterally with China or trilaterally with China and South Korea speaks volumes about Japanese determination not to see China getting further ahead of the pack. A free trade arrangement within Northeast Asia would allow China to benefit even more from gaps between factors of endowment between the Chinese and Japanese economies. A stronger Chinese economy can only enhance China's capacity to integrate with Southeast Asia, and, given Japan's slow record of domestic growth, this will be at a cost to Japan's market influence.

The structural nature of Sino-Japanese rivalry implies that the prospect of joint leadership over deeper economic integration in East Asia is unlikely for the foreseeable future. Indeed, for economic integration to deepen, East Asian countries have to move from the Chiang Mai initiative toward harmonization of macroeconomic policies, and of trade and investment policies. Intra-regional disparities among ASEAN member states in terms of both economic systems and levels of development are basic obstacles to overcome. However, for China and Japan to exercise leadership in the process, the two countries must first be confident in dealing with each other.[55]

Last but not least, neither China nor Japan is in a position to single-handedly provide adequate leadership in moving East Asia toward deeper integration. Anxieties about each other means ASEAN and its member states have an opportunity to choose between one of two large powers, thereby undercutting the prospect of success. China has many domestic challenges to its own stability as well as non-economic disputes with Southeast Asia; and Japan has to overcome its domestic resistance to reform, as well as its reliance on US primacy in diplomacy, which denies it a more active role in regional leadership.[56]

Conclusion

In their post-Cold War evolution, Sino-Japanese relations have followed a derivative rather than a primary pattern in East Asian international politics. The United States continues to be the provider of security for the entire region. With bilateral ties between Beijing and Tokyo deteriorating, it is ASEAN that has provided a necessary platform for bilateral diplomatic engagement between China and Japan. Beijing and Tokyo have also made ASEAN a target of competition in regional diplomacy – that is, an integral part of their bilateral rivalry. The result is that it is ASEAN, not China or Japan, that sets the pace for regional community building.

ASEAN does not ask for and in fact resists a security role for either China or Japan in Southeast Asia. Although ASEAN has been indispensable both for China and for Japan, the 'ASEAN way' of diplomacy obviously has not inspired China and Japan to improve their bilateral ties; instead, it has mainly been employed by ASEAN to expand diplomatic dynamism to Northeast Asia. ASEAN needs to engage China and Japan in order to sustain its own resilience in the region.

In short, ASEAN has emerged as the leader, while China and Japan seek merely to join with it, in community building in East Asia. Moreover, ASEAN is increasingly a stakeholder in Chinese and Japanese designs for the region. But the prospect of ASEAN being a mediator between China and Japan is still far away.

Notes

1 Soeya Yoshihide, *Japan's Economic Diplomacy with China, 1945–1978*, Oxford: Clarendon Press, 1998.
2 For a rich documentation and analysis of Japan–China relations in the 1970s, see Chalmers Johnson, 'The Patterns of Japanese Relations with China, 1952–1982', *Pacific Affairs*, 53:9 (1986), pp. 402–28.
3 Tanaka Akihiko, *ASEAN Factor in Japan's China Policy? A case study of Japan's government loans to China, 1979*, Tokyo: University of Tokyo, Department of Social and International Relations, 1988.
4 For a discussion of Japan's comprehensive security and its application in East Asia, see Akaha Tsuneo, 'Japan's Comprehensive Security Policy: a new East Asian environment', *Asian Survey*, 31:4 (1991), pp. 324–40.
5 Shibuichi Daiki, 'The Yasukuni Dispute and the Politics of Identity of Japan: why all the fuss?', *Asian Survey*, 45:2 (2005), pp. 197–215.
6 Seiichiro Takagi, 'Human Rights in Japanese Foreign Policy: Japan's policy towards China after Tiananmen', in James T. H. Tang (ed.), *Human Rights and International Relations in the Asia Pacific Region*, London: Pinter, 1995, p. 109.
7 Tan Lian Choo, 'Stop Trying Aid to Human Rights, Asian Countries Tell the West', *Straits Times* (Singapore), 3 April 1998, p. 20.
8 Andrew Nathan, 'Human Rights in Chinese Foreign Policy', *China Quarterly*, 139 (September 1994), p. 640.
9 Japan Economic News Agency, 'Asian Rights Declaration Tunes Away From Western Codes', 2 April 1993.
10 Ann Kent, *China, the United Nations, and Human Rights: the limits of compliance*, Philadelphia, PA: University of Pennsylvania Press, 1999, chapter 2.
11 Alan Chong, 'Singaporean Foreign Policy and the Asian Values Debate, 1992–2000: reflections on an experiment in soft power', *Pacific Review*, 17:1 (2004), pp. 95–133.
12 Oishi Mikio and Fumitaka Furuoka, 'Can Japanese Aid Be an Effective Tool of

Influence? Case studies of Cambodia and Burma', *Asian Survey*, 43:6 (2003), pp. 890–907.

13 Soeya Yoshihide, 'Taiwan in Japan's Security Considerations', *China Quarterly*, 165 (March 2001), p. 144.

14 *Ibid.*, p. 145.

15 Liu Jiangyong, '"Maguan Tiaoyu" Bainian Hou de Ritai Guanxi' [Japan–Taiwan Relations One Hundred Years After the Treaty of Shimonoseki], *Riben Xuekan* [Journal of Japanese Studies], June 1995, pp. 9–23.

16 Zha Daojiong, 'The Taiwan Problem in Japan–China Relations: an irritant or destroyer?', *East Asia: An International Quarterly*, 19:1/2 (2001), pp. 207–22.

17 Caroline Rose, *Interpreting History in Sino-Japanese Relations: a case study in political decision making*, London: Routledge, 1998.

18 Shelley Rigger, 'Two Visits, Many Interpretations', *Far Eastern Economic Review*, 168:5 (May 2005), pp. 35–7.

19 Allen S. Whiting, 'ASEAN Eyes China: the security dimension', *Asian Survey*, 37:4 (1997), p. 300.

20 Zha Daojiong, 'China and the May 1998 Riots of Indonesia: exploring the issues', *Pacific Review*, 13:4 (2000), pp. 557–75.

21 Mure Dickie and David Pilling, 'Japan Takes Swipe at China for Official Snub', *Financial Times*, 25 May 2005, p. 7.

22 'Press Conference on 9 October 2001', Japanese Ministry of Foreign Affairs. Report available online at www.mofa.go.jp/announce/press/2001/10/1009. html#5 (last accessed April 2006).

23 'Japan Starts Picking on China', *The Economist*, 8 February 2001, pp. 31–2. For a more in-depth analysis, see Hidetaka Yoshimatsu, 'Social Demand, State Capability and Globalization: Japan–China trade friction over safeguards', *Pacific Review*, 15:3 (2002), pp. 381–408.

24 Ito Motoshige, 'The Challenge of Deindustrialization: responding to imports from China', *Japan Echo*, 29:1 (2002), pp. 40–1.

25 Robyn Lim, 'Between Japan and China, an Irritant Named North Korea', *International Herald Tribune*, 28 January 2002.

26 Wan, Ming, 'Tensions in Recent Sino-Japanese Relations: the May 2002 Shenyang incident', *Asian Survey*, 43:5 (2003), pp. 826–44.

27 Xinhua News Agency, 'China Drills High-Yield Oil Well in East China Sea', 24 July 1995.

28 Eric Watkins, 'Japan, China in Stalemate Over Maritime Boundaries', *Oil and Gas Journal*, 102:42 (2004), p. 28.

29 Martin Fackler, 'Japan Turns to Old Foe Russia for Oil, Finding a Rival in China', *Wall Street Journal*, 17 March 2003, p. A.13.

30 Bobo Lo, 'The Long Sunset of Strategic Partnership: Russia's evolving China policy', *International Affairs*, 80:2 (2004), pp. 295–309.

31 Xinhua News Agency, 'Foreign Ministry Spokesman's Statements', 26 September 2004.

32 Kitaoka Shinichi, 'Answering China's Japan Bashers', *Japan Echo*, 32 (2005), p. 13.

33 Gilbert Rozman, 'Japan's Images of China in the 1990s: are they ready for China's Smile Diplomacy or Bush's Strong Diplomacy?', *Japanese Journal of Political Science*, 2:1 (2001), pp. 97–125; and Gilbert Rozman, 'China's

Changing Images of Japan, 1989–2001: the struggle to balance partnership and rivalry', *International Relations of the Asia–Pacific*, 2:1 (2002), pp. 95–130.

34 Allen S. Whiting and Xin Jianfei, 'Sino-Japanese Relations: pragmatism and passion', *World Policy Journal*, 10:2 (1993), pp. 27–32.

35 Wu Xinbo, 'The Security Dimension of Sino-Japanese Relations: warily watching one another', *Asian Survey*, 40:2 (2000), pp. 296–310.

36 For a description of these and other Chinese overtures, see N. Ganesan, 'ASEAN's Relations with Major External Powers', *Contemporary Southeast Asia*, 22:2 (August 2000), pp. 263–65.

37 Gwen Robinson, 'Singapore's Outspoken PM Appeals to Japan over China', *Financial Times*, 30 August 1997, p. 3.

38 Sudo Sueo, 'The Hashimoto Doctrine, January 14, 1997', in *The International Relations of Japan and Southeast Asia: forging a new regionalism*, London: Routledge, 2002, appendix III.

39 Sudo Sueo, *The International Relations of Japan and Southeast Asia*, pp. 37–9.

40 Joseph Y. S. Cheng, 'China's ASEAN Policy in the 1990s: pushing for regional multipolarity', *Contemporary Southeast Asia*, 21:2 (1999), pp. 176–204.

41 Kathy Chan, 'China's Role in Regional Affairs Grows as Beijing Attempts to Ensure Stability', *Wall Street Journal*, 28 August 1997, p. A.11.

42 Lam Lai Sing, 'A Short Note on ASEAN–Great Power Interaction', *Contemporary Southeast Asia*, 15:4 (1994), pp. 451–463.

43 Hussin Mutalib, 'At Thirty, ASEAN Looks to Challenges in the New Millennium', *Contemporary Southeast Asia*, 19:1 (1997), pp. 74–85.

44 Japan Economic News Agency, 'Hashimoto to Visit China in September, Jiang to Tokyo in '98', 16 January 1997.

45 'Japan–China Joint Declaration On Building a Partnership of Friendship and Cooperation for Peace and Development', Foreign Ministry of Japan website, www.mofa.go.jp/region/asia-paci/china/visit98/joint.html (accessed June 2006).

46 George P. Jan, 'China's Policy Toward Japan: a study of the pattern of Chinese people's diplomacy', *Asian Profile*, 1:2 (1973), pp. 261–70.

47 Japan Economic News Agency, 'Japan, China, S. Korea Leaders Agree to Meet Regularly', 23 November 2000.

48 Chang Li Lin and Ramkishen S. Rajan, 'The Economics and Politics of Monetary Regionalism in Asia', *ASEAN Economic Bulletin*, 18:1 (2001), pp. 103–17.

49 Zha Daojiong, 'The Politics of China–ASEAN Economic Relations: assessing the move towards a free trade area', *Asian Perspective*, 26:4 (2002), pp. 53–82.

50 Akira Kojima, 'How China's Bold Economic Diplomacy Affects Japan', *Japan Echo*, 30:1 (2003), p. 32.

51 There has yet to emerge a systematic study of China and Japan in the ADB when it comes to issues directly affecting Southeast Asian economies. One good case study is Donald E. Weatherbee, 'Cooperation and Conflict in the Mekong River Basin', *Studies in Conflict and Terrorism*, 20 (1977), pp. 167–84.

52 Mely Caballero-Anthony, 'SARS in Asia: crisis, vulnerabilities, and regional responses', *Asian Survey*, 45:3 (2005), pp. 486–8.

53 Otsuji Yoshihiro and Takashi Shiraishi, 'Building Closer Ties with ASEAN', *Japan Echo*, 29:2 (2002), pp. 8–12.

54 For an update on Japan's pursuit of ties with Taiwan, see Michael McDevitt,

Soeya Yoshihide, James Auer, Tetsuo Kotani, and Philip Yang, 'Japan–Taiwan Interaction: implications for the United States', *National Bureau of Asian Research Analysis*, 16:1 (2005), pp. 85–106.

55 One argument sees a 'China–Japan directional leadership' emerging. See Terada Takashi, 'Creating an East Asian Regionalism: the institutionalization of ASEAN + 3 and China–Japan directional leadership', *Japanese Economy*, 32:2 (2004), pp. 64–85.

56 Edward Lincoln, *East Asian Economic Regionalism*, Washington, DC: Brookings Institution, 2004, pp. 231–49.

Chapter 9

Conclusion: building a neighborly community

The subject matter of this book is the endeavor of post-Cold War East Asian states to build a neighborly community among themselves. We argue that East Asian community building is a multi-level, multi-layered construction process in which state cooperation and competition take place simultaneously, and the interaction between regional power politics and the regional integration process (such as ASEAN + 3 and the EAS) has given a unique trajectory to community building in East Asia. ASEAN-led, momentum-driven, multi-layered functional cooperation, centered on the ASEAN + 3 process, has shaped a neighborly community between ASEAN states and their Northeast Asian counterparts – China, Japan, and South Korea. Although structural difficulties between China and Japan do not show signs of early resolution, their bilateral problems have not hampered their participation in East Asian multilateralism. Both Beijing and Tokyo actually use the regional multilateral grouping to hedge against each other's influence in the region.

In East Asia, the US-centered regional security architecture still anchors the regional security order, but the traditional balance of power no longer characterizes the dynamics of the relations between the big powers and the small states in the region. As a matter of fact, although the United States has remained committed to providing regional security and stability, it is no longer trying to manage the course of change in intra-regional political and economic relations. In fact, since the end of the Cold War, the United States has often served as the trigger for East Asian states to seek a means to lessen their differences and to enhance regional welfare. East Asian states do not seek to challenge, collectively or otherwise, US predominance in the military sphere. But they do intend to form platforms for regional cooperation, to advance their common interests without Washington's involvement or endorsement.

A balance of influence, instead, has been redefining rules of the game in East Asian regionalism. ASEAN, as a group of small states, has played a role proportionately larger than its size would suggest in regional community building. The rise of China, more from its 'soft power' and economic clout, does pose a challenge, in different dimensions, to the United States' dominant position in East Asia. But China is nowhere close to replacing the United States' role or that of its principal ally, Japan, in East Asia. As a matter of fact, ASEAN has managed to keep regional dominance by any single power at bay.

The previous chapters have analyzed how East Asian nations cultivated intra-regional cooperation over diplomatic, economic, and social issues in the process of building an East Asian neighborly community in the post-Cold War era. Three tasks remain for this concluding chapter. The first is to reiterate and expand the major theme of the book, linking the building of a neighborly community with the 'ASEAN way' of diplomacy. The second task is to sharpen our distinction between the balance of power and the balance of influence in the multilateral community-building process, with special reference to big power relations in the region. Third, we look at the prospects for East Asian community building.

The 'ASEAN way' of community building

The process of building a neighborly community described in this book has some unique features. We believe the movement toward a neighborly community shows a specific trajectory of intra-regional diplomacy between ASEAN, China, Japan, and other East Asian states. Over the past decade and a half, an 'ASEAN-ized' pattern of intra-regional diplomacy has emerged. Within the ASEAN + 3 framework, nation-states from both Northeast and Southeast Asia have taken steady steps in regional community building. The ASEAN + 3 member states' eligibility for participation in intra-regional discussions is based on geographical proximity and political and diplomatic necessity, rather than on similarity of political systems and/or shared ideological beliefs. The Asian financial crisis of 1997 was a watershed event that compelled them to engage in deeper economic and political cooperation through regularized diplomacy at the highest level and creating forums for discussions at the functional/operational levels. This intra-regional process made it possible for an Asia-only regional structure to emerge, as envisioned by former Malaysian prime minister Mahathir bin Mohamad in 1990.

As discussed in the book, the process of building an East Asian neighborly community has been peaceful and vigorous. The dynamics of the process are quite different from those seen in Europe and North America, where big powers led and small countries followed. In East Asia, however, the small states (ASEAN and South Korea in Northeast Asia) were the driving force and the big powers (China and Japan) were following the small states' lead in regional community building. It is no exaggeration to state that small players have motivated and empowered China and Japan to participate in ASEAN-led institution building. They have initiated ideas and projects to prompt the big powers to act in the interest of the region, against pursuit of their narrowly defined national interests. Indeed, ASEAN's dialogue partnership arrangements with China and Japan have functioned to keep the two big powers engaged and informed about the small states' wish for regional stability and prosperity. Since most initiatives for regional cooperation originated in ASEAN, it has been easier for China and Japan to respond in kind, because the two big powers have less reason to see such initiatives from the prism of their bilateral political relations, which have been difficult over the past decade. In a similar vein, in Northeast Asia, South Korea has played a role much larger than its size would suggest in making APEC include China, Taiwan, and Hong Kong as equal members. It was South Korea that initiated the 'ASEAN + 3' platform when ASEAN was holding separate 'ASEAN + 1' meetings in Manila in 1999. In building the East Asian neighborly community, small states are in the driver's seat while big powers are in the rear. It is the small states that move the region toward regional community building and integration through the group diplomacy ASEAN has pursued.

The emerging East Asian grouping is still very loose by European and North American standards, but the dynamism behind the community building is quite spirited and energetic. Everyone agrees that East Asia is a very diversified region, and that explains why regionalism, especially regional institution building, is difficult to start and sustain. However, as the process of building a neighborly community over the last fifteen years indicates, nation-states in the region have finally come across a new, pertinent way to engage each with other. This 'ASEAN way' of intra-regional diplomacy is modeled on ASEAN's culture and codes of conduct, and the essence of this intra-regional engagement is consultation, mutual respect, consensus building, informality, and refraining from exerting influence and coercion over each other.

Why did the 'ASEAN way' of diplomacy work well in the East Asian community-building process? The 'ASEAN way' has long been criticized for being ineffective and inefficient, and regional integration centered on ASEAN is therefore said to be inherently weak. The ASEAN-ized consultation is said to be fragile because of the informality of meetings, the lack of infrastructure due to the fact that there is little in the way of a paper trail, and the fact that agreements are always reached on the points of principle but with no functional detail.[1] However, it is precisely because of this 'ineffective' and 'inefficient' way that ASEAN has successfully engaged the Northeast Asian big powers in regional community building, at a level they are comfortable with. Both China and Japan have come to feel comfortable with each other and with the ASEAN states in the ASEAN-led regional dialogue. To most East Asian leaders and officials, this is the greatest strength of ASEAN, and it is this asset that has allowed community building in such a vast and diversified region to take root. The beauty of ASEAN-styled consultation and consensus building as the operational modality is that it allows participating states to agree to disagree and escape sanction at the same time. To attain some form of consensus, member states in consultation pursue the lowest common denominator. There is little support for creating the type of supranational institution that exists in Europe. Within the context of consensus building, no nation-state can expect to behave in the kind of hegemonic manner the United States plays in North and South America to obtain regional cooperation. The result, then, is that the sense of regional belonging and community comes from appreciating each other's positions and policies. That appreciation, in turn, prevents the imposition of retaliatory measures when one nation-state's behavior is not in tune with other nation-states' expectations. Simply put, a nation-state functions just as a neighbor in a village: you may not like it but you have to live with it.

Through interactions based on respect and care for each other's interests and concerns, a neighborly community is taking shape in East Asia. In the early 1990s, Mahathir proposed the establishment of the EAEG to counter the development of the Western-dominated APEC forum. But a crucial participant – Japan – withheld support because of concerns that its membership would antagonize Washington, which was excluded from the EAEC. The post-1997 landscape in East Asia has been much changed. Japan's view of its own role in East Asia has shifted as well, from being a supportive partner of the United States to one seeking a more 'normal' role or even a leadership role in East Asia by itself. Tokyo's perceptional change has a great deal to do with the rise of China in the region. As a rising power, China has made swift moves in its relations with ASEAN and other Asian neighbors in recent years. Beijing's growing regional posture put great pressure on Tokyo. Against this background, economic integration and community building in East Asia has gathered momentum, and even cynics have been surprised by a series of moves in the ASEAN + 3 process and the first EAS convened in December 2005.

Balance of influence versus balance of power

Having explained why and how the 'ASEAN way' of diplomacy has facilitated regional community building in East Asia, another major task of this book has been to address how regional states have managed or alleviated the traditional power struggle between Japan, China, and the United States as they were moving on a course of building a regional neighborly community. We argue that East Asian community building is a complex process in which big power competition may correlate with their cooperation. Contrary to the realists' prediction, the East Asian community-building process has demonstrated that the balance of influence matters more than the traditional balance of power in today's East Asian politics. This book has shown how and why Sino-Japanese rivalry and Sino-US power competition have not ruined the process of building a neighborly community since the end of the Cold War.

The post-Cold War East Asian community-building exercise is considered slow and largely ineffective by American and European standards, but one of the significant effects it has produced is to keep big power rivalry between China and Japan in check. After the Cold War's end, diplomatic difficulties and political tension between China and Japan became a structural problem by nature. The persistent trouble over commemoration of the Second World War is just one of the most obvious dimensions of this structural problem. Underlying the problem is the fundamental power competition between China and Japan in East Asia, as seen from the middle of the nineteenth century. As China rises in the region today, how Japan and China should face each other in this changing strategic landscape is becoming one of the dominant themes in Asian international politics, and most people believe an intensifying Sino-Japanese power rivalry in the region is inevitable. However, the growing tension and political frictions between the two countries did not significantly hinder the regional community-building process. Ironically, precisely because Sino-Japanese rivalry keeps resurfacing, both countries find it necessary to respond favorably to ASEAN's initiatives for cooperation in the region.

Since the Asian financial crisis in 1997, regional cooperation under the ASEAN + 3 framework has advanced smoothly from bilateral free trade agreements and currency swap arrangements to the control of infectious diseases like SARS and avian flu. This multi-layered functional cooperation, on the one hand, mirrors the nature of multi-level and multilateral governance problems in the region, and, on the other hand, creates opportunities for regional cooperation not just between ASEAN states, or between China and ASEAN or Japan and ASEAN, but also among the '+ 3' countries themselves, as they hold meetings on the sidelines of the ASEAN + 3 summit every year.[2] ASEAN + 3 has become a good platform on which Beijing and Tokyo can engage with each other in regional cooperation, as opposed to breaking away from the regional community. By participating in the regional forum, both China and Japan can keep their options open and not be left out of the regional organization process. Without the ASEAN + 3 forum, the political atmosphere for Sino-Japanese relations might have become even worse. The bilateral meetings between Chinese and Japanese leaders at the ASEAN + 3 summit and APEC meetings have not led to any great improvement in bilateral relations. But

226

ASEAN + 3 and APEC do provide the necessary mechanism for both Chinese and Japanese leaders to regularly reassure each other and to discuss their common policy concerns.

Today's Sino-Japanese rivalry is not exactly the same as that of more traditional power competition in the nineteenth and twentieth centuries. Instead of a traditional balance of power, Sino-Japanese rivalry is more a matter of a 'balance of influence' in the regional arena. Both want to expand their influence, not military power, to Southeast Asia. They may present their respective acts of regional cooperation as a mode of competition, but neither can afford to upset regional stability for the fear of losing ASEAN's support. On the one hand, both China and Japan have tried to enlist ASEAN's support against the background of increasing tensions in their bilateral relations. On the other hand, both powers want to use the regional multilateral diplomatic platform to hedge against each other's influence in the region. The US–Japanese alliance helps to prolong the Sino-Japanese rivalry, as it makes it difficult, if not impossible, for either China or Japan to become the regional hegemon in East Asia. It also prevents China and Japan from exercising joint leadership in the region. Thus the most likely engine of regional diplomacy continues to be ASEAN. Against this backdrop Sino-Japanese rivalry is more about a subtle balance of influence in the region, rather than a traditional struggle for regional hegemonic dominance. Rivalry of this nature, instead of disrupting regional cooperation, will likely allow East Asian states to continue living in peace and building a neighborly community.

From the 1970s to the mid-1990s, Japan enjoyed a *de facto* leadership role in the East Asian region, mainly through its economic strength. Japan's growing economy and massive foreign direct investment in the region became the invisible hand in regional economic integration. However, with China's increasingly visible rising status in the region since the mid-1990s, Beijing has become a more significant driving force for regional economic integration, and this has made Tokyo rethink its role in East Asia. Before that, Japan's regional thinking was anchored more in the Asia–Pacific framework, rather than a grouping of only East Asian countries. The rise of China and its growing influence in regionalization have compelled Tokyo to be more positive about joining an East Asian community, and to face the challenge of a future Chinese leadership role in the region. However, the structural nature of Sino-Japanese rivalry implies that the prospect of joint leadership for deeper economic integration in East Asia is quite unlikely, at least for the foreseeable future. In regional community building, ASEAN states have thus become the target for Beijing and Tokyo to win over to their side. Against the background of their continuing political difficulties, China and Japan have each quickened the pace of their engagement with ASEAN. Neither Beijing nor Tokyo would allow difficulties in its bilateral diplomacy to affect its engagement with ASEAN. Both have found ASEAN a necessary podium for promoting regional community building and contending for the future leadership role. In the process, the various institutional mechanisms centered on the 'ASEAN way' of diplomacy have served as an alternative means for China and Japan to pursue the pragmatic aspect of their bilateral diplomacy. As ASEAN has taken the liberty to lead the multilateral community-building process, it has increasingly become a key stakeholder in Chinese and Japanese designs for the regional community.

Regional interactions leading to the making of a neighborly community are going to have a life of their own in the foreseeable future. The process of building a neighborly community will not overcome Sino-Japanese bilateral disputes or even conflict, but it adds a layer of precaution for both countries when they think about whether to escalate them. It is not in their interest to have their bilateral problems get out of control. Although ASEAN as a group has not taken up lessening Sino-Japanese rivalry as a key mission, individual ASEAN state leaders have on various occasions made public their preference for an improvement in Sino-Japanese relations. We believe the regional institution building would hold China and Japan together in a long-term process of regionalization. Yet, the prospect of East Asia reaching the level of regional institutionalism of the EU will be a very long one.

Turning to Sino-US power relations in East Asia, we believe there is a 'quiet' but vital power transition taking place in East Asia after the Cold War. Although the construction of a neighborly community did not and will not fundamentally undermine the present deep-rooted regional security structure, it will definitely affect the operation of the existing system in the region. In the security sphere, the US 'hub and spoke' alliance structure in East Asia has dominated regional security affairs since the Second World War, and Washington's reliance on the security architecture is likely to continue as well. Although the Washington-centered structure has been conducive to regional security and stability since it was established, it is not sufficient to prevail over the whole Asia–Pacific region after the Cold War. The 'hub and spoke' architecture was a Cold War product and some major powers, like China and Russia, have been kept outside of it. As China rises in the regional political economy and new forms of multilateral regional institutions are taking shape, the Washington-dominated regional security order is increasingly challenged.

Nevertheless, although the rise of China does pose a challenge to Washington's predominant role in the region, it is mainly in economic and political dimensions, rather than in the regional security order, where the United States is still in a dominant position. The reason why the rise of China in power so far has not caused any head-on confrontation with Washington is in terms of 'balance of influence', not in the traditional 'balance of power'. Correlating directly with US continuous influence and power in the region, Beijing increasingly uses its 'soft power' or uses its power 'softly' to expand its influence in the region. As a result of this 'soft' competition, the US and China have avoided open confrontation in the region. To use a senior Singaporean leader's words, 'The balance of influence in this region is shifting rapidly to China – not yet the balance of power, but the balance of influence'.[3] The rise of China is cutting into the US 'sphere of influence' in economic and political dimensions, where Washington has done little and is less capable to defend it. To use Joseph Nye's term, the increase in Chinese regional influence is largely in 'soft power', not in traditional military power. Nye argues that power competition and the agenda of world politics have become like a three-dimensional chess game: on the top board are classical interstate military issues, in which the United States is likely to remain the only superpower for some years to come. However, on the middle board, of interstate economic issues, the distribution of power is already multipolar. On the bottom board, of transnational issues, power is widely and chaotically distributed between state and non-state actors.[4] With such a scheme it is not difficult to figure out how China can cut into the US 'sphere of influence' in East Asia. For the Chinese leadership it is not in China's interest to have a head-on confrontation with Washington, at least not at present. China's active promotion of regional community building cuts into the US 'sphere of influence' because it did not call for a head-on confrontation with Washington. There is still room for both Beijing and Washington to retain and develop a 'communal space' in Asia–Pacific regional affairs. In this region there is no single issue that does not involve the United States and China, and they have opportunities for both cooperation and conflict. Whether Washington and Beijing can cooperate in regional affairs, exemplified in the Six Party Talks on the North Korean nuclear issue, is vitally important for regional stability and peace.

Major power relations affect regional security, and the regional order is shaped by multilateral regional institution building as well. Driven by strong economic forces and interdependence, East Asian regional cooperation in political and other social dimensions is growing amazingly fast. Given its role as a regional economic powerhouse, China has for the past decade taken over Japan's role as the center of regional economic integration and interdependence. With the Japanese economy on a more certain path of recovery at the time of the writing (January 2006) – which cannot be expected to be sustained without a stable bilateral economic relationship with China – we see the prospect for market-based competition between China and Japan. This, in turn, will be a healthy development for the rest of the region.

In short, the emergence of a multilateral institutional architecture growing out of the ASEAN + 3 process has promoted the sharing of a new set of norms and rules by countries in the region, which is different from that which originated in the Cold War era. In the competition for regional 'influence', not for regional 'power', China's growing economic clout and its good neighborliness policy are giving it an edge in the competition. That is why the Japanese leaders have realized that Japan cannot afford to be left out of the community-building process, and it must gear up its competition for 'influence' with China in the region.

Looking ahead: an East Asian community?

In its report *Toward an East Asian Community* submitted to the fifth ASEAN + 3 summit in Brunei in November 2001, the EAVG envisions an East Asia 'moving from a region of nations to a bona fide regional community where collective efforts are made for peace, prosperity and progress'. The report emphasizes that 'The economic field, including trade, investment, and finance, is expected to serve as the catalyst in this community-building process'.[5] This is so far the most unambiguous declaration of the vision for building an East Asian community.[6] The vision was endorsed by the ASEAN + 3 leaders in November 2001, and it was later further articulated and validated by an EASG study in 2002. The 2002 EASG report provided an overall assessment of the EAVG's recommendations and identified high-priority concrete measures and their implications for East Asian community building.[7] From the ASEAN + 3 leaders' endorsement of these two reports, we can see the East Asian leaders' political will for an East Asian community was clear but the roadmap and substantive steps for achieving the goal are not yet in place. The achievement of this goal would of course take the ASEAN + 3 to a much more advanced stage of neighborly community than we have described here. Furthermore, the multi-level and multi-layered construction process would greatly contribute to regional prosperity and preventing conflict among East Asian nations. It would also help to bolster the identity of an East Asian community in world affairs and to promote regional peace through cooperation, especially between big powers in the region.

As discussed in the preceding chapters, building an East Asian community as envisioned by the EAVG would not be an easy task, given the region's great diversities, large gaps in levels of economic development, and the lack of a mechanism for regional cooperation in Northeast Asia. Yet, in building the regional community, East Asian states have taken some major steps since 1997 in forming regional arrangements and functional cooperation within the framework of ASEAN + 3. These steps have led them to make an important decision in further pushing forward the idea of an East Asian community at the ASEAN + 3 summit in Laos in November 2004. This important decision was to hold the first ever EAS in Kuala Lumpur on 14 December 2005, and invite three additional countries, India, Australia, and New Zealand, to join in, in an ASEAN + 3 + 3 format.[8] With an enlarged membership beyond the ASEAN + 3, does this mean the East Asian leaders agreed to transform the current ASEAN + 3 framework into an East Asian Summit format? Does it represent a step in the right

230

direction of moving community building forward? Will the EAS complicate or facilitate the building of an East Asian community?

The first EAS meeting resulted in little more than confirmation of the value of an ASEAN-led process of discussion. In future, with its enlarged membership, we believe the EAS will pose at least three major challenges for East Asian community building. First, there is a 'vision problem': there are two competing visions of East Asian community building. One path for future community building is embedded in the APEC design, which embraces a larger Asian Pacific community, including the United States, Canada, Australia, New Zealand, and possibly even Latin American states. The other is the East Asian-only grouping, symbolized by the ASEAN + 3 process, which is being developed into a loose East Asian *only* community. The second challenge is that, besides different visions, there are also different models or forms of institution. Should they follow the EU model and transfer national sovereignty to a supranational structure? Or should they continue traveling down the present path and develop an informal and loosely organized community based on consultation and cooperation, while carefully guarding their national sovereignty? The third challenge is, looking further down the road, who will play the leadership role in East Asian community building, China, Japan, or ASEAN? Can the big powers continue to rely on the small states to push forward regional institution building?

The vision problem

To many people, the EAS is an important stepping stone to the creation of an East Asian community. However, for the future course of regional community building, East Asian leaders have to settle on whether the future East Asian community should have non-East Asian member states, especially the United States. The leaders from India, Australia, and New Zealand were invited to the first EAS in December 2005 and the United States was not. Technically, Washington was not invited because, according to the criteria set by ASEAN, all participating states in the EAS must meet three conditions to be eligible. These three conditions were: accession to the ASEAN TAC, a full dialogue partnership status with ASEAN, and considerable trade ties and interest in the region. Washington meets the last two conditions but it did not and probably will not sign the TAC.

The issue of membership of the EAS does not necessarily settle future East Asian community building on any particular course, but it does affect the dynamics of the community-building process. Washington was not happy about being excluded from the first EAS, although it did not show strong annoyance about it. Thus far Washington has not shown much reaction to the idea of an East Asian community, because it is preoccupied with efforts to overcome global terrorism and with developments in Iraq. In addition, the US has not taken the development seriously because there still are problems between China and Japan, despite their increased economic ties. On the other hand, the United States has some of its closest allies in the grouping and the chance of its interests being neglected by EAS participants is low. Washington's most trusted regional ally, Japan, has already raised the issue of 'open regional cooperation' in the ASEAN + 3 process. Tokyo believes, on the basis of the fundamental principle of 'open regional cooperation', that the basic approach to regional community building should be a functional one, with 'respect for and observation of universal values, including freedom, democracy, and human rights, and global rules, and so on'.[9] Tokyo's idea for future community building is obviously distinct from what Beijing has in mind, although there has not yet been an open debate on the issue.

The membership of any future East Asian community has a great deal to do with what a member can bring to the community, if geographic location is not the only criteria for eligibility. Like Australia, New Zealand, and India, the United States has a deep 'footprint' in East Asia, from its vested interest in regional economic, political, and security affairs, and even much stronger economic ties than the other three countries. Thus an East Asian community, viewed from a geostrategic perspective, should not leave Washington out of the regional organization. If the EAS and a future East Asian community are to play a role in the security realm, such as global anti-terrorism and the non-proliferation of weapons of mass destruction, it does not seem to make sense to have India, Australia, and New Zealand in, and the US out. Most East Asian states still believe the US is the guarantor of peace and stability in the region. Thus, how to associate Washington with the East Asian community building is an issue the regional leaders cannot get around.

However, although a broadened membership beyond the ASEAN + 3 could keep a balance among key members in an East Asian community, it would be self-defeating for some ASEAN + 3 states to make just another APEC type of regional forum. For these states, the idea of the EAS is to formally replace the 'ASEAN + 3' framework, thus forging a longer-term Asian-only economic, social, cultural, and political community so as to 'balance' the United States, Europe, and other emerging entities and group-ings. In this light it does not make sense to bring the United States in, and ASEAN + 3 should continue its course of community building in parallel with the APEC process. A broadened regional forum, as seen in the first EAS, should not hinder future substantive development of the ASEAN + 3 process. The EAS should just be a platform for consultation and dialogue on more general and strategic issues, not for functional cooperation-driven community building.

Given the nature of a multilateral and multi-layered construction, East Asian community building is bound to be complex, and the vision problem will not be solved in the short run. East Asia has seen the establishment of many regional institutions at the government and non-governmental levels. At the end of the 1960s, the Pacific Basin Economic Cooperation was formed by regional business leaders, and it was followed by a tripartite process, the Pacific Economic Cooperation Council. Yet, after the Cold War, the most influential and comprehensive regional intergovernmental organization, APEC, was established. These organizations all started with a vision of the creation of an Asia–Pacific community, and their institutionalization processes were developed in a gradual, step-by-step fashion. This was seen as a necessary, pragmatic way to regional community building, given that the region is so diverse and unorganized. When those regional institutions were not able to help the region to overcome the financial crisis of 1997, they lost a lot of credibility. Since then, all of them, including the ARF and APEC, have gone through a process of change and adjustment to reorient their mission and vision. Sub-regional institutions, such as ASEAN, are facing the same challenges. The first EAS did not solve the vision problem, and, instead, it just added a new layer of institutionalized dialogue to the existing regional forums.

Which model?

Mahathir's EAEC proposal was designed to build an Asia-only regional community in response to the rival EU and NAFTA. As a response to the Asian financial crisis, the ASEAN + 3 process mainly promotes functional cooperation among states, and the region is still weak in forming and empowering a common identity. Regional identity requires cultural as well as normative elements to be shared by all states. As some scholars point out, the driving force behind East Asian regionalism is nationalism. Compared with European regionalism, the East Asian version lacks a convincing and acceptable normative framework for regional institutionalization.[10] The further growth of Asian regional institutional building will be constrained by East Asian countries' persistent concerns regarding erosion of their national sovereignty. It would be difficult for these states to give up their sovereignty for a regional order and a supranational structure which looks after regional security.

Moreover, regional cooperation and community building are not just about free trade, exchanges of goods and services, or security dialogue. In the EU case, a common ideology and shared concepts of democracy, human rights, individual freedoms, and the rule of law constitute the normative foundation of its regionalism and regional institutions. Measured by this yardstick, a *bona fide* East Asian community is a long, long way away.

The leadership challenge

The direction of future East Asian community building depends on who is going to lead the process. As East Asia moves further toward community building, the leadership problem will become more intense. The leadership challenge can be viewed in three dimensions. The first dimension concerns ASEAN's own unity and capacity to lead. Based on the vision set out in ASEAN's Concord II,[11] the organization has just embarked on a more in-depth integration and community-building process, which includes building an ASEAN Security Community, an ASEAN Economic Community, and an ASEAN Socio-cultural Community.[12] The goal of Concord II is to make ASEAN more coherent and more integrated. Without internal cohesion and strength, ASEAN would not be able to act together and lead the big powers in regional institution building.

The second dimension is whether East Asia should have two processes with the same purpose, namely ASEAN + 3 and the EAS, and whether ASEAN can still steer the two mechanisms for the purpose of community building. There is no doubt ASEAN has played the leadership role in the ASEAN + 3 process. But will ASEAN continue to lead the EAS and a future East Asian community? What is its legitimacy for doing so? With the regular EAS and ASEAN + 3 in place, the two processes would be redundant, and the presence of two such bodies might even be counterproductive. The centrality of ASEAN is likely to be diluted in the process of building an East Asian community. The idea of an East Asian community based on the ASEAN + 3 + 3 model is not the same as the one envisioned by Mahathir back in 1990. ASEAN + 3 now face new challenges and new realities. Whether a future East Asian community should be embedded in APEC or be strictly an extension of the ASEAN + 3 process is a formidable challenge for ASEAN as well as for the three Northeast Asian states. No matter which one prevails (APEC or an East Asian-only community), the ASEAN + 3 process would need to redefine and relocate its role in regional community building and it would require more leadership responsibility than ASEAN could provide.

The third dimension is, given their current bilateral problems, whether Japan and China are likely to continue and even intensify their competition for the regional leadership role. Under the ASEAN + 3 framework, leadership is being provided by ASEAN. However, in the EAS the ASEAN members are represented separately; ASEAN's leadership role is therefore likely to diminish, and the leadership role will be taken over by the big powers.[13] At the present stage, the ASEAN + 3 countries expect ASEAN to be in the driver's seat, and respect its leadership. But how long that will last? The big powers (the '+ 3' countries) are unlikely to let it continue indefinitely, and would eventually ask ASEAN to pay due attention to their opinions. It is not difficult to imagine the big powers eventually taking the leadership role, either individually or via a co-chair arrangement in agenda setting, and then the EAS being held outside the ASEAN region.

According to the EASG's recommendations in its final report of 2002, pursuing 'the evolution of the ASEAN + 3 Summit into an East Asian

Summit' was a medium-term and long-term measure, and the first EAS was not supposed to take place in the short run, at least not before 2010.[14] Yet, the premature arrival of the first EAS in December 2005 put community building on a faster track than expected, and thus created confusion and complications for regional leaders. East Asian leaders will need some time to sort out priorities on their agenda, and to discuss principles and basic approaches to future regional cooperation and institution building. In our view, although ASEAN + 3 will continue to be the engine for regional functional cooperation and community building, while the EAS is a forum for engaging other countries in general strategic dialogue, whether the EAS and ASEAN + 3 process prove to be complementary or duplicating and countervailing will be a defining issue. More importantly, the growing intensification of Sino-Japanese rivalry for regional leadership, as well as the question of additional members in the EAS, will complicate, if not derail, the existing ASEAN + 3 process, and this will greatly test ASEAN's wisdom and leadership role in the years to come.

Notes

1 Anthony L. Smith, 'ASEAN's Ninth Summit: solidifying regional cohesion, advancing external linkages', *Contemporary Southeast Asia*, 26:3 (2004), p. 421.

2 In protest against the visit of the Japanese prime minister, Junichiro Koizumi, to the Yasukuni Shrine, the Chinese and South Korean leaders boycotted their meeting with their Japanese counterpart at the December 2005 ASEAN + 3 summit. The Chinese Foreign Ministry spokesman later stated that the meeting was 'suspended', with the implication that such meetings would be resumed when the political atmosphere changes.

3 Cited by Clyde Prestowitz, 'The Great Reverse – Part I: after two centuries of Western domination, China and India are poised to claim their places', *Yale Global*, 2 September 2004.

4 See Joseph Nye, Jr, 'U.S. Power and Strategy After Iraq', *Foreign Affairs*, 82:4 (2003), pp. 60–73.

5 The EAVG report *Toward an East Asian Community* is available online at the ASEAN Secretariat's website, www.aseansec.org/pdf/east_asia_vision.pdf (last accessed April 2006).

6 In the EAVG report, the 'bona fide regional community' is still a vague concept, referred as 'an East Asian community', not 'East Asian Community'.

7 EASG, *Final Report of the East Asian Study Group*, ASEAN + 3 Summit, 4 November 2002, Phnom Penh, Cambodia. Available online at the ASEAN Secretariat website, www.aseansec.org/pdf/easg.pdf (last accessed April 2006).

8 It was also agreed that the inaugural EAS in Malaysia would be followed by a second summit held in China, but later the idea was quietly dropped. This was because the choice of venue for the second EAS was considered by some ASEAN + 3 states as giving China the edge in becoming one of the 'core

members' of the East Asian integration process. Japan, as well as an 'outsider', India, had long hoped to lead or at least co-lead (with China) the regionalization process.

9 Japanese Ministry of Foreign Affairs, 'ASEAN + 3 Foreign Minister Meeting (Summary)', 28 July 2005. Available online at www.mofa.go.jp/region/asia-paci/asean/conference/asean3/summary0507.html (last accessed April 2006).

10 See, for example, Baogang He, 'East Asian Ideas of Regionalism: a normative critique', *Australian Journal of International Affairs*, 58:1 (2004), pp. 105–25.

11 On Concord II, see Chapter 5, and for the full text, see www.aseansec.org/15159.htm (last accessed April 2006).

12 Anthony L. Smith, 'ASEAN's Ninth Summit', pp. 422–7.

13 'Challenges of Building an East Asian Community', *Jakarta Post*, 7 April 2005.

14 See EASG, *Final Report of the East Asian Study Group*. According to the report (p. 50), the EASG is of the view that 'as a long-term desirable objective of the ASEAN + 3, the EAS will serve to strengthen regional cooperation in East Asia ... the ASEAN + 3 framework remains the only credible and realistic vehicle to advance the form and substance of East Asian cooperation ... the EAS should be part of an evolutionary and step-by-step process. To ensure the broadest level of acceptance, there is a need to gradually build up a similar comfort level among ASEAN countries, China, Japan, and Korea.'

Select bibliography

Abramowitz, Morton and Stephen Bosworth (2003). 'Adjusting to the New Asia', *Foreign Affairs*, 82:4, pp. 119–31.

Acharya, Amitav (1997). 'Ideas, Identity and Institution-Building: from the ASEAN to the "Asia–Pacific way"?' *Pacific Review*, 10:3, pp. 319–46.

—— (2000). *The Quest for Identity: international relations of Southeast Asia*, Singapore: Oxford University Press.

—— (2002). *Regionalism and Multilateralism*, Singapore: Times Academic Press.

—— (2003). 'China's Charm Offensive in Southeast Asia', *International Herald Tribune*, 8–9 November.

AFP and Carina I. Roncesvalles (2005). 'RP and China to Hold Annual Defense Talks, Swap of Cadets', *Business World* (Manila), 24 May.

Aggarwal, Vinod K. and Charles E. Morrison (eds) (1998). *Asia–Pacific Crossroads: regime creation and the future of APEC*, New York: St Martin's Press.

Ahmad, Hamzah (1997). *The Straits of Malacca: a profile*, Kuala Lumpur: Pelanduk Publications and Maritime Institute of Malaysia.

Akaha, Tsuneo (1986). 'Japan's Response to Threats of Shipping Disruptions in Southeast Asia and the Middle East', *Pacific Affairs*, 59:2, pp. 255–77.

—— (1991). 'Japan's Comprehensive Security Policy: a new East Asian environment', *Asian Survey*, 31:4, pp. 324–40.

Akrasanee, Narongchai and Apichart Prasert (2003). 'The Evolution of ASEAN–Japan Economic Cooperation'. Paper available online at the Japan Center for International Exchange website, www.jcie.or.jp/thinknet/pdfs/asean_narong-chai.pdf (last accessed April 2006).

Allen, Kenneth W. (2001). 'China's Foreign Military Relations with Asia–Pacific', *Journal of Contemporary China*, 10:29, pp. 645–62.

Almonte, Jose T. (1997). 'Ensuring Security the "ASEAN Way"', *Survival*, 39:4, pp. 80–92.

Amer, Ramses (1994). 'Sino-Vietnamese Normalization in the Light of the Crisis of the Late 1970s', *Pacific Affairs*, 67:3, pp. 357–83.

An Xiaohui (2000). 'Xinjiapo "Haidao Duice Huiyi" Jishi' [Report on the 'Measures

Bibliography

Against Piracy at Sea Conference' in Singapore], *Renmin Gong'an* [People's Public Security], December, pp. 11–12.

APEC Economic Leaders' Meeting, Santiago Declaration: 'One Community, Our Future'. Santiago, Chile, 20–21 November 2004.

Aquino, Norman P. (2001). 'GMA Kicks Off China Visit', *Business World* (Manila), 30 October.

Arase, David (1993). 'Japanese Policy Toward Democracy and Human Rights in Asia', *Asian Survey*, 33:10, pp. 935–52.

Askandar, Kamarulzaman, Jacob Bercovitch and Mikio Oishi (2002). 'The ASEAN Way of Conflict Management: old patterns and new trends', *Asian Journal of Political Sciences*, 10:2, pp. 21–42.

Auer, James E. and Robyn Lim (2002). 'The Maritime Basis of American Security in East Asia', *Naval War College Review*, 54:1, pp. 39–58.

Austin, Greg and Stuart Harris (2001). *Japan and Greater China: political economy and military power in the Asian century*, Honolulu: University of Hawaii Press.

Australian Government (2004). *ASEAN and Australia: celebrating 30 years*, Canberra: Department of Foreign Affairs and Trade.

Austria, Benjamin S. and Raymundo A. Reyes Jr (1992). 'Possibilities of W. Bantagas Basin in Philippines South China Sea', *Oil and Gas Journal*, 90:23, pp. 79–81.

Bangsberg, P. T. (1999). 'China Sentences 13 to Death in Hijacking Case', *Journal of Commerce*, 23 December, p. 14.

Barker, Geoffrey (2003). 'APEC Heads Unite in War on Terror', *Australian Financial Review*, 22 October, p. 1.

Barnett, A. Doak (1981). *China's Economy in Global Perspective*, Washington, DC: Brookings Institution.

Bergsten, C. Fred (2001). 'America's Two-Front Economic Conflict', *Foreign Affairs*, 80:2, pp. 16–27.

Bert, Wayne (1993). 'Chinese Policies and U.S. Interests in Southeast Asia', *Asian Survey*, 33:3, pp. 317–32.

—— (2003). *The United States, China and Southeast Asian Security: a changing of the guard?*, London: Palgrave.

Betts, Richard K. (1993). 'Wealth, Power and Instability: East Asia and the United States after the Cold War', *International Security*, 18:3, pp. 34–77.

Bian, Shen (2003). 'New Opportunity for China–ASEAN Trade', *Beijing Review*, 1 May, pp. 18–19.

Blanchard, Jean-Marc F. (2000). 'The U.S. Role in the Sino-Japanese Dispute over the Diaoyu (Senkaku) Islands, 1945–1971', *China Quarterly*, 161, pp. 95–123.

Booth, Anne (1999). 'Initial Conditions and Miraculous Growth: why is South East Asia different from Taiwan and South Korea?', *World Development*, 27:2, pp. 301–21.

Borthwick, Mark (1992). *Pacific Century: the emergence of modern Pacific Asia*, Boulder, CO: Westview Press.

Bradford, John F. (2004). 'Japanese Anti-Piracy Initiatives in Southeast Asia: policy formulation and the coastal states' responses', *Contemporary Southeast Asia*, 26:3, pp. 480–504.

British Broadcasting Corporation (1979). 'USSR Criticizes Japanese Position on PRC–SRV Conflict', 8 March.

Broinowski, Alison (ed.) (1990). *ASEAN into the 1990s*, London: Macmillan.

Brooke, Micool (2002). 'Balancing Act', *Armed Forces Journal International*, March, pp. 38–43.

Buckley, Roger (2002). *The United States in the Asia–Pacific Since 1945*, Cambridge: Cambridge University Press.

Business World (Manila) (1994). 'RP–China Spratlys Study', 21 September, p. 1.

Busse, Nikolas (1999). 'Constructivism and Southeast Asian Security', *Pacific Review*, 12:1, pp. 39–60.

Caballero-Anthony, Mely (2005). 'SARS in Asia: crisis, vulnerabilities, and regional responses', *Asian Survey*, 45:3, pp. 486–8.

Calder, Kent (1996). 'Asia's Empty Tank', *Foreign Affairs*, 75:2, pp. 55–69.

Carino, Theresa C. (ed.) (1998). *China–ASEAN Relations: regional security and cooperation*, Quezon City: Philippine–China Development Resource Center.

Carlson, Allen (2004). 'Helping to Keep the Peace (Albeit Reluctantly): China's recent stance on sovereignty and multilateral intervention', *Pacific Affairs*, 77:1, pp. 9–28.

Catley, Bob (1999). 'Hegemonic America: the arrogance of power', *Contemporary Southeast Asia*, 21:2, pp. 157–75.

Catley, Bob and Makmur Keliat (1997). *Spratlys: the disputes in the South China Sea*, Aldershot: Ashgate.

Chairman's Press Statement of the Sixth ASEAN+3 Foreign Ministers Meeting, Vientiane, Laos, 27 July 2005. Available online at www.aseansec.org/17601.htm (last accessed April 2006).

Chalermpalanupap, Termsak (2002). 'Towards an East Asia Community: the journey has begun', paper presented to the Fifth China–ASEAN Research Institutes Roundtable on Regionalism and Community Building in East Asia, organized by the University of Hong Kong's Centre of Asian Studies, October, pp. 17–19.

Chalk, Peter (1998). 'Contemporary Maritime Piracy in Southeast Asia', *Studies in Conflict and Terrorism*, 21:1, pp. 87–112.

Chalmers, Malcolm (1996). *Confidence Building in South-East Asia*, Boulder, CO: Westview Press.

Chan, Kathy (1997). 'China's Role in Regional Affairs Grows as Beijing Attempts to Ensure Stability', *Wall Street Journal*, 28 August, p. A.11.

Chan, Ronnie C. (1998). 'Asia's Crisis and China's Response', *PacNet Newsletter*, 27 March.

Chen, Qiaozhi *et al.* (2001). *Lengzhan Hou Dongmeng Guojia dui Hua Zhengce Yanjiu* [A Study of ASEAN States' Policy Toward China After the Cold War], Beijing: China Social Sciences Publisher.

Cheng, Joseph Y. S. (1999). 'China's ASEAN Policy in the 1990s: pushing for regional multipolarity', *Contemporary Southeast Asia*, 21:2, pp. 176–204.

Cheng-Chwee, Kuik (2005). 'Multilateralism in China's ASEAN Policy: its evolution, characteristics, and aspiration', *Contemporary Southeast Asia*, 27:1, pp. 102–22.

Cheow, Eric Teo Chu (2004). 'Asian Security and the Reemergence of China's Tributary System', *China Brief*, 18:4. Available online at www.jamestown.org/images/pdf/cb_004_018.pdf (last accessed April 2006).

Chin, James K. and Nicholas Thomas (eds) (2005) *China and ASEAN: changing political and strategic ties*, Centre of Asian Studies, University of Hong Kong.

Chong, Alan (2004). 'Singaporean Foreign Policy and the Asian Values Debate, 1992–2000: reflections on an experiment in soft power', *Pacific Review*, 17:1, pp. 95–133.

Bibliography

Choo, Tan Lian (1998). 'Stop Trying Aid to Human Rights, Asian Countries Tell the West', *Straits Times* (Singapore), 3 April, p. 20.

Christensen, Thomas J. (1999). 'China, the U.S.–Japan Alliance, and the Social Dilemma in East Asia', *International Security*, 23:4, pp. 32–80.

—— (2003). 'China, the U.S.–Japan Alliance, and the Security Dilemma in East Asia', in G. John Ikenberry and Michael Mastanduno (eds), *International Relations Theory and the Asia–Pacific*, New York: Columbia University Press, pp. 25–56.

Christopher, Robert C. (1978). 'America and Japan: a time for healing', *Foreign Affairs*, 56:4, pp. 857–66.

Chung, Christopher (2004). *The Spratly Islands Disputes: decision units and domestic politics*, PhD Thesis, University of New South Wales.

Coleman, William D. and Geoffrey R. D. Underhill (eds) (1998). *Regionalism and Global Economic Integration: Europe, Asia and the Americas*, London: Routledge.

Collins, Alan (2000). *The Security Dilemmas of Southeast Asia*, London: Macmillan/ St Martin's Press.

Conable, Barber B. Jr and David M. Lampton (1992). 'China: the coming power', *Foreign Affairs*, 71:5, pp. 133–49.

Cordenillo, Raul L. (2005). 'The Economic Benefits to ASEAN of the ASEAN–China Free Trade Area (ACFTA)', 18 January, ASEAN Secretariat. Available online at www.aseansec.org/17310.htm (last accessed April 2006).

Crone, Donald (1993). 'Does Hegemony Matter? The reorganization of the Pacific political economy', *World Politics*, 45:4, pp. 501–25.

Cui, Tiankai (2005). *Regional Integration in Asia and China's Policy*, China–ASEAN Project Occasional Paper No. 12, Centre of Asian Studies, University of Hong Kong.

Curtis, Gerald L. (ed.) (1994). *The United States, Japan, and Asia*, New York: W. W. Norton.

Deans, Phil (2000). 'Contending Nationalisms and the Diaoyutai/Senkaku Dispute', *Security Dialogue*, 31:1, pp. 119–31.

Deng, Yong and Thomas G. Moore (2004). 'China Views Globalization: toward a new great-power politics?', *Washington Quarterly*, 27:3, pp. 117–36.

Dent, Christopher M. (2003). 'Networking the Region? The emergence and impact of Asia–Pacific bilateral free trade agreement projects', *Pacific Review*, 16:1, pp. 1–28.

Dickie, Mure and David Pilling (2005). 'Japan Takes Swipe at China for Official Snub', *Financial Times*, 25 May, p. 7.

Dillon, Dana R. (2000). 'Piracy in Asia: a growing barrier to maritime trade', *Heritage Foundation Backgrounder*, 1379, 22 June, pp. 1–5.

Dittmer, Lowell (2002). 'East Asia in the "New Era" in World Politics', *World Politics*, 55:1, pp. 63–4.

Drifte, Reinhard (1999). *Japan's Quest for a Permanent Security Council Seat: a matter of pride or justice?*, New York: Palgrave.

Dupont, Alan (2000). 'ASEAN's Response to the East Timor Crisis', *Australian Journal of International Affairs*, 54:2, pp. 168–70.

East Asia Study Group (2002). *Towards an East Asian Community*, report submitted on 2002 to ASEAN+3 leaders' meeting in Phnom Penh, Cambodia, on 4 November. Available online at www.aseansec.org/4918.htm (last accessed April 2006).

East Asia Vision Group (2001) *Towards an East Asian Community: region of peace, prosperity and progress*, report submitted on 31 October to ASEAN+3 Leaders. Available online at www.aseansec.org/4918.htm (last accessed April 2006).

Economist (1988). 'The Japan Puzzle', 21 March, p. 15.

—— (2001). 'Japan Starts Picking on China', 8 February, pp. 31–2.

Eguchi, Yujiro (1980). 'Japanese Energy Policy', *International Affairs*, 56:2, pp. 263–79.

Elerk, Andrew (1995). 'APEC Beyond Bogor: an open economic association in the Asia–Pacific region', *Asia Pacific Economic Literature*, 9:1, pp. 183–223.

Ellings, Richard J. and Sheldon W. Simon (eds) (1996). *Southeast Asian Security in the New Millennium*, Armonk, NY: M. E. Sharpe.

Elliott, Lorraine (2003). 'ASEAN and Environmental Cooperation: norms, interests and identity', *Pacific Review*, 16:1, pp. 29–52.

Emmers, Ralf (2001). 'The Influence of the Balance of Power Factor Within the ASEAN Regional Forum', *Contemporary Southeast Asia*, 23:2, pp. 276–7.

—— (2003). *Cooperative Security and the Balance of Power in ASEAN and the AEF*, London: Routledge Curzon.

Emmerson, John K. and Leonard A. Humphreys (1973). *Will Japan Rearm? A study in attitudes*, Washington, DC: American Enterprise Institute for Public Policy Research.

Energy Compass (2004). 'Vietnam Objects to Spratlys Deal', 16 September, p. 1.

Fackler, Martin (2003). 'Japan Turns to Old Foe Russia for Oil, Finding a Rival in China', *Wall Street Journal*, 17 March, p. A.13.

Fairbank, John K. (ed.) (1968). *The Chinese World Order: traditional China's foreign relations*, Cambridge, MA: Harvard University Press.

Far Eastern Economic Review (1971). 'Southeast Asia: towards an Asian Asia', 25 September, p. 31.

—— (1990). 'Yankee Please Stay', 150:50, pp. 30–1.

—— (1993). 'The Slowly Rising Sun: what Japan must do to win Asia's trust', 156:21, p. 5.

—— (1994). 'Building Bloc: let's bring NAFTA across the Pacific', 157:22, p. 5.

—— (1997). 'Japan Wants New Asian Pals', 160:6, p. 28.

—— (2000). 'Foot in the Water', 163:10, pp. 28–9.

—— (2004). 'Strait Talk', 167:16, p. 17.

—— (2004). 'A Diplomatic Offensive', 167:31, pp. 28–30.

—— (2005). 'Two Visits, Many Interpretations', 168:5, pp. 35–7.

Feinberg, Richard E. (2003). 'The Political Economy of United States' Free Trade Arrangements', *World Economy*, 26:7, pp. 1019–40.

Foot, Rosemary (1998). 'China in the ASEAN Regional Forum: organizational processes and domestic modes of thought', *Asian Survey*, 38:5, pp. 425–40.

Friedberg, Aaron L. (1993). 'Ripe for Rivalry: prospects for peace in a multipolar Asia', *International Security*, 18:3, pp. 5–33.

—— (2005). 'The Future of U.S.–China Relations: is conflict inevitable?', *International Security*, 32:2, pp. 7–45.

Friedman, Thomas (1995). 'Dust Off the SEATO Charter', *New York Times*, 28 June, p. A.19.

Funabashi, Yoichi (1992). 'Japan and America: global partners', *Foreign Policy*, 86 (spring), pp. 24–39.

—— (1998). 'Tokyo's Depression Diplomacy', *Foreign Affairs*, 77:6, pp. 26–36.

Bibliography

Ganesan, N. (2000). 'ASEAN's Relations with Major External Powers', *Contemporary Southeast Asia*, 22:2, pp. 263–5.

Garver, John W. (1992). 'China's Push Through the South China Sea: the interaction of bureaucratic and national interests', *China Quarterly*, 132, pp. 999–1028.

Gill, Bates (2001). 'Discussion of "China: a responsible great power"', *Journal of Contemporary China*, 10:26, pp. 27–32.

Gilpin, Robert (1989). 'Where Does Japan Fit In?', *Millennium: Journal of International Affairs*, 18:3, pp. 329–42.

Goh, Evelyn (2004). 'The ASEAN Regional Forum in United States East Asian Strategy', *Pacific Review*, 17:1, pp. 47–69.

Goldstein, Avery (1989). 'The Domain of Inquiry in Political Science: general lessons from the study of China', *Polity*, 21:3, pp. 517–37.

Gordon, Bernard K. (1978). 'Japan, the United States and Southeast Asia', *Foreign Affairs*, 56:3, pp. 579–601.

—— (1990). 'The Asia–Pacific Rim: success at a price', *Foreign Affairs*, 70:1, pp. 142–59.

—— (1990). *New Directions for American Policy in Asia*, London: Routledge.

Graham, Norman A. (1998). 'China and the Future of Security Cooperation and Conflict in Asia', *Journal of Asian and African Studies*, 33:1, pp. 94–113.

Green, Michael J. and Patrick M. Cronin (eds) (1999). *The U.S.–Japan Alliance: past, present, and future*, Chicago: Council on Foreign Relations.

—— and Benjamin L. Self (1996). 'Japan's Changing China Policy: from commercial liberalism to reluctant realism', *Survival*, 38:2, pp. 35–58.

Griffiths, Martin and Terry O' Callaghan (2002). *International Relations: the key concepts*, London: Routledge.

Gurtov, Melvin (1971). *China and Southeast Asia: the politics of survival*, Lexington, MA: Heath Lexington Books.

Gyohten, Toyoo (1999). 'East Asian Initiative Needed in Crises', cited in *Institute for International Monetary Affairs Newsletter*, No. 4 (English translation).

Haacke, Jürgen (1998). 'Collective Foreign and Security Policy: the emergence of an ASEANized regional order in East Asia?', paper presented at International Studies Association annual meeting, March. Available online at www.ciaonet.org/conf/haj02 (last accessed April 2006).

Hara, Kimie (2001). '50 years from San Francisco: re-examining the peace treaty and Japan's territorial problems', *Pacific Affairs*, 74:3, pp. 361–83.

Harris, Stuart and James Cotton (eds) (1991). *The End of the Cold War in Northeast Asia*, Melbourne: Longman Cheshire.

He, Baogang (2004). 'East Asian Ideas of Regionalism: a normative critique', *Australian Journal of International Affairs*, 58:1, pp. 105–25.

Hearns, G. S. and W. G. Stormont (1996). 'Managing Potential Conflicts in the South China Sea', *Marine Policy*, 20:2, pp. 177–81.

Hemmer, Christopher and Peter J. Katzenstein (2002). 'Why Is There No NATO in Asia? Collective identity, regionalism, and the origins of multilateralism', *International Organization*, 56:3, pp. 575–607.

Henderson, Jeannie (1994). 'Ideas, Policy Networks and Policy Coordination in the Asia–Pacific', *Pacific Review*, 7:4, pp. 367–79.

—— (1999). *Reassessing ASEAN*, Adelphi Paper No. 328, London: International Institute for Strategic Studies.

Higgot, Richard and Richard Stubbs (1995). 'Competing Conceptions of Economic Regionalism: APEC versus EAEC in the Asia–Pacific', *Review of International Political Economy*, 2:3, pp. 518–22.

Hilpert, Hanns Günther and René Haak (eds) (2002). *Japan and China: cooperation, competition and conflict*, New York: Palgrave.

Ho, Khai Leong and Samuel C.Y. Ku (eds) (2005). *China and Southeast Asia: global changes and regional challenges*, Singapore: Institute of Southeast Asian Studies.

Hogan, Michael J. (ed.) (1992). *The End of the Cold War: its meaning and implications*, New York: Cambridge University Press.

Hoge, James F. (2004). 'A Global Power Shift in the Making: is the United States ready?', *Foreign Affairs*, 83:4, pp. 2–7.

Hongmei, Shen (2003). 'Knocking Down Asian Trade Barriers', *Beijing Review*, 17 April, p. 42.

Hook, Glenn D., Julie Gilson, Christopher W. Hughes and Hugo Dobson (2001). *Japan's International Relations: politics, economics, and security*, London: Routledge.

Hoshino, Takashi (1989). 'Japanese Investment Shifting to ASEAN', *Tokyo Business Today*, 57:10, pp. 58–60.

House, Karen Elliot (1992). 'Japan's Decline, America's Rise', *Wall Street Journal*, 21 April, p. A.16.

Howe, Christopher (ed.) (1996). *China and Japan: history, trends and prospects*, Oxford: Clarendon Press.

Hu, Weixing, Gerald Chan and Daojiong Zha (2000) *China's International Relations in the 21st Century: dynamics of paradigm shifts*, Lanham, MD: University Press of America.

Huai Chengbo (1993). 'Behind the Fear of a "China Threat"', *Beijing Review*, 36:9 (1 March), p. 10.

Huang, Kwei-Bo (2000). *The Association of South East Asian Nations' Confidence and Security Building with the People's Republic of China*, Maryland Series in Contemporary Asian Studies No. 6, Baltimore, MD: School of Law, University of Maryland.

Hughes, Christopher W. (2002). 'Japan–North Korea Relations from the North–South Summit to the Koizumi–Kim Summit', *Asia Pacific Review*, 9:2, pp. 61–78.

Hund, Markus (2002). 'From "Neighbourhood Watch Group" to Community?', *Australian Journal of International Affairs*, 56:1, pp. 99–122.

Hyer, Eric (1995). 'The South China Sea Disputes: implications of China's earlier territorial settlements', *Pacific Affairs*, 68:1, pp. 34–54.

Ikenberry, G. John (2004). 'American Hegemony and East Asian Order', *Australian Journal of International Affairs*, 58:3, pp. 353–67.

—— (2004). 'America and East Asia', *Asian Studies (Journal of the Japan Association for Asian Studies)*, 50:2, pp. 13–23.

—— and Michael Mastanduno (eds) (2003). *International Relations Theory and the Asia–Pacific*, New York: Columbia University Press.

—— and Jitsuo Tsuchiyama (2002). 'Between Balance of Power and Community: the future of multilateral security co-operation in the Asia–Pacific', *International Relations of the Asia–Pacific*, 2:1, pp. 69–94.

Ikuo, Iwasaki (1983). *Japan and Southeast Asia: a bibliography of historical, economic, and political relations*, Tokyo: Library Institute of Developing Economies.

Bibliography

Inoguchi, Takashi and Purnendra Jain (2000). *Japanese Foreign Policy Today*, New York: Palgrave.

Institute of Southeast Asian Studies (2004). *Developing ASEAN–China Relations: realities and prospects* (a brief report on the ASEAN–China forum), Singapore: Institute of Southeast Asian Studies.

Iokibe, Makoto (2002). *The Diplomatic History of Postwar Japan*, Tokyo: Yukihaku Arma.

Ishida, Kakuya (1998). 'Piracy Seen Increasing in Strait of Malacca', *Daily Yomiuri*, 29 December, p. 2.

Ismail, Zaidi Isham (2004). 'ASEAN, China to Complete Talks by June', *Business Times*, 30 March, p. 2.

Ito, Motoshige (2002). 'The Challenge of Deindustrialization: responding to imports from China', *Japan Echo*, 29:1, pp. 40–1.

Jakarta Post (2005). 'Challenges of Building an East Asian Community', 7 April.

Jan, George P. (1973). 'China's Policy Toward Japan: a study of the pattern of Chinese people's diplomacy', *Asian Profile*, 1:2, pp. 261–70.

Japan Economic News Agency (1993). 'Asian Rights Declaration Tunes Away From Western Codes', 2 April.

—— (1997). 'Hashimoto to Visit China in September, Jiang to Tokyo in '98', 16 January.

—— (2000). 'Japan, China, S. Korea Leaders Agree to Meet Regularly', 23 November.

Japanese Ministry of Foreign Affairs website, 'ASEAN+3 Foreign Minister Meeting (summary)', 28 July. Available online at www.mofa.go.jp/region/asia-paci/asean/conference (last accessed April 2006).

Johnson, Chalmers (1986). 'The Patterns of Japanese Relations with China, 1952–1982', *Pacific Affairs*, 53:9, pp. 402–28.

Johnson, Derek and Mark Valencia (eds) (2005). *Piracy in Southeast Asia: status, issues and responses*, Singapore: Institute of Southeast Asian Studies.

Johnston, Alastair Iain and Robert Ross (eds) (2001). *Engaging China: the management of an emerging power*, New York: Routledge.

Johnstone, Christopher B. (1999). 'Paradigms Lost: Japan's Asia policy in a time of growing Chinese power', *Contemporary Southeast Asia*, 21:3, pp. 365–85.

—— (1999). 'Strained Alliance: US–Japan diplomacy in the Asian financial crisis', *Survival*, 41:2, pp. 121–34.

Jones, Randall, Robert King and Michael Klein (1992). *The Chinese Economic Area: economic integration without a free trade agreement*, Paris: OECD.

Kahler, Miles (2000). 'Legalization as Strategy: the Asia–Pacific case', *International Organization*, 54:3, pp. 549–71.

Kallgren, Joyce K., Sopiee Noordin and Soedjati Djiwandono (eds) (1988). *ASEAN and China: an evolving relationship*. Berkeley, CA: University of California Institute of East Asian Studies.

Kamminga, Menno T. (1974). 'Building "Railroads on the Sea": China's attitude towards maritime law', *China Quarterly*, 59, pp. 544–58.

Kang, David C. (2003). 'Getting Asia Wrong: the need for new analytical frameworks', *International Security*, 27:4, pp. 57–85.

Kanishka Jayasuriya (ed.) (2004). *Asian Regional Governance: crisis and change*, London: Routledge Curzon.

Kapstein, Ethan B. and Michael Mastanduno (eds) (1999). *Unipolar Politics*, New York: Columbia University Press.

Karata, Saori N. (2001). 'Why Japan Suspend Aid to China? Japan's foreign aid decision-making and sources of aid sanction', *Social Science Japan Journal*, 4:1, pp. 39–58.

Katada, Saori N. (2002). 'Japan and Asian Monetary Regionalisation: cultivating a new regional leadership after the Asian financial crises', *Geopolitics*, 7:1, pp. 85–112.

Katzenstein, Peter J. and Nobuo Okawara (2001). 'Japan, Asian–Pacific Security and the Case for Analytical Eclecticism', *International Security*, 26:3, pp. 165–93.

—— and Takashi Shiraishi (eds) (1997). *Network Power: Japan and Asia*, Ithaca, NY: Cornell University Press.

Kent, Ann (1999). *China, the United Nations, and Human Rights: the limits of compliance*, Philadelphia, PA: University of Pennsylvania Press.

Khai, Leong Ho and Samuel C. Y. Ku (eds) (2005). *China and Southeast Asia: global changes and regional challenges*, Singapore: Institute of Southeast Asian Studies.

Kim, Samuel S. (ed.) (1994). *China and the World: Chinese foreign policy in the post-Cold War era*, Boulder, CO: Westview Press.

—— (1997). 'China as a Great Power', *Current History*, 96, pp. 246–51.

Kim, Sun Pyo (2003). 'The UN Convention on the Law of the Sea and New Fisheries Agreements in North East Asia', *Marine Policy*, 27, pp. 97–109.

Kinju, Atarashi (1985). 'Japan's Economic Cooperation Policy Towards the ASEAN Countries', *International Affairs*, 61:1, pp. 109–27.

Kitaoka, Shinichi (2005). 'Answering China's Japan Bashers', *Japan Echo*, 32, pp. 12–16.

Kittichaisaree, Kriangsak (2001). 'A Code of Conduct for Human and Regional Security Around the South China Sea', *Ocean Development and International Law*, 32:2, pp. 131–47.

Klinghoffer, Arthur Jay (1976). 'Sino-Soviet Relations and the Politics of Oil', *Asian Survey*, 16:6, pp. 540–52.

Koizumi, Junichiro (2002). *Japan and ASEAN in East Asia: a sincere and open partnership*. 14 January, Singapore. Available online at the ASEAN website, www.aseansec.org/2802.htm (last accessed April 2006).

Kojima, Akira (2003). 'How China's Bold Economic Diplomacy Affects Japan', *Japan Echo*, 30:1.

Kojima, Kiyoshi and Hiroshi Kurimoto (1966). 'A Pacific Economic Community and Asian Developing Countries', in *Report of a JERC International Conference, Measures for Trade Expansion of Developing Countries*, Tokyo: Japan Economic Research Center.

Kojima, Tomoyuki (2001). 'China's "Omnidirectional Diplomacy": cooperation with all, emphasis on major powers', *Asia–Pacific Review*, 8:2, pp. 81–95.

Korhonen, Pekka (1994). 'The Theory of the Flying Geese Pattern of Development and Its Interpretations', *Journal of Peace Research*, 31:1, pp. 93–108.

Krasner, Stephen (ed.) (1983). *International Regime*, Ithaca, NY: Cornell University Press.

Krauss, Ellis (2003). 'The US, Japan, and Trade Liberalization: from bilateralism to regional multilateralism to regionalism', *Pacific Review*, 16:3, pp. 307–29.

Bibliography

Ku, Samuel C. Y. (ed.) (2002). *Southeast Asia in the New Century: an Asian perspective*, Kaohsiung: Center for Southeast Asian Studies, National Sun Yat-Sen University.

Lam, Peng Er (1996). 'Japan and the Spratlys Dispute: aspirations and limitations', *Asian Survey*, 36:10, pp. 955–1010.

Lampton, David (ed.) (2001). *Same Bed, Different Dreams: managing U.S.–China relations, 1989–2000*, Berkeley, CA: University of California Press.

Layne, Christopher (1996). 'Less is More: realistic foreign policies for East Asia', *National Interest*, 43, pp. 64–77.

Leifer, Michael (1983). 'The Security of Sea-Lanes in Southeast Asia', *Survival*, 25:1, p. 16.

—— (1996). *The ASEAN Regional Forum*, Adelphi Paper No. 302, London: International Institute for Strategic Studies.

—— (1996). 'Truth about the Balance of Power', *Structure*, Singapore: Institute of Southeast Asian Studies, pp. 50–1.

Li, Enmin (1997). *Zhongri Minjian Jingji Waijiao, 1945–1972* [Sino-Japanese Private Economic Diplomacy, 1945–1972], Beijing: Renmin Chubanshe.

Li, Yiping (2004). 'Lengzhan Hou Zhongguo yu Dongmeng Guojia Guanxi Tanxi' [An Analysis of Post-Cold War China–ASEAN State-to-State Relations], Proceedings of the 2004 China Association of Southeast Asian Studies Annual Conference, retrieved from Tsinghua Tongfang Optical Disc Databank.

Lim, Robyn (1998). 'The ASEAN Regional Forum: building on sand', *Contemporary Southeast Asia*, 20:20, pp. 115–36.

—— (2002). 'Between Japan and China, an Irritant Named North Korea', *International Herald Tribune*, 28 January.

Lin, Chang Li and Ramkishen S. Rajan (2001). 'The Economics and Politics of Monetary Regionalism in Asia', *ASEAN Economic Bulletin*, 18:1, pp. 103–17.

Lincoln, Edward (2004). *East Asian Economic Regionalism*, Washington, DC: Brookings Institution.

Liu, Jiangyong (1995). '"Maguan Tiaoyu" Bainian Hou de Ritai Guanxi [Japan–Taiwan Relations One Hundred Years After the Treaty of Shimonoseki], *Riben Xuekan* [Journal of Japanese Studies], June, pp. 9–23.

Lo, Bobo (2004). 'The Long Sunset of Strategic Partnership: Russia's evolving China policy', *International Affairs*, 80:2, pp. 295–309.

Lugo, Leotes Marie T. (1996). 'Ramos Meets with China's Jiang', *Business World* (Manila), 27 November.

Lui, Fu-Kuo and Philippe Regnier (eds) (2003). *Regionalism in East Asia: paradigm shifting?*, London: Routledge Curzon.

Ma, Jinqiang, Zhu Zhenmin and Zhang Guangping (2000). *Dangdai Dongnanya Guoji Guanxi* [Modern Southeast Asian International Relations], Beijing: Shijie Zhishi Chubanshe.

Mack, Andrew and Pauline Kerr (1995). 'The Evolving Security Discourse in the Asia–Pacific', *Washington Quarterly*, 18:1, pp. 123–40.

Manupipatpong, Worapot (2002). 'The ASEAN Surveillance Process and the East Asian Monetary Fund', *ASEAN Economic Bulletin*, 19:1, pp. 111–21.

Marshall, Jonathan (1995). *To Have and Have Not: Southeast Asian raw materials and the origins of the Pacific War*, Berkeley, CA: University of California Press.

McAvoy, Audrey (2004). 'Fearing Rivalry with China, Free Trade Agreements Are Suddenly the Rage in Japan', 2 April, Associated Press.

McDevitt, Michael, Yoshihide Soeya, James Auer, Tetsuo Kotani, and Philip Yang (2005). 'Japan–Taiwan Interaction: implications for the United States', *National Bureau of Asian Research Analysis*, 16:1, pp. 85–106.

McGregor, James, *et al.* (1992). 'Major Powers Ponder Change in the U.S.: China, Russia, Japan view Clinton with wariness but see possible benefits', *Wall Street Journal*, 5 November, p. A.9.

Medeiros, Evan S. and M. Taylor Fravel (2003). 'China's New Diplomacy', *Foreign Affairs*, 82:6, pp. 22–35.

Midford, Paul (2004). 'China Views the Revised US–Japan Defense Guidelines: popping the cork?', *International Relations of the Asia–Pacific*, 4:1, pp. 113–45.

Miyagawa, Makio (1996). 'Japan's Security and Development Policy for Southeast Asia', *Japan Review of International Affairs*, 10:2, pp. 158–68.

Miyagi, Daizo (2001). *Bandung Conference and Japan's Return to Asia: between the U.S. and Asia*, Tokyo: Soshisha.

Morrison, Charles (1985). *Japan, the United States, and a Changing Southeast Asia*, Lanham, MD: University Press of America.

Munakata, Naoko (2001). *Evolution of Japan's Policy Toward Economic Integration*, Center for Northeast Asian Policy Studies, Washington, DC: Brookings Institution. Archived at www.brookings.edu/fp/cnaps/papers/2001_munakata. pdf (last accessed April 2006).

—— (2003). 'The Impact of the Rise of China and Regional Economic Integration in Asia: a Japanese perspective', Statement Before the US–China Economic and Security Review Commission (US Congress) Hearing on China's Growth as a Regional Economic Power: Impacts and Implications, 4 December.

Muni, S. D. (2002). *China's Strategic Engagement with the New ASEAN*, IDSS Monograph No. 2, Singapore: Institute of Defense and Strategic Studies, pp. 30–9.

Mure, Dickie and Landingin Roel (2004). 'Oil Pact Marks New Approach to Disputes by China', *Financial Times* (Japanese edition), 3 September, p. 6.

Mutalib, Hussin (1997). 'At Thirty, ASEAN Looks to Challenges in the New Millennium', *Contemporary Southeast Asia*, 19:1, pp. 74–85.

Nathan, Andrew (1994). 'Human Rights in Chinese Foreign Policy', *China Quarterly*, 139, p. 640.

Ng, Francis and Alexander Yeats (2003). *Major Trade Trends in East Asia: what are their implications for regional cooperation and growth?*, World Bank Policy Research Working Paper No. 3084, Washington, DC: World Bank.

Nischalke, Tobias (2000). 'Insights from ASEAN's Foreign Policy Co-operation: the "ASEAN way", a real spirit or a phantom?', *Contemporary Southeast Asia*, 22:1, pp. 89–112.

—— (2002). 'Does ASEAN Measure Up: post Cold War diplomacy and the idea of regional community', *Pacific Review*, 15:1, pp. 89–112.

Nobuo, Shimotomai (1988). 'The Soviet Union and East Asia: toward economic reconciliation', *Japan Quarterly*, 35:4, pp. 390–4.

Nye, Joseph S. (1997). 'China's Re-emergence and the Future of the Asia–Pacific', *Survival*, 39:4, pp. 65–79.

—— (2003). 'U.S. Power and Strategy After Iraq', *Foreign Affairs*, 82:4, pp. 60–73.

Odgaard, Liselotte (2002). *Maritime Security Between China and Southeast Asia: conflict and cooperation in the making of regional order*, Aldershot: Ashgate.

Oil and Gas Journal (1992). 'Vietnam Steps Up Offshore E&D Push', 90:25, p. 38.
—— (1992). 'Territorial Disputes Simmer in Areas of South China Sea', 90:28, pp. 20–1.
Oishi, Mikio and Fumitaka Furuoka (2003). 'Can Japanese Aid Be an Effective Tool of Influence? Case studies of Cambodia and Burma', *Asian Survey*, 43:6, pp. 890–907.
Otsuji, Yoshihiro and Takashi Shiraishi (2002). 'Building Closer Ties with ASEAN', *Japan Echo*, 29:2, pp. 8–12.
Overholt, William H. (1994). *The Rise of China: how economic reform is creating a new superpower*, New York: W. W. Norton.
Palmer, Norman D. (1989). 'United States Policy in East Asia', *Current History*, 88:537, pp. 161–6.
Pang, Zhongying (2005). 'China's Changing Attitude to UN Peacekeeping', *International Peacekeeping*, 12:1, pp. 87–104.
Park, Choon-ho (1983). *East Asia and the Law of the Sea*, Seoul: Seoul National University Press.
—— and Jerome Alan Cohen (1975). 'The Politics of China's Oil Weapon', *Foreign Policy*, 20 (fall), pp. 28–49.
Peou, Sorpong (2002). 'Realism and Constructivism in Southeast Asian Security Studies Today: a review essay', *Pacific Review*, 15:1, pp. 119–38.
—— (2002). 'Withering Realism? A review of recent security studies on the Asia–Pacific region', *Pacific Affairs*, 75:4, pp. 575–84.
PRC Ministry of Foreign Affairs, 'ASEAN Regional Forum (ARF) Concept and Principles of Preventive Diplomacy'. Available online at www.fmprc.gov.cn/eng/wjb/zzjg/gjs (last accessed April 2006).
Prestowitz, Clyde (2004). 'The Great Reverse – Part I: after two centuries of Western domination, China and India are poised to claim their places', *Yale Global*, 2 September. Available online at yaleglobal.yale.edu (last accessed April 2006).
Rajan, Ramkishen S. (2005). 'Trade Liberalization and the New Regionalism in the Asia–Pacific: taking stock of recent events', *International Relations of the Asia Pacific*, 10:2, pp. 217–33.
Rapkin, David P. (2001). 'The United States, Japan, and the Power to Block: the APEC and AMF cases', *Pacific Review*, 14:3, pp. 373–410.
Ravenhill, John (2002). 'A Three Bloc World? The new East Asian regionalism', *International Relations of the Asia–Pacific*, 2:2, pp. 167–95.
—— (2003). 'The New Bilateralism in the Asia Pacific', *Third World Quarterly*, 24:2, pp. 299–317.
Renmin Ribao (1994). 'Over 21,000 Smuggling Cases Prosecuted This Year', 28 December, p. 2.
—— (1997). 'Qian Qichen Unveils New Security Concept at Event Celebrating 30th Anniversary of ASEAN', 16 December, p. 6.
Robinson, Gwen (1997). 'Singapore's Outspoken PM Appeals to Japan Over China', *Financial Times*, 30 August, p. 3.
Robinson, Richard, Gary Rodan, Kevin Hewson and Richard Robinson (eds) (1997). *The Political Economy of Southeast Asia: conflicts, crises, and change*, London: Oxford University Press.
Rose, Caroline (1998). *Interpreting History in Sino-Japanese Relations: a case study in political decision making*, London: Routledge.

Ross, Robert S. (2003). 'The U.S.–China Peace: great power politics, spheres of influence, and the peace of East Asia', *Journal of East Asian Studies*, 3, pp. 351–75.

Roy, Denny (1996). 'The China Threat Issue Major Arguments', *Asia Survey*, 36:8, pp. 758–71.

Rozman, Gilbert (1998). 'China's Quest for Great Power Identity', *Orbis*, 12:3, pp. 383–402.

—— (2001). 'Japan's Images of China in the 1990s: are they ready for China's smile diplomacy or Bush's strong diplomacy?', *Japanese Journal of Political Science*, 2:1, pp. 97–125.

—— (2002). 'China's Changing Images of Japan, 1989–2001: the struggle to balance partnership and rivalry', *International Relations of the Asia–Pacific*, 2:1, pp. 95–130.

—— (2002). 'Japan's Quest for Great Power Identity', *Orbis*, 46:1, pp. 73–91.

Sanchanta, Mariko (2004). 'Gas Provokes Japanese Clash', *Financial Times*, 7 July, p. 10.

Saxonhouse, Gary R. and Robert M. Stern (eds) (2004). *Japan's Lost Decade: origins, consequences and prospects for recovery*, Malden: Blackwell.

Scalapino, Robert A. (1995). 'The End of Communism in Asia: what next?', *Current History*, 375, pp. 16–22.

—— and Jusuf Wanandi (eds) (1982). *Economic, Political, and Security Issues in Southeast Asia in the 1980s*, Berkeley, CA: University of California Institute of East Asian Studies.

Schaller, Michael (1990). *The United States and China in the Twentieth Century*, New York: Oxford University Press.

Schmidt, Gustav (2003). 'Asia, Europe, North America, and the "Asian Capitalist Miracle": changing "power cycles" and evolving roles in regional and international structures', *International Political Science Review*, 24:1, pp. 67–81.

Schofield, Clive (2000). 'The "Oil Rich Spratlys": myth or reality?', paper presented to the Human and Regional Security Around the South China Sea Conference, University of Oslo, Norway, 2–4 June.

Segal, Gerald (1992). 'Opening and Dividing China', *World Today*, 48:5, pp. 77–80.

—— (1996). 'East Asia and the "Constrainment" of China', *International Security*, 20:4, pp. 107–35.

Shambaugh, David (1991). 'China in 1990: the year of damage control', *Asian Survey*, 31:1, pp. 36–49.

—— (1997). 'The United States and China: cooperation or confrontation?', *Current History*, 96:611, pp. 242–3.

Shaplen, Jason T. and James Laney (2004). 'China Trades Its Way to Power', *New York Times*, 12 July, p. A.19.

Shibuichi, Daiki (2005). 'The Yasukuni Dispute and the Politics of Identity of Japan: why all the fuss?', *Asian Survey*, 45:2, pp. 197–215.

Shin, James (ed.) (1996). *Weaving the Net: conditional engagement with China*, New York: Council on Foreign Relations.

Shiraishi, Masaya (1990). *Japanese Relations with Vietnam: 1951–1987*, Ithaca, NY: Cornell University Southeast Asia Program.

Simon, Sheldon W. (ed.) (2001). *The Many Faces of Asian Security*, New York: Rowman and Littlefield.

Bibliography

—— (2002). 'Evaluating Track II Approaches to Security Diplomacy in the Asia–Pacific: the CSCAP experience', *Pacific Review*, 15:2, pp. 167–200.

Sing, Lam Lai (1994). 'A Short Note on ASEAN–Great Power Interaction', *Contemporary Southeast Asia*, 15:4, pp. 451–63.

Singh, Bhubhindar (2002). 'ASEAN's Perceptions of Japan: change and continuity', *Asian Survey*, 42:2, pp. 276–96.

Smith, Anthony L. (2004). 'ASEAN's Ninth Summit: solidifying regional cohesion, advancing external linkages', *Contemporary Southeast Asia*, 26:3, pp. 421–7.

Soesastro, Hadi (ed.) (1995). *ASEAN in a Changed Regional and International Political Economy*, Jakarta: Centre for Strategic and International Studies.

Soeya, Yoshihide (1998). *Japan's Economic Diplomacy with China, 1945–1978*, Oxford: Clarendon Press.

—— (2001). 'Taiwan in Japan's Security Considerations', *China Quarterly*, 165 (March), pp. 130–46.

—— (2003). 'Use Summit to Advance East Asia Strategy', *International Herald Tribune/Asahi Shimbun*, 8 December.

Soh, Chunghee Sarah (2003). 'Japan's National/Asian Women's Fund for "Comfort Women"', *Pacific Affairs*, 76:2, pp. 209–33.

Sokolsky, Richard, Angel Rabasa and C. Richard Neu (2001). *The Role of Southeast Asia in U.S. Strategy toward China*, Santa Monica, CA: RAND.

Solomon, Richard H. (ed.) (1981). *The China Factor: Sino-American relations and the global scene*, Englewood Cliffs, NJ: Prentice-Hall.

Stiglitz, Joseph E. (2001). 'Failure of the Fund: rethinking the IMF response', *Harvard International Review*, 23:2, pp. 14–18.

Stockwin, J. Arthur (2003). 'Why Japan Still Matters', *Japan Forum*, 15:3, pp. 345–60.

Straits Times (1995). 'ASEAN United on Spratlys Issue in Talks with Beijing, Says Manila', 6 April, p. 14.

Stuart-Fox, Martin (2003). *A Short History of China and Southeast Asia: tribute, trade and influence*, St Leonards: Allen & Unwin.

Sudo, Sueo (1992). *The Fukuda Doctrine and ASEAN: new dimensions in Japanese foreign policy*, Singapore: Institute of Southeast Asian Studies.

—— (2002). *The International Relations of Japan and Southeast Asia: forging a new regionalism*, London: Routledge.

Suehiro, Akira (1999). 'The Road to Economic Re-entry: Japan's policy toward Southeast Asian development in the 1950s and 1960s', *Social Science Japan Journal*, 2:1, pp. 85–105.

Sukma, Rizal (1999). *Indonesia and China: the politics of a troubled relationship*, London: Routledge.

Suryadinata, Leo (1981). 'The Chinese Minority and Sino-Indonesian Diplomatic Normalization', *Journal of Southeast Asian Studies*, 12:1, pp. 197–206.

Swain, Michael D. and Ashley J. Tellis (2000). *Interpreting China's Grand Strategy*, Santa Monica, CA: RAND.

Takafusa, Nakamura (1995). *The Postwar Japanese Economy: its development and structure, 1937–1994*, Tokyo: Tokyo University Press.

Takagi, Seiichiro (1994). 'China as an "Economic Superpower": its foreign relations in 1993', *Japan Review of International Affairs*, 8:2, pp. 93–117.

Tanaka, Akihiko (1988). *ASEAN Factor in Japan's China Policy? A case study of*

Japan's government loans to China, 1979, Tokyo: University of Tokyo, Department of Social and International Relations.

—— (1991). *Nitchu Kankei 1945–1990* [Japan–China relations, 1945–1990], Tokyo: University of Tokyo Press.

Tang, James T. H. (ed.) (1995). *Human Rights and International Relations in the Asia Pacific Region*, London: Pinter.

Tanzer, Andrew (1992). 'Asia's Next Flash Point?', *Forbes*, 150:10, pp. 96–8.

Tay, Simon S. C. and Talib Obood (1997). 'The ASEAN Regional Forum: preparing for preventive diplomacy', *Contemporary Southeast Asia*, 19:3, pp. 252–68.

Taylor, Jay (1976). *China and Southeast Asia: Peking's relations with revolutionary movements*, New York: Praeger.

Teitler, Ger (2005). 'Piracy in Southeast Asia: a historical comparison'. Available online at www.marecentre.nl/mast/documents/GerTeitler.pdf (last accessed April 2006).

Terada, Takashi (2004). 'Creating an East Asian Regionalism: the institutionalization of ASEAN + 3 and China–Japan directional leadership', *Japanese Economy*, 32:2, pp. 64–85.

—— (2004). 'Constructing an "East Asian" Concept and Growing Regional Identity: from EAEC to ASEAN+3', *Pacific Review*, 16:2, pp. 251–77.

Thao, Nguyen Hong (2001). 'Vietnam and the Code of Conduct for the South China Sea', *Ocean Development and International Law*, 32:2, pp. 105–30.

Tonnesson, Stein (2000). 'China and the South China Sea: a peace proposal', *Security Dialogue*, 31:3, pp. 307–26.

—— (2005). 'Why are the Disputes in the South China Sea So Intractable? A historical approach', manuscript supplied to the authors.

Valencia, Mark J. (1995). *China and the South China Sea Disputes*, Adelphi Paper No. 298, London: Oxford University Press.

Van Ness, Peter (2002). 'Hegemony, not Anarchy: why China and Japan are not balancing US unipolar power', *International Relations of the Asia–Pacific*, 2:1, pp. 131–50.

Vogel, Ezra F., Yuan Ming and Tanaka Akihiko (2002). *The Golden Age of the U.S.–China–Japan Triangle, 1972–1989*, Cambridge, MA: Harvard University Press.

Wain, Barry (1994). 'Beijing and Hanoi Play with Fire in South China Sea', *Asian Wall Street Journal*, 20 July, p. 5.

Wall Street Journal (1997). 'Japan's Diplomatic Offensive', 24 January, p. A.14.

—— (2005). 'Three State Firms Plan Joint Oil Survey of Disputed Spratlys', 15 March, p. 1.

Waltz, Kenneth N. (1979). *Theory of International Politics*, Boston, MA: Addison-Wesley.

—— (2000). 'Structural Realism After the Cold War', *International Security*, 25:1, pp. 5–41.

Wan, Ming (1998). 'Human Rights and U.S.–Japan Relations in Asia: divergent allies', *East Asia: An International Quarterly*, 16:3/4, pp. 137–68.

—— (2003). 'Tensions in Recent Sino-Japanese Relations: the May 2002 Shenyang incident', *Asian Survey*, 43:5, pp. 826–44.

Wang, Gungwu (1999). *China and Southeast Asia: myths, threats and culture*, East Asian Institute Occasional Paper No. 13, Singapore: World Scientific and Singapore University Press.

Wang, Jianqun. (2003) *Forging Closer China–ASEAN Cooperation at the Regional Multilateral Arena*, China–ASEAN Occasional Paper No. 2, Centre of Asian Studies, University of Hong Kong.

Wang, Liyu and Peter H. Pearse (1994). 'The New Legal Regime for China's Territorial Sea', *Ocean Development and International Law*, 25, pp. 431–42.

Wang, Xinsheng and Yu Changsheng (2005). *Zhongguo Dongmeng Quyu Hezuo yu Gonggong Zhili [Sino-ASEAN Regional Cooperation and Public Governance]*, Beijing: China Social Sciences.

Watkins, Eric (2004). 'Japan, China in Stalemate Over Maritime Boundaries', *Oil and Gas Journal*, 102:42, p. 28.

Weatherbee, Donald E. (1977). 'Cooperation and Conflict in the Mekong River Basin', *Studies in Conflict and Terrorism*, 20, pp. 167–84.

Whiting, Allen S. (1997). 'ASEAN Eyes China: the security dimension', *Asian Survey*, 37:4, pp. 299–322.

—— and Xin Jianfei (1993). 'Sino-Japanese Relations: pragmatism and passion', *World Policy Journal*, 10:2, pp. 27–32.

Woods, Ngaire (1996). *Explaining International Relations Since 1945*, Oxford: Oxford University Press.

World Bank (1993). *The East Asian Miracle: economic growth and public policy*, Washington, DC: World Bank.

Wortzel, Larry M. (1994). 'China Pursues Traditional Great-Power Status', *Orbis*, 38:2, pp. 164–8.

Wu, Xinbo (2000). 'The Security Dimension of Sino-Japanese Relations: warily watching one another', *Asian Survey*, 40:2, pp. 296–310.

Xia, Liping (2001). 'China: a responsible great power', *Journal of Contemporary China*, 10:26, pp. 17–25.

Xinhua News Agency (1995). 'China Drills High-Yield Oil Well in East China Sea', 24 July.

—— (2004). 'Foreign Ministry Spokesman's Statements', 26 September.

Xu, Ke (2002). 'Dongnanya de Haidao Wenti yu Yatai Diqu Anquan' [The Southeast Asian Piracy Problem and Security in the Asia Pacific], *Dangdai Yatai* [Cotemporary Asia Pacific], March, pp. 46–51.

Yahuda, Michael (1983). *Towards the End of Isolationism: China's foreign policy after Mao*, London: Macmillan.

Yamada, Yoshihiko (2003). *Umi no Terrorism* [Terrorism from the Seas], Tokyo: PHP Research Institute.

Yan Xuetong (1995). 'China's Post-Cold War Security Strategy', *Contemporary International Relations*, 5:5, pp. 6–7.

—— (1997). 'Zhongguo de Xinanquan Yu Anquan Hezuo Gouxiang' [China's New Concept on Security and Security Cooperation], *Xiandai Guoji Guanxi* [Contemporary International Relations], pp. 28–32.

Yang Jian (2003). 'Sino-Japanese Relations: implications for Southeast Asia', *Contemporary Southeast Asia*, 25:2, pp. 306–27.

Yee, Herbert and Ian Storey (eds) (2002). *The China Threat: perceptions, myths and reality*, London: Routledge Curzon.

Yoshikawa, Hiroshi (translated by Charles H. Stewart) (2002). *Japan's Lost Decade*, Tokyo: International House of Japan.

Yoshimatsu, Hidetaka (2002). 'Social Demand, State Capability and Globalization: Japan–China trade friction over safeguards', *Pacific Review*, 15:3, pp. 381–408.

You, Ji (2001). 'China and North Korea: a fragile relationship of strategic convenience', *Journal of Contemporary China*, 28, pp. 387–98.

Young, Adam J. and Mark J. Valencia (2003). 'Conflation of Piracy and Terrorism in Southeast Asia: rectitude and utility', *Contemporary Southeast Asia*, 25:2, pp. 269–83.

Zha, Daojiong (2000). 'China and the May 1998 Riots of Indonesia: exploring the issues', *Pacific Review*, 13:4, pp. 557–75.

—— (2001). 'Localizing the South China Sea Problem: the case of China's Hainan', *Pacific Review*, 14:4, pp. 575–98.

—— (2001). 'Security in the South China Sea', *Alternatives: Global, Local, Political*, 26:1, pp. 33–52.

—— (2001). 'The Taiwan Problem in Japan–China Relations: an irritant or destroyer?', *East Asia: An International Quarterly*, 19:1/2, pp. 207–22.

—— (2002). 'The Politics of China–ASEAN Economic Relations: assessing the move toward an FTA', *Asian Perspective*, 26:4, pp. 53–82.

—— (2005). 'Can China Rise?', *Review of International Studies*, 31, pp. 775–85.

—— (2005). 'Zhongri Guanxi yu Dongya Hezuo' [Sino-Japanese Relations and East Asian Cooperation], *Riben Xuekan* [Japan Studies], 89 (October), pp. 8–22.

—— and Mark J. Valencia (2001). 'Mischief Reef: geopolitical context and implications', *Journal of Contemporary Asia*, 31:1, pp. 86–103.

Zhang, Tiejun (2004). 'Self-Identity Construction of the Present China', *Comparative Strategy*, 23:3, pp. 281–301.

Zheng, Bijian (2005). 'China's "Peaceful Rise" to Great-Power Status', *Foreign Affairs*, 84:5, pp. 18–24.

Zou, Keyuan (2000). 'Piracy at Sea and China's Response', *Lloyd's Maritime and Commercial Law Quarterly*, autumn, pp. 364–82.

Index

Lightning Source UK Ltd.
Milton Keynes UK
UKOW030656240313

208075UK00002B/35/P